Twentieth-Century Architecture

Dennis P. Doordan

Twentieth-Century Architecture

 Laurence King

This book is dedicated to Marcia Rickard

Published 2001 by Laurence King Publishing
an imprint of Calmann & King Ltd
71 Great Russell Street
London WC1B 3BP
Tel: + 44 20 7430 8850
Fax: + 44 20 7430 8880
email: enquiries@calmann-king.co.uk
www.laurence-king.com

A catalogue record for this book is available from
the British Library.

ISBN (h/back) 1 85669 234 5
ISBN (p/back) 1 85669 235 3

Senior managing editor: Richard Mason
Interior designer: Tim Higgins
Cover designer: David Stanley
Picture researcher: Sue Bolsom
Typesetter: Marie Doherty
Printed in Hong Kong

Front cover: Santiago Calatrava, TGV Railway Station, Lyon, France,
1989–92. Courtesy Arcaid/Paul Raftery.

Back cover: Zaha Hadid, IBA housing complex, Stessemannstrasse 109,
Berlin, Germany, 1994. Courtesy Christian Richters, Münster.

Frontispiece: Skidmore, Owings, and Merrill (designer Gordon
Bunshaft), Lever House, New York, 1951–52. Courtesy Julius Shulman,
Los Angeles.

Contents

Preface

Books belong in the hands of readers and every author imagines who his or her readers may be. This book is an introductory survey of twentieth-century architecture for students engaged in the study of the subject and its relationship to the social, cultural, and political life of the period. It is the author's hope that this text will provoke students to pursue the subject further. If the book starts the reader on a quest to learn more about the subject and draws him or her ever deeper into the issues, it will have accomplished its principal goal.

A second, equally important group of readers will pick up this book not because they are enrolled in a formal educational program but because they are motivated by curiosity. We spend our lives surrounded by buildings and for most of us those of the twentieth century constitute the largest portion of the architecture encountered on a daily basis. Therefore, it is only natural to wonder about something as pervasive, important, and engaging as architecture. What accounts for its diversity in the twentieth century? What stories, ideals, hopes, and fears were architects trying to convey to their peers and to posterity? The author hopes the general reader will find his or her curiosity rewarded and consequently an appreciation of the world around them enhanced.

This book is divided into three main sections. The first part, "Confronting Modernity," surveys four discrete domains of professional design activity in the period 1900–1940: urban architecture, domestic architecture, the architecture of industry and transportation, and political architecture. This period is described as one of intense debate among architects advocating different approaches such as classicism, modernism, organicism, and craft-based design. The second part, "Modernist Hegemony," reviews developments during the period 1940–1965. During these years, the terms of the debate concerning the character of an appropriate architecture were dramatically revised—and narrowed. It is still a period marked by lively discussion, but the discourse is now predicated almost entirely in terms of modernism and modernist conceptions of appropriate models and design strategies. The third part, "An Era of Pluralism," covers the years 1965–2000. A new consciousness of environmental issues, new scientific paradigms, and critical theories of knowledge called into question the certainties of modernism. This part reviews the spectrum of design movements—postmodernism, deconstructivism, new classicism, "green" architecture, and even a reinvigorated modernism—characteristic of the last decades of the twentieth century.

Although writing is often a solitary occupation, no author of an illustrated history book such as this truly works alone. I wish to thank the following people and institutions for their assistance during the long gestation period of this manuscript. Some of the individuals listed below provided support on a regular basis; others appear here because they asked provocative questions or offered useful advice at critical moments in the process of research and writing. To all I offer my sincere thanks: Richard Buchanan, Richard Bullene, Norman Crowe, Kai Gutschow, Robert Hohl, Judith Hull, Wendy Kaplan, Pekka Korvenmaa, Victor Margolin, Dennis McFadden, Sarah Nichols, Janet Parks, Sidney Robinson, Diane Shaw, Thomas Gordon Smith, John Stamper, Davira Taragin, Carol Willis, and John Zukowsky. I would like also to thank the following reviewers: Linda Hart, Department of History and Theory, Southern California Institute of Architecture; Charles S. Mayer, Department of Art, Indiana State University; Kevin D. Murphy, CUNY Graduate Center and Brooklyn College; Lisa Reilly, Department of Architectural History, School of Architecture, University of Virginia; and Craig Zabel, The Pennsylvania State University.

I received invaluable assistance from Jane Devine and the staff of the Architecture Library at the University of Notre Dame. Part of the research for this project was supported by a grant from the Graham Foundation for Advanced Studies in the Fine Arts. I wish to acknowledge the editorial support (and almost infinite patience) of my editors Lee Ripley Greenfield and Richard Mason at Calmann and King. For their work on the collection and preparation of visual material for this book I thank Sue Bolsom at Calmann and King and Thomas Walker at the University of Notre Dame. For his carefully considered and dynamic design I thank Tim Higgins. At various times in my career I have offered classes on different aspects of twentieth-century architecture and design. I have benefited from the thoughtful questions and sharp observations of students and I thank them for their interest in the subject.

Dennis P. Doordan
January, 2001

Introduction

Most of us will spend our lives in buildings and environments that are designed, that is, purposefully created to support and express a variety of human activities. The manner in which twentieth-century designers, architects, and engineers conceptualized, fabricated, and evaluated these environments has been the subject of very intense debate. This survey is an account of that debate.

It is the book's central thesis that the history of twentieth-century architecture can best be understood as an ongoing discussion about the appropriate architecture for modern times. As an account of that debate, this survey is distinguished from other possible discourses. It is important, therefore, to begin by exploring the implications of different conceptions of twentieth-century architectural history.

One could construct such a history by focusing on masterpieces of design, and so establish a canon of significant modern works. Canons identify paradigms of excellence, validate architectural orientations, and define acceptable criteria for design criticism. In the twentieth century, however, design paradigms proved to be short-lived. No sooner was a canon established than a different vision for the built environment emerged to challenge it.

A second possible approach is predicated on the belief that new materials (reinforced concrete or aluminum), technologies (the elevator, forced air ventilation, computer-aided design software), or dominant economic systems (capitalism) ultimately determined the configuration of new buildings. Histories that privilege such causes as exercising a determining impact on events tend to follow predictable patterns; they describe an impersonal historical process that leads to inevitable conclusions such as the triumph of modern over traditional architecture, or the subordination of the art of architecture to the commercial concerns of real-estate development and the manipulative programs of advertising and political propaganda. However, the volatile nature of twentieth-century architecture, design criticism, and historical scholarship is lost in historical narratives conceived either in paradigmatic or deterministic terms. At any given moment in the past, multiple possible futures existed: nothing was preordained. And, as the reader will learn, for a great many buildings of the twentieth century multiple possible interpretations exist today.

Pluralism

In the last quarter of the twentieth century feminist critiques of design, scholarly interest in colonial and postcolonial experiences, the rise of structuralist and post-structuralist discourses, and the emergence of environmentally oriented criticism have all called into question the validity of efforts to create canons or provide definitive, causal accounts of complex phenomena. This survey, therefore, treats architecture as a broad field of activity in which different conceptions of the built environment coexist and their respective merits are continually debated by designers, patrons, and the general public. Beyond satisfying immediate needs for shelter and service, every building is an argument, expressed in brick and mortar or steel and glass, concerning how the world might be. This argument is not limited to the particular moment in time in which a building's design is first revealed. Once projected onto the stage of history, the debate continues to evolve as critics, historians, and subsequent generations discuss different visions of the built environment. In this book, buildings are presented as examples of arguments to be engaged critically rather than paradigms to be emulated or predetermined results to be accepted. This approach opens up the history of twentieth-century architecture to a variety of design styles and professional issues ignored or marginalized in previous treatments of the topic.

In place of canonical or deterministic histories, this then is a history conceived in the spirit of pluralism. The pluralistic approach is grounded in a definition offered by the design theorists Victor Margolin and Richard Buchanan:

> Pluralism is the principled cultivation of a sustained conversation among individuals with widely differing perspectives on the natural and the human-made worlds. Pluralism keeps alive the ongoing search for truth and understanding by focusing inquiry on common problems encountered in experience—in this case, the experience of the human-made—rather than on the technical refinement, fine points, and stylish polish of a single theory. Pluralism sustains the ecology of culture, maintaining a gene pool of diverse ideas and methods that enables us to avoid entrapment in dogma by forcing our attention to features of the world that might otherwise be ignored by doctrines that are conceived too narrowly—as it seems all doctrines eventually prove to be.
>
> (Margolin and Buchanan, p. xii)

Ultimately, a pluralist history stimulates the intellectual engagement of the reader, drawing him or her into the debates articulated by the buildings selected for inclusion. This type of conversation will nurture an appreciation of diversity. If it succeeds, history will have served its true goal of enriching the present through a critical reflection of the past.

A History of Questions

The range of responses engendered by modernity was considerable. Some designers embraced it. Others sought to blunt its effects and recast the modern in more traditional terms. Modernity presented architects, patrons, and their audiences with questions that demanded answers. How could new, often conflicting bodies of knowledge be incorporated into design practice? How could the received wisdom of the past be preserved and incorporated within new buildings? How could the negative effects of modernization be resisted or ameliorated?

Previous accounts of twentieth-century architecture have searched for answers to these questions. In his seminal study of early modern architecture, *Pioneers of the Modern Movement* (published originally in 1936 and reissued regularly since then), Nikolaus Pevsner identified Walter Gropius's Model Factory (see fig. 3.21) erected at the 1914 "Werkbund Exhibition" in Cologne, Germany, as the critical summation of efforts begun in the mid-nineteenth century to develop an appropriate architecture for the twentieth century. Pevsner was in no doubt as to the epoch-defining significance of Gropius's achievement:

> It is the creative energy of this world in which we live and work and which we want to master, a world of science and technology, of speed and danger, of hard struggles and no personal security that is glorified in Gropius's architecture, and as long as this is the world and these are its ambitions and problems, the style of Gropius and the other pioneers will be valid.
>
> (Pevsner, pp. 216–17)

However, by anointing the work of Gropius and his colleagues as the ideal, Pevsner limited rather than opened up the story of modern architecture. Measured against the Model Factory, traditional architecture and less abstract forms such as Art Deco design lost their claim to serious historical attention (although not, it now appears, their popular appeal). In contrast, this account is as much a history of questions as it is of buildings.

Critical Sets

In order to convey the variety of positions espoused in the design debates of the twentieth century, this text reviews "critical sets" of buildings to tell its story: a critical set consists of three or more projects that demonstrate a range of responses to a common design issue. Chapter 1, for example, begins by examining a range of early twentieth-century urban design proposals that demonstrate different ways of thinking about the city. Buildings in critical sets are grouped together in each chapter, but the reader is encouraged to construct his or her own sets from different chapters. One could juxtapose museums or libraries discussed in different chapters to review developments over a longer span of time than that allotted to an individual chapter.

This is an unconventional approach and the use of critical sets affects the narrative structure. In place of a continuous storyline based on the biography of great designers or the programs and manifestos of significant artistic movements, this survey has an admittedly episodic character. The story shifts continually from one building type, location, or theme to another. It provides the reader with a point of departure and a list of issues, questions, and examples with which to begin exploring the rich and fascinating history of twentieth-century architecture.

The Twentieth Century

This text both steers clear of equating twentieth-century architecture with the story of any single design orientation and seeks to avoid characterizing the century in simplistic terms. In *All That Is Solid Melts Into Air*, the cultural historian Marshall Berman characterized modern life as filled with paradoxical relationships between disparate facets of experience:

> To be modern is to find ourselves in an environment that promises us adventure, power, joy, growth, transformation of ourselves and the world—and, at the same time, that threatens to destroy everything we have, everything we know, everything we are. Modern environments and experiences cut across all boundaries of geography and ethnicity, of class and nationality, of religion and ideology: in this sense, modernity can be said to unite all mankind. But it is a paradoxical unity, a unity of disunity: it pours us all into a maelstrom of perpetual disintegration and renewal, of struggle and

contradiction, of ambiguity and anguish. To be modern is to be part of a universe in which, as Marx said, "all that is solid melts into air."

(Berman, p.15)

Berman's description sets the stage for the treatment of architecture's place in twentieth-century history that informs this book. By its very nature, architecture serves as a manifestation of the factors that shape the modern experience. Architecture begins as a process of design that gives form to a wide range of aesthetic and cultural issues, and concludes as a process of construction intimately connected with economic and material concerns. The study of architectural history, therefore, offers a unique opportunity to gauge the relationship among the cultural, economic, and political dimensions of modernity. Three different historical situations, like "snapshots" from a twentieth-century album, illustrate the intricate interweaving of technological developments, political ideologies, and cultural values that gave the twentieth century its distinctive character.

The first snapshot is a 1937 travel poster advertising dirigible service between Germany and the United States (fig. 1). It depicts a German airship soaring over a skyline dominated by the skyscrapers of a metropolis. Two popular 1930s icons of modernity, the dirigible and the skyscraper, are juxtaposed to evoke a very modern experience. No previous generation of travelers had traversed the Atlantic in the manner described in this advertisement. This is more than an image of speed and travel; it is a portrait of modernity. The experience of modern travel cannot be separated from the means that make it possible. Both the dirigible and the skyscraper represented sophisticated technological achievements in the fields of transportation and construction. Even after noting the references to travel, technology, and architectural typology, the list of themes is still incomplete, for prominently displayed on the tail fins of the German airship is the emblem of Adolf Hitler's Third Reich: the swastika. In an era when political ideologies contended for the allegiance of mass audiences, political images insinuated themselves into all aspects of modern life. The conflation of technology and political ideology evident here was not confined to the Third Reich. Efforts to establish connections between diverse aspects of modernity occurred around the globe as people tried to comprehend, organize, and control what Marshall Berman labeled the "maelstrom" of modernity.

The next snapshot is from 1959 and records the so-called "Kitchen Debate" between American Vice-President Richard Nixon and Soviet Premier Nikita Khrushchev (fig. 2). For centuries, the design of capital cities, government buildings, and civic memorials has been charged with political significance. In the modern age of mass politics, however, the ideological implications of design extend beyond these familiar settings and the political stage is no longer confined to the ceremonial halls of state buildings. As part of an official visit to the Soviet Union, Nixon toured an American-sponsored exhibition depicting contemporary life in the United States. A model kitchen erected as part of the American pavilion provided the

1 Jupp Weirtz, *2 Days to Europe*, 1937. Poster, color lithograph. Wolfsonian Museum, Miami Beach, Florida.

2 Richard Nixon and Nikita Khrushchev, kitchen area of the "American National Exhibition," Sokolniki Park, Moscow, Russia, 24 July 1959. Associated Press.

setting for a debate between the Soviet and American leaders concerning the relative merits of the communist and capitalist systems. The casting of the modern kitchen as a political arena for an ideological debate is not as bizarre as it may at first appear. The mid-twentieth-century kitchen in North America and Western Europe was indeed the most technologically sophisticated room in most homes, and it bore little resemblance to its pre-modern counterpart. In a quiet but insistent way designers had transformed the kitchen into a model modern environment and, thereby, into an emblematic expression of modernity itself. For his confrontation with the Soviet leader, Nixon had chosen his ground well. Surrounded by gleaming new appliances and well-stocked shelves, he needed only to point to the material abundance and technological sophistication of the American kitchen for evidence of the prosperity enjoyed by the average American family.

The final snapshot is a contemporary view of the Chinese city of Shenzhen (fig. 3). In 1979 Shenzhen, located in Guangdong province near Hong Kong, was a fishing village with a population of approximately 30,000 people. As part of the ambitious program of economic development announced in the early 1980s by the Chinese leader Deng Xiaoping, Shenzhen was designated one of the country's new "special economic zones" and became the focus of major development efforts. Two decades later, Shenzhen's population is nearing 4 million and the city's skyline is filled with the types of new office towers, financial centers, and hotels needed to participate in the global economy of the early twenty-first century. Staggering as the rapidity of Shenzhen's transformation from fishing village to modern metropolis may be, it is hardly unique. The twentieth century is a period of ferocious development carried out at a dizzying pace with dramatic long-term social and environmental impacts with which we are still struggling to come to terms. The architectural typologies, constructional materials, and technological systems characteristic of Shenzhen belong not to a millennial tradition of Chinese architecture

3 Shenzhen urban center, China.

Table 1 Largest Metropolitan Areas by Population

1900	*Population millions	2000	**Population millions	2015	**Population millions
London, England	4.21	Tokyo, Japan	26.4	Tokyo, Japan	26.4
New York, USA	3.43	Mexico City, Mexico	18.1	Mumbai, India	26.1
Paris, France	2.53	Mumbai, India	18.1	Lagos, Nigeria	23.2
Berlin, Germany	1.84	São Paulo, Brazil	17.8	Dhaka, Bangladesh	21.1
Chicago, USA	1.69	New York, USA	16.6	São Paulo, Brazil	20.4
Canton, China	1.60	Lagos, Nigeria	13.4	Karachi, Pakistan	19.2
Tokyo, Japan	1.45	Los Angeles, USA	13.1	Mexico City, Mexico	19.2
Vienna, Austria	1.36	Calcutta, India	12.9	New York, USA	17.4
Philadelphia, USA	1.29	Shanghai, China	12.9	Jakarta, Indonesia	17.3
St. Petersburg, Russia	1.26	Buenos Aires, Argentina	12.6	Calcutta, India	17.3

*World Almanac and Encyclopedia (1901)
**World Urbanization Prospects: The 1999 Revision prepared by the United Nations Population Division

but to a modern and international vocabulary of design and construction. Modern environments, as Marshall Berman observed, "cut across all boundaries of geography and ethnicity" (tables 1 and 2).

Late Eighteenth- and Nineteenth-Century Influences

The twentieth century is only the latest chapter in a story that begins much earlier with the political and industrial revolutions of the late eighteenth century, the intellectual revolutions of the nineteenth century, and the demographic changes that accompanied them. The American and French Revolutions introduced the era of mass politics. With their stirring endorsements of the political rights of all people, these revolutions ensured that political affairs could no longer be confined to the activities of the court-centered aristocracies of the old social order. As the nineteenth century unfolded, efforts were made to organize the masses according to class, ethnic, and national identities, but the necessity to enlist the support of mass constituencies transcended the specifics of ideology.

Equally significant for the emergence of the modern world was the Industrial Revolution that began in England in the late eighteenth century. This unleashed the productive capacity of human societies by combining the scientific knowledge, technological know-how, and entrepreneurial spirit of enterprising men and women in unprecedented ways. Whereas the American and French Revolutions transformed the political foundations of the modern experience, the Industrial Revolution established its economic and material bases.

Finally, there was an intellectual revolution that had far-reaching consequences for subsequent architectural history. It was a revolution that can be summed up by citing the work of three men: Charles Darwin (1809–1882), Karl Marx (1818–1883), and Sigmund Freud (1856–1939). Each was responsible for a body of work that fundamentally altered humankind's sense of itself and its place in the world. Darwin's description of the process of natural selection and its role in evolution changed our understanding of humankind's relationship to nature. Marx's contribution to social, economic, and political theory changed our views of the relationship of people to each other and the material world they create. Freud's work suggested a new understanding of the workings of the subconscious mind.

How are any of these political, social, scientific, and economic revolutions manifested in the architecture of the late eighteenth or nineteenth century? For the student of architecture, the enormous range of buildings in these centuries can be both fascinating and bewildering. It is possible, however, to organize this diversity according to four conceptual categories: neoclassicism, historicism, technology, and eclecticism.

In the second half of the eighteenth century a new appreciation of the history of architecture, fueled by fresh archaeological discoveries, prompted a reevaluation of the classical design tradition. The neoclassical movement concentrated on the underlying structural and geometric concepts of classicism rather than superficial stylistic details. French neoclassical architects such as Claude-Nicolas Ledoux (1736–1806) and Etienne Louis Boullée (1728–1799) developed an *architecture parlante* ("speaking architecture") in which the forms of the buildings "spoke" directly of their functions. Ledoux produced designs for craftsmen shelters modeled on the distinctive forms associated with particular crafts; a cooper's house, for example, is shaped like the barrel hoops fabricated by a cooper. Boullée shared Ledoux's interest in the expressive powers of pure geometry. In his 1783 project for a Cenotaph for Isaac Newton, he fused the architectural ideals of French neoclassicism with the aesthetic theory of the sublime in a truly awesome design based on an enormous sphere.

Historicism is the second major thread in the fabric of nineteenth-century architecture. While the flood of new archaeological findings prompted neoclassicists to distill the classical tradition in a quest for a limited set of fundamental forms, the same body of new research inspired others to expand their repertoire of historical styles. Designers felt free to select their models from different periods throughout history. Typically, designers and their patrons took a particular historical period as their model because of a perceived affinity between the cultural or political values of that era and the present. Thus, Napoleon's architects expressed his imperial pretensions by employing Roman models for new buildings. In the United States architects turned to ancient Greece for their models because that civilization was portrayed as the original home of democracy. In each case, ancient models were updated to meet modern needs; thus, Grecian temples acquired windows and chimneys. Nor was historical revivalism confined to classical models; for example, Gothic architecture enjoyed a prestige it had not had since the dawn of the Renaissance. The English architect A. W. N. Pugin (1812–1852) promoted the revival of Gothic architecture under the banner of moral reform and resistance to what he perceived as the corrupt character of modern life. But it was the quest for a national identity that provided Pugin with one of his most significant opportunities to build; together with Charles Barry (1795–1860), he was involved in the design of the new Houses of Parliament in London which were subsequently built in 1836–37 to replace the previous parliament building destroyed in 1834 by fire.

Table 2
World Population
1800–2000

	millions
1800	813
1850	1,128
1900	1,550
1920	1,860
1940	2,300
1960	3,039
1980	4,456
2000	6,080

Source:
United States Census

The material and technological horizons of design also expanded dramatically in the nineteenth century. Iron, steel, and reinforced concrete were now available for architects and engineers. They seized the opportunities provided by world fairs to erect unique monuments to the industrial age such as Joseph Paxton's (1801–1865) famed Crystal Palace in London (1851) and Gustave Eiffel's (1832–1923) epoch-defining Eiffel Tower in Paris (1889). The growing needs of industry and transportation created a steady demand for designs that took advantage of new engineering expertise. As designers learned how to exploit new technologies, they combined structural innovations (the steel frame, for example) with mechanical systems (the passenger elevator), new energy sources (electrical power) with novel communication devices (the telephone) to create taller buildings. Just as the great cathedrals and town halls of the Middle Ages architecturally embodied the gothic spirit, so the skyscraper, the railroad station, and the factory (fig. 4) reflected the onset of the Industrial Revolution.

4 Albert Kahn, Packard Motor Car Company, Building no. 10, interior, Detroit, 1905.

The second half of the nineteenth century also witnessed the emergence of architectural eclecticism. For much of the twentieth century, such eclecticism has suffered from its pejorative connotation as a promiscuous and unprincipled mixing of elements. In the nineteenth century, however, eclecticism identified a hybrid approach to architecture that sought to combine features from different design styles. George Gilbert Scott's (1811–1878) Midland Grand Hotel (1866–76) at Saint Pancras Station in London is an excellent example of eclectic design. Scott combined details from French, Italian, and Flemish architecture to decorate the hotel's enormous bulk. The size and planning of the building incorporated the latest in travel accommodations. Although many of the details refer to medieval models, nothing could be further from the roadside inns and stagecoach stops of premodern Europe than this grand railroad hotel.

As we will see, the twentieth century would add its own distinctive array of architectural orientations to the catalogue of neoclassical, historicist, technology-driven, and eclectic designs of the eighteenth and nineteenth centuries. The diversity of architecture in the modern era reflects the range of attitudes within the design professions concerning its role in society. Some architects saw their role as that of modernisers committed to updating design tools and methods for the purposes of urbanization. Others attempted to integrate architectural and political ideologies in order to promote political systems. Still others embraced the role of visionary designers charged with the task of extending the horizons of the imagination by developing new architectural forms. Architects, of course, are not alone in their concern to make sense of the world; they are unique, however, in their methods. From the stately halls of national capitals to the familial intimacy of domestic kitchens, designers are responsible for the spatial settings in which modern life unfolds. An account of twentieth-century architecture offers, therefore, a revealing portrait of modernity as well as buildings.

Confronting Modernity

1900–1940

Secession Building, Vienna (see fig. 1.32)

Part **1** describes responses to the emerging character of modernity in the first four decades of the twentieth century by reviewing developments in urban, civil, domestic, industrial, and political architecture. While avant-garde designers proclaimed a revolutionary break with the past and proposed radically new models for architecture that would celebrate modernity, traditionally oriented designers continued to argue that classical models could be adapted to contemporary situations.

Chapter 1

The Modern City

As the center of politics, commerce, and art, the city constitutes one of the main arenas in which the modern experience unfolds. However, many of the demographic, economic, and technological trends that shaped the twentieth-century city had their origins in the previous century. The concern of nineteenth-century architects for the health, utility, and beauty of cities remained at the core of the urban design agenda in the early twentieth century, although different strategies for promoting health, facilitating utility, and defining beauty would transform the way designers approached their tasks. As skyscrapers, cinemas, and department stores muscled their way onto the cityscape, dwarfing the churches, palaces, and small shops of the traditional city, new conceptions began to shape both the popular and professional consciousness of the city.

Responses to the Modern City

The configuration of the modern city as a whole, along with the treatment of its constituent parts, provided some of the greatest challenges for an architectural profession committed to the idea that the city could be managed through design. But such a commitment did not mean that architects agreed on a single set of design strategies for shaping the city. In the opening decades of the twentieth century, a variety of proposals ranging from the creation of a new type of settlement altogether to the reconfiguration of the traditional city were advanced by architects and planners. Throughout the twentieth century, the city remained contested ground, with traditional and avant-garde architects offering radically different visions of the modern metropolis.

The Garden City: Ebenezer Howard

In 1898 Ebenezer Howard (1850–1928), an English social visionary, published *Tomorrow: A Peaceful Path to Real Reform* in which he laid out a proposal for what he termed "Garden Cities" (fig. 1.1). Howard wanted to combine the cultural and educational opportunities of city life with the healthy and soul-sustaining benefits of country life in a balanced and self-sufficient form of settlement. This carefully controlled environment would avoid the myriad social and health problems found both in overcrowded cities and in impoverished rural areas. Size was a critical

Richard Shreve, Thomas Lamb, and Arthur Harmon, Empire State Building, New York, 1931.
The Empire State Building, completed in 1931, replaced the Chrysler Building as the world's tallest skyscraper. The structure went from preliminary design to completion of construction in just eighteen months. It is a superb example of rational planning and engineering as well as architectural design. The steel structural frame is clad with Indiana limestone and aluminum spandrel panels.

3

factor for Howard; he envisioned a population of 32,000 inhabitants in his original scheme. Rather than a nostalgic return to premodern settlement patterns, the Garden City concept represented a novel alternative to the traditional city. Howard called for the establishment of limited-dividend companies that would own and manage all the land necessary to sustain a Garden City, thus eliminating land speculation. The provision for factories as well as cultural institutions ensured self-sufficiency for the community and distinguished the true Garden City model from the strictly residential suburbs that began to appear on the periphery of major cities during the nineteenth century.

Within months of publishing *Tomorrow: A Peaceful Path to Real Reform*, Howard established a Garden City Association to promote his ideas. With its faith in the power of enlightened self-interest and private capital, the concept of a Garden City, far from seeming eccentric or utopian, struck many as a viable alternative to overcrowded and unhealthy cities. In 1903 a company was founded in Britain to realize Howard's vision and the architects Raymond Unwin (1863–1940) and Barry Parker (1867–1947) were commissioned to prepare plans for the first Garden City at Letchworth. A second Garden City at Hampstead, also designed by Unwin and Parker, followed four years later.

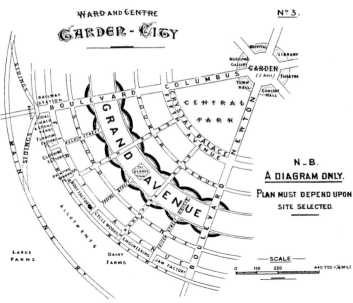

WARD AND CENTRE OF GARDEN CITY

1.1 Ebenezer Howard, Garden City diagram from *Tomorrow: A Peaceful Path to Real Reform*, 1898.

1.2 George Metzendorf, Margarethenhöhe, Essen, Germany, 1914.

Howard's ideas found a receptive audience on the European continent as well. In 1909, for example, the German architect George Metzendorf (1874–1934) presented his plans for Margarethenhöhe, a new community outside of the industrial center, Essen (fig. 1.2). Early Garden City efforts in both England and on the continent shared the reformist impulses that had animated Howard's original vision. As Howard's ideas gained in popularity, however, they were transformed and diluted. Although Margarethenhöhe was surrounded by a greenbelt and included a market square, picturesque streetscapes, and model cottages, all features associated with the Garden City ideal, it functioned more as a suburban housing estate for industrial workers than the novel form of alternative community that Howard originally described in *Tomorrow: A Peaceful Path to Real Reform*.

The City Beautiful: Daniel Burnham and Edward Bennett

1.3 (left) Daniel Burnham and Edward Bennett, Chicago plan elevation after a drawing by F. Janin showing the proposed Civic Center, from *The Plan of Chicago* first published by the Commercial Club of Chicago, 1909.

1.4 (right) Daniel Burnham and Edward Bennett, Chicago plan, 1909.

At the opposite end of the planning spectrum from Howard's sophisticated villages one finds various efforts to promote a new modern civic grandeur. In the United States, Daniel Burnham (1846–1912) and Edward Bennett (1874–1954) produced one of the most influential models of the City Beautiful movement with the publication, in 1909, of a plan of Chicago (figs. 1.3, 1.4), commissioned by Chicago's business elite. Inspired by the deft combination of monumental classicism and coordinated planning demonstrated in the "Columbian Exposition" of 1893 (for which Daniel Burnham had served as director of works), advocates of the City Beautiful movement sought to apply the lessons of the 1893 fair to American cities and recently acquired colonial possessions in order to ameliorate the negative impacts of frenetic and uncoordinated urban growth, improve traffic, protect public health, and provide for enriching recreational and cultural opportunities.

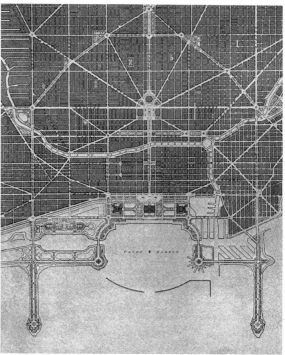

Mindful of the needs of commerce and trade, Burnham and Bennett began by noting the importance of the regional transportation infrastructure. Within the city, therefore, Chicago's orthogonal street plan was modified with the insertion of new diagonal roadways. Features intended to improve sanitary conditions in the city's slums were defended against charges of infringing on property rights; according to the plan's authors, such measures were "just, equitable, and necessary." The Chicago plan subsumed the commercial center of the city into a larger urban whole. The city's east side was dominated by cultural and educational institutions located in an extensive system of lakefront parks; its west side by a new civic center with a towering, domed city hall surrounded by county, state, and federal buildings. The primary architectural image of the city would no longer consist of the Loop's densely packed commercial buildings. Instead civic, commercial, and cultural values would balance one another, thus signaling a new level of sophistication and refinement for the business elite of Chicago.

Much of the persuasive power of the plan rested on a series of renderings depicting grand boulevards, sweeping vistas of lakefront parks, and a proposed civic center west of the Loop. If the renderings clarify central strategies of the Chicago plan, they reveal a significant weakness as well. Civic classicism, an approach based on the design tenets and cultural values of the École des Beaux-Arts in Paris (then approaching the high point of its importance as an educational and design paradigm for American architects), serves as the architectural language or style of the Chicago plan. Civic classicism, ultimately deriving from the Greco-Roman architectural orders, or styles, preferred axial, symmetrical compositions of masonry-clad buildings. In trying to match the scale of this modern metropolis, Burnham and Bennett stretched the classical architectural language to new—and absurd—heights. In order to achieve a commanding presence on Chicago's lofty skyline, the architects exaggerated the verticality of the dome crowning city hall, distorting the proportions of the whole building; the dome stretches upward like an overinflated balloon on the verge of bursting. The result is an awkward rather than an elegant response to the challenge posed by the sheer scale of twentieth-century urban development.

The civic order of schemes such as the 1909 Chicago plan or the proposal of the Finnish architect Eliel Saarinen (1873–1950) for the expansion of Helsinki in 1917, is achieved through the creation of grand boulevards lined by uniform blocks of buildings and punctuated by monumental architecture and imposing civic spaces (fig. 1.5). In the imagery associated with these plans, the city is designed to be apprehended as a coherent, integrated whole structured by the clear, hierarchical relationship of civic, cultural, commercial, and domestic domains. In this urban

1.5 Eliel Saarinen, King's Avenue from the proposed Helsinki plan, Finland, 1917.

hierarchy the public realm of civic and cultural affairs receives a more monumental architectural treatment than the commercial or private worlds of business and family life. The endemic problems of dense urban centers that prompted Garden City advocates to seek an alternative to the traditional city could be resolved, according to Burnham, Bennett, and their colleagues, through the skillful adaptation of traditional planning principles to contemporary situations. Despite the emergence of alternative planning strategies for the modern city, the grand urbanism of the City Beautiful movement would prove to be an enduring ideal in the twentieth century, and we shall note its continuing influence in subsequent chapters.

The Industrial City: Tony Garnier

The debate concerning the fate of the modern city was not, of course, confined to the alternatives of the Garden City or the City Beautiful. Other architects proposed different ways to conceptualize the task of city planning. In 1917 the French architect Tony Garnier (1869–1948) published *Une Cité industrielle: étude pour la construction des villes*, in which he described the design of an imaginary industrial center (fig. 1.6). The concept of demonstrating planning ideas through the description of an imaginary city was hardly a novel idea. In 1804, for example, the French architect Claude-Nicolas Ledoux (1736–1806) published his visionary design for an

1.6 Tony Garnier, plate 2 from *Une Cité industrielle: étude pour la construction des villes*, 1917.

industrial town, and utopian alternatives to existing urban patterns appeared throughout the nineteenth century.

However, in *Une Cité industrielle* Garnier updated and extended this tradition. His urban vision was founded on premises that challenged fundamental definitions of property rights and political power. Garnier posited a future in which, in his words, "a certain progress in the social order has taken place" and control of land, utilities, and food supplies are vested in an administrative agency acting in the best interests of society as a whole. What Garnier meant by "a certain progress" is unclear, although his description suggests some form of socialist system. Garnier's industrial city is generously provided with schools, athletic facilities, hospitals, cultural institutions, and places to accommodate popular assemblies, but includes no churches, military barracks, or prisons. Garnier imagined a population of healthy, athletic, industrial workers committed to participation in the life of their community. Health and sanitation were major concerns: residential quarters were laid out to maximize the amount of light and air available to all the inhabitants.

Garnier was hardly alone in his concern for public health; for nineteenth- and early twentieth-century urban managers, industrialization and urbanization had pushed health and sanitation issues to the forefront of their planning concerns. What distinguishes Garnier's industrial town in terms of physical design is the role assigned to his choice of primary building material—reinforced concrete. Concrete is an ancient material which had emerged in its modern form as reinforced concrete in the nineteenth century. Garnier, however, employed the material in a manner that makes it emblematic of the scheme's modernity—everything from museums to private houses is fabricated of concrete. No previous urban plans used reinforced concrete as extensively nor revealed the material as clearly as Garnier's. He made little or no effort to disguise his chosen material nor to detail it in ways that emulated traditional masonry construction; there are no elaborate moldings nor window surrounds to be seen, for example, and cornice lines and elevations are kept simple.

Compared to the richly articulated buildings illustrated in the Chicago plan, the architecture of Garnier's industrial town initially appears stark and lean. But the cubic severity of his designs was intended to be relieved by ample provisions for landscaping or, in larger public structures, to be lightened by generous porticos. With *Une Cité industrielle* Garnier hoped to demonstrate that health, utility, and beauty—the critical concerns for city planners of the period—could all be achieved through the application of a consistent, rational approach to planning and construction.

The Futurist City: Antonio Sant'Elia

In 1914 a young Italian architect, Antonio Sant'Elia (1888–1916), exhibited a series of drawings entitled *Una Città Nuova* (fig. 1.7). Informed by a very different cultural agenda from Garnier's scheme, they capture the ethos of Futurism, Italy's contribution to the international avant-garde of the early twentieth century. Launched by Filippo Tommaso Marinetti (1876–1944) in 1909, Futurism, like other avant-garde movements, rejected conventional definitions of art and beauty, celebrated the technological and social transformation of modern life, and declared that, because the present was irrevocably different from the past, historical precedents were no longer valid. Avant-garde artists and architects believed that they had a

1.7 Antonio Sant'Elia, from *Una Città Nuova*, 1914. Black ink, blue/black pencil on yellow paper, 20⅝ × 20¼ in (52.5 × 51.5 cm). Museo Civico, Como, Italy.

In the typical skyscraper plan of the early twentieth century, the elevators were located inside at the center of the tower. Sant'Elia reversed this convention and moved them to the exterior in an attempt to add a sense of animation to a stationary building.

special role to play in articulating the true nature and potential of modern life for the rest of society.

Today scholars debate the degree to which the avant-garde constituted a destructive versus a constructive force in the discourse on twentieth-century art and design. With their relentless assault on cultural conventions, avant-garde movements such as Futurism have been described as nihilist efforts devoid of any constructive program. Yet, in their attack on the traditional conceptions of high culture, avant-garde architects presented design as a form of constructive engagement with contemporary life. Throughout the twentieth century, the avant-garde's tireless commitment to provocative positions has done much to shape the agenda of design practice and criticism.

In his renderings for the *città nuova*, Sant'Elia was concerned primarily with scenographic effects and what he described in the Futurist *Manifesto of Architecture* as a "new ideal of beauty, still obscure and embryonic." Missing is the diagrammatic clarity of the Chicago plan or the concern with tectonic logic evident in Garnier's industrial city. In place of traditional avenues defined by a continuous wall of buildings, Sant'Elia depicts isolated towers rising over a complex multilevel network of bridges, rail lines, and streets. His provocative drawings display a radical reformulation of conventional thinking about urban space. The concept of a plan is at the heart of the humanist tradition in architecture as defined in the treatises of Alberti, Palladio, and their followers. A plan conveys the essential idea of the building; it defines positions and establishes coherent relationships. But the Futurist city was predicated on speed, flux, and a complexity of levels that defy two-dimensional mapping. The Futurist city has neither a center nor a clear edge, nor do Sant'Elia's buildings work together to articulate civic space but instead serve as individual nodes within elaborate service and circulation networks. Sant'Elia's *città nuova*, though fragmented and unsettling, is also the most prophetic urban proposal of the early twentieth century.

Expressionist Schemes

In Sant'Elia's cityscape of tall towers one can sense the impact of American skyscrapers on the European imagination. A very different imaginative power, however, informs the slightly later designs produced by Expressionist architects. Since the emergence of reform-minded designers such as A. W. N. Pugin (1812–1852) in the early nineteenth century, architects had argued that the design of environments could influence behavior. Like prophets of a new human sensibility, Expressionist architects promoted a world of crystalline architecture animated with colors and lights. In 1919 Bruno Taut (1880–1938) published *Alpine Architektur*, an ecstatic description of mountain valleys spanned by glass canopies and Alpine peaks carved into abstract, cathedral-like forms (fig. 1.8). In his text, Taut makes clear that the crystalline artifice of the reconfigured landscape heralds an equally dramatic transformation of the social order from an ethos founded on competition and war to one of solidarity and cooperation.

Alpine Architektur can hardly be treated as a practical urban design proposal. It is included here as an indication of the epic scale and imaginative power of visionary design. Throughout the twentieth century, architects created fantastical schemes in which unprecedented (and often unbuildable) forms are offered as utopian models of radical new social, economic, political, and spiritual orders. The history of twentieth-century architecture is as much the history of human imagination and the visual codes developed to express that imagination as it is a history of buildings.

Not everyone shared the Futurists' faith that modernization would lead to a better tomorrow, or the Expressionist belief that the human spirit could be elevated and improved through environmental design. Dark visions of the future metropolis coexisted in the popular imagination with more optimistic views. In the 1926 German film *Metropolis* (fig. 1.9), for example, the director Fritz Lang and his set designers envisioned the city of the future as a dense, congested environment in which the extremes of luxury and deprivation ultimately dehumanized both those who lived high in the lofty towers and those who labored below in the dark bowels of the city. In one scene the movie's heroine, Maria, recounts the biblical story

1.8 Bruno Taut, plate 13 from *Alpine Architektur*, 1919.

1.9 Fritz Lang, scene from *Metropolis*, 1926.

of the Tower of Babel and preaches a message of love and human solidarity. Professional architects, however, argued that comprehensive planning, not quasi-spiritual revivalism, was the way to tame the modern city and impose a rational order on the perceived chaos of urban growth.

The Emergence of the Modern Movement

Le Corbusier

In the 1920s one voice emerged with particular force and clarity: Charles Édouard Jeanneret (1887–1965). Born in Switzerland, he settled in Paris after World War I and adopted the pseudonym Le Corbusier, a name combining "corbeau," French for *crow*, with "Le Corbesier," a relative on his father's side. He is widely considered one of the most influential architects and architectural writers of the twentieth century and his designs were seminal contributions to the development of a new architectural aesthetic. Just as important, he developed a writing style of epigrammatic clarity. Two statements from his important 1923 book *Vers une Architecture*—"A house is a machine for living in" and "Architecture is the correct and masterful play of forms brought together in the light"—capture the range of his thinking. The first conveys his interest in buildings that achieve the functional precision associated with machines while the second expresses his equally strong commitment to architecture as a soul-stirring visual art.

In 1925 he published *Urbanisme*. This treatise on modern town planning brought together various projects and ideas that had occupied Le Corbusier for several years. Just as Burnham and Bennett had presented a striking vision of a reorganized Chicago, Le Corbusier imagined a radically different Paris. In a typically bold rhetorical move, he proposed leveling most of the historic center of Paris and

1.10 Le Corbusier, "The City of Tomorrow and its Planning," from *Urbanisme*, 8e, pp. 246–7.

erecting, in place of the dense, continuous fabric of the old city, cruciform towers set at regular intervals in a gardenlike setting (fig. 1.10). Light and air, the battle cry of urban reformers since the mid-nineteenth century, fill the space of the new city and the whole is governed by a lucid, geometric clarity missing in the Futurist vision of *città nuova*. In a move critical for early twentieth-century design theory, he linked the beauty of geometry and the precision of modern machines.

> Geometry is the means, created by ourselves, whereby we perceive the external world and express the world within us. Geometry is the foundation. It is also the material basis on which we build those symbols which represent to us perfection and the divine . . . Machinery is the result of geometry. The age in which we live is therefore essentially a geometrical one.
>
> (Le Corbusier, *The City of Tomorrow*, p. xxi)

For Le Corbusier, the geometric clarity of his architectural forms ensured they were in harmony with the demands of precision and standardization deemed to be at the heart of the modern means of production.

CIAM

Le Corbusier was hardly alone in his claims that the modern world made new demands of the architect, offered new material and tectonic possibilities and, therefore, required a new architectural aesthetic. Many architects shared his belief that each great civilization ultimately developed its own distinctive architecture and that modern civilization, too, was destined to develop its own authentic architectural language. Le Corbusier and his modernist peers saw their task as the creation of this new architecture. Across Europe, "new" became one of the sacred words of progressive design criticism, expressed in terms of *l'esprit nouveau, lo spirito nuovo, nieuwe bouwen, das neue Sachlichkeit*, or the New Functionalism.

A new organization soon appeared as well. In 1928 two dozen architects committed to the cause of a truly modern architecture assembled in La Sarraz, Switzerland, and founded the Congrès Internationaux de l'Architecture Moderne (CIAM). The organization provided a structure for what had been a loose coalition of like-minded architects and a vehicle for the promotion of the nascent Modern

Movement in Architecture. CIAM met periodically to share research on such topics as low-cost housing, land use, site planning, and the relative merits of low-, medium-, and high-rise housing blocks. In 1933 CIAM drafted a document known as the Athens Charter in which town planning was defined as the organization of collective life according to functional (not aesthetic) criteria applicable to four critical categories: housing, work, recreation, and traffic. The Modern Movement's planning ideology thus emphasized social and economic issues and rejected historical models. CIAM's version of modern architecture cannot be understood in terms of a revival or renaissance. It is a true modernism: the deliberate reformulation of principles and practices in terms different from the humanist tradition of Western classicism.

Despite its august aims, CIAM remained small and never achieved official status in any country. Yet it has always occupied a place in the accounts of modern architecture out of all proportion to its actual size. In part, this is due to the tireless promotional efforts of some of the organization's members, most notably Siegfried Giedion (1888–1968) who served as CIAM secretary for many years.

A flair for self-promotion is however insufficient to explain CIAM's impact. The rise of CIAM coincided with significant changes in the professional identity of architects. Beginning in the late nineteenth century and gaining momentum in the early twentieth century, the modernization of professional practices in many different disciplines (including architecture) emerged as a significant concern. New or revised standards for professional certification, curricular reforms in professional education, and new professional societies and journals combined to redefine the idea of professional competence. CIAM's approach reflected a shift from the notion of architecture as a fine art to design offering the command of techniques required for the rational calculation and control of the built environment. This entailed the development of a new vocabulary for planners along with new sets of analytical categories and methods. The quest for an authentically modern architecture proved to be as much a debate about language and methodology as it was a debate about forms and symbols. For CIAM members, planning lessons were to be drawn from the modern system of industrial organization rather than derived from classical political theories about civic society. (Indeed, the word "civic" virtually disappeared as a critical term from the CIAM lexicon.) Precisely how the lessons of industrial production should be incorporated into design practice remains a central question for the architectural profession to this day.

Housing

Housing design merits special consideration in any account of twentieth-century architecture. With the growth in numbers and potential political power of urban populations, the magnitude of the housing problem in the early twentieth century could not be ignored. It became increasingly clear that neither market forces nor private philanthropy could respond adequately to the demand (increasingly perceived as a right) for decent, sanitary housing. In no other sector of the building economy did state and municipal involvement expand so dramatically. Reformers of various political persuasions seized on housing issues as a critical component of ambitious reform campaigns. Residents of the new housing estates underwent a process of socialization that social historians increasingly recognize as a critical stage in the modernization of urban populations. To survive in the new housing developments, tenants learned to adjust to rhythms and forms of urban life that bore little or no relationship to the customs and practices of small, rural communities or premodern villages. Finally, research concerning optimal design solutions for housing preoccupied professional architects throughout the century. Architects debated the advantages of new versus traditional materials and systems of construction, examined different site-planning strategies, and developed various typological solutions. The projects considered below display a range of the design strategies that emerged during the first third of the century. It is important to remember that, in each case, the chosen strategy emerged in a context determined by local and national legislation, the type of financing employed, and the location of available building sites.

Europe

In 1902 the Netherlands passed important new legislation outlining a national housing program. The Housing Act of 1902 required the preparation of municipal plans in an effort to control urban growth, mandated new building codes for housing, extended state powers of expropriation, and established funds and procedures for financing new housing construction. Although the legislation was national in scope, local solutions varied significantly. In Amsterdam, such architects as Michel De Klerk (1884–1923) extended in novel ways a Dutch tradition of expressive brick architecture (fig. 1.11). De Klerk varied the surface textures of his housing blocks and developed eccentric details that individualized each building. In contrast, the work of J. J. P. Oud   (1890–1963) in Rotterdam reflects his interest in conveying

1.11 Michel De Klerk, Eigen Haard (housing, post office, and school), Amsterdam, Netherlands, 1913–19.
   "Eigen Haard" means "own hearth," a name that embodies the social agenda of modern architects. De Klerk's treatment of the triangular site, with a prow-like design at the narrow end and a mastlike tower at the broad end, earned this project the nickname of "Het Scheep", "the ship."

the rational character of modern construction by using standardized units for maximum economy (fig. 1.12). Encapsulated within the Dutch housing experience is a debate that came to dominate discussions of modern architecture—between the advocates of an exuberant expressive freedom in design and those who favored a limited range of standardized building forms capable of serial production.

The location of large-scale housing projects proved to be another contentious issue. Here, local political and economic conditions were critical in setting the parameters within which design solutions were worked out. Where municipal administrations were able to exercise control over large parcels of land near the city center, superblocks emerged as one strategy. Elsewhere, new satellite communities erected outside historic city centers proved more feasible. Political leaders were desperate to ameliorate the problems caused by inadequate housing and stave off the threat of political turmoil. Le Corbusier deftly summed up the political implications of housing when he concluded *Vers une Architecture* with the admonition: "Architecture or revolution. Revolution can be avoided."

In Germany, reeling from military defeat and the collapse of the monarchy, new housing programs constituted a major part of the Social Democratic agenda. Housing efforts were often conceived as one component of ambitious programs for providing a broad range of social services including new educational and recreational facilities, improved public transportation, and even allotment gardens.

1.12 J. J. P. Oud, Blijdorp housing project plan, Rotterdam, Netherlands, 1931.

In addition to describing the details of a design, architectural plans and drawings often convey other information. Airplanes are instantly recognizable icons of modernity; the inclusion of an aircraft's wingtip in the upper-left corner of this rendering emphasizes the modern spirit pervading the entire housing project.

1.13 Ernst May, Römerstadt, Frankfurt am Main, Germany, 1927. Historisches Museum, Frankfurt am Main.

Under the direction of reform-minded mayor Ludwig Landmann, Frankfurt am Main, for example, embarked on an aggressive program of modernizing the urban infrastructure and expanding the housing stock available to citizens of all classes.

For five years beginning in 1926, Ernst May (1886–1970), an active member of CIAM, served as *Stadtbaurat* or city architect, and during that time he was responsible for the construction of an exemplary series of *siedlungen* (housing estates). Influenced in part by Ebenezar Howard's Garden City concept and constrained by tight finances that rendered large-scale land acquisition in the center of the city difficult, May developed a series of satellite communities on the periphery of the city that earned international recognition for Frankfurt am Main as a center for progressive architecture. Römerstadt, perhaps the finest of May's designs, provided over 1,200 new dwellings along the Nidda river valley northwest of the city center (fig. 1.13). Working with Leberecht Migge (1881–1935), an advocate of allotment gardening not only as a source of food but as a counterpoint to the alienation of modern urban life, May laid out the satellite community in long rows of flat-roofed townhouses along gently curving streets. Early photos suggest a spartan environment, but the maturation of the green spaces and the gardens has softened and enriched the overall effect.

Today, May's efforts in Frankfurt am Main elicit different responses from historians. Marxist historians such as Manfredo Tafuri, although finding much to admire in the Römerstadt scheme and others, ultimately deem Landmann and May's efforts a failure because they were unable to neutralize the role of capital and the power of private landowners in shaping urban development. But other commentators, such as Susan Henderson, see in the complex relationship between housing reform, the allotment gardening movement, and evolving concepts of education, recreation, and family life the essential components of what German reformers of the period identified as the *Neues Leben* (new life). Whether viewed in the political terms of Marxist analysis or from the perspective of social historians, the Frankfurt

experience is crucial to understanding the appeal and the fate of modern architecture in Weimar-era Germany.

At the opposite extreme from the Frankfurt experiment with suburban *siedlungen* stands Vienna. As in the case of Frankfurt, a strong political vision shaped Viennese policies, but unlike Frankfurt's Landmann, the Viennese Social Democrat Otto Bauer pursued a policy of concentration in the Austrian capital. Viennese officials moved aggressively to acquire control of land, control rents, and subsidize new construction. It has been estimated that the public housing authority was responsible for 70 percent of the housing erected in Vienna between the end of World War I and 1934. Completed in 1930, the Karl-Marx-Hof, designed by Karl Ehn (1884–1957), represents the epitome of the Viennese *hof*, or superblock (fig. 1.14). The building stretches for more than a kilometer along the Heiligenstädterstrasse and was designed originally to accommodate more than 5,200 residents. The row of towers along the main facade endows the entire scheme with a monumental quality that some have interpreted as a defiant assertion of the *hof* as a working-class fortress in the heart of "red Vienna."

The United States: Catherine Bauer

In comparison to European efforts, the United States was slower to embrace publicly funded housing programs. It preferred reform legislation designed to impose controls on private developments rather than direct government involvement in new construction. But American architects and social reformers were clearly aware of European developments thanks to the efforts of the architectural critic Catherine Bauer, whose 1934 book *Modern Housing* is a key document in the planning literature of the period. In *Modern Housing*, Bauer described the nineteenth-century origins of the housing problem, evaluated the various typological solutions proposed, and reviewed important contemporary examples. In a cultural and professional

1.14 Karl Ehn, Karl-Marx-Hof, Heiligenstädterstrasse 32–39, Vienna, Austria, 1927–30.

milieu that offered only limited opportunities for women, Bauer epitomized the activist critic. The same year that *Modern Housing* appeared, she was one of the founders, along with the architect Oskar Stonorov (1905–1970) and the labor leader John W. Edelman, of the Labor Housing Conference which lobbied for the creation of a United States Housing Authority. She served briefly as the Director of Research and Information for the Authority and remained an important spokesperson for housing issues until her death in 1964.

Pieces of the City

While CIAM members and other modern architects attempted to recast the terms of city planning, they remained committed to the idea that the city can be planned as a logical and coherent entity. Yet much of the modern city escapes the type of comprehensive planning described above. The construction of the city comes to architects building by building rather than as complete urban schemes, and the city dweller experiences the city as a collection of discrete buildings and environments.

In 1923 the Rudolf Mosse Publishing Company, a major German publishing house and advertising agency, completed the expansion of its Berlin headquarters. The new space, designed by Erich Mendelsohn (1887–1953), appears to rise out of the original office building completed twenty years earlier (fig. 1.15). Mendelsohn made no attempt to harmonize the new and the old; instead the horizontal banding of the Mendelsohn addition stands in stark contrast to the vertical articulation of the original structure. Burnham, Saarinen, and Garnier proposed visions of unified, consistent cityscapes conceived with a sense of civic decorum in which the parts—individual commercial buildings, for example—were subordinate to the urban whole. In Erich Mendelsohn's Berlin Mossehaus of 1922, however, modernity erupts out of the shell of the preexisting building, defiant and assertive.

The appeal of Mendelsohn's design lies in its dynamism and the manner in which it crystalizes an urban aesthetic based on sudden, vivid contrast rather than harmony. Such an aesthetic facilitates the process of modernization, a process that has tended to promote the development of distinct sectors carefully tailored to serve specific functions (work, education, entertainment) and facilitate particular activities (economic production, personal consumption, political participation). In examining these discrete "pieces" of the urban environment—skyscrapers, department stores, apartment buildings, etcetera—we can explore the different forces shaping the modern city: typological innovation, regulatory control, emerging cultural

1.15 Erich Mendelsohn, Rudolf Mosse Building (Mossehaus), Berlin, Germany, 1922.

practices, and the shifting fortunes of style as a central concept in design studios. We can also begin to recognize the cultural dilemma confronting the architectural profession, as traditional conceptions of architects' social status and professional identity are replaced by new expectations concerning professional skills and aesthetic preferences.

In the academic tradition, conformity to precedent legitimizes design decisions; by 1900, however, progressive-minded architects realized that custom and historical precedent were inadequate for meeting the challenge of contemporary building. In 1896 the Viennese architect Otto Wagner (1841–1918) published an important treatise entitled *Modern Architecture*. Two years earlier, Wagner had been appointed Professor of Architecture in the Vienna Academy of Fine Art. His academic credentials ensured that *Modern Architecture* was received as a significant statement by architects and critics across Europe. In *Modern Architecture*, Wagner argued:

> All modern creations must correspond to the new materials and demands of the present if they are to suit modern man; they must illustrate our own better, democratic, self-confident, ideal nature and take into account man's colossal technical and scientific achievements, as well as his thoroughly practical tendency—that is surely self-evident.

(Wagner, p. 178)

1.16 Otto Wagner, Postal Savings Bank, interior, Georg-Coch-Platz 2, Vienna, Austria, 1904–06. Wagner here incorporated the legacy of nineteenth-century engineering into a twentieth-century conception of modern architecture. The glazed vault, exposed structural frame, and new materials such as aluminum establish the modernity of his design.

1.17 H. P. Berlage, Amsterdam Exchange, interior, Damrack and Beursplein, Amsterdam, Netherlands, 1897–1903.

His architectural treatise was inspired, Wagner wrote, by one idea: "that the basis of today's predominant views on architecture must be shifted, and we must become fully aware that the sole departure point for our artistic work can only be modern life." Wagner's own buildings demonstrate his commitment to an authentically modern architecture. His Postal Savings Bank of 1906 quickly gained international recognition as a bold step beyond the eclectic historicism of nineteenth-century Viennese architecture (fig. 1.16). On the exterior, the exposed bolt heads clarified the constructional nature of the panel system used to clad the structure. Once inside the Postal Savings Bank, one has the impression that a cultural threshold has been crossed: the interior has been developed in a new style altogether.

Like Wagner, the Dutch architect H. P. Berlage (1856–1934) pioneered the development of a fresh approach to design conceived in terms of contemporary needs and possibilities. In his handling of masonry and iron, Berlage's Amsterdam Exchange Building (fig. 1.17) builds on the work of such nineteenth-century architectural figures as Eugène Viollet-le-Duc (1814–1879), Gottfried Semper (1803–1879), and Jan Hessel de Groot (1865–1932). With his concern for the articulation of volume, however, and his simplification or elimination of historicist detail, Berlage provided influential support for an emerging architectural aesthetic founded on tectonic issues rather than historical forms. What distinguishes influential figures at the turn of the century such as Wagner and Berlage from the avant-garde designs of younger men such as Sant'Elia and Taut is their attitude to the present. In place of utopian visions of human community or schemes so bold as to exceed any realistic expectations for realization, Wagner and Berlage worked to extend the limits of what was practical in contemporary terms. Both men produced expansion plans for their cities which are realistic proposals carefully developed in light of the practical demands of current conditions.

Skyscrapers

When the Woolworth Building was opened in 1913, one commentator, inspired by the building's soaring gothic tower, proclaimed it a "Cathedral of Commerce." But the cathedral metaphor is misplaced, for unlike the symbolically charged space of a church, space in a commercial building is first and foremost a commodity. In 1900 Cass Gilbert (1859–1934), later the architect of the Woolworth Building, described the skyscraper as "a machine that makes the land pay" and his description neatly captured the essence of the design problem. The optimal solution for the tall office building—like any business machine—could be calculated and the result assessed in quantitative terms. In the nineteenth century, as architects and engineers solved the fundamental structural problems associated with the tall office building, other aspects of skyscraper design received increased attention. In his seminal 1896 essay "The Tall Office Building Artistically Considered," Louis Sullivan (1856–1924) analyzed the problem of providing a vertical stack of identical office floors and proposed the tripartite base–shaft–capital organization of the building's exterior. In his typically lyrical prose, Sullivan then went on to give the tall building its expressive theme: "It must be every inch a proud and soaring thing, rising in sheer exultation that from bottom to top it is a unit without a single dissenting line."

Architects worked closely with real-estate developers and building managers to coordinate office layout, fenestration patterns, and building services in order to maximize the return on investors' money. Lot size and location, provisions for natural light and air, and the height limits imposed by economic rather than engineering considerations did much to fix the terms of the formula: Form follows finance. Early in the century, architects experimented with different architectural treatments for the tall building, including ornate Gothic or classically inspired towers. But it was the passage in New York City of a new zoning ordinance in 1916 that exerted the most profound impact on the design of tall buildings and promoted the skyscraper style of the 1920s and early 1930s.

New York's 1916 zoning ordinance was the first piece of legislation developed to regulate the height and bulk of tall office buildings. The availability of natural light and fresh air were important factors in the design equation of office buildings. The completion, in 1915, of the Equitable Building in Lower Manhattan demonstrated that as constructions rose higher, their bulk blocked sunlight and impeded the circulation of air, thus decreasing the value of nearby commercial space (fig. 1.18). In an effort to mitigate the most negative aspects of skyscraper development, the 1916 zoning ordinance mandated setbacks in the massing of tall buildings and established a formula, based on lot size and the width of the surrounding streets, for establishing the maximum allowable bulk and height for new construction. Other American cities followed New York's lead in regulating the height of tall buildings. Architects were quick to refine design treatments for setback silhouettes as mandated by the ordinance. Today, zoning ordinances continue to be a significant factor in the design of skyscrapers.

Although the formula "Form follows finance" dictated the basic configuration of the skyscraper and developers continued to demand "a machine that makes the land pay," skyscraper architects recognized the importance of individualizing each design. The 1930 Chrysler Building (fig. 1.19) by William van Alen (1883–1954), and Shreve, Lamb, and Harmon's Empire State Building (see page 2), completed in 1931, epitomize the skyscraper style of the post-1916 era. The setback profile rendered the classical cornice line obsolete and the buildings terminated in a distinctive spire. Individual windows were set within brick or masonry curtain walls and ornament remained an integral part of the architectural conception. Chevrons, sun-

1.18 (left) Equitable Building, New York, 1915.

1.19 (above) William van Alen, Chrysler Building (detail), New York, 1928–30.
The Chrysler Building epitomizes the Art Deco skyscraper style. The flamboyant spire creates a unique identity within New York, incorporating references to automotive design including giant radiator caps positioned like gargoyles at the corner of the tower and a frieze composed of car fenders and shiny silver hubcaps.

bursts, setback, and zigzag motifs replaced classical molding and historicist details as skyscraper architects developed a flamboyant, ornamental vocabulary frankly celebratory of the modern metropolis. Originally the product of restrictive legislation, in only a few short years the setback silhouette metamorphized into one of the emblematic features of the modern metropolis. As important as financial considerations were, skyscrapers represented more than the spatialization of capital. When Paul Frankl produced a line of skyscraper furniture in the late 1920s, it was the romance and sophistication of life in the big city he wanted to evoke, not the financial balance sheets of urban real estate (fig. 1.20).

Today, historians use the term Art Deco to identify this amalgam of decorative features, although the sheer range of forms, materials, and motifs employed by Art Deco designers renders the use of any single term problematic. Art Deco combined the formal simplification and abstraction of avant-garde art with exotic materials and a machine age iconography that appealed to a wide range of audiences. Art Deco designs addressed the popular enthusiasm for modernity and celebrated the present rather than the past. Reflecting a persistent bias among critics against the decorative in twentieth-century architecture, Art Deco has been dismissed as a superficial design phenomenon. Yet considered on its own terms, as a style applicable at multiple scales and aimed at a broad audience, Art Deco proved to be enormously successful. Cities as remote from one another as Miami Beach, Florida, and Napier, New Zealand, boast entire Art Deco neighborhoods.

Department Stores

Acknowledging the appeal of Art Deco requires that one address the role of style and fashion in the modern design economy and recognize the importance of department stores in the modern metropolis. Like the tall office building, the department

1.20 Paul Frankl, bookcase skyscraper, circa 1926. Painted plywood, wood, brass hardware, 96¼ × 42 × 15⅝ in (244.5 × 106.7 × 39.9 cm).

1.21 Louis Boileau, Bon Marché Pavilion, "Art Deco Exhibition," Paris, France, 1925.

1.22 Alfred Messel,
Wertheim Department
Store, Leipzigerplatz,
Berlin, Germany,
1896–1904.

store emerged as a distinctive building type in the nineteenth century and grew in size until it often occupied entire city blocks. Cultural historians have noted the role of consumption in the creation of personal, gender, and class identities in the modern era, and department stores played a crucial role in the promotion of all types and styles of goods for an increasingly broad spectrum of consumers. Department stores (often in conjunction with art museums) sponsored exhibitions of contemporary decorative arts and home furnishings which introduced modern design trends to a wide audience. The 1925 "Exposition Internationale des Arts Décoratifs et Industriels Modernes" in Paris, for example, was instrumental in fostering the taste for a stylish modernity; the prominent pavilions erected by Parisian department stores were among the most important examples of an emerging modern sensibility (fig. 1.21).

As places of distribution rather than production, department stores reinforced the trend toward specialization of services and the division of the urban environment into discrete areas designed for separate activities such as production, distribution, and consumption. Here the ephemerality of modern life, the ceaseless flood of novelty and style is concentrated, promoted, and packaged for consumption.

Three examples demonstrate different ways in which architects conceptualized the urban possibilities inherent in the design of a single building type. In his turn-of-the-century design for the Wertheim Department Store in Berlin, Alfred Messel (1853–1909) responded to the urban site with a generous loggia on the Leipzigerplatz (fig. 1.22). The Neo-Gothic design allowed him to open up the walls for the addition of many windows while retaining a recognizable link to traditional architecture.

With the popularity of Art Deco, some department stores assumed a more flamboyant presence in the cityscape. The tower, stepped massing, and decorative details of John (1861–1935) and Donald (1895–1946) Parkinson's design for Bullock's Store in Los Angeles assert its fashionably modern presence on Wilshire Boulevard, while the inclusion of a parking lot reflected the growing importance of

1.23 (opposite) John and Donald Parkinson, Bullock's–Wilshire Department Store, 3050 Wilshire Boulevard, Los Angeles, California, 1928.

1.24 (right) Erich Mendelsohn, Schocken Department Store, Chemnitz, Germany, 1928–30.

the automobile in the modern city (fig. 1.23). Pedestrians entered Bullock's from Wilshire Boulevard while a porte-cochère (a covered, sheltering entrance) on the opposite side of the store accommodated customers arriving by automobile. Clearly this is more than a warehouse for the distribution of goods; it is above all a celebration of stylish modern lifestyles.

For the Schocken Department Store in Chemnitz, Germany, Erich Mendelsohn rejected both the historicist imagery of Messel's Wertheim and the Art Deco motifs of the Los Angeles store (fig. 1.24). The horizontal bands that extend across the curving facade of the Schocken store served both functional and expressive ends. The ribbon windows provided even lighting on the upper floors and ample display areas at street level. For Mendelsohn, the sweeping horizontal emphasis of the facade evoked the dynamism of modern life, which he contrasted with the static compositional schemes of traditional architecture.

Apartment Buildings

Mendelsohn's preference for strong horizontal articulation in his facades reflected a personal conviction concerning the effect on the urban viewer of different types of composition. One of the challenges of any survey is to distinguish between the uniquely personal aspects of an architect's achievement and those design themes, strategies, and typological solutions characteristic of a design movement, a generation, or a particular region. This is clearly so in the case of apartment buildings.

During the nineteenth century, the growing middle class sought to legitimize itself by identifying with many of the elements of high culture traditionally associated with the aristocracy. Apartment buildings were modeled after the palaces of the nobility. By the early twentieth century, however, the inadequacies of this

approach were increasingly apparent. An apartment building occupied by many small families is not the same as the palatial residence of an aristocratic family surrounded by an extensive entourage. Designers turned away from historical models with aristocratic pedigrees and explored other approaches inspired by nature, tectonics, or urban sociology.

The undulating facade of the Casa Milá in Barcelona by Antonio Gaudí (1852–1926) suggests the wave-sculpted face of a seaside cliff while, on the rooftop, the bizarrely twisted shapes of ventilator hoods stand like mysterious sentinels (fig. 1.25). Gaudí's eccentric design language is extremely personal, yet it struck a chord among a generation concerned with promoting the Catalan *Renaixença* (the quest for a cultural identity unique to the region surrounding Barcelona). Gaudí's work combines an interest in rational if unorthodox structural solutions with formal solutions that elicit emotional responses on the part of observers. For Gaudí, the public realm of the modern city—the streets, squares, and parks of Barcelona— embraces both the mundane and the surreal realms of human experience. His buildings unite the rational and the romantic in compositions that vividly assert their presence in the streetscape.

1.25 Antonio Gaudí, Casa Milá ("La Pedrera"), Barcelona, Spain, 1905–11.

Gaudí combined an interest in rational structure, natural forms, religious visions, and eso- teric symbolism in his work. Residents nicknamed this building "La Pedrera" ("the quarry") because of its massive stone façade. Wrought-iron balcony railings suggest dried seaweed clinging to a seaside cliff.

In Vienna, Adolf Loos (1870–1933) adopted a different strategy. His Goldman & Salatsch Building (fig. 1.26) on the Michaelerplatz, completed in 1911, is as restrained as Gaudí's Casa Milá is flamboyant. In the traditional urban palace, the primacy of the *piano nobile* (main floor) was expressed clearly on the facade. Loos chose, however, to privilege the commercial space at street level by cladding the base of the building with marble slabs. As if to guard the privacy of the residents, the stucco-faced upper floors express little beyond the fact of the building's existence. A writer as well as an architect, Adolf Loos was a keen observer of the cultural scene in turn-of-the-century Vienna and his critical essays contain valuable insights into the design debates of the day.

Positioned between Gaudí's expressive intensity and Loos's restrained decorum is the work of the French architect Auguste Perret (1874–1954). Tectonic issues involving the selection of building materials and structural systems are foremost in Perret's work. Like his countryman, Tony Garnier, he employed reinforced concrete extensively in his designs. The addition of metal reinforcing rods, an innovation

1.26 Adolf Loos, Goldman & Salatsch Building, Michaelerplatz, Vienna, Austria, 1909–11.

1.27 Auguste Perret, apartment building, 26 bis rue Franklin, Paris, France, 1902–03.

1.28 Berthold Lubetkin and Tecton, Highpoint One, North Hill, Highgate, London, England, 1935.

of the nineteenth century, completely transformed this ancient material, making it a viable solution for an expanded range of building tasks. In his design for an apartment building on the rue Franklin in Paris, Perret revealed the reinforced concrete frame of the building (fig. 1.27). Ceramic panels impressed with floral patterns filled the interstices of the frame. The result is devoid of any reference to identifiable historical models yet still recognizable as an extension and refinement of the French tradition of structural rationalism committed to the integration of classical design principles with the modern science of building construction.

From disparate examples such as these it would be tempting to describe the story of the middle-class apartment building as the triumphal emergence and widespread acceptance of a genuinely modern architectural type in less than a generation. In Highgate, London, Highpoint One (fig. 1.28), completed in 1935, and Highpoint Two, completed three years later, by Berthold Lubetkin (1901–1990) with the design group Tecton, seem to suggest precisely this. Built of concrete according to a plan that ensures cross-ventilation and ample natural light to all the units, and meticulously detailed in an uncompromisingly modern manner, Highpoint One was hailed by Le Corbusier as "an achievement of the first rank."

But history is seldom as neat as triumphalist accounts would suggest. Shortly after completion of Highpoint One, local residents formed the Highgate Preservation Society and successfully lobbied for a reduction in the size and arrangement of Highpoint Two. Opposition was motivated by hostility to the new architecture and concern over the destruction of the existing architectural character of the neighborhood. Resistance to designs like Highpoint was part of an often fierce debate concerning an appropriate architecture for the twentieth century that would continue well into the late 1930s.

Highpoint's designers challenged social conventions in other ways. Tecton, for example, was created in 1932 by Lubetkin, a Russian émigré architect, and six young English designers. The group's adoption of the impersonal collective name Tecton—a contraction of the Greek term *architecton*—ran counter to the customary practice of identifying a firm by the personal names of the principal partners. Rejecting the customs associated with a gentleman's profession was part of the "cult of the new" characteristic of the period. The gentleman's profession of architecture was changing in other ways: women were now entering the previously male preserve of architectural practice.

Women in Architecture

Wivi Lönn, Jane Drew, and Julia Morgan

One approach to recovering the early history of women architects involves identifying noteworthy "firsts." Take the career in Finland of Wivi Lönn (1872–1966). Although several women had graduated from architectural programs in Finland prior to Lönn in 1896, she was the first to successfully pursue a career as an architect. She established herself professionally with a series of designs for schools. In 1906 she won a national competition for a new fire station in Tampere (fig. 1.29).

1.29 Wivi Lönn, Central Fire Station, Tampere, Finland, 1908.
The tower, picturesque massing, and bold textures identify the fire station as an example of Finnish National Romanticism. During her long career, Lönn designed dozens of schools, timber-framed villas, and two YWCA buildings in Helsinki, and collaborated with Armas Lindgren in the design of a theater in Tallinn. The industrialist Hanna Parviainen commissioned Lönn to design manufacturing facilities in Säynätsalo.

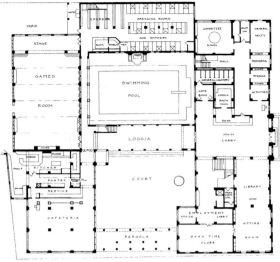

1.30 (left) Julia Morgan, Young Women's Christian Association (YWCA) Recreation Center, Honolulu, 1926.

The YWCA responded to the shortage of reputable accommodations for urban female workers by building housing and recreational centers in cities throughout the US. Between 1913 and 1932 Morgan designed a dozen YWCA facilities along the Pacific coast. Her designs included swimming pools for active recreation as well as reading rooms.

1.31 (right) Julia Morgan, YWCA, plan, Honolulu, 1926.

Along with other women architects, Lönn encountered many problems in the male-dominated profession. Often, routine office decisions such as hiring presented women with dilemmas not experienced by their male colleagues. For example, one of the most successful of American women architects, Julia Morgan (1872–1957), employed women in her office, but limited their number to avoid scaring off potential male clients uncomfortable with an all-female staff. The English architect Jane Drew (b. 1911) had a different experience. When she established her own office in London in the early 1940s, she was determined to recruit women for her staff. Because architecture remained a male-dominated profession, she found it difficult to hire enough women and eventually was forced to bring men into her office.

Morgan was perhaps the most successful woman architect of the first half of the century in terms of the volume of work realized (over 700 buildings). After earning an engineering degree from the University of California, she was the first woman to be accepted in the architectural section of the École des Beaux-Arts in Paris. Returning to the United States, she established an independent practice in the San Francisco Bay Area. In addition to private homes, her list of commissions included a significant amount of institutional work for schools, colleges, and churches. Women philanthropists such as Phoebe Apperson Hearst and women's organizations such as the Young Women's Christian Association (YWCA) were important sources of her commissions (figs. 1.30, 1.31). Morgan also designed scores of YWCA facilities in cities along the American West Coast. Her body of work demonstrates a masterful command of an eclectic range of styles from arts and crafts-inspired work to carefully detailed classical compositions to fabulous romantic designs such as William Randolph Hearst's famous estate at San Simeon, California.

Beyond documenting the achievements of pioneering women in the profession, recent scholarship on gender issues in twentieth-century architecture explores a broad range of topics concerning women's experiences in the world of architecture. While women are acknowledged for their contributions as patrons, critics, and architects, feminist scholars also note their fate as the subjects of masculine speculation concerning the "proper place of women" in the designed environments of the twentieth century.

Cultural Institutions

In contrast to the realm of commerce, dominated by economic competition and monetary values, cultural institutions offered the city dweller a chance to experience the refined world of art and the restorative power of beauty. Museums, theaters, concert halls, and libraries constitute the domain of high culture in the modern city. In the first half of the century, classicism continued to provide the dominant architectural means of celebrating high culture. In many cases, however, it was a classicism modified in novel ways by an emerging modern sensibility. Inscribed over the entry to Joseph Olbrich's (1867–1908) Secession Building in Vienna (fig. 1.32) was the motto: "To the Age its Art—To Art its Freedom." On one level this meant freedom from the strictures of academic rules and established hierarchies. The building was erected to exhibit the work of the Viennese Secession Movement, composed of artists who had defected from the official fine arts institution. In design terms, it meant the freedom to explore the primal elements of geometry, myth, and symbols out of which the language of classical architecture was originally formed. In the romantic conception of design operative here, literal fidelity to historical precedents was seen as a failure of imagination.

To recapture the life-sustaining energy of art, it was necessary to return to the primitive power of elemental form. Olbrich substituted the primary geometry of a sphere for the traditional dome. The metal sphere employed the motif of laurel

1.32 Joseph Olbrich, Secession Building, Vienna, Austria, 1897–98.

leaves, as if to crown the artists whose work was displayed inside. Through the juxtaposition of the perforated volume of the sphere above and the solidity and mass of the building below, Olbrich suggested the struggle between matter and spirit, an enduring theme in reflections on art, yet recast here in fresh terms.

Classical models, transformed through a process of abstraction, continued to appeal to architects throughout

1.33 (left) Erik Gunnar Asplund, Public Library, Stockholm, Sweden, 1920–8.
The plan of a library as a centralized reading room surrounded by book stacks, staff offices, and support services emerged early in the nineteenth century. Asplund adapts this established type and strips it of historicist embellishments. The result is an austere cylinder arising from a low, rectangular box. One of the few historical references appears in the enormous Egyptian-inspired main portal.

1.34 John Russell Pope and Otto R. Eggers, *The National Gallery of Art*, 1937. Gray wash over graphite, 12½ × 46¾ in (32 × 118 cm). National Gallery of Art, Washington, DC.
A pedimented entry portico combined with a saucer-shaped dome recalls the Pantheon in Rome. The dome's low silhouette emphasizes the museum's importance as a repository of art, without challenging the nearby Capitol building with its own tall dome.

the 1920s and 1930s. Stockholm Public Library by Erik Gunnar Asplund (1885–1940) is an excellent example of the Nordic version of this phenomenon (fig. 1.33). But literal renditions of classical forms continued to be proposed as solutions for cultural programs. In the United States, John Russell Pope (1874–1937) was responsible for an outstanding series of monumental classical designs. In his designs for the Jefferson Memorial and the National Gallery of Art, both in Washington DC, Pope handles the full panoply of the classical vocabulary in a masterful manner. In the classical *gravitas* of the National Gallery (fig. 1.34) one can recognize the legacy of the City Beautiful movement.

The International Style

Cultural institutions were not simply refuges from the coarser and more commercial aspects of modernity: many institutions saw themselves as agents of public education, committed to raising popular appreciation of modern conceptions of beauty as well as displaying old master works. New York's Museum of Modern Art, founded in 1929, epitomizes the crusading cultural institution (fig. 1.35). The museum sponsored exhibitions that reflected an unwavering commitment to modernism in the visual arts. In 1932, for example, it staged what in retrospect must be acknowledged as one of the most important architectural exhibitions of the century, "Modern Architecture: International Exhibition" (fig. 1.36). The exhibition celebrated the emergence of what the curators Henry-Russell Hitchcock and Philip Johnson argued was a new style equal in importance to the defining styles of earlier historical epochs. The confused nineteenth-century search for a contemporary style through the adaptation of historical models, they argued, was now over. Architects now had in their grasp the authentic expression of contemporary building technologies and artistic sensibilities.

Three features identified buildings as examples of the International Style. First, an emphasis on volume rather than mass in the articulation of buildings. Second, a regularity in the disposition of compositional elements based on standardization of structural elements rather than the classical concern for symmetry and axiality. Third, applied ornament was avoided as much as possible. Beyond defining the elements of a style, Hitchcock and Johnson provided a historical pedigree for the new style and a roster of its leading practitioners.

Work by more than seventy architects was included in the exhibition. Le Corbusier, the Germans Walter Gropius (1883–1969) and Ludwig Mies van der Rohe (1886–1969), and the Dutch designer J. J. P. Oud were singled out for special praise as leading voices in the International Style. The exhibition traveled extensively in the United States, and the illustrated publication that accompanied the show, *The International Style: Architecture Since 1922*, continued to reach a wide audience long after the close of the exhibition.

The majority of work selected was European. Only a handful of American architects met the strict criteria established by the curators. Frank Lloyd Wright (1869–1959) was acknowledged as a pioneer of the new architecture but, along with an older generation of prominent European designers, was essentially dismissed as a product of a nineteenth-century romantic individualism out of touch with the rational discipline of the new era. While important American architects such as Wright could be excluded, important American building types such as the skyscraper could not. One of the few American buildings included was the PSFS Building in Philadelphia designed by George Howe (1886–1955) and William Lescaze (1896–1969) (fig. 1.37). In a bold departure from the conventional handling of the type, Howe and Lescaze treated the skyscraper's base as if it were separate from the rest of the building. They articulated the tower as a stack of identical horizontal layers of office space. The result clearly breaks with the Sullivan-inspired tradition of the tall building as a single, emphatically vertical unity from top to bottom. The advent of the Great Depression meant that American architects would have little opportunity to explore this new conception of the skyscraper until large-scale commercial building resumed after World War II.

In retrospect it is difficult to accept Hitchcock and Johnson's argument that the International Style was the preeminent architectural expression of the modern age, but the enduring strength of their argument must be acknowledged. The term International Style entered the popular lexicon as synonymous with modern architecture and continues to be employed in general discussions of

1.35 (opposite) Philip Goodwin and Edward Stone, Museum of Modern Art, New York, 1939. Courtesy Museum of Modern Art.

1.36 (below) Installation view of "Modern Architecture: International Exhibition," Museum of Modern Art, New York, 10 February–23 March, 1932. Courtesy Museum of Modern Art.

1.37 George Howe and William Lescaze, PSFS Building, Philadelphia, Pennsylvania, 1928–32.

twentieth-century architecture. By defining it as a style (rather than a movement), Hitchcock and Johnson purged the new architecture of the ethical dimension inherent in architecture understood as a vehicle of social reform, and the political overtones associated with the activities of many architects selected for the exhibit. There is nothing disruptive or threatening in the new architecture as presented by Hitchcock and Johnson; instead, they argue, the International Style resolves the stylistic confusion characteristic of nineteenth-century eclecticism in architecture in an intellectually and aesthetically satisfying manner.

Cinema Architecture

Modernity manifested itself in a variety of ways including novel forms of popular entertainment such as cinema which required an architectural solution to the problem of screening films. From early solutions involving the conversion or adaptation of existing auditoria, movie theaters quickly evolved into exotic environments that reinforced the escapist fantasies nurtured by the film industry. Architects soon began to specialize in the design of movie theaters and quickly mastered the concept of entertainment design for the new medium. John Eberson (1875–1954), an Austrian-trained designer who emigrated to the United States in 1923, is credited with the development of the "atmospheric" theater type. In an atmospheric theater, the interior of the auditorium was rendered illusionistically as an outdoor space—moviegoers were invited to imagine themselves seated in a Mediterranean courtyard, for example, or a Persian garden (fig. 1.38).

The literalness of the atmospheric settings gave way to theaters conceived not as representations of romantic locales but as extraordinary spatial experiences based on the orchestration of light, color, and sound effects. The movie palaces of the interwar period were often enormous theaters capable of accommodating thousands

1.38 John Eberson, Tampa Theatre, Tampa, Florida, 1926.
To enhance the atmospheric feeling of being outdoors, Eberson used birds, a cloud machine, special lighting, and starry effects. Closed in the 1970s, the "theatre" was reopened in 1977 as a non-profit film and special events center.

of patrons. In London, for example, Ernest Wamsley Lewis's (1898–1977) New Victoria Cinema, completed in 1930, included 3,000 seats in a spectacular auditorium with tiers of scalloped lighting fixtures (fig. 1.39).

The development of movie theaters was driven by the evolution of the movie industry itself. The coordination of production, distribution, and exhibition aspects of cinema according to a model of organizational management known as vertical integration, encouraged the rationalization of theater design. A handful of architects working for major theater chains designed literally hundreds of theaters during the interwar period. In England, Harry Weedon (1887–1970) designed over 140 cinemas between 1930 and 1939, most of those for Oscar Deutsch's chain of Odeon theaters, and Deutsch purchased and renovated an additional 130 theater buildings. In a career spanning three decades, the American S. Charles Lee (1899–1990) designed over 250 theaters and John Eberson's list of theater designs exceeds 500.

Producing designs in such volume carries its own challenge for owners and architects. Behind the flamboyant Art Deco facades and colorful interiors of the great movie palaces was a thoroughly rational system, codified in technical manuals developed by various theater chains. These manuals detailed formulas and standards specifying everything from materials for seating and carpeting to fixtures for restrooms and concession areas. If, as Hitchcock and Johnson argued in *The International Style*, only buildings that exhibited a restricted set of formal characteristics could be considered truly modern, then only a handful of movie theaters designed in the first half of the century qualify as such. If, however, we use the term modern architecture to identify work that resolves contemporary functional concerns and expresses a compelling vision of modernity (in this case, enthusiasm for the new medium of film) then the architecture of cinema merits our attention.

One of the primary design strategies employed by theater architects involved the exaggeration of particular parts of a building's exterior. S. Charles Lee neatly summed up the approach of theater architecture with his motto: "The show starts on the sidewalk." Marquees and signage grew in size until these elements dwarfed the structures below. In his 1939

Academy Theater in Inglewood, California, Lee transformed the Academy sign into a beacon visible from a considerable distance (fig. 1.40). In part this reflected the growing influence of an emerging automotive culture on architecture. Signage was enlarged in order to ensure visibility for the passing motorist. The fluid contours and horizontal banding of Lee's Academy Theater also epitomized the streamline version of modern design popularized during the 1930s. In the 1920s modernist designers such as Le Corbusier argued that crisp, hard-edged geometric forms best expressed the precision and rationality of the modern world. But it was the visual form rather than the mechanical logic of industrially produced machines that attracted architects, industrial designers, and the public alike in the 1930s. Inspired by the sleek profiles of transportation vehicles, designers transferred their curving silhouettes to the stationary forms of architecture.

Rockefeller Center and the General Motors Futurama

The economic and political realities of real-estate development after World War I meant that architects remained focused on the potential of individual sites and programs. But the American architectural profession continued to nurture the hope that the new zoning legislation would lead to the more rational design not just of single buildings but of entire urban quarters. Throughout the 1920s, American architects envisioned cityscapes of dispersed towers connected by elevated roadways, extending and refining an American tradition of visionary urban planning already well established by the turn of the century. Hugh Ferriss's 1929 book *Metropolis of Tomorrow* is one of the best examples of this skyscraper urbanism. One notable exception to the process of piecemeal development was the Rockefeller Center, conceived and realized by a team of architects including Wallace Harrison (1895–1981), Raymond Hood (1881–1934), and Harvey Wiley Corbett (1873–1954).

The first schemes for the Rockefeller Center were drafted in 1928, but work on the complex of buildings continued well into the 1930s (fig. 1.41). The multiblock site in midtown Manhattan consists of a series of tall office buildings connected by an underground concourse integrated with the city's mass transit system. The centerpiece of the complex, the RCA Building, rises over a pedestrian plaza which has, as its focal point, Paul Manship's statue of *Prometheus*. In keeping with the spirit of Art Deco, its decorative program was an integral part of the entire conception. The lobby of the RCA Building was the site of Diego Rivera's famous mural *Man at the Crossroads Looking with Hope and High Visions to the Choosing of a New and Better Future*. This mural was eventually destroyed by the building's owners because Rivera included a portrait of the Communist revolutionary Lenin. The iconographic program of the Rockefeller Center is a celebration of commerce and modern technology. From the subterranean concourse to the separation of pedestrian and vehicular traffic at street level to the roof gardens, it is a model of successful skyscraper urbanism and remains vivid proof that tall buildings can sustain a vibrant urban environment.

In 1939 New York City hosted a world's fair. Ephemeral events, the great international fairs of the first half of the twentieth century are nevertheless important historically because they provide unique windows onto the achievements and the aspirations of their times. The theme of the 1939 "New York World's Fair" was

"The World of Tomorrow with the Tools of Today." The most popular exhibit at the fair was the General Motors Pavilion (fig. 1.42). G.M. commissioned the industrial designer Norman Bel Geddes (1893–1958) to develop the exhibit. Bel Geddes, and contemporary industrial designers such as Walter Dorwin Teague (1883–1960), Raymond Loewy (1893–1986), and Henry Dreyfuss (1904–1972), occupy a curious position in American architecture during the 1930s. Their professional practices straddled various design categories and they influenced corporate attitudes towards architecture and the public's understanding of design issues.

For the General Motors exhibit, Bel Geddes rejected the practice established in earlier fairs of creating model assembly lines. Instead of explaining to the visitor how a product was made, he focused on how the product—in this case the automobile—could be used to transform familiar settlement patterns. Bel Geddes created a

1.41 John C. Wenrich, Rockefeller Center, New York, drawing, 1930s.

1.42 Norman Bel Geddes, General Motors Pavilion, "New York World's Fair," 1939.

giant model—the Futurama—measuring more than 35,700 square feet in area, depicting the American landscape as it could be in 1960. Streamlined skyscrapers towered over huge cities and fourteen-lane highways stretched across the landscape. In the Futurama, Bel Geddes harnessed four decades of design thinking about cities, architecture, and products to a peculiarly American model of corporate-sponsored social engineering.

The Rockefeller Center and the Futurama demonstrate two different transportation models operating within American planning. The architects of the Rockefeller Center relied on a sophisticated urban infrastructure of mass transit to service their "city within the city." In the immediate future, however, it would be the automobile that shaped planning policies and guidelines. Despite the social and economic stresses created by the Great Depression of the 1930s, and the looming threat of military conflicts around the world, the message conveyed by the General Motors exhibit was one of optimism about the capacity of private industry to promote prosperity. As they left the General Motors Pavilion, fair goers were handed a lapel pin inscribed with the simple but bold message: "I Have Seen the Future."

Chapter 2

The House

Architecture is one of the primary vehicles through which different social classes and groups assert and maintain their identities. By the beginning of the twentieth century, the single family house had become the architectural embodiment of the middle-class ideal for domestic life in Western culture. The emergence of the detached house or villa, preferably surrounded by some form of intimate green landscape, corresponded in time with the rise of bourgeois patronage as a significant new force in shaping the built environment. For centuries, home had served as both work place and living space for most members of society, whether the setting was rural or urban. In the nineteenth century, the forces of modernization unleashed by the Industrial Revolution began to reconfigure the social and spatial patterns of people in developing countries.

As the distinction between places of employment and habitation grew, the cultural meanings attached to each began to change. Increasingly, the domestic realm was idealized by the middle class as an essential repository of social codes and cultural values which stood in opposition to the commercial mores of capitalism. Thus, the social agenda of middle-class patronage ensured that the single family house would occupy a prominent place in the development of twentieth-century architecture.

In design terms, one of the distinctive aspects of the house as a building type is the lack of limitations imposed on the architect by typological or functional considerations. In contrast to other building types, defined by a stringent set of structural and functional demands, the house is an inherently malleable design problem shaped largely by the circumstances of individual clients, budgets, and sites. The requirements of shelter can be satisfied in diverse ways, ranging from the time-honored to the utterly novel, and the symbolic messages conveyed by domestic architecture can be exquisitely tailored to suit individual tastes. The sheer flexibility of the house-type makes it an extremely attractive vehicle for clients and designers interested in expressing positions on topics ranging from family values to building technologies. In a century characterized by continual debate about the appropriate architectural responses to modern times, few building types are more revealing indicators of the various themes and strategies of this debate than the single family house.

Richard Neutra, Health House (Lovell House), interior, Los Angeles, California, 1927–29.

45

From the Arts and Crafts Movement to the Prairie Style

England: The Arts and Crafts Movement

As the birthplace of the Industrial Revolution and one of the preeminent commercial powers of the nineteenth century, England is also the setting for some of the earliest attempts to articulate a new role for the private middle-class house. It is in its search for an alternative to the perceived inadequacies of contemporary practices that we can recognize the significance of Red House, a modest red-brick house designed by Philip Webb (1831–1915) in 1859 for William Morris and his bride, Jane Burden (fig. 2.1). William Morris (1834–1896) is one of the most important individuals in the story of nineteenth-century design. A prolific writer, political activist, and designer, Morris was a central figure in the Arts and Crafts movement and Red House was a critical early example of the new design ethic that broke with the prevailing Period Revivalism of the day. The arrangement of the house and garden and the decoration of the interior (carried out by Morris, Webb, Dante Gabriel Rossetti [1828–1882], and Edward Burne-Jones [1833–1898]) was inspired by medieval models. Yet the designers of Red House avoided the simple imitation of precedents characteristic of the Neo-Gothic movement, thus establishing a new and freer relationship between contemporary architecture and historical styles.

By the 1890s, British architects had developed an original approach to domestic architecture based on an appreciation of vernacular models, local materials, and craft practices. This so-called Free Style work eventually earned an international

2.1 Philip Webb, Red House, Bexley Heath, Kent, England, 1859.
Red roof tiles and bricks distinguish Red House from the typical yellow-brown brick and stucco houses of nearby villages. Rather than conform to symmetrical order, the varied sizes and locations of the windows reflect the internal arrangements of the rooms. The house is surrounded by flower gardens and an orchard.

2.2 Edwin Lutyens,
Deanery Garden, Sonning,
Berkshire, England,
1899–1902

reputation for British domestic design as practiced by such architects as Ernest
Gimson (1864–1920), E. S. Prior (1852–1932), M. H. Baillie Scott (1865–1945) and
C. F. A. Voysey (1857–1941). The Deanery Garden in Berkshire, completed in 1901
by Edwin Lutyens (1869–1944), weaves together the various threads of this
approach to domestic design in an exemplary manner (fig. 2.2).

For all its freedom from literal imitation of precedents, the Free Style remains
resolutely English in its imagery; the tall chimney, mullioned bay window, and red
brickwork recall Elizabethan models. The subtle asymmetrical adjustments in plan
and the tactile richness of the detailing inside and out are indicative of Lutyens's
appreciation of the lessons of the Red House. The relationship between house and
garden is critical in Deanery Garden. Here, as in over one hundred other commissions, Lutyens worked with the garden designer Gertrude Jekyll (1843–1932) whose
own career demonstrated the application of Arts and Crafts ideals to landscape
design.

Inspired by the writings of William Morris and John Ruskin, their supporters
worked tirelessly to promote the ideals of the Arts and Crafts as a viable social and
economic movement. Various craftsmen's guilds were established, journals
founded, and instructional programs instituted to disseminate models of craft-
based design. Design reformers forged alliances with the settlement house movement composed of neighborhood-based social welfare agencies in England, and
later in the United States, and supported efforts to promote cottage home industries
as part of ambitious campaigns of social reform and economic stimulation. Propo-
nents of the Arts and Crafts movement understood craft as a form of design practice
in which the design and the actual making of objects was indissolubly linked.

According to Ruskin and Morris, the rise of industrialized forms of production disrupted the linkage between the conceptualization and fabrication of artifacts. The result was the alienation of human labor in the factory system and a decline in the quality of machine-made goods. The revival of craft was promoted as a humane alternative to the worst excesses of industrialization and craft practices were idealized as the antithesis of machine production.

The English experience was carefully studied in North America and in Europe. English writers were being translated and published abroad and foreign visitors were recording their impressions of the latest British designs. In 1896, for example, an architect and Prussian civil servant named Hermann Muthesius (1861–1927) was posted to London as an attaché in the German embassy to report on British achievements in architecture and design. In 1904 he published the results of his investigation as *Das Englische Haus*, which remains one of the critical contemporary studies of the subject. Muthesius went on to pursue a career as an important design reformer in Germany. By the early twentieth century, this process of dissemination was also one of transformation. English ideals were scrutinized in light of the distinctive issues and opportunities confronting architects in different countries.

The United States: Greene and Greene

In the United States, the English Arts and Crafts movement proved to be very popular and American versions of Arts and Crafts workshops, schools, and publications soon sprang up. British ideals, however, were modified in significant ways to fit an American context. By the early twentieth century the word "machine" had been invested with a set of diverse connotations. For the supporters of the English Arts and Crafts movement, the word identified the enormous and threatening power of new technologies to overwhelm traditional values and practices. In the American context, however, an alternative understanding emerged. Nowhere is this more evident than in a speech that Frank Lloyd Wright delivered in 1901 to the Chicago Arts and Crafts Society at Hull House, the famous settlement house founded by the social reformer Jane Addams. Wright's talk, entitled "The Art and Craft of the Machine," is one of the critical early modern treatments of the relationship between handcraft and modern machine-based technology. Wright began by praising William Morris but, in a significant departure from the English position, he went on to embrace the machine as an invaluable new tool in the hands of designers. As Morris and Ruskin had before him, Wright acknowledged that when used merely to replicate the forms of handcrafted design, the machine debased product and producer alike. But, Wright argued, the machine could be employed as a tool to enhance the intrinsic qualities of materials and to stimulate the creative imagination of the designer.

In southern California, the brothers Charles (1870–1954) and Henry (1870–1954) Greene established an architectural practice that catered to wealthy easterners seeking a comfortable haven from both the climate and the formality of life in the eastern part of the country. Their work drew on a variety of sources including Ruskin and Morris, Chinese and Japanese architecture, Alpine chalets, the American Shingle Style, and the gospel of craftsmanship as preached by Gustav Stickley (1858–1942) in the pages of *The Craftsman*. This list is revealing of the variety of sources that inspired American Arts and Crafts architects. The freedom with which

2.3 (above) Charles and Henry Greene, David B. Gamble House, Pasadena, California, 1908–09.

With its mild climate, southern California was an ideal setting for the Greene brothers' interest in the integration of architecture and environment. Informal landscaping surrounds the Gamble House. The house features exterior sleeping porches on the upper level. The ends of projecting beams were rounded and polished to bring out the natural beauty of wood in sunlight.

2.4 (right) Charles and Henry Greene, David B. Gamble House, living room, Pasadena, California, 1908–09.

architects combined impeccable craft-based models with the latest technologies for milling lumber, and incorporated the new technologies of domestic comfort such as electric lights, central heating, and telephones, is distinctively American.

Greene and Greene's finest work consists of a series of "ultimate bungalows" executed between 1904 and 1909. The homes were closer to mansions in terms of scale and expense, but they evoked the dominant cultural ideal of a simple life-style enriched by beautiful surroundings that afforded intimate contact with nature. The Gamble House, designed for David Gamble of Proctor and Gamble, included exterior sleeping porches on the upper floor and patios and terraced gardens sur-rounded by a green lawn (fig. 2.3). The architects realized that long after the hearth had ceased to serve as the functional center of the American house, it remained the symbolic heart of the home; they therefore arranged the major space of the house around a great fireplace (fig. 2.4). While English Arts and Crafts designers favored native materials such as oak, Greene and Greene indulged their love of exotic imported woods such as mahogany. Throughout the house, structural members are detailed in ways that celebrate the art as well as the craft of construction. The Gamble House is a catalog of expressive joinery techniques including protruding pegs, exposed mortise and tenon joints, and scarf joints.

The Prairie Style: Frank Lloyd Wright

In the Midwest, a prosperous upper-middle-class clientele provided the patronage necessary to nurture a distinctive school of domestic design and, in Frank Lloyd Wright, they found a designer of rare genius. Wright came to Chicago from his native Wisconsin and, after a brief period in the office of Louis Sullivan, estab-lished his own practice from his home and studio in Oak Park, a western suburb. Like Greene and Greene, Wright absorbed and transformed a broad range of source material including British, European, Oriental, and Mesoamerican models and the American legacy of Sullivan and H. H. Richardson (1838–1886). Transformed is a key word in any discussion of Wright because his work is never reducible to the mere sum of its influences. Over a career that spanned six decades, he created an

2.5 Frank Lloyd Wright, project for "A Home in a Prairie Town" from *Ladies' Home Journal*, February 1901. Watercolor and watercolor wash on paper, 25 x 15 in (16.3 x 38.1 cm).

immense body of work based on his conception of an organic architecture. Notoriously difficult to define precisely, organic architecture is the expression in architectural terms of an American intellectual tradition rooted in the transcendentalist philosophy of Ralph Waldo Emerson (1803–1882). Organic architecture nurtures in the inhabitant a keen awareness of nature's rhythms (captured in the ever-changing quality of light) and of the social dynamics of family and community life.

In 1900 Wright published a design entitled "A Home in a Prairie Town" in the *Ladies' Home Journal* in which it is possible to discern the features of his early domestic work which came to be known as the Prairie Style (fig. 2.5). Wright emphasized the psychological implications of his design: "At that time, a house to me was obvious primarily as interior space under a fine shelter. I liked the sense of shelter in the look of the building." His design emphasizes the horizontal lines of the house with casement windows grouped together under a broad, low roof. On the inside, he replaced the traditional arrangement of the plan as a series of box-like rooms with an expansive sense of space flowing uninterruptedly from one functional area to the next.

The term Prairie Style evokes the mythic role of the land in the development of an American identity. In retrospect, the use of the term Prairie Style to identify this suburban body of work seems ironic given that the actual prairie was rapidly disappearing. It was, after all, short-blade green grass and not the tall grasses of the prairie that took root in the lawns of Oak Park and other suburbs. But irony was alien to the design approach practiced by Wright and his colleagues. Architecture, they believed, could express important cultural values and preserve the memory of seminal national experiences. Home, as Wright wrote, may have been a shelter, but it was also an intellectual program intended to promote a distinctively American identity.

The clients who commissioned Prairie Style homes were equally convinced of architecture's social efficacy. The domestic design agenda endorsed by upper-middle-class clientele that provided the majority of Wright's commissions saw the home as a model environment in which important social values would be instilled. Clients demanded efficient planning and readily accepted the latest in household technologies. Set on its own lot, the single family house afforded daily contact with fresh air, sunlight, and greenery. Inside, the selection of artworks and furnishings reflected the self-conscious cultivation of aesthetic refinement. The suburban home exemplified virtues and interests perceived to be the necessary social antidotes to the corrupting influences and commercial values of the modern business world. It is important to recognize that many of Wright's clients came from this world of business and were an integral part of the rapidly expanding, industrially based bourgeoisie. In the twentieth century, patronage of important new architecture was no longer the exclusive province of an aristocratic elite.

Late in 1906 Frederick C. Robie, a bicycle manufacturer, commissioned Wright to design a new house in Chicago's Hyde Park neighborhood (fig. 2.6). Wright exploited the long narrow corner site to create one of his finest Prairie Style designs. Every detail contributes to the overall effect of shelter and horizontality. Wright selected unusually long narrow bricks for the walls and inserted steel beams which allowed him to cantilever the roof beyond the edge of the house. Despite its prominence on the street corner, how to enter the house is far from clear. There is no apparent front door and the actual entry is hidden along one side of the house. Visitors must follow a winding route up to the main living areas positioned on the

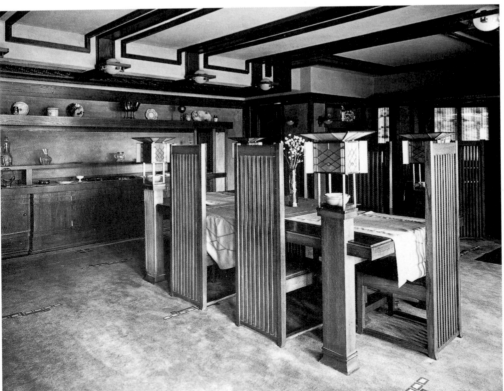

2.6 (above) Frank Lloyd
Wright, Robie House,
South Woodlawn, Chicago,
Illinois, 1908–10.

The structural design of
the Robie House combines
brick piers for vertical
support with concealed
steel beams to support
the cantilevered roof.
In place of a separate
stable for carriage and
horses, Wright provided
a garage for automobiles.

2.7 (left) Frank Lloyd
Wright, Robie House,
dining room, South
Woodlawn, Chicago,
1908–10.

Frank Lloyd Wright
often designed the
furnishings for his houses.
The high-backed chairs
create an intimate space
within the interior's
expansive volume. The
dining table's cornet posts
support electric lamps.

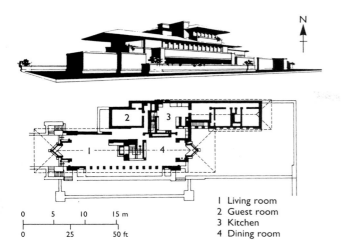

1	Living room
2	Guest room
3	Kitchen
4	Dining room

second level (fig. 2.7) where a huge fireplace serves as the symbolic heart of the entire composition.

Like so much of Wright's work, the experience of moving through Robie House is a complex but deeply satisfying one. There is a sense of security that comes from the fortress-like quality of the house and the contrived entry sequence culminating in the visitor's arrival at the massive hearth. At the same time there is an equally compelling sense of exhilaration triggered by the vistas that open up around every twist and turn. Space ebbs and flows, pooling in cozy inglenooks and then flooding outward from the interior to the porch and beyond in one continuous but artfully modulated composition (fig. 2.8).

European Developments

Charles Rennie Mackintosh

Of the generation of architects active in the first decades of the twentieth century, few have captured both the scholarly and popular imaginations as completely as the Scottish designer Charles Rennie Mackintosh (1868–1928). Mackintosh produced an important body of work in and around Glasgow, Scotland, and gained a following among architects and designers in Central Europe. Following a period of obscurity, the publication of Thomas Howarth's monograph *Charles Rennie Mackintosh and the Modern Movement* in 1952 reinvigorated Mackintosh's reputation. Today, Mackintosh is among the most popular turn-of-the-century figures and there is an enormous market for reproductions of his design, dubbed by some critics the "Mockintosh market."

2.8 (above) Frank Lloyd Wright, Robie House, South Woodlawn, Chicago, plan, 1908–10.

2.9 (below) Charles Rennie Mackintosh, Hill House, southwest view, Helensburgh, Scotland, 1903. Ink, 13 × 21⅝ in (33 × 53.3 cm).

2.10 (right) Charles Rennie Mackintosh, Hill House, main bedroom, Helensburgh, Scotland, 1903.

Mackintosh has been portrayed as a lonely genius working in an isolated provincial setting. Such readings obscure the important role of design collaboration in his work and ignore the stimulating, even cosmopolitan, environment of turn-of-the-century Glasgow. Rather than working alone, Mackintosh was part of an intimate group of artists and designers that included his friend Herbert McNair (1868–1955) and the Macdonald sisters, Margaret (1864–1933) (who married Mackintosh in 1900) and Frances (1873–1921) (who married McNair in 1899). The Four, as the Mackintosh circle came to be known, reflects the influence of the Arts and Crafts movement which valued collaborative design practices in contrast to the hierarchical division of labor typical of large architectural offices. Collaborative practices pose special problems for museums, galleries, and critics because establishing clear attributions to individual designers is important for valuing artifacts in the art market. In addition, individual creation has always been regarded as central to the romantic ideal of creative genius.

In 1902 a wealthy publisher, Walter Blackie, commissioned Mackintosh to design a new house for his family in the Glasgow suburb of Helensburgh. The massing of the design of Hill House reflects Mackintosh's awareness of the Scottish tradition of baronial mansions and castles (fig. 2.9). Like the Free Style work of contemporary English architects, Mackintosh incorporates regional building traditions in his work. The exterior is plastered with harling (cement mixed with small pebbles), a local practice that creates a homogeneous appearance with a rich, tactile quality to the surface. Blackie also commissioned interiors; Mackintosh devoted special attention to the design of the main hall, library, drawing room, and master bedroom (fig. 2.10). The contrast between the light and dark color schemes evident in different rooms has prompted some critics to interpret the binary opposites of black/white, heavy/light, and hard/soft in this—and other Mackintosh interiors— as expressing masculine and feminine attributes. However, the degree to which Mackintosh, McNair, and the Macdonald sisters developed their design in ways that gendered space continues to be debated by scholars. In the gritty atmosphere of an industrial city like Glasgow, the elegant white color scheme found in the drawing room and the main bedroom (which Mrs. Blackie also used as a morning room) clearly identifies Hill House as a special realm. While the urban environment may be shaped by crude commercial values and polluted with industrial grime, for upper-middle-class patrons like Walter Blackie, the domestic realm remained the preserve of beauty and cleanliness. To possess such an elegant environment was a mark not only of the Blackies' wealth but of their refinement and taste as well.

Josef Hoffmann and the Werkstätten Movement

Domestic design fulfilled much the same role for wealthy patrons on the continent as well. Mackintosh's work was prominently featured in important exhibitions including the eighth exhibition of the Viennese Secession in 1900, and the 1902 "Prima Esposizione Internazionale d'Art Decorativa Moderna" in Turin, Italy. In 1905 Adolphe and Suzanne Stoclet commissioned the Viennese architect Josef Hoffmann (1870–1956) to design a new house in Brussels (figs. 2.11, 2.12). Adolphe Stoclet was from a Belgian banking family and the couple were dedicated connoisseurs of the arts. With ample funds at his disposal, Hoffmann designed the mansion, Palais Stoclet, and coordinated the work of craftsmen and artists to complete

2.11 (right) Josef Hoffmann, Palais Stoclet, Brussels, Belgium, 1905–11.

Hoffmann's treatment of the exterior emphasizes the planarity of the elevations. Dark metal mouldings outline the edges of the façade, which is formed of slabs of white marble. A metal dome surrounded by four statues of male nudes crowns the cruciform tower that rises over the stairway on the west side of the house.

2.12 (below) Josef Hoffmann, Palais Stoclet, ground floor plan, Brussels, Belgium, 1905–11.

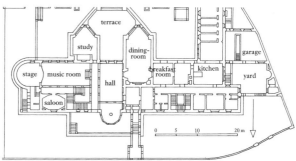

ground floor

first floor

the interiors (fig. 2.13). An analysis that insists on the traditional distinctions between architecture, the fine arts, and the decorative arts will fail to capture the complexity of his design. Hoffmann was committed to creating a *gesamtkunstwerk*—a total work of art—in which every detail of the design contributed to the overall effect. The Palais Stoclet must be experienced as an unified design effort.

The concept of a *gesamtkunstwerk* was one of the animating ideals of progressive architecture and design at the turn of the century. The goal of creating a *gesamtkunstwerk* inspired architects to work closely with craftsmen and artists, and led to the creation of the Werkstätten (workshop) movement in Central Europe. The first workshops were founded in Dresden and Munich in 1898 and, in 1903, Hoffmann participated in the founding of one of the most important *werkstätten*, the Weiner Werkstätte in Vienna. Participants in the Werkstätten movement were committed to the idea of a new, modern design sensibility. In his description of the founding of the Weiner Werkstätte, Hoffmann noted:

> All over Europe, consciousness stirred; to us in Vienna everything seemed moldering and rotting. Everywhere workshops came into existence that made it their duty to be done with eternal imitations of styles and to try to find new forms corresponding to our time . . .
>
> (Sekler, p. 62)

The Werkstätten movement provided an independent distribution system for the work of craftsmen from a wide range of fields including ceramics, furniture,

metalwork, and textiles. The goals of the Werkstätten movement included making modern decorative arts available to the purchasing public and employing artists to elevate the taste of the public by providing contemporary designs for household articles. In Chapter 1, reference was made to the fragmented nature of the modern metropolis; nothing could be further from the unsettling aspects of urban modernity than the reassuring totality of a *gesamtkunstwerk*. It is characteristic of the modern era that new cultural ideals prompt the development of new industries and markets capable of translating those ideals into reality.

National Romanticism

Charles Rennie Mackintosh and Josef Hoffmann were not alone in serving clients interested in protecting themselves from the vulgarity of modern life through the creation of refined and beautiful domestic environments. Hector Guimard (1867–1942), Victor Horta (1861–1947), Ernesto Basile (1857–1932), Joseph Olbrich, and Henry van de Velde (1863–1957) are among the most important members of a generation of designers active in the first decades of the twentieth century whose work promoted the idea of contemporary domestic design. These designers were hardly uniform in their approach; organic and curvilinear forms were popular with some, while others favored more abstract geometric patterns. Working in concert with skilled craftsmen in a variety of fields, however, they all spread the gospel

2.13 Josef Hoffmann, Palais Stoclet, dining room, Brussels, Belgium, 1905–11.

The dining room with mosaics created by the artist Gustav Klimt is one of the most splendid interiors of the twentieth century. Visually the room is divided into two zones by the use of contrasting materials. The lower portion features dark Portovenere marble, macassar wood, and black leather chairs detailed with gold tooling. Above, panels of richly veined Paonazzo marble line the walls.

of the redemptive power of beauty. The novelty of their approach is reflected in the terms used to describe it: Art Nouveau, Le Style Moderne, Jugenstil, and Stile Liberty.

In certain situations, the concept of a *gesamtkunstwerk* could also be pressed into service in support of a quest for national identity. National Romanticism is a term used to identify the adaptation of folk and vernacular forms to express a national identity. The emphasis on craft-based designs and local traditions reflects the influence of the English Arts and Crafts movement. Rather than a reaction to the alienating aspects of modern industry, however, National Romanticism emerged in countries struggling to achieve a measure of cultural and political independence. Because folk traditions were perceived as yet unspoiled by either foreign domination or the emerging modern world, they could provide a vocabulary of forms and motifs for designers seeking an indigenous design language.

At the beginning of the century, Finland formed part of the Russian empire. Eager to separate themselves from Russian hegemony—both cultural and political—Finnish intellectuals sought to establish a distinctive national identity. The

2.14 Eliel Saarinen, Herman Gesellius, and Armas Lindgren, Villa Hvitträsk, near Helsinki, Finland, 1901–03.

A residential and studio compound serving three families, Villa Hvitträsk demonstrates the creative fusion of elements drawn from Finnish vernacular building, contemporary international architecture, and original designs by the architects.

Finnish national epic poem, *The Kalevala*, provided linguistic models for writers and iconographic source material for artists, while the vernacular architecture of remote regions such as Karelia provided architects with "unspoiled" models of indigenous design and construction. One of the greatest examples of Finnish National Romanticism is the complex designed by Eliel Saarinen, Herman Gesellius (1874–1916), and Armas Lindgren (1874–1929) at Hvitträsk, near Helsinki (fig. 2.14).

The three young architects met while students at the Polytechnic Institute in Helsinki and eventually started a professional practice together. They conceived of Hvitträsk as a combination home and studio, where facilities were arranged around a courtyard and sited dramatically along a rocky ridge. In contrast to the elegant refinement of the Palais Stoclet, there is a rugged, rustic quality to the design at Hvitträsk, yet the desire to create a *gesamtkunstwerk* is common to both. The log construction employed for parts of the complex evokes the Finnish vernacular tradition. However, Saarinen, Gesellius, and Lindgren handled the wood in unconventional ways and blended native forms with ideas imported from British and American models of domestic design. The use of wooden columns capped with short segments as capitals to frame the stairway in the main living room is an invention of their own (fig. 2.15).

2.15 Eliel Saarinen, Herman Gesellius, and Armas Lindgren, Villa Hvitträsk, living room, near Helsinki, Finland, 1901–03.

Classicism

National Romantic designers drew upon the vernacular traditions, but another, equally ancient tradition remained available for architects: classicism. While the vernacular models favored by Saarinen, Gesellius, and Lindgren were the products of specific geographic and folk practices, classicism constituted an international heritage based on Greco-Roman and Renaissance models. As we shall see in later chapters, classicism was capable of carrying a wide variety of cultural and political messages. Never entirely absent from architectural culture, classicism was the subject of renewed interest in the early years of the century. In 1903 Lutyens wrote to his friend the architect Herbert Baker (1862–1946): "In architecture, Palladio's the game!" The pedimented central block and the axiality and symmetry of Lutyens's Gledstone Hall in Yorkshire, certainly reflected his appreciation of the sixteenth-century Italian architect's work (fig. 2.16). In his letter to Baker, Lutyens expressed a genuine appreciation for the rigor and challenge of designing classical buildings; classicism, he wrote:

> . . . requires considerable training to value and realize it. . . . It is a game that never deceives, never disguises. It means hard thought all through—if it is laboured, it fails. There is no fluke that helps it . . .
>
> (Hussey, pp. 121–2)

Rather than disappearing from the architectural scene with the advent of newer conceptions of design with claims to represent the authentic spirit of the modern age, classicism continued to exert an attraction for both architects and clients. In the United States, such architects as Charles A. Platt (1861–1933) continued to provide wealthy clients with suburban retreats modeled after Italian Renaissance villas. Villa Turicum, the McCormick family estate in Lake Forest, Illinois, a northern suburb of Chicago, is a good example. Frank Lloyd Wright prepared an

ambitious plan for the McCormick estate which included an elaborate series of terraces overlooking Lake Michigan. But Harold and Edith Rockefeller McCormick
opted instead for the more traditional treatment in what Harold McCormick described as "pure Italian lines" (figs. 2.17, 2.18). In Chapter 1 we noted the appeal of
classical architecture for the City Beautiful movement; in the Villa Turicum we encounter the domestic parallel to the civic classicism of Daniel Burnham. Modern
conveniences are incorporated throughout the house but expressing the spirit of
modernity is not part of the design agenda. If Platt observed the rules of classical
proportion and decorum in the architecture of the villa, he felt less bound by Renaissance models for the landscaping. He combined the traditional idea of the Renaissance garden as a series of formal outdoor rooms with an interest in unusual
arrangements of native horticultural materials. While Wright mythologized the
American prairie in his work of this period, Platt Americanized the European
garden tradition in his.

Some architects demonstrated even more freedom and subtlety in their handling
of classicism. In Sweden, Gunnar Asplund's Villa Snellman fused classical and
vernacular models in an intriguing and sophisticated Scandinavian version of
classicism (fig. 2.19). In general, classicism is a design language based on rule,

2.17 (above) Charles A. Platt, Villa Turicum (McCormick Estate),
Lake Forest, Illinois, 1908–18.

2.18 (left) Charles A. Platt, Villa Turicum (McCormick Estate),
plan, Lake Forest, Illinois, 1908–18.

2.20 (above) Villa Snellman, plan, Djursholm,
Sweden, 1917–18.
  The L-shaped plan creates a courtyard
oriented to the afternoon sun and sheltered
from the prevailing wind.

2.19 (above) Erik Gunnar
Asplund, Villa Snellman,
Djursholm, Sweden,
1917–18.

order, and decorum. Asplund, however, skewed the alignment of the two wings of
the L-shaped plan and then tapered the sides of the interior hallway (fig. 2.20). The
result conveys a relaxed rather than a rigid sense of geometry. The inclusion of two
separate doors on the main facade subverts the order and hierarchy typically
expected of classical compositions, as do the asymmetrical adjustments to the
front and rear fenestration patterns. Asplund's classicism involved striking a fresh
balance between order and invention.

Modernism

In 1915 Le Corbusier proposed a scheme for the rapid erection of housing. Conceived initially as a solution to the problem of replacing housing stock damaged in
the war then raging in Europe, the Dom-ino House is a seminal example of modernism in architecture (fig. 2.21). The skeleton of the house was reduced to a simple
kit of standardized parts, all fabricated of reinforced concrete and capable of rapid
erection. The entire structure consisted of slender columns, square in section, supporting slab floors cantilevered beyond the edge of the
column line. Exterior walls and interior partitions were no
longer load-bearing and could be constructed quickly using a
wide variety of materials. Flexibility in the arrangement of
individual units was combined with the economic advantages
of mass production. Le Corbusier's scheme was an idealiza-
tion of concrete construction; he omitted the flared column
heads and ribbed slabs customarily found in concrete construction in that period. Le Corbusier was more interested in
conveying the potential of modern systems of industrialized
production to transform the way people thought about and
constructed buildings. Like his slightly later plans for the
reconfiguration of Paris (see pages 11–13), the Dom-ino House

2.21 Le Corbusier,
Dom-ino House,
plan, 1914–15.

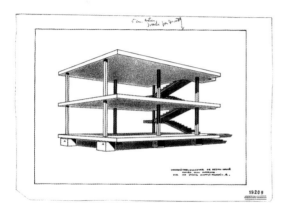

2.22 Ludwig Mies van der Rohe, Barcelona Pavilion, interior, "International Exhibition," Barcelona, Spain, 1929.

Mies combined modern and traditional materials in his design. The columns, cruciform in plan, are fabricated from L-shaped pieces of chrome-plated steel. Onyx, green marble, and travertine as well as clear and frosted sheets of glass were used as partitions. A black area rug, red curtains, and Mies-designed chairs upholstered in white kid leather completed the interior design.

represented a radical rethinking of traditional notions and demonstrated Le Corbusier's enthusiastic embrace of modern methods and ideas.

This enthusiasm for modernity is a central feature of modernism in architecture. Unlike the efforts of some architects to resist the advance of the modern world or create domestic environments opposed to it, modernist architects wished to accelerate the transformation of life provoked by modernization. They seized opportunities afforded by commissions to create spatial experiences and images that brought into focus architectural possibilities inherent in a world no longer bound by historical precedent.

It is in this context that small projects such as Ludwig Mies van der Rohe's German Pavilion for the "International Exhibition," Barcelona, 1929, acquire a significance out of all proportion to their actual size or program (fig. 2.22). Erected originally as a reception pavilion for distinguished visitors to the fair, the Barcelona Pavilion demonstrated the spatial possibilities latent in the simple column and slab system described in Le Corbusier's Dom-ino scheme. In place of the concrete of the Dom-ino design, Mies van der Rohe used chrome-plate metal columns and vertical surfaces of glass alternating with beautifully veined and polished marble slabs. The layering of space, the juxtaposition of transparent, reflective, and opaque surfaces, and the freedom implied by separating column and wall marks the Barcelona Pavilion as one of the paradigms of early-twentieth-century architecture.

Early chroniclers of the modern movement, such as Siegfried Giedion, tended to present the work of modernists such as Le Corbusier, Mies van der Rohe, and Walter Gropius as the manifestation, in architectural terms, of the underlying principles and forces shaping the modern world. In his influential account of the origin and development of modern architecture, *Space, Time and Architecture*, Giedion portrayed modernism in architecture as the synthesis of modern science, technology, and aesthetics.

Today, this equation of modernism and modernity is being challenged by some critics and historians who see tension rather than congruence in the relationship between modernist design ideals and the reality of modern systems of production. Modernism, according to this school of thought, sought to make available models of art and architecture that suggested what was *possible* and *desirable* rather than merely confirming the status quo. There is thus a utopian impulse behind architectural modernism in the first half of the century, and a challenging stance adopted by the modernist to the contemporary world.

Le Corbusier

Le Corbusier was a prolific writer and an accomplished painter as well as an architect who produced an imposing and influential body of work. During the decade of the 1920s he executed a series of designs for private villas that crystalized the International Style. When, in 1903, Lutyens declared "In architecture, Palladio is the game" he meant it literally and his work began to emulate classical forms and models closely. In an insightful essay, published in 1947, the architectural historian Colin Rowe compared the formal organization of Le Corbusier's work of the 1920s with sixteenth-century Palladian villas. For the modernist Le Corbusier, abstraction not emulation was the dominant design strategy underlying every attempt at form-making. In the reductive purism of his work, buildings are drained of mass and solidity and appear as weightless volumes hovering over the ground. Citations of classical iconography are replaced by references to icons of the machine age such as ocean liners, and the perspectival construction of space according to Renaissance models is replaced by a Cubist-inspired spatial aesthetic. In Le Corbusier's work the detailed vocabulary of the classical orders and the solidity and thickness characteristic of classical tectonics are banished. In their place, he proposed a formula he called "The Five Points for a New Architecture:" (1) pilotis (thin columns) that raised the building off the ground, (2) roof terrace, (3) free plan, (4) free facade, and (5) horizontal windows.

2.23 Le Corbusier, Villa Savoye, north corner, Poissy, France, 1928–31.

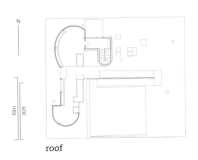

roof   first floor   ground floor

Le Corbusier applied these five points in the design of the Villa Savoye, a week-end retreat located at Poissy, thirty kilometers outside of Paris (figs. 2.23, 2.24, 2.25). A visitor's first impression is of a pristine geometric form lifted off the ground on pilotis so slender that any sense of gravity seems negated. The curve of the recessed ground story was determined by the turning radius of an automobile. Once inside, the visitor is drawn into what Le Corbusier described as *a promenade architecturale*—a carefully orchestrated progression through space—that leads to a rooftop terrace. Because the structural skeleton of the building consists of point support rather than continuous load-bearing walls, internal partitions can be arranged freely. The elevations are treated as thin, taut planes. The horizontal

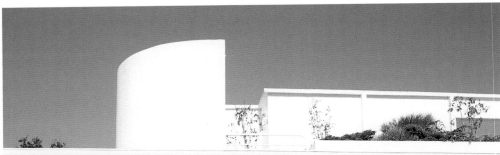

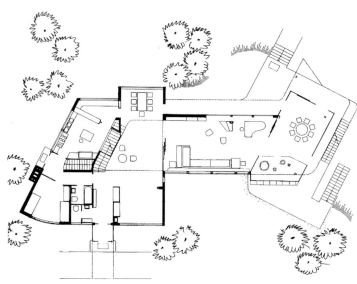

2.26 (above) Hans Scharoun, Villa Schminke, Löbau, Saxony, Germany, 1932–33.

The streamlined profiles of the exterior decks add a nautical flavor to the design. There is a large solarium and interior garden at the east end of the plan (see fig. 2.27). Scharoun positioned round lighting fixtures at strategic spots in the ceilings to create different lighting effects through-out the house.

2.27 (right) Hans Scharoun, Villa Schminke, plan, Löbau, Saxony, Germany, 1932–33.

windows (also termed ribbon or strip windows) signaled a break with the tradition of square or vertically oriented openings. Modern architects maintained that horizontal windows allowed a more even distribution of light throughout interior spaces. The rooftop solarium and the horizontal windows are clear responses to the emphasis on sunlight and fresh air that figured prominently in early-twentieth-century descriptions of modern environments.

Hans Scharoun, Alvar Aalto

As in a Palladian villa, there is a serene and self-contained quality to the Villa Savoye. In both, a clearly delineated geometric volume is set against the surrounding landscape. The pilotis provide an abstract equivalent to the columnar porches of the Palladian model. A different, more dynamic treatment of space can be seen in the slightly later Villa Schminke by the German architect Hans Scharoun (1893–1972) (fig. 2.26). In an attempt to adjust his plan to a difficult site, Scharoun skewed both ends of the composition approximately 30 degrees to the predominant east–west layout of the villa, an adjustment reflected in the diagonal alignment of the stair as well (fig. 2.27). This departure from strict orthogonal and axial relationships introduces an organic quality to what is otherwise a straightforward example of the International Style.

Scharoun's conception of an organic architecture is sharply different from the Prairie Style work of Frank Lloyd Wright and his contemporaries. Scharoun had no interest in developing decorative motifs based on plant forms or providing the same sense of fortress-like shelter that intrigued Wright. This European conception of organic architecture focused more on allowing each volume within the composition to assume its own shape and orientation rather than to conform to a predetermined and rigid geometric scheme. The skewed angles and twisted volumes typical of the organic approach tended to create eccentric spaces within the plans.

In the 1930s some of the finest examples of organic architecture in Europe were being created in Finland by Alvar Aalto (1898–1976). Younger than Gunnar Asplund and Eliel Saarinen, Aalto typified a new generation of modern architects already comfortable with abstract art and eager to incorporate innovations in building technologies. Gone are the romantic trappings found at Hvitträsk and the classical references of Asplund's early work. What remains is a distinctively Nordic version of modernism. A deep humanism infuses many of Aalto's buildings. As he once wrote: "One of the most difficult architectural problems is the shaping of the building's surroundings to the human scale," and his attentiveness to issues of human scale, texture, and the modulation of light is evident throughout his work. For Aalto, the tactile is as important as the visual in the orchestration of the architectural experience.

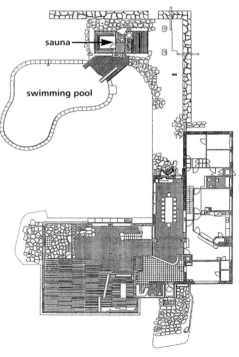

sauna

swimming pool

Aalto produced one of his finest designs for Maire and Harry Gullichsen, the Villa Mairea at Noormarkku, Finland (figs. 2.28, 2.29). The Gullichsens were wealthy clients with extensive business interests in timber, paper, and cellulose products; they were also patrons of the arts and eager to promote new ideas. Mrs. Gullichsen was an early and important supporter of Aalto's furniture designs. For the Villa Mairea, Aalto marshaled a broad palette of materials and techniques and succeeded in striking a balance between refinement and rusticity (fig. 2.30). Rough wooden posts and smooth steel columns, for example, can be found in different parts of the house, and features commonly associated with the International Style exist side by side with elements derived from the Finnish vernacular tradition. Thus, through a process of abstraction, Aalto reconciled the enduring hallmarks of Finnish traditions with the emergent qualities of the modern experience.

2.30 Aalvar Aalto,
Villa Mairea, living room,
Noormarkku, Finland,
1938–39.

American Developments

When, in 1932, the Museum of Modern Art staged the International Style exhibition, which did so much to define architectural modernism for an American audience, the majority of architects featured in the show were Europeans. The American transformation of Arts and Crafts ideals and the innovative work of the Prairie Style receded in importance in the years following World War I. Period revivalism remained a very strong factor in American architecture and versions of Old English, Colonial, and Spanish Revival designs continued to enjoy great popularity. The architectural historian David Gebhard noted that while an American businessman may have worked in an Art Deco skyscraper or supervised a modern factory, in the 1920s and 1930s, more often than not, he returned at the end of the day to the comfort and familiarity of a traditional home. Any discussion of International Style houses must begin by acknowledging, therefore, that such work represents only a small portion of the period's domestic production.

Richard Neutra

One of the few American houses included in the International Style exhibition was the so-called Health House in Los Angeles designed by Richard Neutra (1892–1970) for Dr. Philip Lovell (fig. 2.31 and page 44). Neutra was born and educated in Vienna and came to the United States in 1923. He belongs to a small but influential set of émigré architects who established important design practices in the

United States including Rudolf Schindler (1887–1953), William Lescaze, Josef Urban (1872–1933), and Kem Weber (1889–1943). After working briefly for Frank Lloyd Wright, Neutra established a practice in southern California. Heath House is perched dramatically on a steep hillside and constructed using a steel frame. Transparent volumes negating any sense of mass or weight and the lack of references to historical styles or ornamental enrichment identify this as an example of the International Style. But this is a house that needs to be appreciated in relationship to its client even more than to any European models of modernism.

Neutra's house was actually the second example of modern architecture commissioned by Lovell; several years earlier he built a beach house in Newport Beach according to a design by Rudolf Schindler. Dr. Lovell was interested in the contribution modern environments could make to the psycho-physiological well-being of people. He wrote a regular column entitled "Care of the Body" for the *Los Angeles Times* and founded a Physical Culture Center where he promoted the ideal of a healthy life-style based on vigorous exercise, vegetarianism, nudism, and "natural" remedies. His career was one manifestation of the cult of the body that is such an important part of the culture of southern California. The region's balmy climate made it a perfect setting for Lovell's experiments in lifestyle and the lean, trim appearance of the house captured the athleticism of its owner perfectly. As Aalto did in the Villa Mairea, Neutra infused the attributes of international modernism with the personality of his client and adjusted his design to reflect Lovell's conception of a southern California life-style. In short, Neutra stamped the International Style with a made-in-America brand.

2.31 Richard Neutra, Health House (Lovell House), Los Angeles, California, 1927–29.

The visitor enters this house at the top level and descends an open staircase into a double-height living room. Inside as well as out, Neutra omitted floor and ceiling moldings wherever possible, and treated the walls as simple planes bordering the edges of light-filled volumes. Modern lighting fixtures inside include an automobile headlight inset in a room partition.

Frank Lloyd Wright

In 1909 Frank Lloyd Wright experienced a personal crisis. He abandoned his wife, Catherine, and left Oak Park with Mamah Borthwick Cheney (previously, Mrs. Cheney and her husband had commissioned Wright to design a home in Oak Park). This marked the beginning of a tumultuous period in Wright's life. In the teens and twenties, the volume of his work declined and the location of his most important commissions shifted away from the Chicago area. Early in his career, Wright had established links with Japan, and between the mid-1910s and the early 1920s he devoted an enormous amount of time to the design of the Imperial Hotel in Tokyo.

In a series of houses completed in southern California in the early 1920s, Wright explored what he called his textile block system of construction in concrete (fig. 2.32). Individual concrete blocks were "threaded" together with metal reinforcing rods running in two directions through the wall like the warp and weft of textiles. The relationship between buildings and weaving had been raised by the nineteenth-century architectural theorist Gottfried Semper and the popular use of the term curtain wall to describe the non-load-bearing exteriors of high-rise buildings reflected the strength of the textile metaphor in design. Wright's distinctive twist to this theme was to apply the metaphor to load-bearing construction and to establish an organic relationship between fabrication and ornamentation with his

2.32 Frank Lloyd Wright, Ennis House, 2607 Glendower Avenue, Los Angeles, California, 1923

2.33 Frank Lloyd Wright,
Ennis House, interior,
2607 Glendower Avenue,
Los Angeles, California,
1923.

ground floor

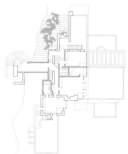

first floor

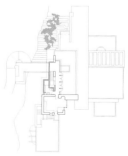

second floor

system. It is in the nature of the material for concrete to be shaped by molds or formwork, and the specially designed molds used to make each block also stamped the blocks with a surface pattern. Thus, whether fabricating an individual block or constructing an entire wall, making and decorating unfolded in the same manner and at the same time. On the outside, the massive and patterned forms of the concrete blockhouses evoked the character of ancient Mesoamerican architecture. On the inside, however, the same expansive sense of space and lightness that was such an important feature of the Prairie Style is evident (fig. 2.33).

Great architecture also requires good patrons, and in Edgar Kaufmann, Wright found one of his best. Kaufmann owned a department store in Pittsburgh and was already attuned to new ideas in design when he met Wright in late 1934. The Kaufmann family owned an extensive tract of land outside of Pittsburgh which the family used as a weekend retreat. A giant boulder overlooking a stream called Bear Run was a favorite spot for family picnics and the Kaufmanns commissioned Wright to design a house on the site. The result, Falling Water, is one of Wright's finest designs and deservedly ranks among the most exciting houses of the twentieth century (figs. 2.34, 2.35). Conceptually, the house can be understood as a series of concrete "trays" cantilevered over the stream. Everywhere the worlds of artifice and nature contend as Wright worked with the primal elements earth, air, fire, and water. A great boulder pushes through the floor in the living room just in front of the hearth, and the combination of earth and fire suggests a warm, secure refuge deep within the house (fig. 2.36). On the terraces, in contrast, one has an exhilarating feeling of being between an ever-changing sky above and water flowing below.

In his analysis of Wright's work, the architectural historian Grant Hildebrand applied the concepts of prospect and refuge, derived from landscape theory, to explain the visceral impact of Wright's architecture. Embedded deep in human

2.34 (opposite) Frank Lloyd Wright,
Falling Water (Edgar J. Kaufmann House),
plan, Bear Run, Pennsylvania, 1934–37.

2.35 (above) Frank Lloyd Wright,
Falling Water (Edgar J. Kaufmann House),
Bear Run, Pennsylvania, 1934–37.

Wright incorporated references to
geological as well as botanical forms.
The rough textures and horizontal
striations evident on wall surfaces recall
the geological formations from which the
stone was quarried. Wright combined
ancient materials such as stone with
modern reinforced concrete to construct
a house both thoroughly modern and
timeless in appeal.

2.36 (right) Frank Lloyd Wright,
Falling Water (Edgar J. Kaufmann House),
living room, Bear Run, Pennsylvania,
1934–37.

consciousness is an innate attraction for landscape settings that offer both prospect—vistas over the surrounding terrain—and refuge from potential threats. In his ability to create artificial "landscapes" that trigger primal human responses we can recognize Wright's genius at work.

Industrialization and the Home

If the assertion of social identity and the pursuit of aesthetic experimentation are two major themes in the history of domestic architecture in the early twentieth century, a third must be recognized as well: the application of methodologies developed originally in an industrial context to the design of domestic environments. In her 1934 study of European and American developments, *Modern Housing*, Catherine Bauer quoted the American architectural critic Lewis Mumford: "The modern house is a biological institution. It is a shelter devoted primarily to the functions of reproduction, nutrition, and recreation." Approached in such strict functionalist terms, the design problem became one of calculating the optimal solution to basic physical needs.

In response, a new kind of design research based on time and motion studies began to circulate internationally. The pioneering figure in this new field was the American industrial engineer Frederick Winslow Taylor (1856–1915). In 1911 Taylor published his major work *The Principles of Scientific Management*. His

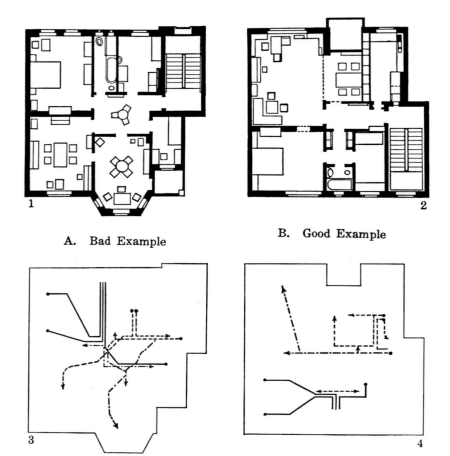

A. Bad Example

B. Good Example

2.37 Alexander Klein, "Functional Housing for Frictionless Living" diagrams, from *Modern Housing* by Catherine Bauer, 1934.

method—dubbed Taylorism—of analyzing task-oriented human activity and re-configuring the arrangement of parts and tools in the interest of greater efficiency proved crucial to the refinement of the assembly-line system of mass production. Taylor's ideas were soon being applied outside the factory as planners, designers, and home economists seized on Taylorism to "improve" the design of domestic environments.

In 1920 home economist Christine Frederick published *Household Engineering: Scientific Management and the Home*, demonstrating the benefits of Taylorism for household management. International interest in Taylorism was so strong that translations of *The Principles of Scientific Management* soon appeared in various Asian and European languages, and Frederick's work appeared in foreign editions as well.

In Germany, Alexander Klein (1879–1961) began to apply the principles of Taylorism to the design of housing. Klein typified the new breed of modernizing expert committed to incorporating into architectural practice scientific advances in other fields. In his research, sponsored by the German Reichsforschungsgesellschaft (National Housing and Building Society), Klein evaluated different apartment layouts by comparing the circulation patterns of each (fig. 2.37). With Catherine Bauer's publication of some of Klein's diagrams in *Modern Housing*, Taylor's ideas completed the round trip from America to Germany and back to America.

Grete Schütte-Lihotzky

In Frankfurt, Grete Schütte-Lihotzky (1897–2000) demonstrated how the principles of task analysis and efficient space planning could be applied to the design of a specific area of the domestic environment: the kitchen. After working for the Vienna Housing Authority in the early 1920s, Schütte-Lihotzky joined Ernst May's staff in Frankfurt in 1926. She was the only woman on the staff and she was responsible for the design of the famous "Frankfurt Kitchen" (fig. 2.38).

2.38 (right) Grete Schütte-Lihotzky, "Frankfurt Kitchen," 1926. Institut für Stadtgeschichte, Frankfurt am Main, Germany.

Grete Schütte-Lihotzky hoped to use modern design to improve the working conditions of women at home. The "Frankfurt Kitchen" reflects her application of industrial techniques of task analysis and her study of models of compact, efficient planning such as galleys in ships and kitchens in railroad dining cars.

2.39 (far right) Lester Beall, "Wash Day," Rural Electrification Administration poster, 1937.

WASH DAY

RURAL ELECTRIFICATION ADMINISTRATION

Introduced in 1927, the Frankfurt Kitchen was a compact, modular work space that represented the ultimate in the rationalization of a task-specific space. Areas for storage, preparation, and clean up of meals were carefully arranged to eliminate wasted effort. Measuring only 1.9 by 3.44 meters in plan, the kitchen was factory-assembled and delivered to the building site ready to be lifted into place by a construction crane. Over ten thousand kitchens were manufactured and installed in the new *siedlungen* erected in Frankfurt under May's supervision.

Schütte-Lihotzky conceived of kitchen design as a way to relieve the drudgery of housework through the careful arrangement of equipment and space. Although the design received a great deal of positive publicity when it was introduced, descriptions of the kitchen did little to challenge basic social conventions concerning women's roles or the gendering of domestic space. Indeed, the degree to which modern "labor-saving" designs actually provided women with the promised benefits of less work and more free time remains a subject of debate among historians of technology, design and gender. What is clear is that, with the introduction of electrification, the kitchen became the most technologically advanced room in the modern home, at least until the advent of the personal computer in the 1970s. Electrification transformed domestic environments in a manner completely unrelated to questions of patronage or style. Whether one is discussing socialist housing in Europe or rural electrification projects in the United States (fig. 2.39), electricity fundamentally altered and modernized the experience of domestic life. A Colonial Revival house or Italianate villa may project a conservative cultural image but the presence inside of a modern kitchen and electrical outlets in all the rooms stamps it as undeniably modern.

R. Buckminster Fuller

Schütte-Lihotzky had successfully reconceptualized the kitchen as a mass-produced modular work station. R. Buckminster Fuller (1895–1983) envisioned extending the same process to the design of the entire house. By harnessing the productive capacity of American industry, Fuller hoped to create a new market for affordable, hygienic, modern housing. The economies of scale made possible by modern systems of mass production, he argued, allowed the manufacture of prefabricated components that could be quickly assembled on site at less than the cost of traditional construction. Clean, bright, and efficient homes could be brought within the financial reach of thousands of potential home buyers unable to afford traditional designs. The modernization and rationalization of design practice in light of the properties of new materials and the engineering logic of new constructional techniques would herald the arrival of a truly modern architecture. For Fuller the advantages of his brand of modern architecture could be quantified using such criteria as weight, time, and cost; indeed, anything that could not be weighed and measured—such as historical precedent, cultural preferences, or architectural aesthetics—was deemed irrelevant (fig. 2.40).

Fuller was certainly not alone in his claim that homes, like

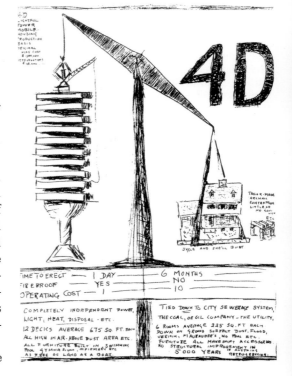

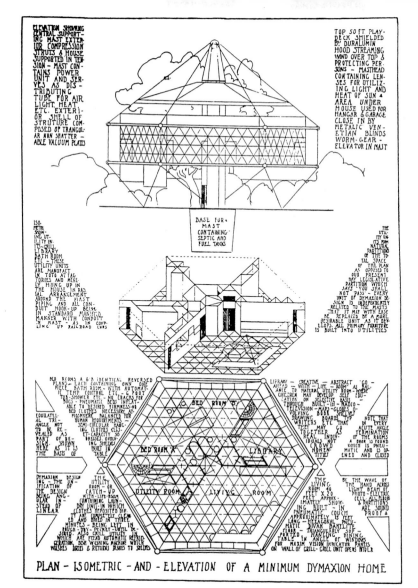

PLAN - ISOMETRIC - AND - ELEVATION OF A MINIMUM DYMAXION HOME

2.40 (opposite)
R. Buckminster Fuller, sketch for The 4-D Tower, 1927.

2.41 (right) R. Buckminster Fuller, project for Dymaxion House, 1929.
  Buckminster Fuller believed that industrial techniques of mass production could be applied to architecture. He invented the term "dymaxion" to describe a prototype house that could be assembled from a kit of mass-produced parts. "Dymaxion" combines parts of "dynamic," "maximum," and "ions" to suggest the technologically sophisticated modernity of the scheme.

cars, could be designed for mass production, but few architects carried this idea to the extreme Fuller did. The Dymaxion House, Fuller's prototypical design unveiled in 1927, bore no resemblance to the traditional image of a house (fig. 2.41). In place of the familiar boxlike structure sitting solidly on the ground, the Dymaxion House was a lightweight single-story hexagonal unit suspended from a central mast containing the utility and power lines. Equipped with the latest labor-saving devices, climate-controlled for comfort, and easily modified as improved components became available in the future, the Dymaxion House was presented by Fuller as the optimal technological solution to the problem of shelter. Few projects capture the uncritical enthusiasm for modern technology shared by many modernist designers as vividly as the Dymaxion House.

Chapter 3

The Architecture of Transportation and Industry

In the manifesto of Futurism, published in 1909, the movement's founder, F. T. Marinetti, proclaimed: "The world's magnificence has been enriched by a new beauty: the beauty of speed." For the Futurists, the sensation of speed evoked the dynamism of the industrial age. Marinetti began his manifesto with a description of racing through the streets of Milan in his automobile—one of the earliest appreciations of the automobile in European literature. The manifesto celebrated the accelerating rhythm of modern life. For millennia, the pace of life had been set by muscle power—either human or animal—and by technological systems for harnessing natural forces, such as the wind for sails or flowing water for water wheels. The Industrial Revolution irrevocably changed this way of life; steam engines now powered factory machines, and steamships and railroads supplanted sailing vessels and horse-drawn wagons.

The process of modernization unleashed by the Industrial Revolution transformed the built environment and altered the relationship between cities and the surrounding countryside. As urban populations grew, cities swelled in size and suburban communities were laid out along new road and rail lines serving the metropolitan centers. To a great extent, the story of nineteenth-century architecture is the story of the efforts of architects and planners to come to terms with the possibilities and problems posed by the urbanization, mechanization, and secularization of modern life.

In the twentieth century, the commitment of the avant-garde to expand the horizons of design, combined with the continued development of new modes of transportation such as the automobile and the airplane, prompted architects to translate the era's fascination with speed into dramatic architectural and urban forms. In *Urbanisme*, published in 1925, Le Corbusier described his vision of "the city of tomorrow" (fig. 3.1):

> A model city of commerce! Is it the mere fancy of some neurotic passion for speed? But surely, speed lies this side of mere dreams; it is a brutal necessity. One can only come to this conclusion; that the city which can achieve speed will achieve success—and this is an obvious truth.
>
> (Le Corbusier, *The City of Tomorrow*, p. 190)

One need not share Marinetti's enthusiasm for speed nor Le Corbusier's conviction concerning its "brutal necessity" to acknowledge that speed and mechanical forms of power exercised a decisive impact on the built environment. The challenge of

Hector Guimard, Porte Dauphine métro entrance, Paris, France, 1900.

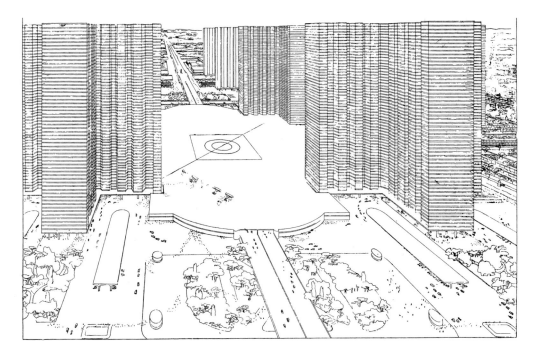

3.1 Le Corbusier, scheme for a future city, from *The City of Tomorrow and Its Planning*, New York, 1929.

giving form to speed and power ranked high on the agenda of modern architects. Equally important, however, were the efforts of modernists to come to terms with the implications of industrial methods of organization and production, for design practice. Thus, this chapter also includes a discussion of the Werkbund movement and the Bauhaus as examples of how major aspects of professional practice, design theory, and architectural education were reconsidered in an effort to integrate architectural and industrial forms of production.

A complete catalog of building types associated with industrial activity and the development of transportation networks is beyond the scope of this survey. Instead, attention is focused on selected building types (such as railroad stations) that allow the reader to sample the range of solutions developed for a single design problem over the course of the entire century. It should be noted, however, that architects and engineers were involved in many different aspects of transportation design. The French engineer Eugène Freyssinet, for example, designed enormous concrete hangars for lighter-than-airships in the late 1910s and early 1920s, while the Italian architect-engineer Pier Luigi Nervi (1891–1979) explored the possibilities of the same material in his designs for airplane hangars erected for the Italian airforce in the 1930s. Sooner or later, airplanes, like ocean liners, must return to land; where and how they do this leaves its mark on the development of architecture.

Railroad Stations

The railroad station was one of the important new building types of the nineteenth century. Rail travel changed the experience of arriving in a city. No longer did the traveler's first encounter with the city occur at a city gate on the periphery; instead, the urban gateway was now located in the heart of the city. Nineteenth-century architectural treatments of the station reflected the era's various architectural movements, and therefore no one single railroad station style emerged to define this building type. Railroad stations provide an index of contemporary design positions and reveal shifting attitudes within architectural culture. Some of the most impressive of early-twentieth-century stations demonstrate the appeal of civic classicism.

New York: Pennsylvania Station, Grand Central Station

New York City boasted two of the era's grandest stations: Pennsylvania Station and Grand Central Station. Pennsylvania Station, designed by McKim, Mead, and White between 1902 and 1911, was demolished in 1963–64 (a loss that did much to stimulate a renewed interest in historic preservation) but Grand Central remains as beautiful and serviceable today as it was upon completion in 1913. Both stations were conceived as monumental classical compositions and possessed a spatial grandeur intentionally reminiscent of imperial Roman architecture. Credit for the design of Grand Central Station belongs to two architectural firms: Reed & Stem, and Warren & Wetmore. Whitney Warren (1864–1943) had studied at the French École des Beaux-Arts and in the design of the station we can see the adaptation of academic models to modern programs that is the hallmark of American classical architecture in the first decades of the new century. The imposing monumentality of the columns and arches on the facade of Grand Central signal its importance as one of the main gateways to the city; beneath the stone veneer, however, a steel frame supports the building (fig. 3.2).

The design of large metropolitan railroad facilities involves more than serving up civic symbolism or satisfying the desire for corporate aggrandizement: stations must work. Providing for an efficient circulation of people and trains was the chief

3.2 Grand Central Terminal and Hotel Commodore, East 42nd Street, New York, 1913.

challenge facing the station's designers. Grand Central took almost a decade to complete and was complicated by the fact that train service had to be maintained during construction. In the station, intercity rail lines connect with local subway and surface transit routes, and vehicular as well as pedestrian traffic must be accommodated. A sectional view of Grand Central reveals the sophisticated planning of multiple pathways designed to move large numbers of people through the building (fig. 3.3). The station sits astride Park Avenue so an elevated roadway bridges 42nd Street and carries automotive traffic around the terminal. Inside passengers move through the building's multiple levels via a series of gently sloping ramps. There is no incompatibility between the functional and engineering demands of station operation and the classical language of architecture employed by the designers. The architects of Grand Central Station showed that modern classicism could accommodate the demands of a complex program and resolve issues of form and function successfully.

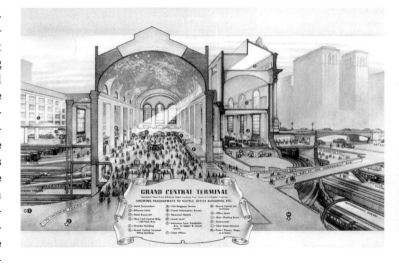

3.3 Grand Central Terminal and Hotel Commodore, sketch of north-south section, East 42nd Street, New York, 1913.

Helsinki and Stuttgart Railroad Stations

In 1904 Eliel Saarinen won a competition for the design of a new railroad station in Helsinki, Finland. Like Grand Central, work on the new Helsinki terminal stretched over years and the station was only finished in 1919 (fig. 3.4). Saarinen's original proposal, with a rough-hewn texture for the granite facing of the building and an

3.4 Eliel Saarinen, Railway Station, Helsinki, Finland, 1904–19.

ornamental program that included sculptures of bears, fitted comfortably within a National Romantic conception of design but it soon became the target of fierce criticism. Two Finnish architects, Gustaf Strengell (1878–1937) and Sigurd Frosterus (1876–1956), published a pamphlet attacking Saarinen's design. They cited Otto Wagner's call for a modern architecture based on modern life in support of their appeal for a less romantic approach. Saarinen's willingness to rethink his competition design in light of Strengell and Frosterus's argument reveals just how shallow the roots of National Romanticism were in the soil of the modern age.

Saarinen's revised scheme reflected his growing appreciation for the structural possibilities of reinforced concrete. He remained reluctant, however, to reduce architectural design to engineering and material considerations. Throughout the building, surfaces are incised with linear patterns that modulate the basic rhythm established by the facade bays and the grand entry arch (fig. 3.5). Significantly, Saarinen rejected the Beaux-Arts classicism of American models. A pervasive theme in early-twentieth-century cultural debates about form was the inadequacy of classical models for modern life and, while classicism had its defenders, the tide was steadily shifting in the direction of alternate approaches to design. As the Helsinki station demonstrates, one could forsake classical models and move beyond the fanciful imagery of National Romanticism while still remaining committed to the principle that surface patterns and applied ornament were an integral part of any building.

The tendency to eliminate ornament gained momentum after World War I. In 1911 the German architect Paul Bonatz (1877–1956) won a competition for the design of the Hauptbahnhof (central station) in Stuttgart. Once again, years were required to bring the project to fruition; Bonatz, now working with Friedrich Eugen Scholer (1874–?), submitted a revised plan in 1913, but the design continued to evolve and the station was not completed until 1928 (fig. 3.6). In Bonatz's own words, his architecture was "purified by the gravity of war": the result is a composition based on massive undecorated shapes. Like the architects of Grand Central Station, Bonatz resolved the complex traffic and operational requirements of a large station; however, while function determined significant aspects of plan and section, it did not dictate the final form of the design. In contrast to the ornate grandeur of Grand Central Station, Bonatz achieved a monumental effect through the bold simplicity of his masonry forms. In the 1920s such simplicity increasingly came to be equated with modernism in design. With its thick, solid walls, the mural modernism of Stuttgart's Hauptbahnhof is a far cry from the International Style and demonstrates that the movement away from historicism did not lead solely or inevitably to an architecture of transparent volumes and revealed structure.

3.5 Eliel Saarinen, Railway Station, detail of portal, Helsinki, Finland, 1904–19.

3.6 Paul Bonatz and Friedrich Scholer, Railway Station and Hotel, Stuttgart, Germany, 1911, 1917–19, 1922–28.

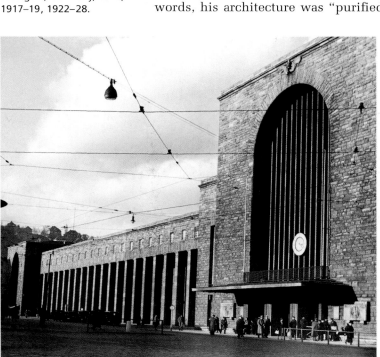

Los Angeles: Union Station

The last station to be considered here reminds us that Period Revival architecture continued to appeal well into the twentieth century. Period Revivalism involves the selection of models and images on the basis of their association with a particular era or place in the history of architecture. (In the early nineteenth century, for example, American architects favored Greek architectural models because of the implicit link between American and ancient Greek democracy.) Architects then adapt the models to accommodate new programs, materials, and structural systems.

In southern California, architecture suggestive of the region's Spanish colonial past proved popular. John and Donald Parkinson's Union Station in Los Angeles,

3.7 John and Donald Parkinson, Union Passenger Railroad Terminal, 800 North Alameda, Los Angeles, California, 1934–39.

completed in 1939, evoked the romance of the region's past rather than the rational-ism of modern transportation technology or the modernity of its reinforced concrete construction (fig. 3.7). The contrast between the classicism of Grand Central and the romanticism of the Los Angeles station reinforced regional identities.

While architectural imagery may address issues of differentiation, however, the functional demands tended to promote strong similarities among stations of compa-rable size. Ignore the tilework and Spanish detailing of the interior spaces, and the Los Angeles Station reveals strong affinities with the solid, simple massing of the Stuttgart Hauptbahnhof.

Urban Mass Transit Systems

The growth of cities spurred the development of mass transit systems to facilitate the movement of ever greater numbers of people across the expanding urban area. These systems entailed the construction of elevated, surface, and subway lines along with all the necessary supporting facilities such as transit stations, power houses, and maintenance yards. While many of these facilities could be sited out-side of the city center, passenger stations had to be inserted in the midst of the urban fabric. Traveling on subway, surface, or elevated lines quickly became part of daily experience as people adjusted their life-styles to the routines of modern living. Far from being unassuming parts of the built environment, stations became integral links in the transportation infrastructure of major urban centers. Increas-ingly, architectural design was only one facet of the development of entire systems, and the complexity of systems engineering demanded that architects grapple with an expanded set of design considerations. Architects and designers worked with engineers to develop facilities that not only satisfied functional considerations but contributed to a coherent identity for entire transit systems.

Paris, Vienna, and London

In Paris, the architect Hector Guimard designed stations and canopied entrances for the Parisian métro using cast iron (see page 76). Iron had been used throughout the nineteenth century, but Guimard shaped it in a way that reflected his involvement with the international art and design movement known as Art Nouveau. The term Art Nouveau captures the era's yearning for a fresh design identity. In the 1890s artists and architects began to explore alternatives to the prevailing historicist styles and they turned to nature rather than history as a source for formal inspira-tion. Natural forms can be interpreted in a variety of ways. Any survey of Art Nou-veau work from the 1890s reveals a wide range of treatments from the literal reproduction of plant or animal forms to highly abstracted designs. The origin of the term Art Nouveau is often traced to an art dealer named Siegfried Bing who, in 1895, opened a shop of that name in Paris. Bing's Salon de l'Art Nouveau special-ized in fine decorative arts and Art Nouveau designers certainly aspired to the cre-ation of artfully coordinated environments. But Guimard's métro stations hardly qualify as examples of the decorative arts nor, given their settings on busy city streets, can they satisfy the definition of a *gesamtkunstwerk*.

What is worth noting here is that a discussion of Art Nouveau cannot be con-fined to the realm of high art and elite culture. The same design concerns evident in

examples of the fine arts or monumental architecture appear in works that belong to the domain of utilitarian infrastructure such as subway stations. The blurring of the distinctions between traditionally separate categories of artistic endeavor is one of the distinctive features of twentieth-century architecture and design.

Guimard's version of Art Nouveau shares an affinity with the contemporary work of such Belgian designers as Victor Horta (1861–1947) and Henry van de Velde (1863–1957). Slender pieces of iron were detailed to appear plantlike with the fluid curves and organic lines of plant stems or tall grasses. Springing from a simple base, the structural elements "blossom" and grow richer in detail as they approach the station's canopy, infusing the simple cast-iron system of construction with the morphology of organic forms.

A very different spirit pervades contemporary work in Vienna where Otto Wagner designed stations for the city's new Stadtbahn (railroad) (fig. 3.8). In place of Guimard's curving forms that appear to spring from the ground, Wagner placed a

3.8 Otto Wagner, Karlsplatz Stadtbahn, Vienna, Austria.

greater emphasis on geometric order and tectonic clarity. Despite their formal differences, both Wagner and Guimard worked with frame-and-panel building systems using a limited number of prefabricated elements. As the contrast between Wagner and Guimard's stations illustrates, far from being predetermined or fixed, the relationship between visual form and physical structure could be configured in a variety of ways. The question of the appropriate relationship between form and structure was central to the architectural debates of the twentieth century.

In terms of a comprehensive design strategy encompassing an entire transit network, however, few systems approached the coherence and design quality of the London Passenger Transport Board (LPTB), thanks to the efforts of Frank Pick (1878–1941). Pick joined the Underground Electric Railway Ltd. (the predecessor to the LPTB) in 1906, rose to be managing director of the system and eventually was named vice-chairman of the LPTB in 1933. During his years with the LPTB he supervised the development of a consistent visual identity for everything from buildings to rolling stock to graphic design. Pick valued order, unity, and consistency in design. He had little interest in the ornamental work of Guimard and preferred a leaner, less ornate style for LPTB facilities. Edward Johnston's (1872–1944) famous sans serif typeface, commissioned by Pick for use in signage throughout the entire system, is a perfect expression of Pick's commitment to legible, functional design.

Beginning in the mid-1920s, the architect Charles Holden (1875–1960) was responsible for the design of LPTB stations. In preparation for the expansion of underground lines, Pick and Holden toured Germany, the Netherlands, and Scandinavia in 1930 to study continental developments. Upon their return, Holden developed a simple formula that has been described as a "brick box with a concrete lid" for new stations on the Piccadilly Line. The Arnos Grove Station is a typical Holden solution; this simple, well-lighted brick cylinder is the architectural counterpart to Johnston's typeface (fig. 3.9).

3.9 Charles Holden, Arnos Grove Underground Station, London, 1930s.

This station reveals the impact of Holden's European tour. The simple brick-and-glass exterior demonstrates an affinity with Willem Dudok's work in Hilversum (see fig. 4.5). The arrangement of a low base and tall cylinder echoes Erik Gunnar Asplund's design for the Stockholm Public Library (see fig. 1.33).

Automobile Service Stations

When F. T. Marinetti began the founding manifesto of Futurism with a description of speeding through the streets of Milan, he employed the automobile as a potent symbol of modernity. More than an abstract symbol, however, the automobile proved to be a decisive agent in the transformation of the built environment; the impact of the car is a theme we shall note throughout this account of twentieth-century architecture. At times, the form-determining quality of the automobile was idiosyncratic; the ground-floor curve of Le Corbusier's Villa Savoye, for example (see fig. 2.24), was determined by the turning radius of an auto.

But the automobile also had a more substantial impact on existing building types. In the era of horse-drawn carriages, stables were kept at a distance from the residence. The automobile required no such separation—the attached garage appeared early in the century. Frank Lloyd Wright included one in his design of Robie House, yet another indication that modern technologies were compatible with the Emersonian spirit of the Prairie Style. As the number of automobiles increased, urban and suburban settlement patterns were adjusted to accommodate the spatial requirements of automotive technology, such as wider, paved roads and parking facilities.

Although architectural historians have noted the impact of the automobile on traditional building types and settlement patterns, they have tended to ignore the

3.10 Walter Dorwin Teague, Texaco Gas Station, Texaco, type "M," Milwaukee, Wisconsin, 1948.

3.11 The Coffee Pot, Tacoma, Washington, 1931.

development of new building types specifically created to serve the automobile, such as the service station. However, articles treating the service station as a design problem appeared frequently in professional architectural reviews and oil industry trade journals beginning in the 1920s.

A pervasive presence in the roadside landscape, the service station (also called the filling or gasoline station) constitutes an industrial vernacular type of architecture. The development of the service station is intimately related to the rise of an automotive culture and the pattern of development varies from country to country. In the United States, the basic features of the new type emerged between 1907 and 1913. Early stations included a canopy over the pumps and a small building containing sales and service facilities. Standard Oil of California launched the first chain of service stations in 1914 and individual stations soon reflected corporate attitudes toward image as well as function. In an effort to blend into residential settings, early service stations often showed a hipped roof and window shutters.

By the 1930s, more attention-grabbing design strategies were adopted by most oil companies. Stations were conceived as streamlined boxes with flat roofs, large display windows, and wide service bays. Prominently displayed corporate logos and signature color schemes quickly established brand identity for passing motorists. Standardization served corporate interests in ensuring uniformity, efficiency, economy, and brand recognition.

Oil companies soon realized that the development of standardized facilities did not require the services of architects; they therefore turned to industrial designers because of their expertise in coordinating advertising and product design. In the 1930s Texaco commissioned the industrial designer Walter Dorwin Teague (1883–1960) to prepare pattern books outlining design solutions for different types of sites and markets (fig. 3.10). Teague developed five different models that shared the same features. Although they varied in size, the models all had a horizontal band of three lines running around the top of their simple rectangular volumes. Below the band, signage identified different functional areas such as service bays, and restrooms. Above the band, in larger letters, only the corporate name appeared.

Standardized design according to corporate norms is only one aspect of automotive architecture. Roadside America also featured whimsical designs based on familiar objects inflated to an unfamiliar scale in order to grab the attention of passing motorists. A building shaped like a giant coffee pot, for example, fuses architecture and signage into a single, startling form (fig. 3.11). Today, in the wake of Pop Art and postmodernism, this wacky roadside commercial architecture is celebrated by enthusiasts of American popular culture.

But the advent of commercial design along America's roadways sparked resistance as well as affection. In the 1920s a roadside reform movement emerged committed to maintaining the aesthetic appeal of the landscape by controlling roadside development. In 1923 Elizabeth Boyd Lawton founded the National Committee for the Restriction of Outdoor Advertising (later renamed the National Council for the

Protection of Roadside Beauty). Lawton forged a coalition of civic associations and women's clubs to promote the cause of roadside beauty. "The great stream of automobile traffic," she wrote in 1926, "increasing at a rate almost incredible, is trailing the commerce of the cities out along every country road, and the quiet beauty of our rural roads is fast giving way to the sordid ugliness of cheap commerce." If Marinetti's Futurist manifesto demonstrates an enthusiastic embrace of modernity, Lawton's crusade against "the sordid ugliness of cheap commerce" is a reminder that the story of twentieth-century architecture includes episodes of reaction and resistance to the forces shaping the built environment.

Factory Architecture

The modern history of the factory unfolds in step with the history of the Industrial Revolution. Initially, factories occupied a strictly marginal position in the thinking of the architectural profession which distinguished between architecture, understood as a fine art practiced by gentlemen, and the construction of other less noble forms of utilitarian building. With only rare exceptions, the design of factories was left to engineers or contractors. In the early twentieth century, however, this situation began to change as the factory system of mass production began to register a significant impact on popular consciousness. Pioneers of modern mass production such as Henry Ford became cultural figures of international renown, and the condition of an increasingly factory-based labor force became the concern of social reformers, labor organizers, and efficiency experts. Factory design came to occupy a much higher profile within architectural culture. As we shall see, however, the "problem" of factory design assumed slightly different definitions in Europe and America.

The United States: Albert and Julius Kahn, Robert Derrah

The brothers Albert (1892–1942) and Julius (1861–1924) Kahn are key figures in the story of American factory architecture. Born in Germany, they immigrated to the United States as young men and settled in Detroit. Albert was largely self-educated as an architect but Julius studied engineering at the University of Michigan. Over the course of four decades, the Kahn design firm was responsible for the design of over 1,500 buildings; the majority of these were industrial facilities.

3.12 Julius Kahn, the Kahn system of reinforced concrete, detail.

However, quantity of production is only one aspect of the Kahn story. Julius Kahn invented an improved system of reinforced concrete construction; by reconfiguring the arrangement of steel reinforcing bars, the Kahn system simplified construction and increased the space to structure ratio (that is, it provided more room with less structure) (fig. 3.12). In 1905 Julius Kahn founded the Trussed Concrete Steel Company (later renamed Truscon) to market the new constructional system and the Kahns began using it for the design of new factories. The Kahn Daylight System of Factory Design developed by Albert Kahn involved the construction of a regular grid of widely spaced structural columns supporting a beam and slab floor structure and enclosed by extensively glazed exterior walls.

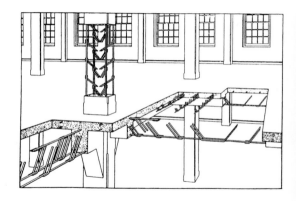

Albert Kahn enjoyed a close working relationship with Henry Ford and thoroughly understood the spatial requirements of Ford's automotive assembly lines. Kahn's great contribution was to harmonize two separate processes of conceptualization central to modern forms of production: the production engineer's technical definition of the production process—the actual making of a product—and the architect's design of the physical space of production. Ford insisted on the rationalization and simplification of the flow of materials throughout the manufacturing process from the arrival of raw materials to the departure of the finished product. Kahn's approach to design allowed the diagram of the manufacturing process to establish the basic design of an entire industrial installation such as Ford's famous River Rouge plant in Dearborn, Michigan. For heavy manufacturing, the Kahn system tended to generate single-story factories which facilitated the movement of materials through the manufacturing process. The extensive glazing of the perimeter walls and the provision of skylights ensured that ample natural light reached the working areas inside.

Albert Kahn's 1937 Chrysler Corporation's Half-Ton Truck Plant in Warren, Michigan, is one of his most famous designs (figs. 3.13, 3.14). The crisply defined volumes of this design with its wide, horizontal band of clear glass encircling the building could be identified as features of the International Style. But the aesthetic concerns of European architects that figure so prominently in the International Style are alien to Kahn's industrial design approach. He summed up his own approach to factory design in strictly functionalist terms:

> Industrial architecture must necessarily deal with the practical first, with proper functioning of the plant, with the best working conditions, efficiency and flexibility, with economical and safe construction, and only last with external appearance.

(Kahn, p. 501)

3.13 Albert Kahn, Half-Ton Truck Plant, interior, Dodge Division, Chrysler Corporation, Warren, Michigan, 1937.

Throughout his career, Kahn carefully distinguished between industrial and civic architecture; his designs for campus buildings at the University of Michigan, for example, conform to traditional tastes.

Factory design involves more than configuring the place of production: factory buildings also serve as the architectural image of the company. Beginning in the nineteenth century, promotional literature for products often includes an illustration of a company's production facilities, intended to convey the impression of a substantial operation capable of satisfying market demand. Modern advertising relies heavily on memorable images to capture attention and reinforce name recognition. A vivid example of this design strategy is a bottling plant designed in 1936

3.14 Albert Kahn, Half-ton truck plant, Dodge Division, Chrysler Corporation, Warren, Michigan, 1937.

Kahn emphasized pragmatic, not dogmatic, solutions to design problems. Although he owed his early success to innovations in reinforced concrete construction, Kahn never restricted himself to working only with a single material. This Chrysler facility is steel-framed; the raised center bay provides clerestory windows and ensures adequate light across the interior's entire width.

3.15 Robert Derrah, Coca Cola Bottling Plant and Office, Los Angeles, California, 1936.

by Robert Derrah (1895–1946) for Coca Cola (fig. 3.15). Derrah remodeled several existing structures into a single building fashioned to look like a giant ocean liner. In the 1930s nautical imagery was very popular among modern architects as it evoked an aura of streamlined power and rational engineering. Few designers carried nautical themes to the extreme that Derrah did, however, and the incongruous image of a giant ship "moored" along a city street is indicative of a quixotic rather than a rational conception of industrial design.

England and Holland: Thomas Wallis's Factories, the Van Nelle Tobacco Factory

3.16 Wallis, Gilbert and Partners, Hoover Factory, Perivale, London, England, 1931–35.
   The front of the factory is organized like the façade of a palace. The piers suggest an enormous colonnade supporting an entablature and flanked by corner towers. This palace of labor is the antithesis of the dreary nineteenth-century factory.

In England, Thomas Wallis (1873–1953) designed a series of factories dubbed "fancy factories" by contemporary critics for his eye-catching treatments of facades. Wallis founded his own practice in 1914 when he was approached by the Trussed Concrete Steel Company, which was then seeking to gain entry to the English market. Wallis entered into an agreement with Moritz Kahn (Albert and Julius's younger brother) to introduce the patented Kahn system of concrete construction in England and he soon established a thriving business. His factory designs show the same careful attention to lighting, ventilation, and efficient arrangement of spaces as those of Albert Kahn. For factories located along prominent roadways such as the 1931–35 Hoover Factory on London's Western Avenue, Wallis designed monumental Art Deco facades in a contemporary style (fig. 3.16). He insisted that the extra money invested in the architectural embellishment of a factory attracted public attention and served as good advertising.

The Art Deco style of the Hoover Factory is more than a clever advertising ploy, however; industrial architects such as Albert Kahn and Thomas Wallis worked hard to erase the popular image of factories as dark and brutal workplaces. Wallis's sense of style was one aspect of his efforts to change this popular perception. Better factory lighting and ventilation were hailed as signs of more humane working environments in much the same way that housing reforms had trumpeted their commitment to providing natural light and fresh air to the residents of new housing projects.

In Rotterdam, J. A. Brinkman (1902–1949) and L. C. van der Vlugt (1894–1936) with Mart Stam (1899–1986) designed one of the most acclaimed factories of the era: the Van Nelle Tobacco Factory (figs. 3.17, 3.18). Situated along a narrow strip of land between the access road and a shipping canal, the plan of the Van Nelle Factory consists of a straightforward grid of structural columns, by then the standard solution for the plans of commercial and industrial buildings. The floor slabs are cantilevered beyond the edge of the column line and the exterior walls are opened up as much as possible with glass. In contrast to the vertical piers and colorful ornamental details of Wallis's design, smooth surfaces, broad planes of glass, and an emphasis on the horizontal sweep of the design set the tone of the Van Nelle Tobacco Factory.

This difference in approach is significant. In his famous 1908 essay "Ornament and Crime" the Viennese architect and critic Adolf Loos claimed, "The evolution of culture is synonymous with the removal of ornament from utilitarian objects"; this

3.17 Johannes A. Brinkman, Leendert Cornelius van der Vlugt, and Mart Stam, Van Nelle Tobacco Factory, Rotterdam, Netherlands, 1926–30.

European modernists believed that factories should be models of progressive social design. Le Corbusier argued that humane, rational, and efficient designs such as the Van Nelle factory would improve relations between labor and management. Although his assessment of labor-management relations was naive, his description of this factory as an outstanding example of modernism was correct.

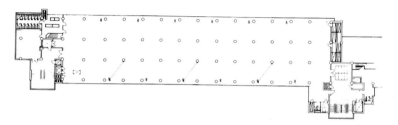

3.18 Johannes A. Brinkman, Leendert Cornelius van der Vlugt, and Mart Stam, Van Nelle Tobacco Factory, plan, Rotterdam, Netherlands, 1926–30.

puritanical attitude took root among young European modernists. Factories are first and foremost utilitarian buildings, and the ornamental flourishes of Wallis's "fancy factories" struck many as superficial. For the members of the CIAM, the German word *sachlich* (objective) best captured the essence of what they were trying to achieve. The social agenda of modern architecture may have brought architects together in their commitment to better working conditions for factory labor, but the role of style in factory design proved to be a divisive issue among designers and critics.

The German Experience

The discussion of industrial architecture must be broadened to include more than a review of the planning formulas, structural designs, and architectural treatments imposed on individual buildings. Progressive architects were convinced that civilization was on the threshold of a new age characterized by new modes of production along with novel social and political systems which rendered traditional ways of problem solving obsolete. The design profession struggled to come to terms with the logic of industrial systems of production. What were the implications for architecture of the rationalization of process and standardization of form typical of mass production? What was the role of the design profession in promoting national prosperity and prestige? Beyond satisfying programmatic requirements, how could architecture represent the emerging industrial order? In the first third of the century, the German experience provides a valuable case study of the effort to answer these questions.

Behrens and AEG

After almost eight years as a cultural attaché in London, Hermann Muthesius (see page 48) returned to Germany and quickly emerged as an influential voice in design discussions. In Central Europe the discussion of industrial form was charged with a cultural significance it did not have in America. "Without a total respect for form, culture is unthinkable," wrote Muthesius, "and formlessness is synonymous with lack of culture." The cultivation of form was a role traditionally performed by creative artists and, in an effort to enhance the competitive position of German manufactured goods in world markets, design advocates sought to foster closer links between German industry and designers. The list of people concerned about the design quality of German goods was not limited to artists and architects but included such political leaders as Friedrich Naumann and such industrialists as Emil Rathenau. Unlike England, where craft-based design continued to exercise a strong appeal and design critics assailed industrially produced goods as debased forms of design, the design debate in Central Europe followed a different course.

The AEG company, the largest German manufacturer of electrical products, founded by Emil Rathenau, provided the model for the kind of coordination between creative design and industrial production advocated by Muthesius. In 1907

AEG hired the architect Peter Behrens (1868–1940) to serve as artistic advisor. Behrens was consulted on everything from the design of factories to the form of products to advertising and graphic design. In 1909 he designed the AEG turbine factory in Berlin (fig. 3.19). To satisfy the requirement for a tall, unobstructed space, Behrens employed a system of steel arches 25 meters tall. Along the building's flanks, he left the steel frame exposed and filled the intervening bays with glass. For the facade, however, Behrens encased the steel frame in massive corner pylons made of concrete. Issues of representation rather than function motivated this design decision. With its polygonal gable, the facade suggests an abstracted version of an ancient temple, with the AEG logo substituting for the statue of the deity in the pediment. Behrens thus elevated industrial design to the level of a culturally significant high art.

The German *Werkbund*

Efforts to promote a rapprochement between art and industry continued to gain momentum. In 1907, the same year Behrens joined AEG, a national organization known as the German *Werkbund* was formed in Munich. The *Werkbund* sought to bring designers and manufacturers together, educate the public about industrial design, reform design education, and raise the quality of German manufactured goods. The organization held annual conferences, published a yearbook, and periodically staged exhibitions. Two dozen industrialists and artists attended the founding meeting but the membership roster grew quickly; only two years later there were 731 members and by 1914 the number had risen to 1,870. *Werkbund* membership included both artists and industrialists, and from its inception a range of viewpoints was represented within the organization. Other countries followed the German example. In 1910 an Austrian *Werkbund* was founded; in 1913 a Swiss *Werkbund* appeared. An English equivalent, the Design and Industries Association (DIA), was founded in 1915 (with Frank Pick as an active member).

In 1914 the German *Werkbund* organized a major exhibition in Cologne. At its annual conference convened during the exhibition, an important public debate occurred between two of the organization's leading figures, Hermann Muthesius and Henry Van de Velde. Van de Velde, a Belgian artist and designer with an international reputation, had been active in Germany since the 1890s. In 1902 he was appointed head of the Weimar Art Academy where he began to reformulate the educational program and he was among the original members of the *Werkbund*. At issue in the debate was the position designers ought to assume in relationship to the logic of modern industrial production. Muthesius presented the case for standardization as the design strategy best suited to systems of mass production:

> Architecture, and with it the whole area of the *Werkbund*'s activities, is pressing towards standardization, and only through standardization can it recover that universal significance which was characteristic of it in times of harmonious culture.

(Conrads, p. 28)

3.19 (opposite) Peter Behrens and Karl Bernhard, AEG turbine factory, Berlin, Germany, 1908–09.

But standardization was perceived by many as limiting the artistic freedom of designers. Van de Velde responded to Muthesius with an impassioned plea for individual creativity:

> The efforts of the *Werkbund* should be directed toward cultivating . . . the gifts of individual manual skill, joy, and belief in the beauty of highly differentiated execution, not toward inhibiting them by standardization.

(Conrads, p. 30)

Standardization versus differentiation: this is the essence of a debate that would occupy not only members of the *Werkbund* but modern architects in general throughout the twentieth century.

Pavilions erected for the exhibition included a model factory building designed by Walter Gropius and a domed pavilion housing an exhibit of glassware designed by Bruno Taut. Improvement in factory conditions went hand-in-hand with the desire to raise the standard of production among *Werkbund* reformers. Walter Gropius's model factory, for example, included provisions for a workers' canteen on the rooftop of the administrative block (fig. 3.21). Taut's Glass Pavilion, on the other hand, expressed an almost mystical faith in the power of materials to transform not just the workday routine of factory labor but life itself. The display of glassware produced by *Werkbund* members provided an opportunity for Taut to erect what amounts to a shrine to a new glass culture (fig. 3.22). Around the base of the pavilion, Taut arranged a series aphorisms drawn from the utopian writing of the author Paul Scheerbart extolling glass: "glass brings a new era," "colored glass destroys hatred," and "building in brick only does us harm." Like an alchemist's stone, according to Taut, glass held the potential to transform the crude reality of the built environment into a crystalline paradise. This theme of the transformative power of new materials is a major one in the story of modern architecture.

With a membership that included representatives from small companies as well as industrial giants like AEG and designers who worked in a variety of scales from furniture to buildings, the *Werkbund* was a diverse organization that served multiple agendas. Rather than limiting themselves to deliberations about specific building types such as factories, *Werkbund* designers tended to concern themselves with establishing an appropriate formal language for the modern era. In the years following World War I, the focus of deliberations shifted to the field of housing, and in 1927 the *Werkbund* staged a major exhibition devoted to this theme in Stuttgart. For this occasion, the *Werkbund* solicited support from local housing officials and erected a model housing settlement called the Weissenhof Siedlung (fig. 3.20). Ludwig Mies van der Rohe, then

3.20 Ludwig Mies van der Rohe, Weissenhof housing development, "Deutscher Werkbund Exhibition," Stuttgart, Germany, 1927.

vice-president of the *Werkbund*, supervised the project and Richard Döcker (1894–1968) served as technical director. On a sloping site outside of Stuttgart, seventeen architects were invited to erect model homes including detached single-family houses, row houses, and four-story apartment buildings. Participants included Peter Behrens, Le Corbusier, Walter Gropius, Hans Scharoun, and Bruno Taut. With work by so many different architects in one place, the Weissenhof Siedlung offers a critical "snapshot" of progressive architecture in the late 1920s. In general, it is clear that the expressionist quality of so much German design from the 1910s and early 1920s characterized by vivid color schemes, contrasting textures, and multifaceted or crystal-like forms has given way to a *sachlich* mentality that favored flat roofs, standardized details, and rational planning criteria.

The Bauhaus

Few institutions in twentieth-century architecture have achieved the enduring recognition associated with the Bauhaus. The name alone has become synonymous with modern design. More than six decades after its closing, schools of architecture and design around the world continue to define themselves in relationship to "the Bauhaus model" of design education. An enormous body of literature has appeared describing the Bauhaus and assessing its legacy for modern architecture. The skeleton of facts at the core of the Bauhaus story is clear. The school was created in 1919 by merging two existing educational programs in Weimar, the Academy of Art and the School of Arts and Crafts, with the goal of providing a comprehensive design education. After losing the financial support of the local administration in Weimar due to criticism of the radical nature of the Bauhaus program, the Bauhaus relocated to Dessau in 1925. In Dessau, Walter Gropius designed a new facility for the school—the result is one of the seminal examples of architectural modernism (fig. 3.23). The Bauhaus moved once more, to Berlin in 1932, after the National Socialists gained control of local government in Dessau. The Berlin chapter of the Bauhaus story was brief and the school, then housed in a rented factory building, closed in August 1933. During its lifetime, the Bauhaus had three directors: Walter Gropius from 1919 to 1928, Hannes Meyer (1889–1954) from 1928 to 1930, and Ludwig Mies van der Rohe from 1930 to 1933.

The Bauhaus curriculum underwent a series of revisions during the school's history as faculty members and directors changed. In the early years, the animating

3.21 (left) Walter Gropius and Adolf Meyer, factory and office building, "Deutscher Werkbund Exhibition," Cologne, Germany, 1914.

3.22 (right) Bruno Taut, Glass Pavilion, "Deutscher Werkbund Exhibition," Cologne, Germany, 1914.
From a windowless, grotto-like room in the base of the pavilion, visitors climbed a curved stairway to the upper level under the glass dome. For Taut, the passage from darkness to light symbolized the dawn of a new era made possible by modern materials.

spirit was based on an appreciation of craft ideals. Later, however, the focus shifted to teaching students to exploit the potential of industrialized forms of production. Gropius hoped to finance the school, in part, by marketing student and faculty designs to manufacturers. In terms of the architectural history of the twentieth century, however, what is most important about the Bauhaus is what remained consistent in the school's approach: learning through experimentation. In 1926 Gropius described the Bauhaus workshops as "laboratories" and argued:

> It is only through constant contact with newly evolving techniques, with the discovery of new materials and new ways of putting things together, that the creative individual can . . . develop a new attitude toward design which is a resolute affirmation of the living environment of machines and vehicles.

(Conrads, p. 95)

Throughout its brief history, the Bauhaus remained committed to the idea of design as a form of constant experimentation with materials and techniques. Gropius, Meyer, and Mies van der Rohe all recognized that in the modern era technological and material progress presented designers with a range of choices unprecedented in history. In such a situation, they concluded, historical precedents no longer provide adequate models. Previously, architectural education began with the study of historical models. Education through emulation of paradigms was replaced, at the Bauhaus, by education through experimentation with materials and techniques.

3.23 Walter Gropius, Bauhaus, workshop wing, Dessau, Germany, 1926.

The Bauhaus looks more like a factory building or research laboratory than a conventional school. Because the floor slabs project beyond their supporting columns, the exterior curtain wall is uninterrupted by the building's structural frame. The result is an International Style design that emphasizes volume rather than mass, regularity rather than symmetry, and omits decorative embellishments.

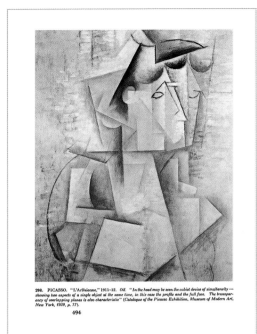

3.24 Siegfried Giedion, *Space, Time, and Architecture: The Growth of a New Tradition*, Harvard University Press, 1941, copyright © Harvard College, 1941. Copyright © A. and V. C. Giedion, 1982.

Giedion's book is one of the most influential works on modern architecture. It was based on a series of lectures originally delivered in 1939 at Harvard University. This page spread illustrates Giedion's argument that there was a strong connection between modern architecture, avant-garde art, and modern science.

Experimentation is the hallmark of the scientific method; the appeal of science resided in its supposed objectivity as a way of examining and acting upon the world. For modernists in search of alternatives to premodern ways of conceptualizing design, the application of scientific methods to design held the promise of accelerating the pace of material and social progress through the reformulation of design methods.

The Bauhaus was only one of a number of attempts to found new or to reform existing educational programs in the twentieth century, yet its story dominates most discussions of modern architecture and design. Recent evaluations of the Bauhaus have noted the disproportionate influence of the school and have suggested its record concerning equal opportunity for women was disappointing, but its reputation endures nonetheless. Multiple reasons can be advanced for this. First,

3.25 Laszlo Moholy-Nagy, book jacket for Bauhausbauten Dessau showing Walter Gropius's Törten housing project, Dessau, Germany, 1926–28.

The Bauhaus published a series of small books documenting the work of the school's faculty and students. This particular book describes a project by Walter Gropius for row houses that could be erected quickly. The houses are shown at various stages of completion in order to illustrate the simple structural system: concrete slabs wall-braced by thin concrete beams.

much of the Bauhaus's reputation can be attributed to the fact that members of its faculty went on to assume prominent positions in design education after World War II. Second, the antagonistic relationship between the Bauhaus and the Nazi regime established the school's moral authority in the eyes of postwar historians seeking to preserve modernism free of any taint of association with totalitarianism. (The leftist political orientation of Bauhaus members during the 1920s and 1930s was conveniently downplayed in later discussions of the Bauhaus, particularly in the United States.) Third, the Bauhaus successfully integrated the three primary concerns of modern architecture: formal invention, technological innovation, and a progressive social agenda.

In his influential discussion of modern architecture, *Space, Time and Architecture*, Siegfried Giedion compared the Dessau Bauhaus, designed by Gropius, with Picasso's *L'Arlésienne* (fig. 3.24). Giedion argued that the transparent corner of the Bauhaus revealed not only a modern system of construction related to contemporary factory design, but could be linked to a Cubist conception of space and form. Schemes such as Gropius's Törten Housing project in Dessau demonstrated how this fusion of art and tectonics could be applied to the solution of design problems such as prefabrication and serial construction (fig. 3.25). For modernists, the Bauhaus demonstrated how the aesthetic achievements of the artistic avant-garde and technological advances in building construction could be incorporated into architectural culture without stifling the spirit of innovation deemed critical for design.

Bridges

Throughout history bridges have been hailed as expressions of humankind's ability to overcome natural obstacles and transform the natural environment in ways that facilitate human purposes. The triumphalist theme that figures prominently in bridge literature and the public celebrations surrounding the completion of modern spans would be just as familiar to an ancient Roman engineer. In the premodern era, bridges often ranked among the most sophisticated engineering achievements of their day. In the modern era bridges continue to exert a particular fascination for both the professional design community and the general public. Such striking achievements as San Francisco's Golden Gate Bridge achieve an iconic status as instantly recognizable images of their cities or settings. One approach to the study of bridges focuses on physical dimensions and ranks bridges by criteria such as length of span or height of supporting towers. Such ranking systems remain in a state of permanent flux as specific details are disputed or new spans completed. In terms of a history of twentieth-century architecture, one can also appreciate bridges for what they reveal about design thinking as engineers and architects turn to time-tested formulas or apply new insights to old problems.

San Francisco: Golden Gate Bridge

After more than five years of construction, the Golden Gate Bridge opened to pedestrian traffic in May 1937, and automobiles one year later (fig. 3.26). Although suspension bridges were not new, the scale of the achievement was noteworthy. Upon its completion, the Golden Gate Bridge boasted the tallest towers, the longest,

thickest cables, and the largest underwater foundation piers ever built. But the enduring appeal of the Golden Gate Bridge is in its graceful form soaring across the dramatic opening into San Francisco Bay. One need not be an engineer to understand intuitively how a suspension bridge works. With the Golden Gate Bridge one can appreciate what David Billington, a historian of structural engineering, identified as the elements of structural art: efficiency, economy, and elegance. Billington defined efficiency as the use of the minimum materials necessary. The quest for efficiency tends to reduce the weight and visual mass of a structure. The quest for economy promotes integrated forms that are straightforward in construction and easy to maintain. Billington's third criterion, elegance, reflects his belief that the design of beautiful structures involves more than numerical calculations. Like any other kind of designer, engineers must refine shapes to achieve expressive form. In the twentieth century, steel and concrete have replaced masonry as preferred materials. As a result, structural elements with thinner section can be used and slender, graceful forms have replaced the massive solidity of masonry as the ideal of structural and formal elegance.

3.26 Golden Gate Bridge, San Francisco, California, 1937.

3.27 Robert Maillart, Tavanasa Bridge over the Rhine, Grisons, Switzerland, circa 1905, destroyed 1927.

The profile of the Tavanasa Bridge is an elegant expression of the three-hinged arch form applied to bridge design. The triangular openings in the side reduce the weight of the bridge and enhance its aesthetic character. The bridge spans 168 feet (51.25 meters) with a rise of only 19 feet (5.79 meters). An avalanche destroyed it in 1927.

Robert Maillart's Tavanasa Bridge

If the Golden Gate Bridge demonstrates the survival of familiar bridge types in the twentieth century, the work of the Swiss engineer Robert Maillart (1872–1940) serves as an example of structural invention. Maillart employed reinforced concrete in his bridge designs. Although he was not the first to use reinforced concrete for bridge work, Maillart broke with the prevailing mode of handling concrete. To appreciate Maillart's achievement, one must take note of a pattern in the history of materials; new materials are often employed initially in the same form as the materials they are designed to replace. Thus, early examples of reinforced concrete construction often imitated masonry forms. Maillart broke with the masonry-inspired tradition of bridges and instead invented forms uniquely suited to the properties of concrete. Around 1905 he built a small bridge over the Rhine in Tavanasa, Switzerland. He designed the bridge as a three-hinged arch to accommodate the expansion and contraction of the structure. While the three-hinged arch was a familiar structural concept, he refined it with an innovative approach to concrete slab construction. In determining the final form of the bridge's design, Maillart combined a calculating approach to structure with an intuitive appreciation of form that pushed the limits of prevailing engineering practice. In a bold move, he dispensed with the solid longitudinal walls present in masonry construction and detailed the profiles of the arch and roadway to emphasize the thinness of the structural members (fig. 3.27).

In the Golden Gate Bridge, the massive stone towers of nineteenth-century suspension bridges such as John Roebling's (1806–1869) Brooklyn Bridge are replaced by a slender, open steel framework. In the bridge at Tavanasa, Maillart abandoned the weighty strength of masonry construction in favor of a lithe concrete structure that seems to spring across the river. Both bridges testify to a common interest shared by twentieth-century engineers and their modernist counterparts in the architectural profession in the development of a design language that combined strength with lightness and suggested the unbounded horizons of modern vision.

ДВОРЕЦ СОВЕТОВ

Chapter 4

Architecture and Politics

The state has been an increasingly important patron of architecture in the modern era. The nineteenth-century debate concerning the appropriate style for an emerging modern consciousness of time and place carried over directly into a twentieth-century search for persuasive representations of authority and political identities. The age of kingdoms was drawing to a close and a royal palace could no longer serve as both the symbol and site of government. Faced with the necessity of building popular support for novel political creeds, the advocates of revolutionary ideologies turned to architecture as a powerful propaganda tool.

But the discussion of the relationship between architecture and politics cannot be limited to the design agenda of revolutionary movements. The process of modernization affected established as well as revolutionary regimes at every governmental level from the municipal to the imperial. Just as distinctly modern forms of commerce stimulated the development of tall office buildings and large department stores, efforts to rationalize and control urbanization and industrial development prompted the growth of governmental bureaucracies. This in turn led to the need for more extensive office space to house administrative and clerical staffs.

Scandinavia and the Netherlands

National Romanticism, Classicism, Modernism: Stockholm, Helsinki, Hilversum

The design of government buildings reveals both programmatic needs and symbolic aspects in architecture as two Scandinavian examples demonstrate. Stockholm's Town Hall is an example of National Romanticism (figs. 4.1, 4.2). The architect, Ragnar Östberg (1866–1945), had traveled extensively prior to receiving the commission for a new city hall and admired the design ethic of the British Arts and Crafts movement. In his design for the Stockholm Town Hall he combined a sensitivity to materials and a concern for craft with his own clearly expressed commitment to developing a national architecture for Sweden. Östberg integrated Swedish motifs with lessons learned from the study of Italian medieval architecture. The simple massing and slight irregularities in the alignment of different wings of the building recall Swedish castle architecture of the sixteenth and seventeenth centuries. The tower, like those on Italian town halls, functions as an architectural sign of civic identity. The building is planned around two courtyards, one for

Boris Iofan, Palace of the Soviets, Moscow, competition project, unexecuted, 1934.

4.1 (above) Ragnar Östberg, Town Hall, Stockholm, Sweden, 1902–23.

4.2 (left) Ragnar Östberg, Town Hall, Golden Chamber, Stockholm, Sweden, 1902–23.

The Golden Chamber, 144 feet long (43.89 meters), 46 feet wide (14.02 meters), and 39 feet high (11.88 meters), serves as the ceremonial setting for formal occasions. In the tradition of medieval town halls, the walls are decorated with scenes from the city's history, government, industries, and crafts on a gold mosaic background.

the municipal administrative offices and the other for more public and ceremonial uses. The use of two courtyards instead of a single monumental axis to organize the interior results in an informality that suggests a democratic sense of accessibility. At the same time, the decorative treatment of the council chamber and the Blue Hall establishes an appropriately impressive aura for the seat of municipal government. Initial plans for a new town hall and law courts were discussed in 1902 and, after revisions in the program, Östberg began to develop the design for the present building in 1908. Construction commenced in 1911 and work continued until 1923.

Between the conception and completion of the Stockholm Town Hall, however, the appeal of National Romanticism began to fade, so when newly independent Finland considered plans for its parliament, a very different type of building was proposed. Its architect, J. S. Sirén (1889–1961), turned to the time-honored paradigms of the classical tradition for the design of the Finnish National Parliament Building, erected between 1924 and 1931 (fig. 4.3). The visitor approaches the

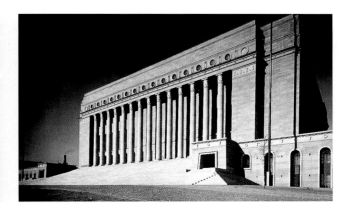

building up a flight of stairs and through a monumental colonnade, before entering the grand lobby and proceeding on to the legislative chamber. The compact, symmetrical massing and a processional experience culminating in a domed central legislative chamber (not visible on the exterior) reflects Sirén's familiarity with the work of the nineteenth-century German master Karl Friedrich Schinkel (1781–1841). At the same time, his stylization of classical details combined with the selection of tubular metal furniture for interior spaces such as the cafeteria stamps the parliament building with an undeniably modern sensibility (fig. 4.4). The Finnish

4.3 (above) J. S. Sirén, National Parliament Building, Mannerheimintie 30, Helsinki, Finland, 1931.

4.4 (right) J. S. Sirén, National Parliament Building, cafeteria, Mannerheimintie 30, Helsinki, Finland, 1931.

National Parliament Building is only one of many examples that demonstrate the continued vitality of the classical tradition in twentieth-century architecture. Classicism answered the desire of politicians and architects alike for monumental images of enduring order and stability.

Östberg and Sirén were charged with the design of individual buildings and the results represent significant but singular moments in the development of modern Nordic architecture. The experience of the Dutch architect Willem Dudok (1884–1974) illustrates another facet of the relationship between architecture and politics: design as a growth-management tool. Dudok's best known work, the Hilversum Town Hall, completed in 1931, reflects his familiarity with a wide range of modern work including Frank Lloyd Wright's Prairie Style designs and, on the interior, the use of color and geometric patterning associated with Art Deco (figs. 4.5, 4.6).

But the town hall was only one piece of a larger mosaic of work executed by Dudok in Hilversum. Like Ernst May in Frankfurt, Dudok was a designer in the employ, not of a princely patron eager to adorn his kingdom, but of a municipal government charged with managing a period of tremendous growth. In 1915, when Dudok arrived to assume the post of Director of Public Works, Hilversum was a small town with a population of approximately 35,000 people. By 1934 the population had nearly doubled; it would reach 100,000 within two more decades. Housing and an adequate urban infrastructure had to be developed and managed as efficiently as possible within real political restraints regarding finance and property rights. In fifteen years, Dudok designed thirteen public housing estates, eleven schools, athletic facilities, an abattoir, and water, sewage, and public utility installations. The simple massing of plain brick volumes characteristic of the Hilversum Town Hall is evident in much of Dudok's work and established a coherent identity for municipal facilities. Dudok's role in managing the built environment typifies the growing involvement of the architectural profession in the design and coordination of large urban systems, an involvement with obvious political implications.

By the early twentieth century, the belief that the form of the built environment could influence human behavior was an accepted tenet of design theory. Architects were eager, therefore, to explore ways to integrate political and architectural ideologies in the hope of shaping the development of political culture. Both the ground-

4.5 (above) Willem Dudok, Town Hall, Hilversum, Netherlands, 1928–31.
The broad planar surfaces, crisply defined geometric volumes, and complex massing reveal the impact of Frank Lloyd Wright's architecture. The severity of the boxlike exterior is softened by the surrounding landscaping and a shallow reflecting pool.

4.6 (below) Willem Dudok, Town Hall, reception, second floor, Hilversum, Netherlands, 1928–31.

breaking design strategies of the avant-garde and the timeless models of classical architecture were pressed into political service by architects. Historians and architectural theorists debated—and continue to debate—whether the political significance or meaning of architectural form is socially constructed or invariably fixed by the inherent properties of particular formal languages. "Constructionalists," for example, argue that since classical architecture has been used to represent democratic, imperialist and totalitarian regimes, classicism cannot be identified exclusively with any one political ideology. Different political systems appropriate classicism for their own purposes and each "constructs" an explanation that legitimizes their choices. Contrarily, "essentialists" maintain that the emphasis on formal order, spatial hierarchy and historical precedent in classical design (properties deemed to be inherent in the essence of classicism) renders it the inevitable expression of political systems based on a model of strong centralized authority and sweeping control.

Political leaders defined the design problem in different terms. First and foremost on their agenda was the issue of legibility, that is, the degree to which a particular design conveyed the desired political message clearly to the intended audience. Lenin expressed the concern of political patrons when he wrote:

> What matters is not what art gives to several hundred or even several thousand members of a population of millions. . . . It must penetrate with its deepest roots into the very heart of the broad working masses. It must be understandable to these masses and loved by them.
>
> (Golomstock, p. 174)

The familiarity of architectural imagery based on classical models or rooted in national vernaculars ensured legibility in ways the novel forms of avant-garde design often could not. The varying fortunes of traditional and radical design languages in twentieth-century architecture reflected the constant tension between avant-garde and mass cultures.

The "Architecture of Empire"

Historians use phrases such as the Machine Age and the Age of Revolutions to characterize the modern era but the Age of Imperialism is an equally appropriate description. Between 1876 and the outbreak of World War I, one quarter of the earth's land surface was governed by the colonial powers of Europe and the United States. Although great empires had existed throughout history, the scale of the colonial venture in the late nineteenth and early twentieth century was truly global and peculiarly modern in character. Economic considerations, above all the exploitation of resources and the expansion of markets, rather than dynastic pride or religious faith provided the main impetus for modern colonialism. The design agenda of modern imperialism addressed the requirements for infrastructure, administrative control, and conceptual as well as physical domination. As the developed economies of the colonial powers came to depend on raw materials unavailable in Europe (such as rubber for tires), roads, bridges, harbor facilities, and new settlements were needed to support resource extraction. The administration of huge tracts of territory and resident populations spurred the development of colonial bureaucracies which required the provision of appropriate administrative and domestic accommodations. Finally, as a representation of authority, architecture contributed to the conceptual domination of non-European races that was the cultural counterpart to their military subjugation.

England: Herbert Baker, Edward Lutyens, Aston Webb

In the nineteenth century, British architects adapted a variety of architectural styles to serve colonial purposes ranging from Gothic Revivalism to a curious hybrid of Indian elements labeled Indo-Saracenic architecture. In the early twentieth century, however, classicism emerged as the preferred architectural expression of British imperialism, with the architect Herbert Baker (1862–1946) as one of its most vocal champions. An ardent supporter of British imperial policy, Baker went out to southern Africa in the early 1890s where he formed close ties with Cecil Rhodes. In 1900 Rhodes sent Baker on a grand tour of the Mediterranean to study classical architecture in preparation for future commissions. Baker returned convinced that a natural affinity existed between the principles of order and composition on which classical design is based and the British imperial system. In an essay entitled "Architecture of Empire" Baker wrote:

> Our rule confers order, progress and freedom within the law to develop national civilizations on the lines of their own traditions and sentiment: so in architecture there is infinite scope within the limits of order, true science, and progress for the widest self-expression in every field of art; but without the orderly control of the great principles, there might result a chaos in the arts such as in governments which History records our rule was ordained to supersede.
>
> (Irving, p. 278)

In 1909 Baker had the opportunity to apply the "great principles" of classical architecture when he began designing the Union Building in Pretoria (fig. 4.7). He rejected the proposed flat site in the center of town for a hillside location a mile away. The south-facing slope of the Meintjes Kop was carved into a series of terraces that combined the European tradition of formally landscaped gardens with

4.7 Herbert Baker, Union Building, Pretoria, South Africa, 1909.
  Early in his career Baker was attracted to the ideals of the Arts and Crafts Movement. However, Arts and Crafts design models lacked the imposing scale required for imperial commissions. Baker eventually turned to classical design as the most effective way to express architecturally the colonial theme of the superiority of Western civilization.

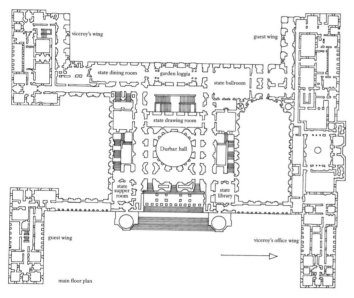

4.8 (above) Edwin Lutyens, Viceroy's House, New Delhi, India, 1912–31.

4.9 (below) Edwin Lutyens, Viceroy's House, plan, New Delhi, India, 1912–31.

a Mediterranean model of a sacred acropolis (citadel) raised above the city. With Christopher Wren's Royal Naval Hospital at Greenwich in mind as a model, Baker designed the Union Building as two blocks united by a curved colonnade and crowned by twin domes. The identical office blocks symbolized for Baker the "two races" of South Africa: the Dutch and the English. Missing from Baker's grand vision, of course, is any sign of South Africa's black population. In racial terms, Baker understood classicism as the expression of the inherent superiority of Western values and experience. Applied to architecture, the normative principles of classicism ensured order and represented authority in a way that validated the claim of white colonialists to be "ordained" by history to rule over allegedly inferior races.

In an elaborate imperial pageant staged in 1911 in India, King George V announced the transfer of the British colonial capital from Calcutta to Delhi. One year later, Edward Lutyens sailed for India to join the Delhi Planning Commission. He eventually assumed responsibility for the design of the centerpiece of the capital ensemble, the Viceroy's House (figs. 4.8, 4.9). Herbert Baker joined his friend Lutyens in India and designed a pair of buildings flanking Kingsway, the main axis of New Delhi, to house the colonial secretariat. Baker and Lutyens shared the same conviction regarding the appropriateness of classical architecture for representing Great Britain's imperial authority. In contrast to Baker's work in South Africa, however, Lutyens made an effort to incorporate clear references to various historical traditions of monumental architecture on the Indian subcontinent. The dome on the Viceroy's House recalls the first-century BCE Buddhist stupa at Sanchi, and Lutyens adapted Mughal designs for pavilions in the new building.

To British observers, this fusion of Western and Indian architectural elements suggested a benevolent new cultural synthesis that ennobled the imperial venture. The critical issue, however, involves not simply Lutyen's acknowledgment of indigenous traditions but the balance he struck between Western and Indian imagery. Overall the Indian motifs constitute minor accents in an overwhelmingly Western and classical design. Following independence, Indian political leaders would pursue a fundamentally different synthesis of foreign and native elements in their quest for a modern Indian identity.

The plan of New Delhi carried the European Baroque tradition of monumental town planning into the twentieth century. As at Versailles, in Wren's 1666 plan for London, and in Pierre L'Enfant's 1791–92 plan for Washington DC, a network of broad avenues radiates from a series of monumental squares each distinguished by

a different geometric form. While the Viceroy's House mixed European and Indian motifs, the plan of New Delhi stood in stark contrast to the urban form of the original Delhi, maintaining a clear distinction between the European enclaves and the indigenous settlements. This was an important part of the imperial design strategy, in which the layout of colonial cities represented the spatialization of social hierarchies. The rational character of European settlements and the congested conditions of the "native quarters," a recurrent theme in the European literature on colonial experience, was often cited as evidence of the superiority of Western ways. In the colonial context, the concept of modernity is no longer linked to industrialization nor expressed in the cultural forms associated with modernism. Instead, it becomes equated with the Westernization of colonial regions, an equation that allows the entire Western classical tradition to be enlisted in the service of modern Imperialism.

The imperial system created networks of economic and cultural exchange that linked central and peripheral areas of the various national empires. Colonial outposts were not the only places to be reshaped by the imperial venture; colonialism left its imprint on the home countries as well. In London, for example, Aston Webb's (1849–1930) Admiralty Arch completed the monumental axis linking Buckingham Palace with Trafalgar Square (fig. 4.10). The Roman quality of Webb's triumphal arch reflects the imperial ethos of Great Britain before World War I. When the indigenous elements of various colonized cultures were brought back to the various European centers of power they were never treated with the same respect as Western designs such as the Admiralty Arch. Instead, Europeans displayed their colonial possessions as exotic trophies and cultural curiosities.

The 1931 "Exposition Coloniale Internationale"

In 1931 the colonial powers staged the "Exposition Coloniale Internationale" in Paris. While other international fairs of the period focused on the advances of modern technology and promoted the idea of consumer culture, the colonial exposition celebrated European hegemony over nonwhite races. Tribal customs and

native arts were displayed as ethnographic case studies rather than as sophisticated cultural achievements. The Netherlands held extensive colonies among the islands of the East Indies and motifs derived from the islands of Java and Bali are evident in Dutch decorative arts of the late nineteenth and early twentieth century. The Netherlands Pavilion at the 1931 Paris fair revealed an amalgam of elements derived from various Dutch possessions (fig. 4.11). Its architect, W. J. G. Zweedijk, combined wooden carved doors from Bali with the distinctive Minangkabau roof form found in Sumatra and the ironwood shingle pattern from Borneo. The result is a collage of disparate elements composed to satisfy a Western taste for the exotic.

The Soviet Union

Before World War I, architecture in Russia reflected the same influences as we have already noted elsewhere: National Romanticism, Art Nouveau, and a vibrant avant-garde. The October Revolution in 1917, however, irrevocably changed the cultural as well as the political scene in Russia. National Romanticism and Art Nouveau faded away, and members of the Russian avant-garde allied their program of cultural transformation with the political program of the revolution. Designers put their talent to work in the service of the Soviet state.

Vladimir Tatlin and Constructivism

4.12 Vladimir Tatlin, Project for the Monument to the Third International, 1919–20.

In 1919 Vladimir Tatlin (1885–1953) proposed a Monument to the Third International that would both represent and facilitate the agencies of the revolution (fig. 4.12). Over 400 meters tall, Tatlin's model invited comparison with the Eiffel Tower and other great engineering monuments of the nineteenth century. The combination of an inclined spine thrusting up through a spiraling latticework created a dynamic composition. Three volumes—a cube, a pyramid, and a cylinder—set within the open skeletal frame housed various agencies of the Third International. Each volume was to rotate at a different speed designed to coincide with the frequency of the scheduled meetings for each agency: once a year for the legislative, once a month for the administrative, and once a day for the information agency. This transparent, kinetic composition, the antithesis of the solid, earthbound forms of tradition, illustrates the formal character and the spirit of what, in the 1920s, came to be called Constructivist architecture.

Constructivist architects sought to extend the formal language of abstract art to the design of buildings. The buildings were "constructed" conceptually as well as physically of the basic visual elements such as lines, planes, and volumes. This new syntax of form, according to the Constructivists, was grounded in a scientific understanding of human perception and social organization. For Russian architects, a potent combination of political revolution, material progress, and aesthetic innovation held the promise of a new universe of possibilities. By developing a new formal language for design, architects believed they were answering the revolution's call to bring into existence a new Communist society.

However, Constructivism was more than simply a response to the revolution. Convinced that the built environment influences everyone who inhabits it, Constructivist architects believed they could affect the development of the new society. In the design of buildings and spaces (both public and private), architects could encode the basic elements of the new social order and vividly convey to all members of society the enormity of the political, economic, and social changes unleashed by the October Revolution.

ASNOVA and OSA

Enthusiasm does not guarantee consensus, however; Constructivism hardly constituted a uniform movement. In the early 1920s different orientations emerged within Soviet architecture and crystalized around several professional societies. In 1923 the Association of New Architects (identified by the Russian acronym ASNOVA) was formed, followed shortly by another group, the Union of Contemporary Architects (OSA). Both groups emphatically rejected the notion that traditional (now labeled bourgeois) forms could give proper shape to socialist culture, but they differed over the relative weight to give expressive versus functional concerns.

Konstantin Melnikov (1890–1974) was a prominent member of the ASNOVA group. He achieved international success with his design for the Soviet Pavilion at the 1925 "Exposition Internationale des Arts Décoratifs et Industriels Modernes" in Paris which contrasted sharply with the Art Deco style characteristic of other fair pavilions. Between 1927 and 1929 he built six workers' clubs in Moscow. The workers' club was an important building type; it was conceived as a center—literally a "social condenser"—for the formation of the new proletarian culture of Communism. For the Rusakov Workers' Club in Moscow, Melnikov allowed the blocks of auditorium seating inside to project through the front of the building so that the building reads as a sculpturesque composition of solids and voids (fig. 4.13). He also provided a system of moveable partitions that allows the interior spaces to be reconfigured in a variety of ways.

Moisei Ginzburg (1892–1946), one of the leading figures of the OSA group, was responsible, together with Ignatii Milinis (1899–1974), for the design of the Narkomfin Communal House in Moscow, erected as housing for dependents of the Russian Ministry of Finance (fig. 4.14). Ginzburg conceived this project as prototypical Communal House (Dom Kommuna). In the Constructivist vision, communal housing would serve as the incubator of the new socialist society and facilitate the transition from bourgeois to Communist conception of personal and social space. The Narkomfin included a communal kitchen, dining and laundry facilities, and a gymnasium and library

4.13 Konstantin Melnikov, Rusakov Workers' Club, Moscow, Russia, 1927–28.
Like a machine capable of being adjusted to perform various tasks, this workers' club was designed to be flexible. Each of the projecting blocks contained a small auditorium seating 200 people. In Melnikov's original scheme, retractable partitions allowed the three small auditoria to be combined with a fourth internal theater to create a single large hall for 1,200 people.

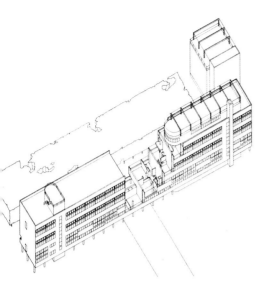

4.14 Moisei Ginzburg, Narkomfin Communal House, Moscow, Russia, 1929.

(a communal childcare center was projected but never built). Accommodation for 200 households in a variety of configurations was provided. As an acknowledgment of the transitional state of Russian society, a handful of Narkomfin units included small kitchens to satisfy traditional conceptions of private family life. Like Grete Schütte-Lihotzky's work in Frankfurt (see fig. 2.38), OSA designers planned these kitchens as small, functional workstations. With its long horizontal bands of windows, flat roof, and slender pilotis, the design of the Narkomfin reflected the impact of Le Corbusier's work in Russia.

VOPRA and Socialist Realism

The contrast between the expressive plasticity of Melnikov's Rusakov Workers' Club and the lean, almost puritanical severity of the Narkomfin design is indicative of the respective orientations of the ASNOVA and OSA groups. In 1929, however, a new association, the All-Union Society of Proletarian Architects (VOPRA), was founded signaling a new direction on the debates concerning revolutionary architecture. VOPRA began to undermine the position of both ASNOVA and OSA architects, charging them with ignoring the real conditions of Soviet society in favor of exercises in abstract formalism. In Soviet terms, formalism was a feature of bourgeois art that reinforced the distinction between popular and elite cultures. The VOPRA attacks paralleled similar criticism against the experiments of the avant-garde in literature and art. In the early 1930s, the Communist Party began to reformulate its approach to artistic activity. In 1932 all independent groups were suppressed and the memberships of various cultural organizations were combined into unions representing the interests of each discipline. By 1934 the regime had adopted socialist realism as the official cultural policy.

Defining socialist realism in architectural terms is not as easy as it is for other visual arts because one can attach various meanings to the word realism in building. However, the issue of legibility is central to the socialist realist view of design. One party edict stated: "In its search for an appropriate style, Soviet architecture must strive for realistic criteria—for clarity and precision in images, which must be easily comprehensible by and accessible to the masses." While projects like Tatlin's Monument to the Third International were impractical given the economic and technological state of the Soviet Union at the time, ultimately it was the pursuit of a novel language of form based on abstraction rather than tradition that doomed the Constructivist vision. In Stalin's Russia, to be avant-garde—literally in front of the mass audience—was to court danger.

In 1931 an international design competition was announced for the Palace of the Soviets in Moscow. The program called for meeting halls and offices for various state agencies and identified the projected building as the preeminent architectural symbol of the Soviet Union. The competition progressed through a series of rounds and attracted entries from around the world. Many Constructivist architects submitted proposals and the entries included a broad spectrum of traditional and modern designs. Finally, in 1934 a team headed by Boris Iofan (1891–1976) was awarded the prize. The result influenced the development of Russian architecture for decades (see page 102).

Iofan's enormous tower had the setback silhouette of an American skyscraper which, by then, had become an instantly recognizable image of modernity. But Iofan's palace would never be mistaken for a capitalist office building; a statue of Lenin over one hundred meters tall crowned the design and brought the total height of the tower to more than four hundred meters. Iofan rejected the Constructivist language of form and relied on the traditional elements of monumentality such as mass, symmetry, and axiality for effect. The vivid contrast between Tatlin's Monument to the Third International and Iofan's Palace of the Soviets reveals the trajectory of political architecture in Russia.

Russian modernists, however, continued to enter major architectural competitions. The 1934 competition for the People's Commissariat for Heavy Industry Headquarters (NKTP) in Moscow included a range of Constructivist entries. In his proposal, Melnikov moved away from the more abstract forms characteristic of his earlier work and transformed machine parts into giant architectural elements which he combined with enormous figural sculpture (fig. 4.15). But his efforts to match the epic scale and popular iconography of the Palace of the Soviets were no more successful in gaining official support than the bold abstractions submitted by other Constructivists. Ultimately, socialist realism in architecture was equated with the application of classical models in the service of proletarian society. The leaders of

4.15 (below) Konstantin Melnikov, Narkomtiazhprom (People's Commissariat for Heavy Industry) competition project, Moscow, Russia, 1934.

4.16 (opposite) Grigorii Zakharov and Zinaida Chernysheva, Kurskaya metro station, central hall, Moscow, Russia, 1949.

the recently constituted Union of Soviet Architects explicitly identified the classical heritage of Greco-Roman antiquity and the Renaissance as the appropriate model for Soviet architecture.

Stations designed for the Moscow subway system provided a vivid demonstration of this new design doctrine of palaces for the people. The new underground system was an important part of the modernization program for the city; the first completed stations date to the mid-1930s and work continued for decades. The imposing Doric columns of the Kurskaya metro station's central hall, opened in 1949, transform this transit facility into a patriotic shrine (fig. 4.16). Like a cult figure, the statue of Stalin dominates the space and the words of a new national anthem are incribed on the colonnade. The decorative programs of other stations celebrated Russian military and industrial achievements.

Fascist Italy

In the twentieth century, revolutionary movements have emerged on the right as well as the left of the political spectrum and have appealed to racial as well as class identities to build support.

In Italy, Benito Mussolini founded the Fascist Party in 1919. Fascism was a curious amalgam of reactionary and progressive ideas. The nationalistic program of Fascism rejected the liberal political tradition of the nineteenth century yet embraced an ambitious program of modernization. Representations of Fascism as the revival of ancient Roman glory coexisted with unequivocally modern portrayals. Like their counterparts in the Soviet Union, Italian Fascists tried to develop a political culture that pervaded every aspect of life; it is important to recognize that architecture was only one element in a larger program to coordinate all the arts in the service of the state.

Nationalism, Modernism, and Classicism: Marcello Piacentini, Giuseppe Terragni, and "E'42"

The Fascist Party adopted an ancient Roman symbol—the fasces—as its emblem. In antiquity, the fasces was a bundle of reeds bound together with an axe; it was carried by certain Roman officials as a sign of their authority. During the 1920s and 1930s, the fasces appeared in countless images and designs and soon became an unavoidable element in the material culture of Fascism. In 1929 Marcello Piacentini (1881–1960) employed this motif in his design for a triumphal arch in Bolzano (fig. 4.17). Piacentini was one of the most powerful figures in Italian architecture during the Fascist era. In professional architectural circles, power can be measured not only in terms of the number and prestige of designs executed, but also in terms of the control exercised over the awarding of commissions and the publication of work. Piacentini exercised his power through his role as jury chief for important architectural competitions and as the editor of the leading professional journal, *Architettura*.

From its inception in 1919, close links existed between the Fascist Party and the cultural avant-garde. F. T. Marinetti, the founder of Futurism, participated in the founding of the Fascist Party and stood for election on the first electoral slate presented by the party. Marinetti's association with Mussolini encouraged modern architects in their assumption that the belief systems of Fascism and architectural modernism could be reconciled. Reflecting, in 1962, on the appeal of Fascism for members of his generation, the Italian architect and critic Ernesto Rogers (1909–1969) wrote: "We based ourselves on a syllogism that went roughly thus: fascism is a revolution, modern architecture is revolutionary, therefore it must be the architecture of fascism."

The Casa del Fascio in Como, by Giuseppe Terragni (1904–1942) illustrates how modern architects attempted to turn revolutionary theories into buildings (figs. 4.18, 4.19). A Casa del Fascio served as the local party headquarters and the regime erected scores of these buildings throughout the country. Terragni transformed the traditional palace block with an internal courtyard into a very personal interpretation of Fascism. Parts of the building were extensively glazed: transparency as a metaphor for direct contact between the leadership and party cadres was the primary theme of Terragni's design. But he explored other architectural themes with political implications. Terragni established a series of dialectical relationships between key features of the design: strip and sash windows, natural and artificial light, parts of the elevation framed as an open grid of posts and lintels and sections

4.18 (left) Giuseppe Terragni, Casa del Fascio, Como, Italy, 1932–36.

4.19 (above) Giuseppe Terragni, Casa del Fascio, plan, Como, Italy, 1932–36.

4.17 (opposite) Marcello Piacentini, Monument to Victory, Bolzano, Italy, 1928.

Political emblems are a pervasive presence in the visual culture of the twentieth century. In place of classical columns, Piacentini employs the design of the fasces (an ancient Roman emblem of official power, adopted as the symbol of the Fascist Party). The arch was erected to commemorate the tenth anniversary of Italy's victory in World War I.

4.20 Giovanni Guerrini, Ernesto Bruno la Padula, and Mario Romano, Palace of Italian Civilization, EUR, Rome, Italy, 1937–42.

Like Piacentini's design for the Bolzano Monument (see fig. 4.17), this modernized version of a classical model portrayed the Fascist regime as the modern equivalent of Imperial Rome. All elevations of the palace are identical and the result has the haunting quality of Giorgio de' Chirico's early twentieth-century metaphysical paintings.

of continuous wall (mural) surfaces. The result was a synthesis of traditional and contemporary forms. This represented the architectural equivalent of the political equation—implicit for Terragni in the Fascist revolution—of the strength of tradition and the vitality of modernity.

At issue in any discussion of political architecture is the relationship between design as a personal expression and design as an officially sanctioned representation of culture. In the provincial setting of his home town, Terragni was able to realize his unique interpretation of the program, but the result attracted criticism even from other modern architects for its esoteric and abstract treatment of the theme. Architects more interested in ensuring public legibility than personal expression turned to Italy's classical heritage for their models.

In the late 1930s, planning began for a projected 1942 world's fair to be staged on the outskirts of the nation's capital. Known originally as "E'42" (and today identified by the initials "EUR" for "Esposizione Universale di Roma"), it was one of the most prestigious building campaigns undertaken by the regime. The fairgrounds were planned as the permanent nucleus for a new neighborhood. The Palace of Italian Civilization, designed by the architectural team of Giovanni Guerrini (1925–1972), Ernesto Bruno la Padula (1902–1969) and Mario Romano, served as the major theme building for "E'42" (fig. 4.20). Nicknamed "the square

Colosseum" by the Romans, its references to Italy's classical past are unmistakable, but the treatment of the classical language is distinctively modern. The marble arches are applied over a reinforced concrete frame. Stripped of their structural role along with any details such as moldings or impost blocks, they exist as pure signs referring to a classical past while ignoring the tectonic principles of classicism.

The Third Reich

When the Weimar Republic fell in 1933 and the National Socialists led by Adolf Hitler came to power, Germany already possessed a sophisticated modernist design culture. The relationship between the design legacy of the Weimar Republic and the architectural programs of the Third Reich is a major theme in the scholarly literature on Nazi cultural policy. The National Socialists appealed to racial identities and national traditions in an effort to counter the unsettling effects of modernization. As a result, premodern artistic traditions—classical, medieval, and folk— were enlisted in the service of political rhetoric. Particular building features such as roofs and windows were charged with political significance. A pitched roof and vertical windows represented "German-ness" while the flat roof and horizontal strip window were rejected as signs of a degenerate "internationalism."

The achievements of such modernists as Ernst May in Frankfurt or Walter Gropius at the Bauhaus were too closely identified with the Weimar Republic to be embraced as models by the Nazi leadership, although individual modernists such as Ernst Neufert (1900–1986) and Herbert Rimpl (1902–1978) were employed by the Nazi regime. The buildings completed under the Third Reich reveal how the Nazis manipulated architectural imagery to convey a variety of messages. Modern materials and building systems were incorporated into the building programs of the Air Ministry, for example, while rustic buildings symbolized the party's idealiza-tion of rural virtue and the "sacred soil" of Germany. Place, patron, and program affected the choice of architectural style and the balance established by the regime between rustic, modern, and classical representations of the Third Reich remains a critical issue in any discussion of Nazi architecture.

4.21 Albert Speer, Grand Avenue, Dome, and Arc de Triomphe, model for Berlin, Germany, 1937–43.

Albert Speer's Berlin Plan

Hitler himself took a strong interest in architecture and worked closely with his architect Albert Speer (1905–81) on the redesign of Berlin to conform to Hitler's vision of the city as the capital of the Nazi "thou-sand-year Reich" (fig. 4.21). A plaza and an enormous domed hall were positioned at the intersection of an

4.22 Albert Speer, Great Hall, plan for Berlin, Germany, 1937–43.

existing east–west and a new north–south axis. The projected capacity of the Great Hall was 150,000 people and the dome measured 825 feet in diameter (fig. 4.22). The scale of the entire undertaking was enormous: the north–south axis stretched three miles and required a massive demolition campaign to open up ground for new construction. The Berlin Plan is often described as a manifestation of Hitler's megalomania. Hitler justified the scale of his architectural vision in terms of national pride.

> Why always the biggest? I do this to restore his self-respect to each individual German. . . . I want to say to each of you: we are not inferior, on the contrary, we are completely equal to every other nation.
>
> (Krier, *Speer*, p. 225)

Yet size alone fails to distinguish this scheme from equally grandiose proposals such as Boris Iofan's Palace of the Soviets. Megalomania is a feature of totalitarian architecture in general and reflects a way of thinking in which size is equated with power, majesty, and virility.

The Berlin Plan may exemplify the architectural aesthetics of totalitarianism, but it can also be positioned within the tradition of the City Beautiful movement. In the plan a monumental civic center is approached along a grand boulevard lined with imposing buildings. The plan called for two new railroad stations (one at either end of the north–south axis) and a large airport located near the center of town. Thus a Beaux-Art conception of architectural and urban composition was allied with a plan for the modernization of the city's transportation infrastructure much as in the Chicago Plan of 1909 (see page 5).

While Speer's classicism is sterner stuff than either Lutyen's work in New Delhi or Burnham's Chicago scheme, ultimately it is process rather than form that distinguishes Nazi architecture. In 1938 the SS (secret police) established the German Earth and Stone Works (Deutsche Erd-und Steinwerke Gmbh) to produce building materials for use in Reich construction projects, employing concentration camp labor to quarry stone and make bricks. Prisoners were literally worked to death in order to maximize productivity. As an art form, architecture can be analyzed in the same formal terms as other visual arts. As building, however, architecture can also be investigated in terms of labor policies and resource consumption. The failure at the heart of totalitarian architecture is not a question of style but a moral issue of the human costs of rendering ideology into stone.

Only small portions of the Berlin Plan were completed before the Third Reich collapsed. One of the largest surviving pieces is Tempelhof Airport, designed by Ernst Sagebiel who had previously worked in Erich Mendelsohn's office. The huge terminal was positioned between a circular plaza that linked the airport to the north–south axis of the Berlin Plan and the elliptical airfield that covered more than 1,300 acres. Tempelhof shows two faces to the world. On the side facing the city, Sagebiel designed a limestone-clad facade in a stripped-down classical style

4.23 (below) Ernst Sagebiel, Tempelhof Airport model, Berlin-Tempelhof, Germany, 1936–39 (now slightly altered).

4.24 (opposite) Ernst Sagebiel, Berlin-Tempelhof, Tempelhof Airport, Germany, 1936–39.
The design of windows acquired special significance in twentieth-century architectural debates. Modernist architects advocated the alignment of windows in continuous horizontal bands across the facade. In keeping with Hitler's conservative taste in architecture, windows in the Tempelhof have a vertical orientation.

matching the general architectural character of the Speer plan (fig. 4.23). On the airfield side, he provided an enormous steel canopy, forty feet high, that covered the entire boarding area (fig. 4.24). The city side responded to the urban rhetoric of the Berlin Plan while the cantilevered steel canopy on the airfield side matched the technological sophistication of the world of aviation.

The United States

Beginning with his role as Director of Works for the Columbian Exposition of 1893, Daniel Burnham (1846–1912) played a crucial role in promoting the ideals of the City Beautiful movement. As the United States began to acquire territories abroad, Burnham extended the ideals of the City Beautiful to America's colonial possessions: in addition to major plans for San Francisco and Chicago, he worked on city plans for the colonial centers of Baguio and Manila in the Philippines. But it was in the nation's capital that the City Beautiful movement exercised its most lasting impact. Burnham, along with the architect Charles Follen McKim (1847–1909), the sculptor Augustus Saint-Gaudens (1848–1907), and the landscape designer

Frederick Law Olmsted, Jr. (1822–1903), served on a special commission established by Senator James McMillan to review the status of L'Enfant's plan for Washington DC. The McMillan Commission published its report in 1902. The report was instrumental in reestablishing the principles of Pierre L'Enfant's original vision for the capital; while modifying and enlarging specific details of L'Enfant's 1791–92 plan. Nineteenth-century intrusions on the Mall were removed, the Mall was extended, and new buildings and memorials were planned.

Classicism: Lincoln Memorial

One of the most important proposals, both formally, as the western terminus of the Mall, and symbolically, as a memorial to one of the nation's most beloved presidents, called for the erection of a memorial to Abraham Lincoln. In 1912 Henry Bacon (1866–1924) received the commission for the Lincoln Memorial, construction began two years later, and the memorial was dedicated in 1922 (fig. 4.25). The result is one of the finest classical designs of the early twentieth century. Bacon did not feel constrained by the rules of classical composition; instead, he exploited the elements of the classical language to create an eloquent but very unorthodox secular temple for a democratic hero. Rather than create a temple front facing the Mall, Bacon turned the memorial ninety degrees so that the long side closes off the perspective from the Mall. A recessed attic story rather than the traditional temple pediment crowns the Doric colonnade and, in a bold departure from type, the main entrance is located in the middle of the long side rather than at one end.

The contrast between the classical design of the Lincoln Memorial and Albert Speer's Great Hall is instructive. Speer inflated the familiar classical paradigm of the domed, centralized building to satisfy Hitler's craving for grandeur; the Lincoln Memorial would have been dwarfed by it. Bacon's building rises only eighty feet above its foundation—one could stack eleven Lincoln Memorials under Speer's dome with room to spare—yet the memorial works well on its site. Bacon's design is large enough to provide a visual and symbolic focal point for mass rallies but not so large that the solitary visitor or family group feels overwhelmed. The contemplative aura of tranquility and reverence that pervades the Lincoln Memorial is the antithesis of the bombastic bigger-is-better rhetoric of Nazi architecture.

The appeal of classical architecture for an American audience in the early twentieth century has been explained in different ways. For some critics and historians, marble colonnades masked a sense of cultural inferiority and satisfied a yearning to legitimize new wealth and power by imitating European traditions and conventions. One can also read Bacon's deft handling of the classical language, however, as the expression of a new-found self-assurance that invites comparison with the best of the old world's achievements. In this interpretation, it is confidence rather than anxiety that is displayed by the powerful Doric order of the memorial. Finally, classicism claimed to

4.25 Henry Bacon, Lincoln Memorial, Washington, DC, 1912–22. The Lincoln Memorial demonstrates the vitality of the classical tradition in the early twentieth century and is a critical element in the urban design of the Mall in Washington, DC. It terminates the view from the Capitol building and provides a solemn architectural setting for political rallies.

be a universal design language and it is possible to interpret American classicism as the assertion of national priorities and images over regional or local forms in an ongoing quest for an American identity recognizable from coast to coast.

Period Revivalism: Santa Barbara County Courthouse

The tension between national and regional forms of expression in America is evident throughout the first half of the twentieth century as Period Revivalism remained a favorite design strategy for government buildings across the country. William Mooser designed the Santa Barbara County Courthouse in the Spanish Colonial style then popular in southern California (fig. 4.26). But no Spanish

4.26 William Mooser, Santa Barbara County Courthouse, Santa Barbara, California, 1929.

mission or presidio (garrison) in colonial California was ever as elaborate as Mooser's building. As the architectural historian David Gebhard has demonstrated, it was a romanticized past that Mooser evoked with whitewashed walls, red tile roof, and ornate iron and tile work.

In the United States, with its diverse ethnic mixture, the question of national identity is charged with political significance. If representing America is an important theme for American architects, the debate concerning the appropriate design language cannot be confined to the contrast between the classicism of the Lincoln Memorial and the picturesque period revivalism of the Santa Barbara County Courthouse. Instead the terms of the debate must be expanded to include various conceptions of modern architecture. Louis Sullivan and Frank Lloyd Wright, for example, had pleaded with their audiences to embrace organic architecture as uniquely American. Organic architecture, predicated on an appreciation of materials and new techniques and inspired by nature, could, its advocates claimed, represent a national identity responsive to local conditions but not dependent on historicist imagery for effect. There are relatively few examples of government buildings conceived in the spirit of organic design, but other versions of modern architecture did appear in municipal, state, and federal building programs.

Modernism: Nebraska State Capitol

The Nebraska State Capitol, Lincoln, designed by Bertram Goodhue (1869–1924) and erected between 1922 and 1932, is an example of the tall office building adapted for governmental purposes (fig. 4.27). It is not the first time that the tall building type was pressed into government service; McKim, Mead, and White's Municipal Building in New York City and Palmer, Hornbostle, and Jones's City Hall in Oakland, California, both predate the Nebraska Capitol. Nor would it be the last, as Louisiana and North Dakota soon followed Nebraska's lead by erecting tower capitols of their own. In part, towers could accommodate the growing bureaucratic apparatus associated with governmental authority, and, in the 1920s, few building types were as emblematic of American modernity as the skyscraper. But the tall office building was clearly associated with commercial, not civic, pursuits; Cass Gilbert had described the skyscraper as "a machine that makes the land pay." In the 1920s, however, government buildings were still expected to put civic ideals ahead of profit and express a political rather than a commercial identity.

The Nebraska Capitol is the most successful in resolving the inherent contradiction between commercial and civic architecture. Goodhue proved that the tall building could escape its typological definition as a machine for making money and could, instead, represent the ideal of a community bound together by a common heritage and mutual respect for the rule of law. Goodhue worked with a team of decorators including the sculptor Lee Lawrie, the mosaicist Hildreth Meiere, and the painter Augustus Tack to create an iconographic program appropriate for the state capitol. In New Delhi, Lutyens incorporated Indian motifs into his classical design. In Lincoln, Nebraska, Goodhue and his team of decorators blended personifications of abstract virtues such as wisdom, justice, power, and mercy with themes drawn from the history and agriculture of Nebraska.

Memorials, courthouses, and capitals are obvious examples of architectural designs in which programmatic and symbolic concerns have clear political overtones. In the 1930s, Franklin Delano Roosevelt's New Deal administration embraced

4.27 Bertram Goodhue, Nebraska State Capitol, Lincoln, Nebraska, 1922–32.

Goodhue combined the visibility of a skyscraper with the accessibility of a low two-story podium that houses branches of state government. The dome is covered in gold tile and crowned by the sculptor Lee Lawrie's statue "The Sower," which celebrates the state's agricultural heritage.

ambitious programs of regional planning that dwarfed even the grandest of City Beautiful schemes. The New Deal enlisted all of the design professions—engineering, architecture, industrial and graphic design—in coordinated efforts to extend the role of the central government in managing economic and social development.

The Tennessee Valley Authority

One of the most important examples of the new scope of federal design efforts to manage both the natural and the built environment was the Tennessee Valley Authority. Established as a government agency in 1933, the TVA was created to oversee the development of the area drained by the Tennessee river and its tributaries (fig. 4.29). It was an undertaking on an enormous scale which covered parts of seven states in one of the poorest areas of the country. The TVA was given a broad

mandate to reconfigure environmental conditions and exploit the energy resources of the region. Plans were drawn up to establish flood control and improve navigation along the river. The TVA instituted erosion control and reforestation programs. Public health issues were also addressed through programs to reduce the incidence of malaria. Finally, the TVA produced hydroelectric power and used the energy generated to raise living standards in the region.

The TVA built roads, navigation locks along the river, factories to produce fertilizer, and a planned community (Norris, Tennessee), but the heart of the TVA

4.28 Roland Wank, Norris Dam, Tennessee Valley Authority, 1933–36.

programs was a series of dams erected to control river levels and generate power. More than works of civil engineering, the dams became symbols of a new level of federal involvement and responsibility in the life of the region—and popular tourist attractions.

As Chief Architect for the TVA from 1933 to 1944, Roland Wank (1898–1970) was involved in the planning of new facilities. Wank carefully considered the siting of new dams and the design of powerhouses, visitor centers, and approach roads to dramatize the visual impact of the entire scheme. The Norris Dam, one of the first TVA projects, is typical of the bold massing and simple forms that Wank favored (fig. 4.28).

4.29 (right) Roland Wank, water control system diagram, Tennessee Valley Authority, 1933–36.

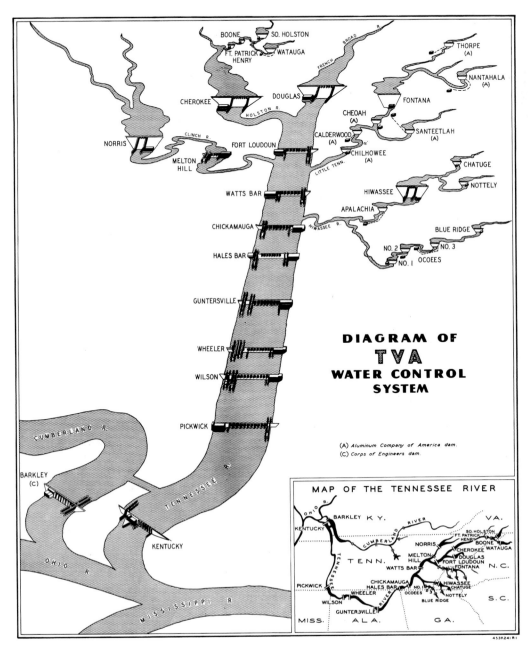

DIAGRAM OF TVA WATER CONTROL SYSTEM

(A) *Aluminum Company of America dam.*
(C) *Corps of Engineers dam.*

MAP OF THE TENNESSEE RIVER

Neither the classicism of the Lincoln Memorial nor the romanticism of the Santa Barbara County Courthouse could adequately express the modern spirit of federal projects like the TVA. As a design theme as well as a design problem, the modernization of the nation's infrastructure under the aegis of the federal government tended increasingly in the 1930s to favor the adoption of a frankly modern conception of form. The efforts of the TVA and related federal engineering projects in the American West captured the popular imagination and provided subject matter for popular music, literature, and artwork such as the mural programs sponsored by the Works Project Administration (WPA). The forces of nature, it seemed, were at last being harnessed to serve human needs and the subjugation of nature became a source of national pride. The arrival of electrical power, running water, better roads, and radio eased the hardships of rural isolation and raised hopes that the future would be better. After visiting the Hoover Dam near Las Vegas, Nevada, the English writer J. B. Priestly described his impression of the massive structure: "It is the symbol of the new giant man, a new world, a new way of life."

Part 2

Modernist Hegemony
1940–1965

Solomon R. Guggenheim Museum, New York (see fig. 6.23)

After **World War II** the terms of the debate in Europe and North America about an appropriate architecture were dramatically narrowed. It was still a period of lively discussion, but design discourse was now predicated almost entirely in terms of rationalist versus expressionist versions of Modernism. The political implications of design were shaped by the Cold War, which sharpened the contrast between capitalist and communist systems, and by the end of colonial rule in many areas. In Asia, Western conceptions of architecture were modified to satisfy local needs.

Chapter 5

The Triumph of Modernism

Worable orld War II was a major turning point in the twentieth century—one can identify distinctive pre- and postwar phases in many disciplines, including architecture. The differences involve more than a psychological perception of the chasm between the world before and after the atomic bomb. Waging global war required the mobilization of peoples, industries, and resources on a vast scale and the architectural profession was deeply involved in the war effort. In America, Franklin Delano Roosevelt's description of the United States as the "arsenal of democracy" committed the nation to expanding its industrial and military establishments.

Architects and engineers were involved in the design of new factories, military installations, and workers' housing projects. Speed, once glamorized by the Italian Futurists as an aesthetic value, was now vital to the war effort. Anything that could accelerate the pace of design and construction was incorporated into design practice. A generation of architects quickly learned to appreciate the virtues of design methods predicated on standardization of types, prefabrication of elements, and substitution of new materials that facilitated rapid construction. The victors returned convinced of the efficacy of rationalized design methods, enamored by the power of technology, and eager to apply their wartime experiences to peacetime tasks. The debate—so important in the 1920s and 1930s—between the defenders of tradition and the advocates of new approaches was resolved; modern design methods had contributed to the defeat of Hitler and modernism now shared in the victory over Fascism. The point of departure for postwar discussions of architecture was neatly stated in the September 1948 issue of the British journal *Architectural Review* (September 1948, p. 117): "Modern architecture has now won its battle against period revivalism and against the denial of the technical revolution that the use of reminiscent styles implies."

The Industrialization of Design

Materials as well as people were transformed by the war. Modern warfare consumed enormous amounts of material and the nations involved hurriedly expanded their productive capacities and searched for synthetic substitutes for suddenly scarce raw materials. Wartime research and development accelerated the pace of innovation and led to substantial new developments in material technologies.

Oscar Niemeyer, Plaza of the Three Powers, Brasilia, Brazil, 1958.

Already by 1943, experts recognized the need to begin planning for a return to peacetime conditions, while trade journals and architectural periodicals carried articles enthusiastically describing postwar possibilities. Design competitions were staged as a way to get architects creatively engaged with materials. All of the parties involved in the planning and construction of the built environment envisioned a future transformed by the innovations spawned by the war. When peace finally arrived, the architectural profession and the building industry were eager to get on with the job of redesigning the world. In a 1983 essay about the London school of architecture known as the AA, the architect Peter Cook described the spirit of the immediate postwar years:

> Rushing back to qualify as architects, the first post-war generation were full of enthusiasm for technology. . . . to build: to incorporate all those wonderful ways in which glued-together bombers had flown, rivets had been punched, rivers had been crossed by weird objects; this was the stuff of architecture. To suggest a better and special world was no arrogance — merely their inheritance.

(Cook, *Architectural Review*, October 1983, p. 33)

One of the most dramatic stories concerning materials in the 1940s and 1950s involves aluminum. Spurred by the voracious military demand for this strong, lightweight metal, the production of aluminum increased by 600 percent during the war years. The aluminum industry was eager to develop new peacetime applications to absorb this increased production volume. Architecture (along with aviation and automotive design) was considered a potentially lucrative market. First the economic depression of the 1930s and then the war had interrupted the construction of tall office buildings. When building resumed after the war, new aluminum panel systems for curtain wall construction soon appeared.

In 1950 Alcoa — one of the largest primary producers of aluminum — commissioned a new headquarters facility in Pittsburgh, Pennsylvania (fig. 5.1). The entire building was treated as a giant catalog of architectural uses for aluminum. Everything that could be was fabricated of aluminum, including the exterior curtain wall. Aluminum had been used to a limited degree in curtain wall construction before the war; the spandrel panels beneath the windows of the Empire State Building, for example, are aluminum. The Alcoa Building, however, represented a significant technological advance over prewar curtain wall systems. Prefabricated aluminum panels were shipped to the site and bolted directly to the steel structural frame (fig. 5.2). Aluminum's light weight meant the panels could be hoisted into place and assembled with a minimum of heavy construction equipment.

As the modernists' dream of industrialized building became a reality, it brought with it a new set of concerns for the architectural profession. If critical building components and systems were now to be fabricated at the factory and assembled on site rather than constructed in the traditional manner, then important design decisions were to be made in situations that bore little resemblance to traditional architectural practice. In a building culture increasingly oriented to technologically sophisticated systems of industrially produced elements, critical design parameters were now being established not in the architect's studio but in the research and development laboratories of such major material producers as Alcoa. The implications of emerging construction practices were clear to many architects. As the original director of the Bauhaus school in Germany and, beginning in 1938, chairman of the Department of Architecture at Harvard University, Walter Gropius was one of

5.1 (opposite) Wallace Harrison and Max Abramovitz, Alcoa Building, Pittsburgh, Pennsylvania, 1952.

The Alcoa Building is sheathed in thin aluminum panels. Each panel measures 6 x 12 ft (1.82 x 3.65 m) and is only $\frac{1}{8}$ in thick. Aluminum's light weight facilitated rapid construction. The novelty of this aluminum panel curtain wall attracted unusual public attention during construction, and a temporary spectators' gallery was erected to accommodate the curious.

5.2 (opposite, right) Wallace Harrison and Max Abramovitz, Alcoa Building, curtain wall diagram, Pittsburgh, Pennsylvania, 1952.

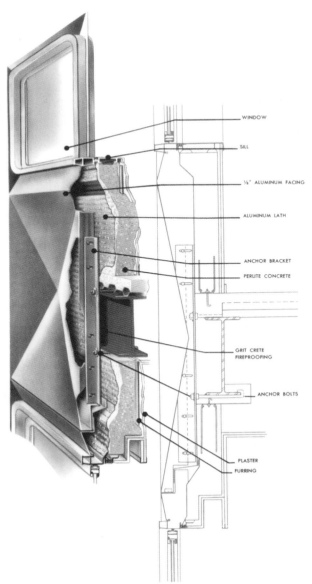

the most respected postwar leaders of the architectural profession. In *Scope of Total Architecture*, he expressed genuine concern about the marginalization of the design profession in the industrialized world:

> So it might be appropriate to investigate how far our professional framework fits the condition of our time . . . Let's see if the gigantic shift in the means of production has been sufficiently recognized by us. For we have to see our case in the light of techno-logical history . . . The architect is in a very real danger of losing his grip in competi-tion with the engineer, the scientist and the builder unless he adjusts his attitude and aims to meet the new situation.

(Gropius, p. 73)

Rather than resist the overtures of industry, Gropius urged the architectural pro-fession to embrace the opportunities and technical support offered by industry.

Sydney Opera House

The industrialization of building design is not the only theme in postwar architecture, however, and within the modernist framework, design followed various paths. Professional journals published flamboyant examples of expressionism next to austere exercises in reductive rationalism. One could structure a historical account of this period according to an expressionist–rationalist polarity that juxtaposes corporate office buildings such as the Alcoa Building to individual buildings of unique or exceptional design quality such as the Opera House designed by the Danish architect Jørn Utzon (b. 1918) for Sydney, Australia (fig. 5.3). Utzon won an international competition for the Sydney Opera House in 1957 with a design that split the building into two main parts: a substructure (labeled the "podium" by Utzon) containing all the building's services, and a superstructure covering the performance and public spaces. The superstructure consisted of a series of thin shells which created the building's striking silhouette.

5.3 Jørn Utzon, Opera House, Sydney, Australia, 1957–73.

The unconventional shape of the roof and the building's dramatic site on Sydney's harbor evoked nautical associations, and the shell-forms have been described as like the spinnaker of a yacht under sail or a series of upturned boat hulls leaning one against the next. The same shell forms that elicit such allusive poetic verbal descriptions proved extremely challenging to calculate and Utzon worked with the engineer Ove Arup on the design. Bringing the design to completion proved to be a long and arduous process and in 1966 Utzon was forced to withdraw from the commission. Arup eventually resolved the difficulty of calculating the shell by modifying Utzon's original scheme slightly and the opera house finally opened in 1973.

The Sydney Opera House provides an interesting case study of modern architecture for several reasons. First, it demonstrates the international scope of professional practice. The design involves a Danish architect working with London-based engineer for a building in Australia. Second, the difficulty of reconciling the expressive potential of Utzon's original design with the practical problem of calculating structural performance illustrates the parameters within which formal imagination and building tectonics interacted prior to the advent of computer-assisted means of calculation. Third, the Sydney Opera House demonstrates the iconic power of modern architecture to represent the identity of a place (some would say of an entire nation) in the same manner that great building traditions throughout history have done. No longer an intruder in the traditional city, modern architecture now provides the crowning features of urban settings around the globe.

New Directions

The postwar design agenda facing the profession was daunting. Architects and planners confronted three major tasks. First and most pressing was the need to rebuild or repair cities ravaged by the war. Second, architects were called upon to design new cities or reconfigure existing ones to express new political identities, particularly in the context of postcolonial developments. Third, avant-garde architects set themselves the task of reconceptualizing the form of cities in order to accommodate a new type of dense urban conglomeration for which specialists in the social sciences coined the term "megalopolis." Four designs—in New York City, Hiroshima and Tokyo in Japan, and Jakarta in Indonesia—suggest the new directions postwar architecture would follow.

New York: United Nations Building

In the aftermath of the war, perhaps no single building embodied the vision of a new world order better than the United Nations Building in New York City. The United Nations Charter was signed in June 1945, and in 1947 work began on a permanent home for the organization (fig. 5.4). An international team composed of architects from eleven countries was created to come up with the design for the UN headquarters. Although Le Corbusier played an active role in the preliminary design stage, the final design reflects Wallace Harrison's commanding role as director of planning and executive architect for the project. Harrison brought his experience with the design of the Rockefeller Center and his close ties with the

Rockefeller family (who were instrumental in securing the site along Manhattan's East River) to bear on the project.

The original UN complex consists of three buildings: one for the General Assembly, one housing conference rooms, and an office building for the Secretariat. While the General Assembly and conference facilities were arguably the most important parts of the program in terms of symbolism, the Secretariat, 544 feet high and only 72 feet in width, provided the dominant architectural image of the complex. The UN Secretariat demonstrated the new geometry, materials, and mechanical systems that were to transform the American skyscraper. Gone are the distinctive spires and exuberant decorative programs of Art Deco towers such as the Empire State and Chrysler Buildings. The air-conditioned Secretariat is a simple slab form with no setbacks and a flat top. In place of the masonry exterior walls that were typical of prewar construction, the UN Secretariat's east and west walls are clad in an aluminum and glass curtain wall that reflected advances in building technology prompted by wartime research and development.

5.4 Wallace Harrison and Max Abramovitz, United Nations Headquarters, New York, 1947–50.

Hiroshima: Peace Center

In Japan, Kenzo Tange (b. 1913) designed a Peace Center in Hiroshima, the first city to be destroyed by an atomic bomb (fig. 5.5). Tange's vision was for a new center for the city dedicated not just to the memory of the victims but also to the promotion of peace studies and international cooperation. On a plaza near the epicenter of the bomb blast, Tange arranged a group of buildings housing conference, exhibition, and library facilities. Raised on pilotis, the buildings clearly demonstrate the impact of Le Corbusier's ideas in Japan. Tange's designs, however, cannot be dismissed as copies of the master's work; the proportions and the detailing of the concrete structure reflect traditional Japanese timber-framed construction. This original synthesis of Japanese and Western models captured the attention of architects around the world and established Tange as a significant new figure in the international culture of design.

He was not the first in Japan, however, to explore the principles and techniques of modern architecture. Beginning with the Meiji Restoration in 1868, Japan had embarked on its own program of modernization. Foreign architects including Josiah Conder (1852–1920), Antonin Raymond (1888–1976), and Frank Lloyd Wright executed important work in Japan and Japanese architects began to travel abroad. In the early 1930s, Kunio Maekawa (b. 1905) and Junzo Sakakura (1901–1969) studied with Le Corbusier in France. Tange, however, was the first Asian to achieve international recognition as an important formal innovator within the modern movement. In the geography of modern architecture, Asia occupied a peripheral position during the first half of the century. In the wake of World War II, however, the map would be redrawn. The Hiroshima Peace Center marked the beginning of Japan's emergence as one of the important centers of modern architecture.

5.5 Kenzo Tange, Peace Center, Hiroshima, Japan, 1950–56.

Ancient Japanese and modern Western forms are combined in Tange's design for the Peace Center at Hiroshima. The saddle-shaped memorial at the plaza's center recalls the curved forms of the ancient Japanese *haniwa* house-type. The vertical louvers on the long walls of the Peace Museum are a contemporary rendition in concrete of traditional Japanese lattice screens.

Jakarta: The Monas

Political as well as cultural maps were being revised after 1945 as European countries slowly surrendered their grip over colonial possessions and former colonies embraced the challenge of nation-building. The Dutch were finally driven out of Indonesia in 1949 and the archipelago was united under the leadership of Achmed Sukarno. Nationhood ushered in a new era of development; in the twenty-five years following independence, the population of the capital, Jakarta, increased sevenfold; by 1976 it had reached 5.7 million. Against this background of tremendous population pressure, Sukarno set out to transform the former colonial city (known as Batavia during the Dutch period) into a modern capital. The symbolic centerpiece of the capital plan was a national independence monument known as the Monas (fig. 5.6). The enormous Medan Merdeka (Freedom Square), the site of the Monas, occupies a pivotal position between the old and new parts of Jakarta.

5.6 The Monas (Indonesian National Monument), Medan Merdeka Square, Jakarta, Indonesia, 1961–72.

The monument has a long, complicated building history; designs were solicited as early as 1955, but construction did not begin until 1961. Before turning to politics, Sukarno was trained as an architect and the final design is based on a concept he originated that was subsequently developed by the Indonesian architect Soedarsono. The base houses a museum exhibiting artifacts associated with the struggle for independence, while the tall obelisk symbolizing the flame of freedom asserts the monument's presence on the city's skyline. The clean lines and abstract form of the Monas suggest an affinity with modernist conceptions of monumentality, but in Indonesia the memorial's form was perceived in different and more complex ways. With its tall obelisk rising over a base housing relics from the birth of the nation, the Monas combines the lingam (the Hindu phallic image of the god Siva) and the yoni (an image of the female genitalia), two forms with deep symbolic associations in south Asia, as expressions of male and female principles. Indonesian independence was proclaimed on August 17, 1945 and the numbers 17–8–45 were used to establish the major dimensions of the monument. The recourse to ancient principles of male and female spatial types and the specification of dimensions based on an esoteric belief in numerology distinguish the Monas from Western secular attitudes concerning form.

As the formal language of modern architecture spread outward from its cradle in Europe and the United States it was transformed and enriched by the encounter with traditions and cultures from around the world. The September 1948 issue of the *Architectural Review* quoted above announced that modern architecture had won its battle against historicism, but continued by noting that this "victory" was only a first stage in the development of a truly modern architectural language.

> The second positive stage has still to be undertaken, the development of an idiom rich and flexible enough to express ideas that architecture—especially representational architecture—ought to be capable of expressing. . . . In its next phase modern architecture will blossom in several new directions.
>
> (*Architectural Review*, September 1948, p. 117)

Tokyo: National Gymnasium

In the 1950s and 1960s, Tange's work captured the attention of an international audience because his fusion of Eastern and Western elements demonstrated one exciting possibility of such new directions for modern architecture. One of his most dramatic works in these years was the National Gymnasium complex in Tokyo, site of the 1964 Olympic games (fig. 5.7). On a large plaza, Tange arranged two athletic facilities, one accommodating 15,000 spectators and a smaller arena seating 4,000. Working with the engineers Yoshikatsu Tsuboi and Mamoru Kawaguchi, Tange adapted the structural principle of a suspension bridge for his design. Two steel cables stretched between piers set 125 meters apart carried the roof structure of the larger hall, while the covering for the smaller hall was suspended using a single mast and cable system. Tange was not the first to apply the structural concept of tensile suspension systems to building design; in the late 1950s, both Le Corbusier and the American architect Eero Saarinen (1910–1961) had successfully used the idea. But as the largest tensile structure in the world at the time of its completion, the main gymnasium building served as vivid testimony to Japan's assimilation of modern technology.

5.7 Kenzo Tange, National Gymnasium, 1964 Olympics, Tokyo, Japan.

The sweeping rooflines of the two Olympic sports facilities combined sophisticated engineering and graceful design. The streamlined curvature of the roofs reduced wind-generated loads on the structures. The roofs were suspended from a network of cables stretched between tall masts and the upper edge of the stadium seating.

The form of the National Gymnasium also acquired a particular resonance in the context of Japanese building traditions. The curved silhouette of the gymnasium recalled the graceful curvature of Japanese temple roofs, and the stone-faced walls of the plaza podium were detailed in the same way as Japanese castle walls. Formal analysis, however, conveys only part of the story. No site is without history, and location as well as form is often charged with significance. The National Gymnasium complex is located in Tokyo's Yoyogi Park. During the military occupation of Japan, the park was known as Washington Heights and was the site of a major housing estate erected for US military personnel. In 1964 Japan celebrated more than a summer of athletic competition: it celebrated its recovery from the devastation of war and a regained sense of national sovereignty.

The Decline of Tradition

The triumph of modernism came, of course, at the expense of more traditional conceptions of architecture. Isolated examples of classical design such as Raymond Erith's (1904–1973) Provost's Lodgings for Queen's College, Oxford, can be cited (fig. 5.8), but such efforts registered no impact on the larger design scene. While modernism shared in the victory over Hitler, classicism was tainted by its association with the rhetoric of totalitarianism. A quarter century would elapse before Western architects demonstrated any interest in architecture's classical heritage. The modernization of design education, a process initiated during the 1930s, gained momentum. Walter Gropius and Ludwig Mies van der Rohe, for example, were appointed to influential positions as heads of architectural programs in the United States and they began to revise the curriculum of their schools to bring them into line with the Bauhaus model of design education. Elements of the traditional, Beaux-Arts system survived well into the 1950s, but the influence of such "academic" models steadily waned.

The newfound strength of the modern movement is reflected in the literature of architecture as well. Manuals and handbooks began to replace manifestos as textual tools for promoting modern design. The publication program of the CIAM served as a precedent, but the scope of the new publications dwarfed that of prewar efforts. No adequate bibliography of post-1945 design manuals exists but their importance cannot be ignored. As an example, one can cite the Italian *Manuale dell'Architetto* first published in 1946 (fig. 5.9). Compiled by a team of Italian architects headed by Mario Ridolfi (1904–1984) and working under the auspices of the Italian National Research Council, the *Manuale dell'Architetto* was a handbook consisting of graphic standards for indicating different building materials, standard construction details suitable for windows, doors, and related tectonic aspects of architectural design, typical plan types and relevant ergonomic criteria for different building purposes—and uniform standards for sanitation, ventilation, and other building services. Conceived as a replacement for outdated manuals and handbooks, it established the new technical norms and graphic standards that would shape postwar building practices in Italy.

5.8 (below) Raymond Erith, Provost's Lodgings, Queen's College, Oxford University, England, 1958–59.

5.9 (opposite) Mario Ridolfi et al, from *Manuale dell'Architetto*, plate 3c, 1946.
   The literature of building is an important part of the story of twentieth-century architecture, and often *who* published a book proved as significant as who wrote it. Part of American efforts to support the modernization of European industries after World War II involved the United States Information Services (USIS) paying for the publication and distribution of this modern architectural manual.

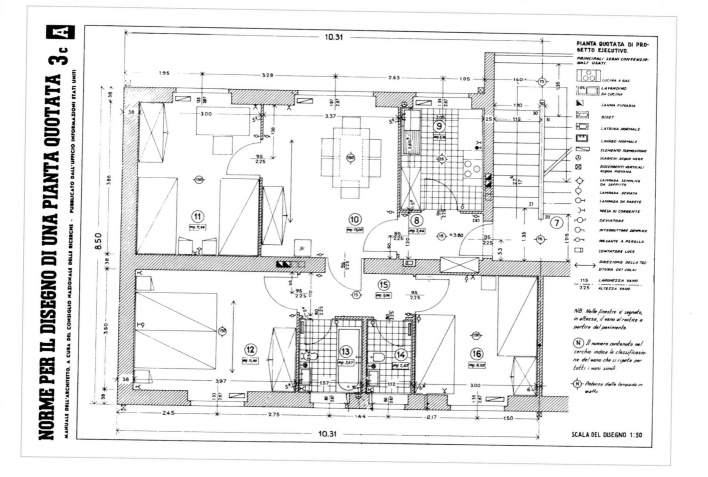

Rebuilding

Modern warfare renders the distinction between the front lines and the home front meaningless. Cities and civilian populations were subjected to sustained campaigns of bombardment by both sides during the war. When the dust finally settled, huge swathes of urban fabric had been destroyed and the first task facing architects and planners was rebuilding. A comprehensive account of this important episode in twentieth-century urban history remains to be written. The debate over rebuilding came into sharp focus over the question of restoration versus new construction and the degree to which the prewar conditions of buildings and cities should be the model for postwar efforts. Each city constituted a unique case shaped by the extent of the damage, the cost of reconstruction, and the political orientations of local administrations. In Milan, Italy, for example, the Galleria—one of the masterpieces of nineteenth-century urbanism—and La Scala opera house had been badly damaged by Allied air raids. Both of these structures were critical ingredients of Milan's architectural identity and were restored to their prewar appearances.

The experience of Florence, Italy, illustrates a different approach to the same problem. In August 1944 German troops withdrawing from Florence dynamited five of the six bridges over the Arno river including Bartolomeo Ammannati's Renaissance design for the Ponte Santa Trinità. Perversely, the retreating Germans left the medieval Ponte Vecchio intact. In order to deny its use to the approaching Allies, however, they dynamited the buildings lining the street approaching the

5.10 (left) A street view along the via Por San Maria near the Ponte Vecchio, Florence, Italy, reconstructed after World War II.

Rebuilt after the war, the via Por San Maria is an outstanding example of a sensitive solution to inserting new buildings into an historic setting. Although traditional materials were used in the rebuilding, details such as larger windows, wider structural bays, and updated mechanical systems reveal the modern quality of new construction.

5.11 (opposite) Otto Apel, 25 Berlinerstrasse, Frankfurt am Main, Germany, 1956.

bridge. After the war, an intense debate erupted over plans to restore the devastated portions of Florence's historic center. What should be the character of new construction in the old city? With the slogan "Dove erano e come erano" (Where they were and how they were), traditionalists advocated the exact reconstruction of lost buildings. With "Indietro non si puo" (You can't go back) as their rallying cry, modernists argued for a modern treatment of the damaged areas.

Today, the streets and bridges of the affected part of Florence represent a compromise. Ammannati's Ponte Santa Trinità was meticulously reconstructed, while other spans were replaced with new designs. Along the via Por San Maria leading up the Ponte Vecchio, traditional materials, particularly at street level, recalled the character of the prewar fabric and masked new structures (fig. 5.10). Progressive Italian architects considered the rebuilding of Florence a lost opportunity to shape the development in their country along the lines of a CIAM-inspired vision of urbanism. Rather than dismissing the rebuilding of the via Por San Maria as a timid compromise, however, it should be recognized as an excellent example of a contextually sensitive approach to new construction in a historic urban setting.

In other cities entire quarters and not just individual buildings or streets were destroyed. Suddenly the early twentieth-century visionary schemes of Sant'Elia and Le Corbusier, created originally as imaginative exercises, seemed like blueprints waiting to be implemented. The war created unprecedented opportunities to recast the form and character of cities. During the years of the Weimar Republic,

Frankfurt am Main in Germany emerged as a major center for modern design. Much of the work that made the city a showcase for the new architecture consisted of housing estates erected around the periphery of the expanding city. The historic center was destroyed during the Allied air campaign against Germany, and although isolated buildings of cultural significance such as Goethe's House were reconstructed, most of the damaged area was rebuilt along clearly modern lines. Wider, straighter streets such as the Berlinerstrasse formed a new street pattern. The contrast between the stereometric purism of Otto Apel's (1906–1966) mixed use building at 25 Berlinerstrasse and the traditional gabled structures characteristic of prewar Frankfurt am Main symbolized the new direction German architects pursued (fig. 5.11). Across Europe and parts of Asia, surviving historical monuments existed as lonely islands floating in a modern sea of concrete, steel, and glass.

Reconfiguring Capitals

The political role of city planning after 1945 is most apparent in the remodeling of existing and the design of new capital cities. The form of a capital city—indeed, of any city—is a revealing indicator of a society's social and political organization. As the global community realigned itself in power blocs after 1945, social scientists began to speak in terms of first- (developed capitalist), second- (socialist), and third- (developing) world experiences. Political leaders employed design as a powerful tool in their campaigns to distinguish new regimes from the preceding power structures and to suggest the broad outlines of emerging political cultures.

The debate about the relationship between space and ideology was particularly acute in the socialist bloc where socialist planning theory described public spaces as the explicit representation of the sociopolitical order. In the early years of the Russian Revolution the avant-garde designers combined artistic and political agendas under the banner of Constructivism with the goal of developing a new art for a new socialist society. By the mid-1930s, however, socialist realism had replaced Constructivism as the officially sanctioned image of the Soviet Union. With the extension of Soviet hegemony after World War II, the principles of socialist realism became the basis for monumental architecture and urban planning throughout the socialist bloc. From Beijing to Berlin streets and plazas were charged with a political significance lacking in the CIAM-inspired planning models used in the capitalist West.

Beijing

In 1949 the People's Republic of China was established with Beijing as the capital. The future of Beijing was soon the subject of an intense debate. Liang Sicheng, vice-director of the Beijing City Planning Commission and an authority on China's architectural history, proposed a plan for Beijing based on the concept of the city as an

administrative and cultural center for Communist China. Liang's plan called for preserving Beijing's walls and the Forbidden City intact, limiting the height of new construction to no more than three stories and banning industrial development. The plan also called for the creation of a new governmental center to be built west of the Forbidden City and aligned along a north–south axis. Liang's plan would have preserved the character of the imperial capital and applied the principles of traditional Chinese design to new construction. Mao Zedong, however, had a dramatically different vision of the future. Liang was informed by Beijing mayor P'eng Chen: "Chairman Mao wants a big modern city: he expects the sky there to be filled with smokestacks" (Fairbanks, p. 170). In 1953 the Communist Party announced a five-year plan for the transformation of the capital with the slogan: "utility, economy, and, if conditions allow, beauty." China's leadership now demanded bold symbols of a Communist conception of modernity and decisively rejected Liang's vision of a city characterized by the continuity of forms and traditions. In 1958, as the tenth anniversary of the Communist victory approached, the Chinese Communist Party announced the Great Leap Forward program and plans were unveiled for the rebuilding of Tian'anmen Square and the widening of Chang'an Avenue. These projects constitute the spatial representation of China's Communist revolution.

The decision to create a huge square for public rallies and political celebrations signaled a dramatic break with China's imperial past. Originally Tian'anmen Square was a small T-shaped space leading up to Tian'anmen Gate, the southern entry to the Imperial Palace. Surrounded by a high wall, it conformed to traditional Chinese design practices that privileged the north–south axis in planning and restricted access to spaces associated with government. As a result, orientation, size, and accessibility were charged with political significance that was culturally specific.

5.12 Tian'anmen Square with Mao-tse-Tung's Mausoleum and the entry to the Forbidden City, Beijing, China, 1950s.

As part of the reconfiguration of the city center, Chang'an Avenue, the east–west street that crosses Tian'anmen Square, was broadened and lined with new government buildings. Today, Tian'anmen Square occupies an area of 440,000 square meters, capable of accommodating crowds of up to 500,000 people (fig. 5.12). In the context of Chinese history, the planning of Tian'anmen Square and Chang'an Avenue resonated with specifically Chinese meanings and associations. But the results also conform to the tenets of political design that shaped planning in the socialist bloc after World War II. The necessity to create places of mass assembly was explicitly recognized in socialist planning theory. In 1950, for example, the German Democratic Republic (East Germany) issued a planning directive entitled "Sixteen Principles for the Restructuring of Cities." This document describes large central plazas as the "political midpoint" of urban life:

> At the city's center lie the most important political, administrative, and cultural spaces. On the city center's plazas, political demonstrations, parades, and popular celebrations take place. . . . Plazas are the structural foundation of city planning and the city's overall architectural composition.
>
> (Ockman, pp. 127–8)

Understood in these terms, Tian'anmen Square conforms to the model of planning evident throughout the socialist world after 1945.

Berlin

Following the war, Berlin was partitioned among the four occupying powers (France, Great Britain, the Soviet Union, and the United States) and quickly became a focal point of Cold War tensions. Both East and West Germany embarked on campaigns to turn Berlin into a showcase for their respective social systems. In 1949 work began on the development of a major new axis for the Communist eastern zone of the city known originally as the Stalinallee (today called the Karl-Marx Allee and Frankfurter Allee). Some of the earliest buildings erected on the Stalinallee and designed by Ludmilla Herzenstein (b. 1906) demonstrated an affinity for prewar modernist models as if to reconnect with the Weimar legacy of progressive planning quashed by the Nazi regime. However, the character of design soon changed. In 1950 East German architects returned from a planning conference in Moscow committed to a program of monumental urban design. Under the general

5.13 Stalinallee (1961, Karl-Marx-Allee), former East Berlin, Germany, 1949–57.

direction of Hermann Henselmann (1905–1995), work on the Stalinallee continued throughout the 1950s (fig. 5.13). In the supposedly classless society of socialist countries such as the German Democratic Republic, bourgeois and aristocratic models are freed from their elitist connotations and pressed into service on behalf of the proletariat. Construction along the Stalinallee depended on modern industrialized building techniques, but the urban design reflects a more traditional conception of monumental planning, in which individual buildings create a continuous street facade and changes in height or decorative detailing define a clear spatial hierarchy.

Developments in East Berlin were matched by corresponding efforts to develop the architectural character of West Berlin in a way representative of Western conceptions of urban space and economic planning. In 1955 work began on a new residential quarter in the western sector of the city known as the Hansaviertel (fig. 5.14). Conceived as a showcase development for the 1957 "Interbau Housing Exhibition" in West Berlin, Hansaviertel consisted of a series of apartment blocks to accommodate a projected population of 5,000. An international roster of modern architects provided designs for an entire range of housing types from detached single-family units to high-rise apartment buildings.

An analysis of postwar architectural developments in Berlin reveals not only differences in design approaches between Eastern and Western architects but also the way in which the politics of the Cold War shaped architectural criticism and the public perception of design values. In reviews shaped largely by the antagonistic climate of the Cold War, the "free" arrangement of the Hansaviertel buildings was contrasted with the "regimented" alignment of buildings along the Stalinallee and the variety of designs was portrayed as evidence of the artistic freedom enjoyed by Western architects.

5.14 Hansaviertel, "Interbau Housing Exhibition," Tiergarten Klopstockstrasse and Altonaerstrasse, formerly West Berlin, Germany, 1955–61.

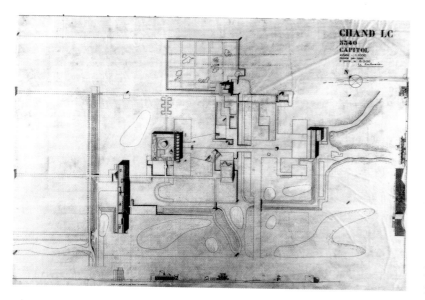

5.15 Le Corbusier, Chandigarh, capitol complex, plan, India, 1950–65.

Chandigarh, India

In India, architecture and capital planning reflected the postcolonial agenda of the country's first Prime Minister, Jawaharlal Nehru, and his commitment to the modernization of the newly independent country. Anxious to distance the country from its recent colonial past, Nehru rejected the argument advanced years earlier by the British architects of New Delhi that Western and Indian forms could be blended together under the rubric of a Western classical conception of architecture. Nehru also rejected the option of reviving in any literal sense the precolonial traditions of monumental architecture to represent the new state. In a country filled with ethnic, religious, and caste distinctions, he reasoned, what native tradition could be pressed into service without antagonizing some elements of the diverse society? An eclectic approach that mixed elements from different traditions seemed clumsy and ill-suited to the task of creating a new coherent identity for the country. In modernism Nehru found an architectural approach capable of expressing his vision of a rational, secular political culture. The partition of territories between India and Pakistan at the time of independence created the necessity of providing a new regional capital for the Punjab. Chandigarh was selected as the site. Nehru seized the opportunity to give form to this vision, and in Le Corbusier he found an architect of international stature and impeccable modernist credentials ready to give India a modern image.

Le Corbusier began work on the plan of Chandigarh in 1951 (fig. 5.15). His cousin Pierre Jeanneret (1896–1967) and the British couple Jane Drew and Maxwell Fry (1899–1987) worked with him on the scheme. The involvement of Drew and Fry is particularly noteworthy. In the 1950s they made important contributions to the development of climatically appropriate modern housing typologies for the Third World; thus they carried forward the social agenda of early modern architecture into the design of the new capital. The entire city was laid out using a gridded street pattern adjusted to accommodate different types of traffic. Once the main elements of the plan were established, Le Corbusier devoted most of his energy to the design of the capitol complex consisting of the Governor's Palace, the High Court, and the Parliament and Secretariat buildings (fig. 5.16). While the emphasis on

5.16 Le Corbusier, Chandigarh, Parliament Building, India, 1950–65.

zoning and circulation is rooted in the principles of the CIAM, Le Corbusier's design for the capitol group reflects a new sculptural handling of form uniquely his. Gone is the interest in smooth, taut surfaces delineating transparent volumes lifted off the ground on slender pilotis apparent in his work of the 1920s and 1930s. The monumental architecture of Chandigarh is closer to Le Corbusier's definition of architecture as "the correct and masterful play of forms brought together in the light" than it is to the machine age imagery of his prewar work.

Although the plan of the capitol complex reveals a series of axial relationships, the effect of the whole cannot be explained in terms of a simple set of diagrammatic relationships. Rather than develop the political buildings as a civic forum near the center of Chandigarh's gridded plan, Le Corbusier located the capitol complex to the north of the city. There buildings are seen against the backdrop of distant mountains. The result has more in common with the concept of a sacred precinct than a civic center, and the individual designs possess the sculptural presence and solemnity of temple architecture. Le Corbusier incorporated elements drawn from his study of the indigenous building traditions of India but always transformed in a personal and idiosyncratic way. For the Parliament building he inverted the traditional profile of the Indian "parasol" roof and created a striking troughlike form that reaches up to catch the sunlight even as it shades the portico below. Le Corbusier also proposed a curious monument in the form of an open, upturned human hand located on the capitol plaza. The image of an open hand possessed a great personal significance for Le Corbusier—he repeatedly stamped his postwar architecture with a personal iconography representing humankind between nature and culture. The capitol buildings at Chandigarh are the work of a modern artist pursuing formal invention through a process of abstraction that unfolds according to self-constituted rules of composition rather than conforming to traditional models of civic buildings and public spaces.

Chandigarh is a complex achievement. It answered Nehru's call for a modern representation of India but did so in a way that seemed to willfully disregard concerns with cultural legibility and shared symbolic languages. It conflated the personal design agenda of the designer with the political agenda of the patron to an unprecedented degree. Nehru summed up the Chandigarh experience in the following words:

> It hits you on the head, and makes you think. You may squirm at the impact but it has made you think and imbibe new ideas, and the one thing which India requires is being hit on the head so that it may think.

(Khilnani, p. 135)

If Chandigarh makes one squirm and think about India's postcolonial identity, it also calls on the viewer to reconsider some popular conceptions about modernism. In the minds of many, modernism is associated with techno-idolatry, a position crystalized in Le Corbusier's own dictum that a house is a machine for living in. But there is another vital pulse animating modern art: the belief that abstraction and formal invention could recover for architecture a primal language of form not dependent upon advanced technology for its realization and capable of speaking to men and women everywhere. At Chandigarh, Le Corbusier's forms exhibit a brute, sculptural power in spite of the esoteric and convoluted process that generated them. Unfortunately, the same cannot be said for other exercises in modern capitol design.

Brasilia

In 1957 Lúcio Costa (b. 1902) won a competition for the design of Brasilia, the capital of Brazil. One of the leading modernists in Latin America, Costa had developed a close working relationship with Le Corbusier in the 1930s. Proposals for a new capital in the center of this vast country had been advanced since the 1880s, and in 1955 presidential candidate Juscelino Kubitschek de Oliveira made it a key element of his campaign. Kubitschek was an advocate of state-directed industrialization and saw the construction of a new capital as a way to advance his nationalist agenda. Following his election, Kubitschek moved quickly to implement his vision, and the new capital was inaugurated in 1960.

More than a symbol, the capital was to be an active agent promoting change. The enormous construction project would provide a focus for national identity and stimulate development in allied fields such as transportation, communication, and hydro-electric power generation. Costa, like Le Corbusier at Chandigarh, sought to combine CIAM principles of planning with an expressive formal vocabulary. Following CIAM practice, Costa separated the residential zone from the area reserved for major institutions and organized each zone along a dominant axis (fig. 5.17). The automobile replaced the pedestrian as the standard for establishing distances between significant points. In its reliance on the automobile, Brasilia is a thoroughly modern city with no links to the pace, scale, or form of premodern urbanism. Costa described the cross-axial plan of Brasilia in terms of the primal human act of taking possession of a site by inscribing a geometrical diagram on it. As if to balance the ancient gesture of foundation, he likened the final form of the plan to that of an airplane, thus asserting the essential modernity of the scheme. Important institutional buildings were aligned along the straight east–west axis while the curved north–south axis (the "wings" of the airplane) was lined with residential superblocks.

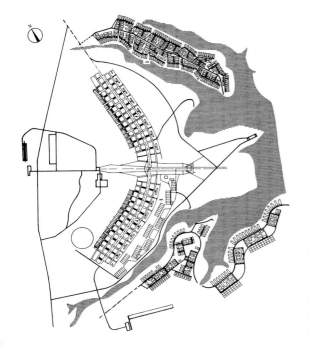

5.17 Lúcio Costa, Brasilia, plan, Brazil, 1957.
Brasilia expresses national aspirations for social and economic progress in an international design language heavily influenced by Le Corbusier. The "superquadras" (housing blocks) of Lúcio Costa's plan are pure rectangular forms lifted off the ground by piers.

Oscar Niemeyer (b. 1907) was responsible for the design of the main group of government buildings clustered, again as at Chandigarh, in a plaza—the Plaza of the Three Powers—located at the east end of the monumental civic axis (see page 130). Niemeyer conceived of the Presidential Palace, the Supreme Court, and the National Congress buildings as pure modernist forms meant to be perceived against the natural backdrop of the towering sky and distant horizon of Brazil's central plateau. For the National Congress building, Niemeyer designed low saucer-shaped domes and inverted one to distinguish between the two chambers.

Rather than speaking eloquently of a modern conception of authority, however, the result is awkward and strangely mute. The twin domes are neither close enough to historical precedents to be effective symbols nor different enough to suggest a radical new interpretation of the type. Dwarfed by the twin slabs of the Secretariat, the Plaza of the Three Powers is an unwitting expression of the triumph of bureaucracy over democracy. Since its completion, Brasilia has occupied an equivocal position in the literature on modern architecture. The modernist historian and critic Bruno Zevi, for example, described it as "Kafkaesque," yet it remains one of the landmark achievements of modern architecture in Latin America.

In chapter 4, the term megalomania was used to describe the 1930s building campaigns of totalitarian regimes. Compared meter for meter, however, Chandigarh and Brasilia rival anything conceived by Speer or Iofan for size. If size is the only criterion, then one set of plans cannot be labeled megalomaniacal and a comparable set exempted from a similar judgement. In fact, one can discern both similarities and some important differences between the capital designs of the middle third of the century.

First, the common thread is the adamant refusal of all involved to recognize limits. No past is too sacred to be challenged, no place too venerable or remote to be left untouched, no problem too intractable to be solved; this is the creed of modernity and, for better or worse, it has shaped the twentieth century. Second, creating or reconfiguring capital cities requires the commitment of strongwilled political patrons regardless of the specifics of political ideology. Nehru and Kubitschek, however, cannot be compared with Hitler and Stalin; critics need to recognize the implications of various types of patronage. The cult of the leader operates within totalitarian systems and hence shapes totalitarian architecture in different ways than leadership exercised in parliamentary systems. Third, the architectural form that the rhetoric of power assumes is important. Speer's Berlin is different from Le Corbusier's Chandigarh and being in the Plaza of the Three Powers in Brasilia is a different experience than being in Tian'anmen Square in Beijing. Employed as forms of design rhetoric, classicism and modernism convey different conceptions of legitimacy and authority and promote different kinds of experiences. The solemnity of Speer's monumental axis was meant to intimidate visitors to the Reich's capital and serve as the setting for the type of military pageantry the cinematographer Leni Reifenstahl brilliantly captured in her documentary *Triumph of the Will*. In contrast, Kubitschek envisioned speeding along the roadways of Brasilia as an exhilarating celebration of Brazil's newly achieved industrial power and freedom from colonial models.

Säynätsalo, Finland

Capitals are stagesets created for global as well as national audiences, and issues of grand scale are inevitably bound up with their design. The last building to be considered in this section demonstrates a very different and more modest scale of design. Between 1948 and 1952 Alvar Aalto designed and built a new town hall for the small community of Säynätsalo, Finland (fig. 5.18). In addition to a council chamber, the program included a library and small shops that could be converted to municipal office space as needed. Aalto conceived the building as a series of simple brick boxes arranged around a courtyard crowning a small rise in the terrain. The Säynätsalo Town Hall can be read as Aalto's reworking of a series of archetypal images and forms. Native Finnish traditions of rural buildings clustered around courts are blended with the Mediterranean-inspired images of an acropolis. The attention to detailing and the elaborate trusswork supporting the roof of the council chamber celebrates both a local tradition of woodcraft and the ritual of democratic assembly (fig. 5.19).

Aalto excelled at creating rich sensory experiences for the users of his buildings. As the visitor moves from the brick paving of the corridor to the wooden flooring of

5.18 (right) Alvar Aalto, Town Hall, western entrance to the inner courtyard, Säynätsalo, Finland, 1949–52.

5.19 (below) Alvar Aalto, Town Hall, Council Chamber, Säynätsalo, Finland, 1949–52.

the council chamber, for example, the sound of footsteps changes as if to announce arrival at the ceremonial heart of the community. Adjustments in the fenestration pattern modulate the quality of light and the selection of materials creates a rich tactile experience. The Säynätsalo Town Hall comes naturally out of Aalto's concern with the aural and tactile as well as visual aspects of spatial experience apparent in his prewar work. It also picks up the theme of a less grandiose, more accessible public architecture marked out by Ragnar Östberg in the Stockholm Town Hall and updated by Willem Dudok at Hilversum (see figs. 4.1, 4.5).

The Säynätsalo Town Hall is important as an early indication of what would become a major theme in postwar discussions of architecture: the development of modern architecture along more humane lines. As classical and traditional models receded in importance after 1945, the debate within architectural circles was reconfigured along new lines. The triumph of modernism brought with it a dawning awareness of its own excesses. The CIAM-inspired approach to planning with its narrow focus on zoning and circulation, and the increasingly single-minded quality of modernist architecture that placed formal abstraction at the service of technological rationalism, began to attract criticism from within the ranks of the modern movement. In a 1950 eulogy for Eliel Saarinen, Aalto argued:

Regardless of which social system prevails in the world or its parts, a softening human touch is needed to mould societies, cities, buildings, and even the smallest machine-made objects into something positive to the human psyche, without bringing individual freedom and the common good into conflict.

(Schildt, p. 246)

The sculptural power of Le Corbusier's work at Chandigarh and the sensuous richness of Aalto's design for Säynätsalo were important reminders of the potential inherent in the modern language of architecture to resist both technological determinism and the loss of a sense of self to the political concept of the masses.

Reconceptualizing the City

Megastructures and Megalopolis

In 1960 Kenzo Tange unveiled a plan for the future development of Tokyo (fig. 5.20). The occasion was the "World Design Conference" convened in Tokyo that year which attracted an international roster of architects and designers and focused global attention on the city. Tange proposed to direct the city's future expansion into Tokyo Bay by erecting a series of enormous buildings on artificial islands in the bay. A network of roadways graded to handle different levels of traffic would tie the entire scheme together. Not since Bruno Taut proposed carving

5.20 Kenzo Tange, Tokyo Bay plan, Japan, 1960.
  Tange used the metaphor of a skeleton to describe his visionary plan for Tokyo. Commercial and recreational facilities would, like vertebrae, be linked to form a central spine that crossed Tokyo Bay. Large residential buildings, like ribs, branched out on either side of this spine.

mountains into giant crystalline forms in his *Alpine Architecture* (see fig. 1.8), had an architect visualized such a bold transformation of a natural environment into a designed one.

In the Tokyo Bay plan, Tange combined the philosophy of the CIAM with the emerging concept of megastructures. A megastructure is an enormous framework in which all the functions of a city or of any part of a city can be arranged using modular units. The frame defines the basic form of the settlement, provides structural support, and contains utility and power lines serving the individual parts. Within the framework, the modules can be rearranged, renovated, or replaced as needed. The concept of a megastructure combines the idea of a fixed form with the promise of limitless flexibility. The sudden rise (and equally sudden collapse) in popularity of megastructures in the 1960s is a curious and revealing chapter in the history of modernism after 1945. It is an episode that demonstrated the extreme measures that the architectural profession was willing to consider in order to satisfy its own sense of responsibility to manage the built environment.

For architects, the cruel lesson of wartime destruction was that no physical thing is permanent. Buildings, neighborhoods, and entire cities could be destroyed and rebuilt in a different manner. This is the immediate background against which they contemplated an ominous new problem: global population growth. In the late 1950s, United Nations-sponsored population studies began to describe both an increase in population numbers and a significant shift in human settlement patterns. According to UN demographers and social scientists the future was predictable and the timeline short: more people would be living in larger cities than ever before. Humanity's future was now an urban one.

In 1961 the French geographer Jean Gottmann coined the term megalopolis to describe a form of continuous, dense urban development in which individual settlements merge seamlessly into one another along transportation corridors linking major cities. As it moved from the descriptive domain of the social sciences to the prescriptive orientation of design, the "problem" of the megalopolis was recast in architectural terms and megastructures were advanced as the solution. Tange's Tokyo Plan was only the first in a series of Japanese megastructural projects. In 1960 Japanese architects Kiyonori Kikutake (b. 1928), Kisho Kurokawa (b. 1934), Fumihiko Maki (b. 1928), and Masato Otaka (b. 1923) along with the graphic designer Kiyoshi Awazu (b. 1929) issued a manifesto describing their conception of megastructural urbanism which they called Metabolism:

> We regard human society as a vital process, a continuous development from atom to nebula. The reason why we use the biological word *metabolism* is that we believe design and technology should denote human vitality.
>
> (Kurokawa, p. 27)

Metabolism was predicated on the belief that human societies could be modeled in biological terms and that design could mediate the intersection of technological and biological processes.

The dream of technology as a beneficent tool that could enhance "human vitality" was very much alive in the early 1960s. In England, the concept of megastructures was popularized by Archigram. Peter Cook launched the journal *Archigram* in 1960 and a few years later along with Warren Chalk, Dennis Crompton, Ron Herron, David Greene, and Mike Webb began a series of projects that stamped English megastructures with a distinctive pop sensibility. *Archigram* magazine was filled with images drawn from popular culture and Archigram projects eroded the distinction between permanent buildings and disposable consumer products.

Archigram's 1964 project Plug-In City conceptualized the city as a set of dynamic relationships rather than a defined place in space (fig. 5.21). Plug-in City adapted the consumer-product concept of planned obsolescence; residents could treat their modular units like automobiles or appliances and replace them with newer models as desired. Later Archigram projects included mobile cities and ephemeral encampments that subverted any notion of architecture as the creation of enduring monuments.

Archigram projects such as the 1959 Entertainment Centre proposed for London's Leicester Square reflected the group's fascination not just with space-age technology but with advertising and consumer culture as well. A more complex and critical examination of contemporary trends emerged in the work of the Italian group Superstudio.

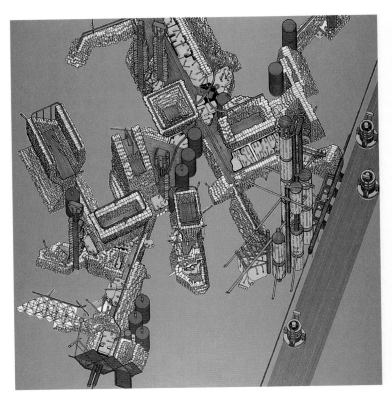

5.21 Peter Cook, Plug-In City, 1964. Print on board from ink drawing with felt-tip pen color, 28 × 27 in (71 × 68 cm).

The members of Archigram interpreted literally the frequently cited dictum of modern design: a building is like a machine. Their projects synthesize ideas drawn from a variety of sources including Futurism, Buckminster Fuller, the Frankfurt Kitchen, and the American space program.

Founded in Florence in 1966, Superstudio included Adolfo Natalini, Gian Piero Frassinelli, Roberto and Alberto Magris, Alessandro Polis, and Cristiano Toraldo di Francia. Like the Metabolists and Archigram, Superstudio produced a series of dramatic schemes for alternative forms of human settlement. By the late 1960s, however, an articulate critique of the excesses of consumer culture had begun to emerge. Superstudio projects were not so much solutions to the problem of megalopolis as they were dystopian warnings about an over-rationalized future. While Archigram's images of megastructures are filled with elaborate space-frames, cranes, and moving parts, Superstudio tended to package its designs in sleek, abstract shapes and eventually dematerialized the concept of megastructures completely.

For "Italy: The New Domestic Landscape," an important 1972 exhibition at the Museum of Modern Art in New York, Superstudio contributed a series of panels labeled Microevent/Microenvironment in which they described a form of technological nomadism that raised questions about the meaning of place and building in the context of global networks of energy and information (fig. 5.22). In Microevent/Microenvironment, Superstudio brought into sharp focus the contrast between the object-fixation of consumer culture and the anti-materialism of the youthful counter-culture of the late 1960s.

In less than a decade megastructures went from providing answers to posing questions. Initially, the concept promised to be a solution to pressing concerns about the explosive growth of cities. The concept of megastructure struck a responsive chord among architects because it suggested a strategy for resolving the conflict between spontaneity and order inherent in the design of human environments. Megastructures applied Le Corbusier's dictum that a house is machine for living in

5.22 Superstudio, Micro-event/Micro-environment, 1972.

Like the drawings in Bruno Taut's *Alpine Architecture*, executed fifty years earlier, Superstudio's images describe a world transformed by design. In this image exhibited at the Museum of Modern Art in New York, the world of human artifice is juxtaposed with primal nature. The grids and satellites symbolize global networks of energy and information relentlessly encroaching on the natural world.

to the scale of an entire city. But cities are not machines, and by pushing technology to an extreme megastructures also brought into sharp relief the weaknesses of modernism's faith in technology. Treating cities likes appliances that wear out and require replacement is an extravagant use of resources and denies the cultural importance of memory and permanence. The alleged permissiveness and spontaneity of the system was illusory and conditioned by the materialist parameters of capitalism. Superstudio's haunting images challenged architects to question both the means and the ends associated with modernism's vision of a relentlessly new world. The story of megastructures indicates just how tenuous the triumph of modernism proved to be.

Housing

In 1923 Le Corbusier concluded *Vers une Architecture* with the admonition: "Architecture or revolution. Revolution can be avoided." The architectural profession never lost sight of this truism and by the 1950s it was an axiom of social planning in both the socialist and capitalist camps. In the 1920s and 1930s modern architects developed rationalized housing typologies that could provide ample light, fresh air, and sanitary living conditions, and governments had begun to play a more active role in housing construction. The concerns of postwar architects remained the same but the debate over the optimal design strategies to achieve these goals continued to evolve.

The debate was driven by several factors. New developments in building and domestic technologies inspired designers to reconsider their approaches. As architectural modernism made the transition from the status of an emerging ideology to that of the dominant model of design thinking in schools and bureaucracies as well as the architectural profession, the legacy of prewar modern design was subjected to critical reevaluation. A combination of personal design agendas, individual national contexts, and the overarching political reality of the Cold War shaped the course of development of postwar housing.

Sweden: New Empiricism

The distinctive Scandinavian contribution to the housing debate came out of Sweden and was identified with the term New Empiricism. In 1944 Sweden established a Home Research Institute, followed four years later by the creation of a National Housing Board charged with developing norms to govern public housing construction. By the early 1950s, the board had established minimum room dimensions, studied kitchen layouts, and tested various materials and finishes. In

establishing an institutional framework for design research, Sweden was following the modernist model of rationalizing the design, construction, and management of the entire built environment.

But the New Empiricism signaled a willingness to reconsider the paradigms of modernism. In the first half of the twentieth century, when modern architects used the word "new" it was intended to denote novel ideas and forms that could be distinguished from classical and traditional architecture. In the second half of the century, however, the meaning of new changed. In design criticism, the use of the word new increasingly identified the effort to reevaluate modernism. The New Empiricism described a more flexible approach to housing design in which a commitment to research and experimentation was tempered by an equally strong commitment to human scale and spatial diversity.

Per Ekholm (b. 1920) and Sidney White's (1917–1982) design for the Baron-backarna Housing project in Örebro is typical of the New Empiricist approach (fig. 5.23). Baronbackarna consisted of 1,230 apartments for a town in the midst of making the transition from a small farming community to a manufacturing center with a growing population. Rather than spread the housing units across the site in a simple geometric diagram, the architects arranged the apartments in a meandering pattern around the periphery. The buildings define a series of U-shaped courtyards that open onto a generous communal space in the center of the site. Flat roofs and horizontal windows—iconic features of the International Style—give way to shallow pitched roofs and vertical windows at Baronbackarna. Such "adjustments" to the formal language of prewar modernism were described as an effort to soften and render less abstract the rationalized and standardized imagery of CIAM models. Swedish design efforts were covered extensively in the international architectural press and the New Empiricism became an influential model in postwar housing debates in Britain and on the continent.

5.23 Per Ekholm and Sidney White, Baron-backarna housing project, Örebro, Sweden, 1953–57.

Within New Empiricism, the rationalization of technique is combined with a concern for environmental features and practical effects. The site plan was arranged so as to preserve existing trees, boulders, and other natural features. Inside, the layout of individual apartments was calculated to facilitate as much as possible the housewife's daily routine.

France: Le Corbusier

As he did so often, Le Corbusier provided one of the most important points of reference for the postwar discussion of housing with the design of the Unité d'habitation in Marseilles, France, commissioned in 1945 and finally completed in 1952 (fig. 5.24). The Unité was conceived initially as a prototype for government-sponsored housing in postwar France and Le Corbusier received government support for its construction. The experimental nature of the project meant that the design was exempt from compliance with existing housing regulations and allowed to exceed standard budgetary guidelines.

In many ways, the Unité grew naturally from Le Corbusier's earlier work. The building is an eighteen-story block containing 337 housing units. It is lifted off the ground on massive pilotis and the rooftop is developed as a sundeck and play area for the residents. The design of individual units to include double-height living rooms with single-story bedroom and service areas was also based on earlier housing studies. Le Corbusier kept the Unité slab narrow (only 24.5 meters wide) and arranged the apartment units to ensure cross-ventilation. Individual units are slotted into the framework in a way that also minimizes the number of corridors needed (fig. 5.25).

5.24 (below) Le Corbusier, Unité d'habitation, Marseilles, France, 1945–52.

5.25 (bottom) Le Corbusier, Unité d'habitation, model, Marseilles, France, 1945.

The Unité is more than merely a summation of Le Corbusier's earlier work, however. The aesthetic quality of the design reveals a different sense of mass, texture, and surface than his International Style work of the 1920s and 1930s. The rough surfaces created by leaving the marks of the wooden construction forms exposed on the surface endowed the building with a rugged quality absent in earlier designs such as the Villa Savoye. In French, the term *béton brut* is used to describe this handling of concrete, and critics soon spoke of a "brutalist" conception of architecture. The heroic scale, bold massing, and rough textures of brutalist buildings such as the Unité represent the antithesis of the New Empiricism.

Like an ocean liner, one of Le Corbusier's favorite models of rational planning, the Unité was a self-contained world comprehensible largely in terms of his own formal development and the planning tenets of CIAM. The extent to which the Unité could serve as a model for the creation of viable neighborhoods soon emerged as a major issue within modernist design circles.

England: the Smithsons

In England, the husband and wife team of Alison (1928–1993) and Peter (b. 1923) Smithson tried to combine the reductive clarity of modernist design paradigms with what they claimed was an objective acknowledgment of the messy vitality of English working-class life-styles. Their 1952 Golden Lane Housing Project conformed to the Unité model of a narrow, multistoried housing block. The Smithsons imagined the corridors as "streets-in-the-air" capable of sustaining the same type of community life as the earthbound streets of older working-class neighborhoods. In their renderings for the Golden Lane scheme, the Smithsons tried to evoke the sociological reality of street life and popular culture at the same time as they described the formal elements of the design (fig. 5.26). The Smithsons' attempt to combine elite and popular models of cultural forms focused renewed discussion on the sociological basis of modern architecture. It is precisely the issue the Smithsons raised—the relationship between avant-garde and popular cultures—that would prove so difficult for architects and critics in the postwar period.

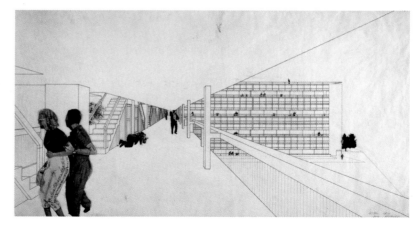

5.26 Alison and Peter Smithson, Golden Lane Housing Project, England, 1952. Drawing and collage with Joe Di Maggio and Marilyn Monroe, 20½ × 38⅓ in (52 × 97.5 cm). Collection Centre Georges Pompidou, Paris, France.

Following the ninth congress of the CIAM in 1953, Peter Smithson organized (along with the Dutch architects Aldo van Eyck [b. 1918] and Jacob Bakema [b. 1914]) Team X, a group of younger members of the organization. Team X assumed the task of preparing the agenda for the tenth CIAM congress, to be held in Dubrovnik in 1956. Team X criticized the CIAM approach, codified in the 1933 Athens Charter drafted at the fourth CIAM meeting, that analyzed the city according to a set of simplistic functional categories: dwelling, work, recreation, and transportation. Wary of reducing vibrant communities of human beings to anonymous statistics, the younger members of the organization were interested in developing ways to include the complexity of social relationships and group identity in their calculations. Rather than revitalizing the organization and bringing it in line with the new social reality created by the unprecedented material prosperity of the postwar era, the Team X critique split the CIAM along generational lines. The differences between generations proved too intractable to be resolved and the CIAM disbanded after a final meeting in Otterloo in 1959.

The United States

In America the growing tension between the idealist premises and social reality surrounding modernist planning came to a head in the field of public housing. In 1955 the Pruitt-Igoe Housing Project in Saint Louis, Missouri, was opened. The design by Minoru Yamasaki received favorable reviews in the professional architectural press. Like postwar housing projects across the country, however, crime, high vacancy rates and tenant dissatisfaction plagued the Pruitt-Igoe community. Seventeen years later, in a brutally frank acknowledgment that the scheme was a failure, the housing authority authorized the demolition of the problem-plagued project (fig. 5.27). The famous press photograph of the dynamiting of Pruitt-Igoe captured more than the collapse of a few derelict buildings—it captured the end of an era of modernist hegemony.

The stress within modern architecture built quickly in the 1950s and 1960s as the dream of housing projects erected in parklike settings gave way to the grim urban reality of disenfranchised communities trapped in dreary modernist buildings. Team X's efforts revealed the fault lines within the European Modern Movement, while the Cold War directed any significant public discussion of architecture and urbanism in the West into simplistic and unchallengeable categories of free (capitalist) versus totalitarian (socialist) approaches.

In the United States, the publication of Jane Jacob's *Death and Life of Great American Cities* provided critics of modernist planning with a powerful new voice. The postwar triumph of modernism brought little change in the status of women within the profession and the number of female architects remained small. Criticism, therefore, remained one of the few avenues available to women interested in issues of architectural and urban design. In the United States, for example, Ada Louise Huxtable, Esther McCoy, and Mildred Schmertz wrote regularly on a variety of design topics. Jacobs, a journalist by profession, argued that what made cities great and neighborhoods liveable could not be reduced to a limited set of physical planning criteria described in strictly quantifiable terms. Furthermore, she argued, the CIAM-inspired emphasis on traffic flows, single-use zoning, and the concentration of population in high-rise towers dispersed in parklike settings actually undermined the social and economic vitality of cities.

While Jacobs provided a powerful critique of the shortcomings of modernism, responsibility for the manifest failures of American public housing projects such as Pruitt-Igoe cannot be attributed entirely to modernist design theory or the choice of building typology. If high-rise design proved to be a disaster as public housing, the

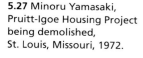

5.27 Minoru Yamasaki, Pruitt-Igoe Housing Project being demolished, St. Louis, Missouri, 1972.

same building type was far more successful in wealthier neighborhoods. Given sufficient investment in building services and maintenance, the high-rise building type can be a decent and desirable place to live.

To what, then, can the failure of projects like Pruitt-Igoe be attributed? Architecture inevitably bears the stamp of the society that brings it into existence. Racism, not typology, is the critical factor in explaining the failure of postwar public housing in America. Subsidized public housing formed an integral part of massive postwar campaigns of urban renewal in American cities. The clientele served by public housing consisted of predominately poor and non-white communities politically powerless to defend their own interests. Tragically, American architecture and urbanism in the 1950s and 1960s reflected the situation of a country still unwilling to extend the same political and social considerations to African-America, Latino, and Asian communities as those enjoyed by more affluent sectors of society. The public will to spend sufficient sums of money on public housing to ensure the same level of basic habitability evident in privately developed high-rise apartments for an affluent market simply did not exist. Evicted from neighborhoods targeted for redevelopment and resegregated in poorly funded housing projects, these communities were the victims of institutional racism as much as they were of modernist idealism.

Skyscrapers

The Alcoa and United Nations Buildings announced new directions in postwar skyscraper design. Twin high-rise apartment buildings at 860–880 Lakeshore Drive in Chicago designed by Ludwig Mies van der Rohe crystalized the new paradigm and boldly carried forward the International Style conception of transparent prismatic volumes into the postwar world (fig. 5.28). The identical treatment of the twin apartment towers reflected Mies's interest in standardization. Subtle adjustments in bay widths, a concern for proportion, and the attachment of I-beams to the surface are the sole means employed by Mies to enrich the otherwise spare design. Mies shared Bruno Taut's early enthusiasm for glass and had exhibited sketches for glass towers as early as 1919. While the vision of glass towers emerged early in the century, the means to realize those visions had to await the development of adequate glass products along with the gaskets and sealants required to fabricate metal and glass curtain walls. As in other areas of construction, it was wartime research and development that accelerated the introduction of new building technologies. Now installed as Dean of the School of Architecture at the Illinois Institute of Technology, Mies was instrumental in training a generation of young architects to work in the new design idiom of steel and glass.

Beginning in the 1950s, the firm of Skidmore, Owings, and Merrill (SOM) designed numerous International Style buildings for corporate clients. For the Lever House in New York City (fig. 5.29), SOM revived the distinctive design solution of Howe and Lescaze's 1931 PSFS Building (see fig. 1.37). The Lever House consists of two parts: a tall narrow slab containing offices and a low, two-story podium. The slab is positioned off-center over the podium and both units are sheathed in a green-tinted metal and glass curtain wall. Air conditioning, a rarity in offices before the war, became a standard feature in new office buildings: the Lever House, like most postwar skyscrapers, has no operable windows. The building's

5.28 Ludwig Mies van der Rohe, 860–880 North Lake Shore Drive Apartments, Chicago, Illinois, 1951.
Mies arranged the two rectangular slabs at right angles to each other. From different vantage points along the lake shore the visual relationship between the towers changes as the slender opening between them disappears from view. The absence of any distinction between the fronts and backs of the buildings adds to the abstract quality of the design.

5.29 Skidmore, Owings, and Merrill (designer Gordon Bunshaft), Lever House, New York, 1951–52.

The Lever House was the first postwar office building to develop an idea (originally suggested in the design of the PSFS Building) of treating the building's base and shaft as separate elements. Rather than the building resting on the ground, short piers lift it off the earth to create the image of glass-enclosed volumes floating over the street.

initial reception was very positive, the distinguished critic Lewis Mumford describing it in glowing terms:

> The Lever House is a building of outstanding qualities, mechanical, aesthetic, human . . . it has used to the full all the means now available for making a building comfortable, gracious, and handsome.
>
> (Mumford, p. 156)

Mumford concluded his review of the Lever House with a curious acknowledgment of the climate created by the Cold War:

> Fragile, exquisite, undaunted by the threat of being melted into a puddle by an atomic bomb, this building is a laughing refutation of "imperialist warmongering," and so it becomes an implicit symbol of hope for a peaceful world.
>
> (Mumford, p. 165)

The building won the first Honor Award bestowed by the American Institute of Architects in 1952 and, in 1956, the American journal *Architectural Record* ranked the Lever House as one of the most influential buildings of the preceding one hundred years. The Lever House epitomizes the International Style corporate glass box that came to dominate skyscraper design in the 1950s and 1960s. While buildings endure, often their reputations do not. With the advent of postmodernism, however, critics began to assail the glass box as inefficient in terms of energy consumption and disparage it as a symbol of a corporate culture of conformity and depersonalization. The Lever House remains an outstanding example of the postwar International Style—today the viewer's response to it is a revealing indication of his or her critical preferences and attitudes.

Strategies of Display

The 1951 "Festival of Britain"

World fairs and smaller national exhibitions provide valuable insights into the prevailing cultural themes and design strategies of their historical moments, as well as serve as nurseries for new ideas. To commemorate the centenary of the "Great Exhibition" of 1851, the British organized the "Festival of Britain" in 1951 (fig. 5.30). Staged on London's South Bank, the fair captured the ethos of postwar Britain. The festival's theme structures, the saucer-shaped Dome of Discovery designed by Ralph Tubbs (1912–1996) and the needlelike Skylon by Philip Powell (b. 1921) and John

5.30 "Festival of Britain," London, England, 1951.

Hidalgo Moya (b. 1920), invited comparison with the trylon and perisphere structures of the "1939 New York World's Fair." Like the original "Crystal Palace" of 1851 and the "1939 New York fair," the "Festival of Britain" celebrated scientific and technological progress. Pavilions were erected using lightweight metal frames covered with aluminum, concrete-asbestos, or stretched canvas panels.

As Director of Architecture for the "Festival of Britain," Hugh Casson (b. 1910) was responsible for the general plan of the twenty-seven-acre fairgrounds. Casson conceived of the event as an opportunity to provide a suitable model for the planning of new English towns. He rejected the Beaux-Arts tradition of axial avenues, regular cross streets, and *rond-points* (traffic circles). Instead, he developed an informal layout that reflected both an English affinity for picturesque compositions and the growing influence of Sweden's New Empiricism. The overall arrangement of the festival supported its didactic program concerning the benefits and responsibilities of consumer-citizens in modern England. Visitors were encouraged to follow a designated path through the festival visiting the various pavilions in sequence like chapters in a book. Concerned that the attempt to program the visitor's experience should appear too heavy-handed, the *Official Exhibition Guide* assured the festival goer: "This is a free country; and any visitors who . . . feel impelled to start with the last chapter and zig-zag their way backwards to the first chapter, will be as welcome as anyone else." This statement is yet another indication of the way in which the relationship between structure and choice as features of spatial experience was equated with the principles of freedom or totalitarianism in Cold War criticism. It is not that the "Festival of Britain" lacked structure; rather, the mechanisms for imposing order were less overtly formal than the monumental axes and precisely defined civic plazas that Western critics identified with the Communist design programs.

The 1959 "American National Exhibition," Moscow

While the architectural style of the fair may have been novel, Casson and Misha Black (1910–1977) employed a familiar design strategy for the "Festival of Britain." Individual pavilions devoted to different themes were arranged on the fairgrounds and visitors moved from one to another (hopefully) in the intended sequence. The same strategy, executed in various styles, had underlain the design of fairs since the nineteenth century.

One of the themes of this book deals with the modernization of design practice and this applies to exhibition design. Techniques of description and display continued to evolve. In 1959 the United States staged the "American National Exhibition" in Moscow as part of a program of cultural exchange. This was the site of the famous "kitchen debate" between Vice-President Richard Nixon and Soviet Premier Nikita Kruschchev in which the two leaders debated the respective merits of their political systems against the backdrop of a "typical" American kitchen filled with modern appliances. Just as the Alcoa Building and the Lever House solidified the relationship between corporate America and modern architects, the "American National Exhibition" signaled the federal government's embrace of modern design as the preferred mode for representing contemporary American values and culture.

George Nelson, chief exhibition designer, turned to the husband-and-wife team of Charles (1907–1978) and Ray (1912–1988) Eames for one of the most challenging projects in the exhibition. The Eames were asked to create an exhibit that would

5.31 Charles and Ray
Eames, US Pavilion with
film monitors showing
Glimpses of the USA,
from "American National
Exhibition," Moscow,
Russia, 1959.

depict a typical American day. They responded with a twelve-minute film entitled
Glimpses of the USA, describing twenty-four hours in seven different parts of the
country. The film combined still photography with short film clips in a rapidly
paced collage of 2,200 images; featured sequences described supermarkets, factories, skyscrapers, suburbs, dams, and houses of worship. Inside a geodesic dome
designed by Buckminster Fuller, the Eames arranged seven giant screens and
projected different parts of the film story simultaneously on all seven screens
(fig. 5.31).

Glimpses of the USA compressed an enormous amount of information into a relatively brief film and overwhelmed the visitor with a flood of images. The juxtaposition of Fuller's geodesic dome and the multiscreen format suggested a new
dialectic between space and screen that went beyond the traditional perspectival
concerns of cinema architecture in which the architecture framed the screen and
focused the viewer's attention on a single surface. The triumph of modernism represented not only the installation of modern architecture as the leading form of
design in the postwar world but also the triumph of continually evolving forms of
modern visual culture. Camera and the screen now begin to emerge as fundamental
tools in design practice and, as the second half of the century unfolds, they start to
rival pen and paper in importance.

Chapter 6

Trends in Postwar Architecture

As nations recovered from global war and adjusted their economies for peace-time, the developed world entered a period of unprecedented prosperity. The rate of recovery varied from place to place, but in general the third quarter of the twentieth century was a prosperous period for architects and builders, especially in the United States. The war increased America's prominence around the world; with the atomic bomb, America had ended the conflict as the dominant global military power. But American influence rested on more than force of arms. The United States controlled almost two thirds of global industrial production and American forms of both popular and elite culture reached every corner of the globe. When, in a famous editorial in the February 17, 1941 issue of *Life* magazine, Henry Luce declared that the twentieth century was now "The American Century" it was more than an idle boast; it represented a recognition of how pervasive American products such as Coca Cola, Hollywood films, and American pop music had become.

Through such economic programs as the Marshall Plan, educational exchanges as the Fulbright Program, and aggressive cultural campaigns involving traveling exhibitions, concert tours, and publications, the United States projected an Americanized version of the good life around the world. The majority of buildings discussed in this chapter are, therefore, American. This chapter explores trends, patterns, and concerns characteristic of the period by focusing on developments in a limited set of designed environments including domestic, campus, museum, and church designs. This list is suggestive rather than exhaustive, but like the tesserae of a mosaic, each contributes a piece to the larger story of architecture in the third quarter of the twentieth century.

While the United States projected American models abroad, in the 1940s and 1950s the American design community began to register the impact of recently arrived European architects driven from their homes in Central Europe by Fascism. With impeccable modernist credentials based on their association with the Bauhaus, Ludwig Mies van der Rohe and Walter Gropius assumed influential positions as directors of architectural programs in American universities. Enjoying a degree of institutional support and professional acceptance that exceeded anything they had experienced in prewar Europe, they could now formalize and transmit their conception of modern architecture to a younger generation of architects.

In 1938 Mies van der Rohe accepted the post as Director of the School of Architecture at the Illinois Institute of Technology (IIT) in Chicago where he combined

Charles and Ray Eames,
Eames House, interior,
Santa Monica, California,
1945–49.

6.1 Daniel Brenner, Concert Hall Project (based on Mies van der Rohe's "Concert Hall Project," 1942), 1946. Perspective view, foil, and wood veneer on photo enlargement, mounted on board, 14⅛ × 29¼ in (36 × 74.2 cm). Art Institute of Chicago.

teaching with professional practice. A 1946 student project by Daniel Brenner (1917–1977) for a concert hall illustrates just how thoroughly IIT students absorbed Mies's lessons (fig. 6.1). Brenner's project was based on a 1942 Mies design for a concert hall. Mies's proposal took the form of a collage in which he superimposed a series of planar elements on a photograph of a factory interior designed originally by the industrial architect Albert Kahn. In subsequent years Mies assigned the same design problem as a studio exercise at IIT. Although Brenner suggested different surfaces for several of the planar elements, his version of the concert hall faithfully adheres to Mies's original design, including the sculpture of a seated nude figure in the foreground.

The rational, flexible, and technologically sophisticated qualities of American industrial building allowed Mies to realize his concept of a universal spatial paradigm for the modern age. The Miesian concept of space was based on a clear span structure that, ideally, provided maximum flexibility by reducing to a minimum the number of fixed internal partitions. The concert hall project elevated Albert Kahn's system of industrial architecture to the status of high art by transforming space for industry into space for culture through the insertion of a series of planar elements that articulate the interior without compartmentalizing it. In contrast to the seemingly weightless planes, the human figure provides the only note of gravity and mass in the design.

The presence of the figure (in the form of a sculpture by the artist Aristide Maillol) brings into sharp relief the contrast between classical and modernist conceptions of architecture. The classical tradition asserts the anthropomorphic basis of architectural form, in which basic units such as columns and capitals ultimately referred to the human figure. The huge steel trusses and thin planes of the concert hall, however, owe nothing to the organic form and proportions of the human figure. As a viable design for a concert hall, the scheme is flawed; serious questions about the acoustical quality of the design remained unresolved. As an architectural statement of a philosophical issue, however, the design is eloquent. The contrast between the human figure and its spatial setting suggests the existential problem of humankind creating a sense of place within the universalizing space of modernist architecture. As a studio exercise, Brenner's design indicates how literally the Miesian aesthetic was passed on to a younger generation of students.

Domestic Architecture

As it did throughout the twentieth century, the detached house served as a revealing index of postwar design thinking about a variety of architectural issues. Following the economic depression of the 1930s and wartime restrictions on new construction, there was an enormous demand for housing. Developers were eager to provide affordable models for a lucrative private market. But many of the most famous house designs of the 1950s and 1960s bore little or no relationship to the developers' mass-market designs. Architects continued to approach the design of a house as an opportunity to articulate larger concerns about the nature of modern architecture and, by extension, contemporary life.

Mies van der Rohe

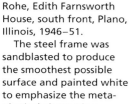

6.2 Ludwig Mies van der Rohe, Edith Farnsworth House, south front, Plano, Illinois, 1946–51.
The steel frame was sandblasted to produce the smoothest possible surface and painted white to emphasize the metaphysical abstraction of the design. The floor and exterior deck were paved with Roman travertine.

Mies van der Rohe transferred his interest in steel-framed construction and uninterrupted space directly to domestic architecture. In 1946 he designed a weekend retreat for Dr. Edith Farnsworth in Plano, Illinois, near Chicago (fig. 6.2). A number of architects including Richard Neutra and Buckminster Fuller had grappled with the practical problems of using metal-framed structural systems for domestic design but no one idealized the concept to the degree Mies did in the Farnsworth House. Mies distilled the concept of house to a single glass-enclosed volume, recasting the idea of the primitive hut in terms of modern tectonics and materials. The Farnsworth House weaves together various threads in the fabric of postwar art and design, including the minimalist aesthetic of abstract modern art, an interest in industrial materials, and the elegant simplicity of Japanese design.

Mies's treatment of living space as a single transparent volume provoked harsh criticism as well as praise. *House Beautiful* editor Elizabeth Gordon attacked the International Style as un-American in an April 1953 article entitled "The Threat to

the Next America." Gordon blasted what she called a "self-chosen elite" of museum curators, academics, and architectural critics for promoting the most extreme forms of modernist design such as the Farnsworth House:

> They are all trying to sell the idea that "less is more," both as a criterion for design, and as a basis for judgement of the good life. They are promoting unlivability, stripped-down emptiness, lack of storage space and therefore lack of possessions.
>
> (Gordon, p. 128)

Gordon's essay serves as a reminder that even during the postwar decades when modernism constituted the dominant model for design thinking, it did not go unchallenged. If history is to provide an intelligible portrait of complexity, then episodes of resistance as well as acceptance must be included in the account.

Philip Johnson

While the impracticalities of life in a glass box rendered the Farnsworth House an unlikely model for the mainstream housing market, the concept fascinated many architects. In 1949 Philip Johnson (b. 1906) began work on his own residence in New Canaan, Connecticut (fig. 6.3). In some ways, the Farnsworth and Johnson houses studies in contrast. Painted white and lifted off the ground on eight steel I-beams, the Farnsworth House appears to float serenely over its grassy site. Johnson's Glass House, in contrast, rests firmly on the ground. The black steel frame and brick cylinder containing a fireplace and bathroom define the volume and anchor the composition in a manner different from Mies's more ethereal design. But Johnson conceived of his house as the centerpiece of a large estate; rather than

6.3 Philip Johnson, Glass House, New Canaan, Connecticut, 1949–50.
Due to the opaque ceiling and transparent walls of the Glass House, visitors have the uncanny sensation of being definitely under a roof but not quite inside a building. The house's steel framework, painted black, frames views of the surrounding landscape just as the black steel easel frames the landscape painting visible in the living area.

possessing the self-contained quality of the Farnsworth House, Johnson House is meant to be seen as part of an ensemble of buildings that grew over the years to include a solid-brick guest house, lake pavilion, and galleries to display Johnson's extensive collection of painting and sculpture.

Philip Johnson is a critical figure in any account of twentieth-century architecture. Along with Henry Russell Hitchcock, he organized the Museum of Modern Art's influential "International Style" exhibition in 1932 and worked tirelessly to promote the cause of modern architecture. In the late 1940s, he studied architecture under Walter Gropius at Harvard and with his New Canaan residence he launched a very successful career as a professional architect. In addition to his own significant body of work, Johnson became one of the most powerful figures in the American architectural community. His extensive network of personal connections with corporate, educational, and political leaders allowed him to promote emerging talent, validate new directions in architecture, and influence design discourse.

6.4 Charles and Ray Eames, Eames House, Santa Monica, California, 1945–49.

Charles and Ray Eames

The third steel-framed house to be considered here, like Johnson's Glass House, was conceived as the designers' own residence, but it represents a very different model of design. The husband-and-wife team of Charles and Ray Eames ranged effortlessly across the boundaries of different design fields with a professional portfolio that included architecture, furniture, toy, graphic, and exhibition design. Their own home and studio in Santa Monica, California, was part of a series of steel-framed houses erected in southern California in the late 1940s and early 1950s (fig. 6.4). Known collectively as the Case Study Houses, they explored the application of modern construction technology to residential designs which were attuned to the region's climate and life-style.

Although Mies van der Rohe and Philip Johnson used industrial materials, their houses were realized with uniquely designed details and represented a curiously handcrafted approach to modern building. When the Eames began work on their residence, they rejected the craft-based approach of Mies and Johnson. Instead, they worked with regular stock items such as the light steel joists that were available in steel manufacturer's catalogs. They substituted colorful opaque panels fabricated of plywood, plaster, or asbestos for the glass walls of Mies and Johnson's designs. The result is not constructed in the traditional sense of that word; rather the house is assembled out of a kit of parts drawn from the world of material possibilities. Design here is understood more as a process of perceptive selection from an existing array of materials and systems than as original creation.

The same artful process of selection and arrangement governs the interior design of the Eames House (see page 166). The Miesian aesthetic of *beinahe nicht* (almost nothing) is rejected in favor of a lively interior landscape filled with furniture, artwork, and artifacts; contemporary furniture shares space with folk art and peasant crafts from around the world. The result is a radical rethinking of the image of standardization developed in the 1920s and 1930s. At the Bauhaus, for example, the industrialization of design was visualized in terms of the repetition of identical units (see fig. 3.25), and Bauhaus designers developed standardized designs for furniture that could be mass produced. The image of standardization was one of coordination and uniformity at every scale from furniture to urban design. Charles and Ray Eames, however, took standardized building elements and combined them with their own tastes in a way that suggested variety rather than uniformity. Peter Smithson recognized the Eames's distinctive achievement. In an insightful essay in the September 1966 issue of *Architectural Design*, he wrote:

> The Eames-aesthetic . . . is based on an equally careful selection but with extra-cultural surprise, rather than harmony of profile, as its criteria. A kind of wide-eyed wonder of seeing the culturally disparate together and so happy with each other. This sounds like whimsy, but the basic vehicle—the steel lattice frame in the case of the house, the colour film and the colour processing in the graphics work, the pressings and mouldings in the case of the furniture—are ordinary to the culture.
>
> (Smithson, *Architectural Design*, September 1966, p. 443)

Bruce Goff

Characterized by a visceral, tactile richness, the work of Bruce Goff (1904–1982) represents the Dionysian counterpart to the cerebral and abstract Apollonian qualities of the Farnsworth House. Goff's Bavinger House of 1950 is conceived as a spiral around a central fifty-five-foot tall mast from which the roof is suspended by cables

6.5 Bruce Alonzo Goff, Eugene Bavinger House, Bartlesville, Oklahoma, August 6, 1950. Elevation showing bridge, colored pencil on Diazo lineprint, 25½ × 34½ in (65 × 87.5 cm). Art Institute of Chicago.

(fig. 6.5). Inside, circular platforms are arranged at different levels within a single continuous interior volume. The rough stone surfaces, unexpected choices for materials, and spatial dynamics of the house provoke a rich, sensuous experience. The Bavinger House eludes easy description; references to primitive and archetypal forms such as caves and tents compete with futuristic images of science fiction castles as the visitor tries to decipher the eccentric quality of the design. Such resistance to simple description is an important feature of the organic tradition in American architecture which continued, in the postwar years, to offer an alternative to the rationalized imagery and conventions of modernism in design.

Frank Lloyd Wright

Frank Lloyd Wright remained the preeminent figure among practitioners of organic architecture. The war had less impact on the direction of Wright's work than on that of most other architects active in the middle third of the century. The buildings examined here, in fact, have their roots in the decade of the 1930s but acquire a special significance in terms of Wright's place in postwar design discourse.

In the 1950s, Wright came to personify for many the romantic ideal of the creative genius in architecture. His highly personal approach to life and work was often contrasted in the press with the corporate model of organization and architecture adopted by large firms such as SOM. Wright's commitment to organic architecture, his belief in the centrality of nature-awareness for American culture, and his sensitivity to material and place are the important threads of continuity that define his entire career and, at the same time, marginalized him in professional circles during the 1950s. Philip Johnson sardonically described Wright as the greatest American architect of the nineteenth century.

6.6 Frank Lloyd Wright, Taliesin West, Scottsdale, Arizona, 1938.
Low masonry walls constructed by Wright's apprentices using local materials define different zones within the sprawling Taliesin complex. The rugged and earthy beauty of Taliesin represents Wright's response during this period to the pristine and abstract forms of the increasingly popular International Style.

The rugged texture and rough-hewn forms of Taliesin West, his residence near Scottsdale, Arizona, reflected his response to the desert terrain of the American Southwest (fig. 6.6). Like Goff's Bavinger House, Taliesin West represented the rejection of the pristine form and industrial precision of the steel-framed glass box, whether that box served as an office building or a private house. Wright began work on Taliesin West in the 1937 and the design of the compound continued to evolve until his death in 1959. His annual routine involved spending part of each year at his home, Taliesin in Wisconsin, and wintering in Arizona. In 1932 he founded the Taliesin Fellowship, a school for young architects which moved with him on his annual migration from Wisconsin to Arizona and back. Taliesin West included a drafting studio that doubled as school room for

the Fellowship (fig. 6.7). Wright's model of design education balanced manual labor and agricultural fieldwork with time spent in the studio and on construction sites. The Taliesin Fellowship could be criticized for exploiting student labor for Wright's personal benefit but it is important to recognize that Wright treated his life as a seamless fabric of living, working, and teaching. The students became integral members of the unique community that Wright fashioned around himself. The Taliesin Fellowship remains a rare postwar American example of an alternative model for architectural education. Architecture was by now firmly installed as an academic program in American institutions of higher education, with accreditation standards and degree options that distanced the profession from the apprentice system associated with the building trades.

Also in the 1930s, Wright developed a new formula for domestic architecture which he continued to work on for the rest of his career: the Usonian home. Usonia was a neologism coined by Wright to describe his vision of an egalitarian society based on the principles of organic architecture. Wright's Usonian house was intended to serve as the cradle of Usonian democracy and culture. In 1935 he exhibited a model of Broadacre City, his name for the settlement pattern he envi-

6.7 Frank Lloyd Wright, Taliesin West, drafting room, Scottsdale, Arizona, 1942.

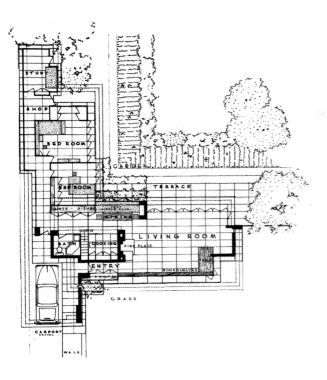

6.8 Frank Lloyd Wright, Herbert Jacobs House, plan, Madison, Wisconsin, 1936–37.

sioned as the setting for Usonia. A year later, Wright designed the Jacobs House in Wisconsin, the first of his Usonians to be built (figs. 6.8, 6.9). He used a simple planning grid based on a two-by-four foot module, and set the house directly on a concrete floor slab equipped with radiant heating. Still committed to innovative approaches to building, Wright designed a novel composite wall system. He lined both sides of a plywood slab with insulation material and then sandwiched this core between board and batten siding on both exterior and interior surfaces. All the elements of later Usonian houses are present in the Jacobs House—planning grid, floor slab, and composite wall—although later Usonian designs would use different geometric modules and replace the pine boards of the Jacobs House with cypress. Wright scholar and archivist Bruce Brooks Pfeiffer has counted fifty-eight built and more than one hundred unbuilt designs by Wright for Usonians. More modest in size and price than the Prairie Style homes, the Usonian house was the equal to Wright's earlier work in the claims he made for it as an exemplar of the Emersonian ideal in American culture.

Wright was a prolific author as well as designer but he was not the only one with first hand knowledge to write about his work. Client accounts offer valuable insights into the reception of architecture and provide a critical balance to descriptions of the designer's intent. Wright's clients have described eloquently the experience of living in a Wright-designed house. In a 1969 essay, Marjorie Leighey, the

6.9 Frank Lloyd Wright, Herbert Jacobs House, Madison, Wisconsin, 1936–37. Pencil, colored pencil, and ink on tracing paper, 21 × 31¾ in (53.3 × 80.6 cm).

second owner of the Pope-Leighey Usonian house, described the process of coming to terms with life in a Wright-designed house:

> At first there is the quiet pleasure and thankfulness for being surrounded by something so admirable to look upon—the four walls of any of the rooms. Then comes the business of living. The need for storage space is felt almost to desperation. Mr. Wright's own teaching that possessions merely clutter one's life is recalled, and an attempt is made to reduce possessions. . . . Comes a time of rebellion, an anger at any dwelling-place that presumes to dictate how its occupants live. Comes the time for decision. Do we truly like the house. . . . Again the beauty spoke. It held, compelled. . . . Possessions continued to be reduced. . . . Great freedom and ever greater simplicity follow once simplicity has been entered upon as a deliberate choice. . . . In simplicity the individual comes at last to the place from which he started, the human level. He recognizes that it is only as himself, another created being, that he meets all creatures, animal or human. He has an increased awareness of every aspect of life and that God is the Lord of life. . . . Beauty and truth co-mingle in this house.

(Leighey, pp. 60–2)

Elsewhere in this survey, architecture's role in promoting modernization or propagandizing on behalf of political ideologies has been noted, but Wright's career reminds us that architecture has always had the power to focus experience and intensify perception in ways that enrich the lives of men and women. While Marjorie Leighey acknowledged the very problem that concerned Elizabeth Gordon—the lack of storage space in modern houses—she responded in a different way. Rather than finding it a threat to America's culture of material abundance, Marjorie Leighey found a renewed appreciation of life, truth, and beauty in the Usonian ideal of simplicity.

With its low, horizontal configuration, informal living space, and intimate connection to its site, Wright's Usonian house proved to be prophetic of postwar developments. In the mid-1940s, as numerous competitions were staged soliciting designs for new homes, the ranch house began to emerge as a popular choice. A prize-winning entry for one such competition sponsored by the *Chicago Tribune* illustrates the distinctive ranch house type (fig. 6.10). The ranch house fused elements of Western vernacular with Wrightian interest in the continuity of indoor and outdoor spaces. Like the Usonian, the ranch house was set directly on the ground and one did not have to navigate steps to enter and exit. Large expanses of plate glass created a visual continuity between inside and out that complemented the continuity of the ground plane. The patio and yard area functioned as outdoor "rooms" and were direct extensions of the interior living spaces, making the ranch appear larger than it really was. Popular shelter and women's magazines were filled with articles extolling the virtues of modern kitchens and describing how to entertain in the informal domestic settings of the ranch house.

While there are strong affinities between the Usonian and ranch

6.10 R. R. Burns, Jr. (delineated by I. Floyd Yewell), Ranch house, Chicagoland Prize Homes Competition, *Chicago Tribune*, 1945. Watercolor on illustration board, 16½ × 22½ in (42 × 57 cm). Gift of D. Coder Taylor. Courtesy Art Institute of Chicago.

house types, it is important to recognize their differences as well and to distinguish between the realms of high design and popular architecture. Wright's Usonian ideal was transformed by developers to accommodate the demands of an unprecedented mass market for new houses after the war. The tectonic innovations and modular geometry of the Jacobs House, for example, were abandoned in favor of more traditional framing and mechanical systems better suited to the constructional systems adopted by such developers as William Levitt, Cliff May, or Joseph Eichler, each of whom built thousands of new homes in the two decades following 1945.

Wright knew his clients and they shared his lofty Emersonian idealism, but in developer-driven programs of new home construction such architect–client relationships were rare. The client became an abstraction, a creation of marketing studies and demographic profiling. It is an indication of Wright's genius that his Usonian homes strike a delicate balance between features common to all and details unique to each. Such subtlety of design is lost in the developers' approach based on appealing to the common denominators of defined market segments.

6.11 Victor Gruen, Northland Center, Detroit, Michigan, 1954.

Suburban Developments

No account of the postwar American house is complete without an acknowledgment of the larger settlement pattern of which it was a part. While European countries tended to adopt the model of direct state intervention in the field of housing, the United States pursued a different route. The Federal Housing Administration (FHA) ensured that mortgage money was readily available but left middle-class buyers to operate within the private real-estate market. FHA lending policies favored the development of so-called virgin sites on the periphery of cities rather than the refurbishing of existing housing stock in the urban core. This accelerated the growth of suburbs and the development of life-styles dependent upon the automobile. Originally, suburbs clustered along commuter rail lines that radiated like spokes from urban centers. The automobile altered the linkage between center and periphery, however, and new developments sprawled outward in all directions. Suburban shopping malls specifically designed to serve customers that arrived by automobile began to compete with urban retail districts.

The Northland Center near Detroit, designed by Victor Gruen (1903–1980) is typical of the suburban shopping mall that brought together under one roof large department stores, small speciality shops, and dining and entertainment facilities (fig. 6.11). The contrast between Northland and earlier suburban retail developments vividly illustrates the new character of postwar developments. In 1916 Harold Van Doren Shaw (1869–1926) designed Market Square for Lake Forest,

Illinois (fig. 6.12). Market Square is located across the street from the railroad station that provided commuter rail service to nearby Chicago. The U-shaped development originally included twenty-five shops, twelve offices, and twenty-eight apartments above the shops, with parking spaces lining the inside of the square. While Shaw provided for the automobile, the mixture of residential and commercial uses and his picturesque design reinforces the traditional character of the village. By contrast, surrounded by acres of parking, Northland reflects the enormous scale of postwar developments; the charming streetscape of Market Square is replaced by modern storefronts devoted to maximizing the display of merchandise.

6.12 Howard Van Doren Shaw, Market Square, Lake Forest, Illinois, 1916. Courtesy Art Institute of Chicago.

Accommodating the automobile was only part of the new challenges that suburban developments posed for the architectural profession. In an August 1950 feature article on suburban retail development, the American journal *Architectural Forum* described the task confronting such architects as Gruen:

> For his new job, he needs to combine skills ranging from those of traffic engineer and city planner to those of the chain store leasing specialist—not because he will dream of undertaking these jobs in his own firm, but because he will need to coordinate the work of experts in a dozen fields.

(Gruen, *Architectural Forum*, August 1950, p. 110)

Not everyone was enamored with the new suburban lifestyles. Design critics and sociologists warned their readers about the culture of conformity and social isolation that they saw emerging behind the crisply manicured lawns and picture windows of suburban communities. Consumers, however, responded to the developer-driven pattern of suburban homes with enthusiasm. In the wake of the Great Depression and the war, there was an enormous demand for new homes. FHA money made the purchase of a home possible for many and stimulated the market for new construction. The various models proposed by developers were perceived as superior to existing prewar housing stock because they provided increased living space and modern amenities unmatched by older apartment buildings and bungalow neighborhoods.

The sheer material abundance of American consumer culture both attracted and repelled foreign observers. The British Pop artist Eduardo Paolozzi captured this ambivalence in his 1948 collage *It's a Psychological Fact Pleasure Helps Your Disposition* (fig. 6.13). Paolozzi's collage can be read as both a critique of the shallowness of Amer-

6.13 Eduardo Paolozzi, *It's a Psychological Fact Pleasure Helps Your Disposition*, 1948. Collage on paper, 14 × 9 in (36.2 × 24.4 cm) Tate Gallery, London, England.

ican culture with its fixation on hygiene and, at the same time, a denunciation of the deprivation and drudgery of postwar life in Britain and Europe. Nothing could be farther from the "less is more" aesthetic of Mies's Farnsworth House or the Usonian simplicity of Wright's Jacobs House than this image of the American home as a warehouse for the modern consumer.

Central and South America: Oscar Niemeyer and Juan O'Gorman

Consumerism and developer-driven design were not the only forces at work subverting the purity of modernist design ideals. Outside the United States, questions of regional and racial identities shaped the development of modern architecture.

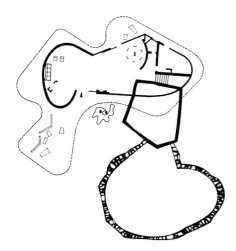

Designers in Central and South America began to enjoy international recognition only rarely achieved before the war. In Brazil, Oscar Niemeyer began describing his work in terms of an uninhibited "plastic freedom." In an interview, Niemeyer explained his architecture as "one which makes an appeal to the imagination, to things that are new and beautiful and capable of arousing surprise and emotion by their very human creativeness." His own house in Rio de Janiero, designed in 1953, expresses his sense of plastic freedom in the undulating outline of the plan (figs. 6.14, 6.15). In his handling of the relationship between the structural columns and the glazed walls, and the incorporation of a boulder into the interior, Niemeyer demonstrated a sophisticated understanding of the work of architects as different as Mies van der Rohe and Frank Lloyd Wright. Yet Niemeyer's house is hardly derivative in character. The austerity of the Farnsworth House and the earthiness of Falling Water is replaced by a flamboyance and a fluidity

6.14 (above) Oscar Niemeyer, Niemeyer House, plan, Canoa, Rio de Janeiro, Brazil, 1953.

Set amidst dense vegetation on a steep hillside, the site's shape is conveyed in the eccentric, curvilinear outline of this plan. Like Frank Lloyd Wright at Falling Water (see figs. 2.35, 2.36), Niemeyer incorporated a boulder in his design as a way of establishing a creative tension between the domains of nature and human artifice.

6.15 (right) Oscar Niemeyer, Niemeyer House, living room, Canoa, Rio de Janeiro, Brazil, 1953.

6.16 Juan O'Gorman, O'Gorman House, El Pedregal, Mexico City, Mexico, 1953–56.

of space and form that European and American critics tended to categorize (and not always in approving terms) as Latin.

Another facet of Latin American modernism is revealed in a house that Juan O'Gorman (1905–1982) designed for himself in the El Pedregal neighborhood of Mexico City (fig. 6.16). Early in his career, O'Gorman's work reflected his interest in the ideas of Le Corbusier. His house and studios for Diego Rivera and Frida Kahlo, completed in 1932 in the San Angel district of Mexico City, follows the tenets of the International Style. O'Gorman subsequently abandoned Eurocentric models and began to develop a distinctively Mexican conception of modern architecture in which modernism was equated with freedom both from Mexico's colonial heritage and from the more positivist and technocratic aspects of the European program of modernization. He admired the indigenous character of Taliesin West and once described his own development as an architect in terms of a shift from Le Corbusier to Frank Lloyd Wright as sources of inspiration.

It would be an oversimplification, however, to treat O'Gorman as a Mexican disciple of Wright's organic philosophy. His postwar work is rooted in an appreciation for the rich legacy of ancient Mesoamerican civilizations. O'Gorman began to incorporate elements of the mythology and iconography of pre-Conquest cultures in his designs: his house is encrusted with mosaic decoration and the mask-like facade is based on the image of the Aztec deity Tlaloc. O'Gorman's telluric version of modernism attempts to enlist the primal energy of ancient Mesoamerican civilizations in the development of a fiercely independent cultural identity for modern Mexico. The contrast between Niemeyer's and O'Gorman's designs indicates the multiple forms of modernity evident in Central and South America after the war.

Campus Architecture

In the third quarter of the twentieth century, the number of young people attending universities rose dramatically. Before the war, the population of university students in western Europe could be numbered in the low hundred thousands. The historian Eric Hobsbawm estimates that Germany, France, and Britain, three of the most developed countries in Europe, *together* had no more than 150,000 students pursuing a university degree at any one time. Within decades, the number of students in western Europe had grown into the millions. The phenomenal growth in higher education was not confined to Europe. The end of colonialism created opportunities for formerly subject countries to nurture their intellectual resources, and higher education was an important part of national agendas for development. The modern economy required more administrators, technical experts, and teachers than in the past and therefore was favorable to the expansion of higher education. Finally, access to higher education also served an important social function in defining class status and demarcating hierarchies of exclusiveness within the growing middle class. This expansion of higher education inevitably entailed a corresponding increase in new university construction. Furthermore, campus architecture became a critical microcosm of the values, ideals, and strategies shaping the postwar world.

The United States

The Graduate Center at Harvard University, designed by Walter Gropius and completed in 1950, signaled the new direction of postwar campus architecture in the United States (fig. 6.17). In place of the closed quadrangles of traditional campus planning, the Graduate Center consists of eight buildings arranged to create a series of informally linked courtyards. Seven of the buildings serve as dormitories; the eighth is a commons building equipped with dining facilities, lounges, and meeting rooms. The architecture is unabashedly modern, with flat roofs, horizontal windows, and smooth surfaces on the exterior.

The vast majority of American campus architecture in the first half of the century consisted of variations on classical, Georgian, or Collegiate Gothic models. In

6.17 (left) Walter Gropius, Harkness Commons, Graduate Center, Harvard University, Cambridge, Massachusetts, 1948.

6.18 (below) Skidmore, Ownings, and Merrill, Air Force Academy, Colorado Springs, 1954.

the Harvard Graduate Center, however, Gropius enlisted the prestige of one of the nation's oldest and most respected universities in the cause of modern architecture just as one of the greatest periods of campus construction was about to get underway. The Graduate Center launched postwar campus design on a new course. And its lessons were clear: physical context and institutional traditions were either to be ignored or filtered through a process of abstraction that ultimately eroded the distinctive sense of place and continuity which had been an integral part of prewar campus architecture. In the 1950s and 1960s, new campus architecture introduced the materials, forms, and environments of modernism to a generation of students.

As an addition to an existing campus, the Harvard Graduate Center was one part of a larger whole and coexisted (however awkwardly) with buildings conceived according to other architectural principles. A second category of university architecture involved the design of new campuses according to a single unified design vision. In 1954 the architectural firm of Skidmore, Ownings, and Merrill received the commission for the design of the new United States Air Force Academy in Colorado Springs (fig. 6.18). The same building technology used to fabricate metal and glass curtain walls for high-rise office buildings was utilized in the construction of the Air Force Academy. In formal and tectonic terms, its uncompromisingly modern design shows more affinity with the commercial construction of the period than it does with the building traditions of either the Military Academy at West Point, New York, or the Naval Academy at Annapolis, Maryland. The main academy buildings are designed as rectilinear volumes along a central parade ground. When the cadets parade, the military precision of their formations resonates with the precision of modern building technology and the entire campus can be understood as a modernist *gesamtkunstwerk* of the highest order. Set on a large terrace, the self-contained order and consistency of the campus is juxtaposed to the rugged landscape of the nearby mountains. There is an epic quality to the site at the Air Force Academy as the epitome of modern technology and sublime nature confront each other beneath the vast western sky.

Italy

In Italy, Giancarlo De Carlo (b. 1919) designed a master plan for the growth of the Free University at Urbino that demonstrates a very different approach. The swelling population of students necessitated the creation of a new campus and De Carlo developed a plan that took into account not only the projected enrollment figures but also the topographical and historical context of Urbino. Construction work on a series of new residential colleges began in the mid-1960s and continued in stages until 1980.

Each college contains dormitories, eating facilities, and meeting rooms. To relieve congestion in the city center, the various colleges were laid out along the crest of a hill just outside the center, adjacent to a former Capuchin monastery (figs. 6.19, 6.20). De Carlo sited each college to maximize available views and adjusted the layouts to harmonize with the hillside contours. Absent here is any sense of the confrontation established at the Air Force Academy between civilization and nature. Instead of the aggressive modernism of the Academy, De Carlo explored the possibility of creating a modern restatement of the typical formal elements and spaces of Italian hill towns. Within the campus, a variety of informal spaces are created. To achieve the unity and material consistency displayed by

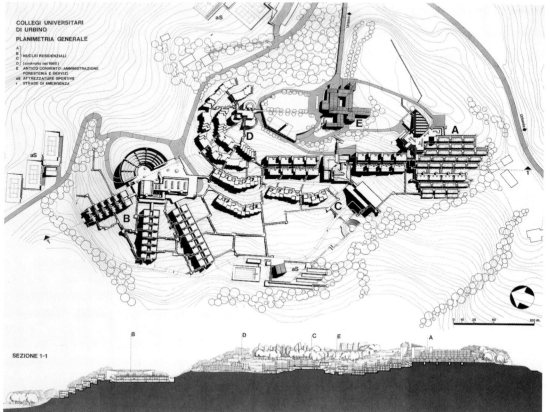

medieval towns, De Carlo restricted his choice of building materials to brick and reinforced concrete. De Carlo's work at Urbino is an important early example of a growing interest among modern architects in contextually sensitive designs informed by an appreciation of historical patterns of developments.

Mexico

The construction of the new Ciudad Universitaria in Mexico City, begun in 1950, represents another noteworthy variation on the internationalism of postwar modern architecture. Enrique del Moral (1905–1987) and Mario Pani (1911–1993) were responsible for the master plan; they coordinated the efforts of one hundred and fifty architects, engineers, and landscape architects involved in the design and construction of the new facility. Separate zones were provided for academic, residential, and athletic facilities, and the various schools within the university were designed as freestanding buildings around a central plaza. The new campus was erected on the ruins of Cuicuilo, an ancient settlement from the period 600–200 BCE. The historical significance of the site as the cradle of ancient civilization in central Mexico and the mythic dimension of racial identity were important components of the iconographic program for the Ciudad Universitaria. Carlos Lazo, the general administrator for the university project, stressed this theme of connection with the past in his remarks at the cornerstone ceremonies:

> In this same site where the Nauhuas and Olmecas met in the Valley of Mexico, in the pyramid of Cuicuilco, the most ancient culture of the continent appeared from the contemplation of this land and this sky. . . . We are not laying the first stone of the first building of Ciudad Universitaria, we are laying one more stone in the fervent construction of our Mexico.

(Burian, p. 94)

6.21 Juan O'Gorman and Gustavo Saavedra, Library, Ciudad Universitaria, Mexico City, Mexico, 1951–53.

This desire to establish a connection between the ancient, revered past and a thoroughly modern present stamped the architecture of the Ciudad Universitaria with a distinctive character, a character evident in such buildings as the main library, designed by Juan O'Gorman and Gustavo Saavedra (fig. 6.21). In place of the transparent curtain walls of metal and glass typical of postwar modernism, the library (along with other university buildings) was provided with expansive surfaces suitable for mural decoration. Abstraction is rejected in favor of representational imagery which fuses ancient and modern signs and symbols. The goal expressed in the architectural and decorative program of the Ciudad Universitaria to be both modern and Mexican—to find a national version of the International Style—appears contradictory only if modernity is equated strictly with a single international version of modernism. The emergence of multiple forms of modernity is an important development in the history of modernism in the second half of the twentieth century.

The USSR

Soviet architecture in the immediate postwar years followed a different path than design in the West. The Moscow State University, for example, demonstrates a very different solution to the problem of housing an academic institution. Rather than conceived as a group of buildings, the university was planned as a single, enormous structure (fig. 6.22). The university building was one of eight such towers (of which seven were ultimately built) to be erected at key points around the city. There is no strict relationship between architectural type and functional program for these towers and they served a variety of purposes including government offices, hotels, and apartments. According to Soviet planning ideology of the late 1940s and early 1950s, the dispersal of tall buildings across the city would distinguish Moscow, as a model Communist city, from the concentration of skyscrapers in the urban center characteristic of Western capitalist cities. The site atop the Lenin Hills overlooking the city provides the university with an imposing presence on the city's skyline, but the ornate setback tower appears anachronistic in the context of postwar design. The undecorated glass box characteristic of American skyscrapers in the 1950s represents the wedding of the formal and tectonic preferences of modern architects with the concerns of real-estate interests for maximizing the profitability of land in the urban center. However, neither the autonomous aesthetic preferences of the design profession nor a concern for profit were factors in Soviet architecture during the Stalinist era. The Moscow State University reflects the continued significance of Boris Iofan's prizewinning design for the Palace of the Soviets as a model for Russian architects (see page 102). It was not until after Stalin's death in 1953 that Russian architects could begin to reconsider the premises of socialist realism and explore alternative design strategies to promote the modernization of the Soviet Union.

6.22 State University, Lenin Hills, Moscow, Russia, first variant 1948.

Museum Architecture

In the history of architecture, different periods can often be characterized in terms of particularly representative building types such as the temple in antiquity or the cathedral during the medieval era. In the second half of the twentieth century, museums emerged as major showcases for design thinking. They captured both popular and professional attention and became internationally recognized attractions for their cities. More than warehouses for art, museums are architectural representations of the cultural institutions. For many communities, the erection of a new museum often signaled a level of cultural aspiration and civic pride that identified the host city as both prosperous and sophisticated. While certainly not a new building type, the museum underwent a metamorphosis after the war. Museum buildings became celebrations of the creativity and imagination of their designers as much as they were the repositories of cultural heritage. In place of the classical decorum and meditative aura that surrounds earlier buildings such as John Russell Pope's National Gallery, there is a dynamic, often brazen, quality to the new designs that threatens to overwhelm the art on display.

New York: Guggenheim Museum

Dynamic is certainly an appropriate term to describe Frank Lloyd Wright's design for the Solomon R. Guggenheim Museum in New York City (fig. 6.23). Wright's concept of organic architecture is most often associated with domestic designs created in the context of regional identities; the Guggenheim Museum offered him an opportunity to realize his vision in a large institutional building located in one of the nation's most important cities. Wright began working on the commission for a museum to house Guggenheim's collection of non-objective art in 1943, but the

6.23 Frank Lloyd Wright, Solomon R. Guggenheim Museum, New York, 1943–52.

Wright tended to organize his public buildings such as the Guggenheim Museum in New York around large atriums that emphasized the vertical dimension and provided visitors with a consistent reference point (see also fig. 6.24).

building was not finished until shortly before his death in 1959. Wright exploited the malleable quality of reinforced concrete to create a fluid, shell-like volume that expands in size as it rises over its site. Wright declared:

> Here for the first time architecture appears plastic, one floor flowing into another (more like sculpture) instead of the usual superimposition of stratified layers cutting and butting into each other by way of post and beam construction.
>
> (Curtis, p. 413)

Plastic continuity is the primary spatial theme of the design; inside, the main exhibition space is defined by a spiral ramp that coils around a central skylit volume (fig. 6.24). The experience of moving through the space is exhilarating but the Guggenheim has its limitations in terms of the display of art. Sloping surfaces complicate the installation of art works, for example, and circulation is restricted to the single path created by the spiral ramp. Visitors typically ascend to the top of the museum by elevator and walk down the ramp; the only alternative is to begin one's journey at the bottom of the ramp. Wright's philosophy of organic design requires an extraordinary commitment on the part of the building's users to his vision of the relationship between form and function.

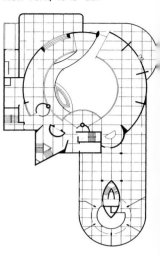

6.24 Frank Lloyd Wright, Solomon R. Guggenheim Museum, plan, New York, 1943–52.

Paris: Pompidou Center

At the opposite extreme from the organic plasticity of the Guggenheim stands the industrialized technology of the Centre Culturel d'Art Georges Pompidou in Paris. In 1970 French authorities staged an international competition for the design of a new cultural center which attracted more than 680 entries. The presence of Philip Johnson and Oscar Niemeyer on the competition jury is one indication of the

importance attached to this project. The program called for a multipurpose facility to house a museum of modern art, a public lending library, centers for industrial design and audiovisual research, cinemas, and restaurants. The building was intended to be a catalyst for the cultural life of the city and to propel Paris, once again, to the forefront of the international avant-garde. In July 1971 the commission was awarded to the partnership of Renzo Piano (b. 1937) and Richard Rogers (b. 1933) and, in January 1977, the center opened to the public. Piano and Rogers conceived the building as a giant steel skeleton erected in a manner that created huge unobstructed interior spaces (fig. 6.25). Two parallel layers of structure, seven meters wide and forty-eight meters apart, supported the clear-span floor decks. Threaded through the structural layer on one side of the building were provisions for vertical circulation, including a giant escalator that snaked its way up the west front and carried visitors to the rooftop observation level. The building's mechanical services ran through the corresponding zone on the opposite side. In between, a system of moveable partitions was installed so that the interior could be configured in a variety of ways. The Pompidou Center pulled together ideas drawn from a variety of sources such as the Miesian concert hall project discussed above (see fig. 6.1). The kinetic quality of the giant escalator on the front, the bright color scheme, and the brawny steel armature of the building's design reflect an affinity for the work of Archigram and earlier prophets of high-tech design such as Buckminster Fuller.

6.25 (opposite) Richard Rogers and Renzo Piano, Centre Georges Pompidou, Paris, France, 1971–77.

6.26 (above) Richard Rogers and Renzo Piano, Centre Georges Pompidou, detail, Paris, France, 1971–77.

The building occupies only half of its site on the Place Beaubourg; the other half was transformed into a public square and functions as the center of a lively street scene attracting jugglers, musicians, and street artists of all kinds. Originally, the contrast between the Pompidou and its surroundings was stark (fig. 6.26). The center's bulk and exposed steel framework appeared out of place in the traditional urban fabric of Paris's Marais district. Precisely because of its enormous size, its ambitious program (including the first public lending library in Paris), and the number of people it attracts each day, the Pompidou Center has generated a new context and identity for the surrounding neighborhood. The building has proven to be an outstanding popular success and ranks among Paris's leading tourist attractions, but an evaluation of its performance as an exhibition center is more problematic. The huge spaces and lack of wall surfaces present a challenge to anyone attempting to install exhibitions. It is also questionable to what degree the Pompidou Center can be seen as a representation of French culture. The building is more recognizable as a representation of the design culture of advanced building technology than it is emblematic of the literary, visual, and performing arts.

Verona: Castelvecchio Museum

The Guggenheim Museum and the Pompidou Center represent organic and high-tech approaches to museum design. The third example to be considered—the restoration of the Castelvecchio Museum in Verona, Italy, by Carlo Scarpa (1906–1978)—demonstrates a craft sensibility applied to museum design. Because a craft-based approach does not advance any larger program of modernization nor expand the domain of professional expertise claimed by architects, it is often discounted in accounts of late twentieth-century architecture. However, Scarpa's work is widely admired by architects of various orientations. The Castelvecchio was a medieval castle altered repeatedly during the course of centuries and damaged during World War II. Beginning in 1956, Scarpa was commissioned to restore the castle and reorganize the museum's installation. His involvement continued into the early 1970s.

Scarpa was not as dismissive of the existing context as Wright, Piano, and Rogers, but he shared their commitment to expressing contemporary conditions and sensibilities. For Scarpa, restoration did not imply a literal return to an original premodern condition; there is no illusion of escaping the present in his work. Instead, restoration called for pruning the cumulative effect of centuries of use in order to clarify spatial and temporal relationships within the building. Walls added in the eighteenth and nineteenth centuries to create additional rooms, for example, were removed and original windows bricked-up at different moments in the building's long history were reopened. However, not all post-medieval additions were removed and traces remain from every period of the castle's use. The result is an architectural palimpsest, revealing layers of the structure's history.

6.27 Carlo Scarpa, Museo Castelvecchio, Verona, Italy, 1956.

Scarpa's palette of materials included traditional ones such as stone and wood, but steel and reinforced concrete also appear as clear indications of the museum's modernity. He lavished great care on details such as the pattern of paving stones and the hardware for mounting artwork on the walls in order to generate a visual dialogue between distinct moments in time—past and present. He used one of the museum's most important works, the fourteenth-century equestrian statue of Cangrande della Scala, to concentrate attention at a point that subverts spatial hierarchies within the museum, installing it on a specially designed reinforced concrete plinth set in a critical juncture between two wings of the castle (fig. 6.27). The patches visible on adjacent walls remind the visitor of the vicissitudes of time. The poignant quality of Scarpa's work is at odds with the furious rush of the avant-garde into the future; nonetheless, he captures an important aspect of the modern experience: the coexistence of ephemeral and enduring cultural achievements in the same place.

Religious Architecture

Religious architecture occupies a curious position within the story of twentieth-century architecture because of the perceived incompatibility between the spiritual focus of ecclesiastical design and the secular values associated with modernism and modernity. The first half of the twentieth century has been characterized in these pages as a period of lively debate between advocates of traditional and avant-garde architectural approaches, and examples of church design can be cited for both sides. Frank Lloyd Wright's 1904 Unity Temple in Oak Park, Illinois, and Auguste Perret's 1922 Notre Dame du Raincy extended the modernist involvement with new materials and spatial conceptions into the realm of ecclesiastical design. Traditional approaches to church architecture survived as well in the work of such architects as Ralph Adams Cram (1863–1942). It was in the third quarter of the century, when modernism's hegemony within design circles was at its strongest, that the possibility of a modern religious architecture was questioned most seriously. This process of questioning is also revealing for the light it sheds on design criticism in the 1950s.

Mexico City: Church of the Miraculous Virgin

Religious commissions provided architects with opportunities to apply modern materials and methods to the design of sacred communal spaces. The Church of the Miraculous Virgin in Mexico City, designed by Felix Candela (1910–1998) consists of a series of hyperbolic paraboloids supported on flared columns (fig. 6.28). Candela belongs to the same expressive tradition in twentieth-century engineering as the bridges of Robert Maillart, characterized by thin, light structures that appear to spring upward in apparent defiance of gravity. Candela became a master of thin shell construction: the concrete vaults of the Church of the Miraculous Virgin are only $1^1/_2$ inches thick. Candela's design suggests a modern reinterpretation in abstract terms of the integral relationship between rational structure and expressive space characteristic of Gothic architecture. Ecclesiastical commissions represent only a small number of the more than one thousand structures designed by Candela, however, and the application of thin shell design to a variety of building types did little to clarify the relationship between the rational and secular world view represented by modernist architecture and the religious values of traditional religious buildings.

England: Coventry Cathedral

In 1950 Basil Spence (1907–1976) won a competition for the design of a new cathedral for Coventry, England, to replace the previous building destroyed during the war (fig. 6.29). Spence envisioned stone walls surrounding an interior defined by slender concrete columns carrying a concrete vault. In a critical review of the initial design in the January 1952 issue of *Architectural Review*, the influential critic

6.28 (left) Felix Candela, Church of the Miraculous Virgin, Mexico City, Mexico, 1953.

6.29 (below) Basil Spence, Cathedral Church of Saint Michael, interior, Coventry, England, 1950–62.
  Stained-glass windows illuminate the interior of the new cathedral built adjacent to the ruins of the earlier one. The sequence of colors along the nave symbolizes the stages of life from birth to the afterlife. The figure of Christ, designed by the artist Graham Sutherland and executed as a tapestry 72 feet (22 meters) high, fills the wall behind the main altar.

J. M. Richards noted the challenge of designing religious buildings in a secular age:

> The question is next asked whether, architecture being today in a state of experiment and flux and religious worship being so largely a matter of fixed traditions, rooted in the past, there is any common ground on which the two can meet.

(Richards, *Architectural Review*, January 1952, p. 4)

Richards concluded that Spence's attempt to bring the two together by combining stone walls and concrete columns was an unconvincing marriage of a static, earthbound outer shell with a soaring, interior volume. For Richards, the awkward qualities of Spence's Coventry Cathedral indicated that modern architecture had yet to develop a fully resolved expressive language. Other reviewers were more sympathetic. The new Coventry Cathedral was dedicated in 1962; six years later another British architectural critic, Lance Wright, published a more favorable analysis of the building in the August 1968 issue of the *American Institute of Architects Journal*. He noted the disparity between popular and professional responses to the design and suggested that the "problem of religious architecture" was really rooted in the prevailing tendency of

architectural critics to privilege innovation above all else in assessing new designs:

> As a consequence of this determined opinion, we tend to value each separate building less for what it is than for the promise it holds for the future development of its building type, for its innovations. Another consequence is that we find it difficult to focus on buildings which are frankly regressive, which do not pretend to any deep rethinking of the brief, and which not only fail to bring new architectural values into the world but deliberately reassert old ones.
>
> (Wright, p. 50)

France: Notre Dame du Haut, Ronchamp

Coventry Cathedral was not the only religious building to become the focus of so much critical debate. In 1953 construction began on the new pilgrimage chapel of Notre Dame du Haut, designed by Le Corbusier and located on a hilltop near Ronchamp, France (fig. 6.32). Le Corbusier's design replaced an earlier chapel on the site destroyed during the war. Instead of the engineering aesthetic of Candela and the tentative union of traditional and modern typologies pursued by Spence, Le Corbusier adopted a bold sculptural approach. Curved walls of varying thickness outline the main body of the church and, as they curl inward, create smaller chapels along the periphery of the plan (fig. 6.31). Each elevation is different and the roofline changes constantly as one moves around the building. There is an intentionally crude and primitive quality to the building; the floor slopes and the roof dips, creating a cavelike interior. Light filters into the interior through splayed openings arranged randomly on the south wall (fig. 6.30). Abundant clear light was always an important feature of modern architecture, but here the lighting is muted and evocative rather than revealing.

6.30 Le Corbusier, Notre Dame du Haut, interior, Ronchamp, France 1950–54.

Because of Le Corbusier's stature as one of the premier figures of modern architecture, the church attracted international attention and it remains one of his most important designs. It has been included in every survey of modern architecture published since its completion and is ranked by most critics as one of the key buildings of the second half of the twentieth century. Not everyone, however, was enthusiastic about the design initially. In his March 1956 review of the building in *The Architectural Review*, the British architect James Stirling (b. 1926) wondered whether this design by "Europe's greatest architect" should "influence the course of modern architecture." He conceded that the chapel had a "sensational impact" on most visitors but he was suspicious of the building's emotional appeal and he found few lessons that could be applied to new buildings. Like Mannerist architecture of the sixteenth century, Stirling concluded, Notre Dame du Haut was "symptomatic of a state when the vocabulary is not being extended." Stirling's critique of the building was directed at the inability of many modern architects to come to terms with architecture that addressed other dimensions of human experience besides pragmatic and rational concerns.

By contrast, the Italian architect and critic Ernesto Rogers (1909–1969), among the most astute observers of modern architecture in the period, recognized the power of Le Corbusier's design to provoke reflection. After visiting the chapel, he wrote a small book about the work in which he concluded:

> Whether orthodox or otherwise, a believer in immanentism or transcendentalism, all sensitive men are aware of a growth in their spiritual potential within the walls of this architectural work.
>
> (Rogers, p. 8)

Whatever the effect the chapel has on visitors, however, it is questionable whether such spirituality was intended by the architect. Le Corbusier avoided appealing to religious values in his explanation of the design, which was based on landscape, not religious creed. He patiently explained different facets of the hilltop chapel as

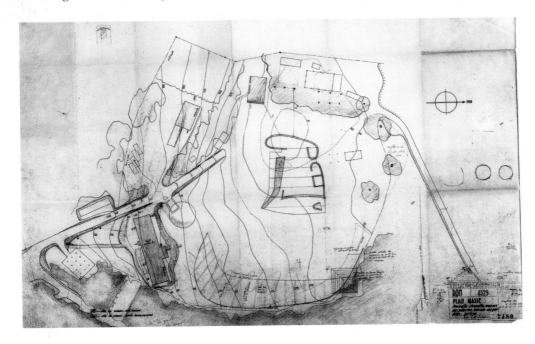

6.31 Le Corbusier, Notre Dame du Haut, plan, Ronchamp, France, 1950–54.

6.32 Le Corbusier, Notre Dame du Haut, Ronchamp, France, 1950–54.

responses to the surrounding landscape and maintained that he was interested in the "psycho-physiological" dimension of design and not religious cult. The artistry of Le Corbusier's response to the site is clear—as is the power of his design to provoke reflection and prayer. Although it was commissioned as a Catholic pilgrimage shrine to Mary, the sense of sacredness that animates the design is not bound to a particular sectarian doctrine. The appeal of Notre Dame du Haut is primal and testifies to the ability of modern architects to successfully address the enduring human interest in the spiritual as well as the material dimension of life.

"The Style for the Job"

The contrast between the Platonic abstraction of the Farnsworth House and the robust tactility of the Bavinger House, or the structural rigor of the Church of the Miraculous Virgin and the sculptural freedom of Notre Dame du Haut, indicates the broad spectrum of design thinking within postwar modernist architecture. When one shifts the focus of analysis from isolated examples by prominent architects to broad patterns in the built environment, however, a different impression of the period emerges. Mies van der Rohe and Bruce Goff operated in very different professional contexts and it was the reductive rationalism of the Miesian approach that exercised by far the greater impact on architectural production. In general, developers, corporate clients, and architectural firms developed standardized solutions to typical design problems. As a result, problems were often defined in ways that fit predetermined solutions.

It is in this context that the career of Eero Saarinen, the son of Eliel Saarinen, acquires particular interest as a model of professional practice. Eero's practice included some of the largest and most discussed commissions of the period. He inherited the commission for the General Motors Technical Center in Warren, Michigan (near Detroit), following his father's death in 1950. The GM Technical Center housed research and design facilities for the automotive giant (fig. 6.33). Saarinen's design involved the creation of an "office campus" with an undeniable Miesian quality in its low, steel-framed rectangular buildings arranged around a central pool.

6.33 Eero Saarinen, General Motors Technical Center, Warren, Michigan, 1949–55.

Saarinen employed a consistent vocabulary of metal and glass curtain walls for the long elevations, and colorful, glazed brick walls on the short ends of simple rectangular volumes, to unify this enormous research complex. Variations in the color scheme, the entrance canopies, and lobby arrangements individualize the office blocks without disrupting the overall uniformity of the design.

6.34 (right) Eero
Saarinen, TWA Terminal,
JFK Airport, New York,
1962.

6.35 (below) Eero
Saarinen, TWA Terminal,
interior, JFK Airport,
New York, 1962.

Saarinen was wary of the tendency in many architectural firms to repeat successful design solutions. In 1958 he wrote:

> I feel strongly that modern architecture is in danger of falling into a mold too quickly—too rigid a mold. What was once a great hope for a great new period of architecture has somehow become an automatic application of the same formula over and over again everywhere. I feel, therefore, a certain responsibility to examine problems with the specific enthusiasm of bringing out of the particular problem the particular solution. . . . In this sense, I align myself humbly with Le Corbusier and against Mies van der Rohe.
>
> (Saarinen, p. 6)

His commitment to approaching each problem in search of a fresh solution became known as "The Style for the Job."

If the GM Technical Center follows the example of Mies van der Rohe, Saarinen's TWA Terminal at New York City's JFK Airport (fig. 6. 34) reflects the sculptural qualities of Le Corbusier's Ronchamp chapel (see fig. 6.32). He exploited the plastic quality of reinforced concrete and conceived the terminal as four segmental vaults springing from four Y-shaped pylons. The vault segments converge to envelope the terminal in a great birdlike form which Saarinen felt captured the idea of flight. The fluid, streamlined character of the design continued in the interior, evoking the exoticism and romance of travel (fig. 6.35). The TWA Terminal was designed for propellor aircraft and the dawn of the jet age revealed the design's functional limitations. The sculptural quality of the design made it difficult to modify the terminal to handle the larger jets and the increased passenger traffic that followed. Saarinen addressed these problems in his subsequent design for Dulles International Airport in Washington DC.

The oscillation apparent in Eero Saarinen's work between a sober rationalism and an evocative expressionism neatly sums up the situation in the postwar years as modern architects explored the range of possibilities within modernism. Others shared Saarinen's concern that architecture was in danger of falling into a rigid mold; they would soon propose new challenges to the hegemony of modernist doctrine.

Part 3

An Era of Pluralism
1965–2000

Jean-Marie Tjibaou Cultural Center, Nouméa, New Caledonia (see fig. 9.27)

Disappointed with modernist design, architects in the mid-1960s began to reassess their allegiance to its principles. Driven by changes in the global economy, poststructuralist theories of knowledge and culture, environmental issues, computer-aided design tools, architecture entered a period of diversity and critical debate unmatched since the early years of the century. This section reviews the spectrum of movements including Postmodernism, Deconstructivism, Classicism, "green" architecture, and a reinvigorated Modernism characteristic of the last decades.

Chapter 7

Postmodernism, Deconstructivism, and Tradition

For twenty-five years following the end of World War II, the philosophical ideals and design strategies of modernism dominated professional practice in the developed world. The era of modernist hegemony proved to be short-lived, however. This chapter describes the series of challenges to modernist design doctrines that began to appear in the late 1960s. In sharp contrast to modernist architecture, for example, postmodern architects proposed designs that drew upon historical sources for formal inspiration and demonstrated a renewed commitment to the idea that ornament should be an integral part of architecture. Once the universal applicability of modernist design was called into question by postmodern architects, other voices soon joined the debate. A new avant-garde based on novel theories of culture and language, and initially labeled Deconstructivism, emerged to challenge the normative basis of modern architecture. Finally, architects once again began to assert the validity of designs based on classical paradigms that were untouched by either a postmodernist sense of irony or an avant-garde rejection of certainty.

While in the 1970s and 1980s modernism was assailed by critics outside the modern movement, the process of critical reassessment really began from within. In 1966 the Italian architect Aldo Rossi (1931–1997) published *The Architecture of the City*, one of the most influential architectural books of the decade. Rossi treated the city not as an economic entity nor as a demographic problem, but as the locus of collective identity. He criticized functionalist planning theory as naïve and, in place of the modernist dictum "form follows function," he argued that form precedes and exists independently of function. For Rossi, the enduring lessons of form-making are distilled and preserved in architectural types. While the functional and symbolic programs of urban buildings may change over time, architectural types endure and can accommodate new functions and symbols. Rossi freed the discussion of typology from a narrow concern with programmatic and technological issues and forcefully reintroduced the study of premodern urban morphology into the European architectural debate. The term Neo-Rationalism was used by critics to distinguish Rossi's approach from the functionalist and materialist biases of the rationalism characteristic of modernist design theory.

In 1971 Rossi won a competition for an addition to the cemetery of San Cataldo in Modena, Italy, and the project soon became one of the paradigms of Neo-Rationalist architecture (fig. 7.1). The elemental language of geometric figures characteristic of the Modena cemetery recalled the austere projects of the eighteenth-

Peter Eisenman, Wexner Center, Ohio State University, Columbus, Ohio, 1983–89.

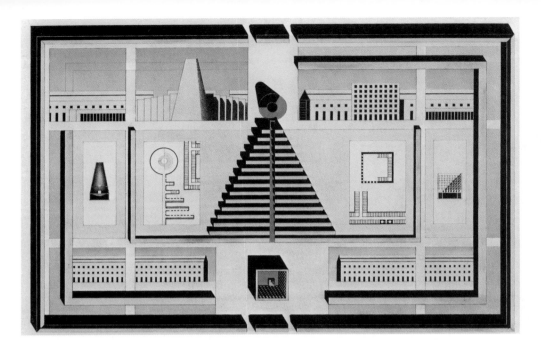

7.1 Aldo Rossi, San Cataldo Cemetery, Modena, Italy, 1971–73.
Rossi here combines a detailed plan of the entire cemetery with elevations of its different parts. Abstract geometric forms provide the cemetery's basic design vocabulary. The buildings in this "city for the dead" consist of linear forms of varying length. A roofless cube and a truncated cone establish a short cross-axis within the rectangular enclosure.

century French architect Etienne-Louis Boullée, whose work Rossi knew well. Rossi's design can also be compared with specific Italian monuments. For example, the pattern of identical openings repeated on all four sides of the simple cube that serves as an ossuary recalled the Palace of Italian Civilization erected as part of the Fascist program for E'42 on the outskirts of Rome (see fig. 4.20).

Renewing Modernism from Within: Housing

Ralph Erskine

By the late 1960s the shortcomings of modernist housing schemes were readily apparent: banal buildings, alienating environments, and broken communities. Some architects who still identified with the modern movement and saw themselves as extending the legacy of modernism were nonetheless concerned about such shortcomings. Ralph Erskine (b. 1914) was one such architect. Born and educated in England, Erskine began his professional career in the late 1930s. He moved to Sweden in 1939 and gained extensive experience in housing and related social design programs. As a member of Team X in the mid-1950s (see p. 158), he was involved in the final stages of the CIAM. In a 1984 essay, he reflected on the experience of his generation of architects:

> We fought for the new world of Modern Architecture and functionalism as we understood it. It was at that time an architecture of analysis, but also with strong emotional ties to the new techniques and materials of the industrial age, and to Cubism in the Arts. We fought for freedom, and our faith was strong, but in retrospect it would seem that our understanding was naïve, our analysis limited, and that our freedom from old styles was rapidly and willingly exchanged for the dictates of the new.
>
> (Lasdun, p. 72)

When, in 1968, the Newcastle-upon-Tyne Housing Council commissioned Erskine to design a new housing estate for the Byker community, the municipal authorities were anxious to preserve the cohesive social fabric of the existing community

7.2 Ralph Erskine,
Byker Wall, Newcastle-
upon-Tyne, England,
1968–74.

while improving their living conditions. Erskine brought his extensive experience with housing and social planning in Sweden to bear on the project. Significantly, he opened an office in the community and included as part of the design process extensive input from the residents. The result is a mixture of high- and low-rise housing units arranged to create a variety of outdoor spaces on the carefully landscaped site. Byker Wall, the most prominent feature of the scheme, is a high-rise block of flats that runs along the northern perimeter of the site (fig. 7.2). This block screens the community from an adjacent highway and, like the protective walls of a medieval village, shelters the housing terraces within. Color and bold patterning are used to animate the huge expanse of brick wall facing the highway, while projecting balconies provide depth and rhythm to the inner face of the high-rise units. At Byker, the abstract formulas of CIAM-inspired housing schemes are replaced by a participatory process of user input and intimate on-site involvement by the architect.

Aldo van Eyck

The Dutch architect Aldo van Eyck was also concerned that modern architecture had succumbed to formulaic methods of design. One of the founders of Team X, van Eyck emerged as a leading figure in the critical reassessment of modernism from within. He recognized that the industrialization of building threatened to reduce architecture to little more than the packaging of space. Rather than reject the material and constructional advantages of modern technology, however, van Eyck urged architects to accept modern building systems as the new vernacular of the industrial age. Architects, he argued, should learn how to manipulate the elements of this industrial vernacular in order to enrich and humanize their designs.

An important theorist as well as talented designer, van Eyck criticized the tendency of modern architects to quantify and categorize programmatic elements, thus losing the rich complexity of human experience. In a 1962 essay entitled "Steps Towards a Configurative Discipline," he warned that important design values were in danger of being "hollowed out" by contemporary practice:

> I am again concerned with twinphenomena; with unity and diversity, part and whole, small and large, many and few, simplicity and complexity, change and constancy, order and chaos, individual and collective; . . . as conflicting polarities or false alternatives these abstract antonyms all carry the same luggage: loss of identity and its attribute—monotony.
>
> (Ockman, p. 348)

Architects, he suggested, must solve the aesthetic problems created by modern technology and seek to integrate what he labeled the "twinphenomena" (the integral relationship between seemingly contradictory qualities) that modern design methods tended to treat in isolation.

Hubertushuis in Amsterdam provides an excellent illustration of van Eyck's approach (fig. 7.3). Commissioned in 1973 but not completed until 1981, Hubertushuis provides temporary housing and social services for single parents and their children. The project is an example of urban in-fill design in which a new building is inserted between existing structures in order to complete a row of buildings along the street. Hubertushuis occupies a deep midblock site and incorporates an existing townhouse adjacent to the new construction. The recessed entry bay leads to an internal street that serves the apartments. Van Eyck employed a vibrant color scheme to articulate the frame construction, and skillfully balanced the transparency of the street facade with a circuitous entry sequence to reveal the depth of the project while maintaining a sense of enclosure to respect the privacy of the residents. This careful measuring of transparency against enclosure demonstrates what van Eyck has in mind when he speaks of the integration rather than the separation of "twinphenomena" in design. Details often treated by many architects in a prosaic manner received special attention from van Eyck. His treatment of stair treads, paving patterns, transoms, and door frames, for example, enriches the experience of moving through the space and gives the design a distinctive identity.

7.3 Aldo van Eyck, Hubertushuis, Amsterdam, Netherlands, 1973–81.

Silence and Light: Louis Kahn

In 1959, the American architect Louis Kahn (1901–1974) presented a paper at the final CIAM meeting in Otterlo, Holland. His talk was typical of the criticism that led to the demise of the CIAM and, at the same time, a very personal statement of his own thinking about the nature of architecture. Kahn drew a distinction between the quantitative aspects of building and the qualitative nature of architectural space:

> If you get a program from a school board, the first thing it will say, in our country, is that it must have a nine-foot fence around it . . . and the corridors must be no less than nine feet wide, and that all the classrooms must be well-ventilated and have good light and all be a certain size. They will give you many things which help the practitioner make a pretty good profit out of his commission by following the rule of rules. But this is not an architect at work. An architect thinks of a school possibly as being a realm of spaces within which it is well to learn.

(Latour, p. 83)

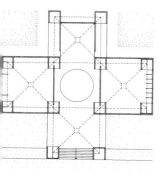

7.4 Louis Kahn, Bathhouse, Jewish Community Center, plan, Trenton, New Jersey, 1955.

7.5 Louis Kahn, Jonas Salk Institute for Biological Sciences, plan, La Jolla, California, 1959–65.

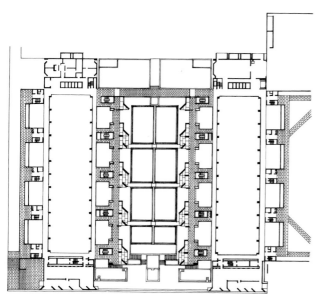

For Kahn, good design required more than economical solutions to the enclosure of space; architects, he argued, gave form and order to important human institutions, and design, therefore, dealt with significant philosophical issues. Kahn expressed his ideas in evocative rather than technical language. He spoke of silence as the primordial beginning point of the creative process and light as the animating spark that endowed architectural form with life. Beginning in the mid-1950s, his work emerged as an influential alternative to the stale functionalism of the CIAM and the slick professionalism of the "style for the job" approach to professional practice.

A simple bathhouse for a Jewish Community Center near Trenton, New Jersey, commissioned in 1955, reveals the distinctive character of Kahn's work. Four square pavilions, each capped by a pyramidal roof, are arranged symmetrically around a central unroofed atrium (fig. 7.4). Kahn hollowed out the huge piers at the corner of each pavilion, thus creating spaces for circulation and building services while retaining the monumental effect created by the massive squat piers. Kahn was trained before World War II in the American version of the Beaux-Arts system, and the sense of order and spatial hierarchy evident in this centralized plan is Palladian rather than modern in spirit. Kahn often spoke of a building plan as "an assembly of rooms"; his interest in mass and the differentiation of space distinguished his approach from the typical modernist strategy of using transparent planes and volumes to establish spatial continuity. The insertion of building services within the hollowed-out piers demonstrates Kahn's concept of servant and served spaces within a building, in which a hierarchical distinction is established between the primary rooms of a building (the served) and zones devoted to secondary or supporting functions (servant).

In December 1959 Kahn met Dr. Jonas Salk (the man responsible for the development of the first effective polio vaccine). Kindred spirits in terms of their shared interests in the philosophical issues raised by modern science and technology, they developed a deep friendship and Salk invited Kahn to prepare a design for a new research facility he was creating on a magnificent ocean bluff site in La Jolla, California. The patron's role was fundamental; inspired by a visit to a Franciscan monastery in Assisi, Italy, Salk wanted to create a center where scientists would enjoy both privacy and community. In addition to laboratory facilities, the final program for the Salk Institute for Biological Studies included individual studies for each scientist and a plaza which served as a gathering place and as the symbolic core of the institute (figs. 7.5, 7.6). The studies were arranged in two rows flanking the central plaza and the huge laboratory wings were positioned on the outer edges of the scheme. A thin ribbon of water emphasized the longitudinal axis of the plaza and drew the viewer's gaze from the entrance to the ocean vista in the distance. The contemplative aura of the plaza brilliantly captures Kahn's concept of architecture between silence and light.

Kahn's ability to compose space with light and to coordinate the conceptual order of a design with the structural system of a building is evident in the Kimbell Art Museum in Fort Worth, Texas. In a museum, controlling the level of natural light in the exhibition space is a critical design concern. In the Kimbell, the basic structural unit is a barrel-vaulted bay that measures 104 feet by 23 feet. Kahn pierced the long axis of each bay with a skylight and inserted a curved aluminum light baffle below to control light levels and illuminate the galleries with what he described as silver light (fig. 7.7). Landscaped courtyards adjacent to some of the galleries allow what Kahn described as green light to filter in from the sides. Like the pyramidal roofs of the Trenton bathhouse, the barrel vaults reinforce the spatial identity of each gallery yet maintain the uniformity of the overall system.

In his absorbing interest in the tectonic logic and formal possibilities inherent in modern materials such as reinforced concrete, and in his lack of interest in applied ornament, Kahn demonstrated his commitment to architectural modernism. At the same time, his interest in spatial differentiation instead of continuity, his appreciation for the design qualities of mass and monumentality and, most importantly, in the poetic quality of both his writing and his designs, Kahn enriched the vocabulary of modern architecture. He remains among the most influential architects of the second half of the century.

7.6 Louis Kahn, Jonas Salk Institute for Biological Sciences, La Jolla, California, 1959–65.
Ocean, sky, and architecture are drawn together in the plaza's design. Preliminary plans included trees, but Kahn decided to leave the space open. He described the plaza as a façade to the sky. From the entrance, the narrow channel of water leads the visitor's eye to the ocean and the horizon beyond.

7.7 Louis Kahn, Kimbell Art Museum, south gallery, Fort Worth, Texas, 1966–72.

Postmodernism

Postmodernism is an awkward term. The prefix "post-" suggests that the phenomenon comes "after" modernism, without describing it any further. The continued vitality of modernism as an architectural and cultural phenomenon only increases the confusion. In popular usage, however, the word modern is still used to describe the present era and the concept of a post-present condition is difficult to grasp. Nonetheless, the term postmodern entered widespread architectural usage in the mid-1970s in an effort by critics to confirm the existence of a significant alternative to modernism in architecture. It is used in a general way to identify a broad spectrum of work by architects who rejected orthodox modern architecture (an orthodoxy that critics equated with the International Style). In a more limited sense, postmodern describes a particular design orientation that depends upon the creative manipulation of symbols and explicit references drawn from history or popular culture. In the first, broad sense, both Charles Moore and Thomas Gordon Smith (two architects whose works are discussed below) are postmodernists. Although both architects turned away from modernist concepts, Moore's whimsical exaggeration of historical paradigms is different from Smith's literal classicism. In the narrow sense of the term, therefore, Moore is a postmodernist while Smith is not. It is the second, more precise usage of the term that is adopted here.

Robert Venturi

The foundational document for postmodernism in America is the book *Complexity and Contradiction in Architecture* written by the architect Robert Venturi (b. 1925) and published in 1966 by the Museum of Modern Art. *Complexity and Contradiction in Architecture* revealed Venturi's sophisticated understanding of the history of architecture—his work is filled with recondite as well as obvious historical references. In his enthusiastic introduction to the book, the architectural historian Vincent Scully observed: "Like all original architects, Venturi makes us see the past anew." In the opening section, entitled "Nonstraightforward Architecture: A Gentle Manifesto," Venturi declared his polemical intent:

> Architects can no longer afford to be intimidated by the puritanically moral language of orthodox Modern architecture. I like elements which are hybrid rather than "pure," . . . I am for richness of meaning rather than clarity of meaning; for the implicit function as well as the explicit function. I prefer "both-and" to "either-or," black and white, and sometimes gray, to black or white. A valid architecture evokes many levels of meaning and combinations of focus: its space and its elements become readable and workable in several ways at once.
>
> (Venturi, *Complexity and Contradiction in Architecture*, pp. 22–23)

While Venturi's interest in an architecture of "both-and" evokes a strong parallel with Aldo van Eyck's concept of "twinphenomena," he applied the idea in a very different manner. In 1962 Venturi designed a house for his mother in Chestnut Hill, Pennsylvania (fig. 7.8), which embodies many of the concepts in *Complexity and Contradiction in Architecture*. Within the simple gabled silhouette of the house the apparent symmetry of the facade is contradicted by the fenestration pattern and the position of the chimney. Sudden shifts in scale and the use of wood moldings on the planar stucco surface create multiple possible readings of the composition.

Six years after the publication of *Complexity and Contradiction in Architecture*, in *Learning from Las Vegas*, co-authored with his wife Denise Scott Brown (b. 1931) and their associate Steven Izenour, Venturi challenged the design profession to take an unbiased look at the flamboyant commercial architecture of Las Vegas. In *Learning from Las Vegas*, the authors went beyond the description of spatial configurations to discuss the informational and symbolic dimensions of design (fig. 7.9). The lessons to be learned dealt with the importance of symbolic communication in architecture and the insights to be gained from studying American commercial vernacular design. There were other, unintended lessons as well. In her preface to the 1977 revised edition of the book, and, later, in a 1990 essay "Room at the Top? Sexism and the Star System in Architecture" which appeared in the British journal *Architectural Design*, Denise Scott Brown described her experiences as a female practitioner in the still male-dominated world of professional practice. Critics, she noted, routinely attributed the work of the Venturi and Scott Brown partnership to him alone and ignored her role in the firm. While new ideas about architecture entered the discourse of design, old concepts of architecture as a white male profession endured.

Communication emerged as a major theme in the architectural criticism surrounding the rise of postmodernism. Charles Jencks, one of the most astute and prolific critics of the period, approached the topic by applying concepts rooted in literary criticism and semiotics to architectural form. In his widely read book *The Language of Post-Modern Architecture* (published in 1977 and revised several times since), Jencks articulated the concept of multivalence in architecture. He described multivalence as the imaginative fusion of multiple meanings in a single design, and criticized modernism as an impoverished architectural language capable of expressing only a limited set of meanings. He cited the work of Antonio Gaudí as an example of multivalent design and contrasted this with the buildings of Mies van der Rohe which he described as univalent in terms of their ability to convey meaning. For Jencks, the architect's primary role was the expression of culturally significant

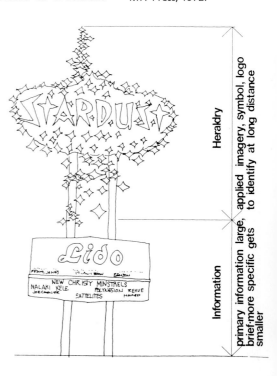

meanings. He concluded *The Language of Post-Modern Architecture* with the admonition that "no other profession is specifically responsible for articulating meaning and seeing that the environment is sensuous, humorous, surprising and coded as a readable text."

Charles Moore

7.10 Charles Moore, Piazza d'Italia, New Orleans, Louisiana, 1975–80.

Charles Moore was fascinated by fountains. In graduate school at Princeton University he wrote a doctoral dissertation on the relationship between water and architecture. The design of the Piazza d'Italia includes an enormous fountain (much like the Trevi Fountain in Rome) set within an elaborate architectural backdrop.

Sensuous, humorous, and surprising perfectly describe the Piazza d'Italia by Charles Moore (1925–1994) in New Orleans (fig. 7.10). Planned by the city as the hub of a proposed redevelopment project, the Piazza d'Italia was conceived by Moore as a festive public space celebrating New Orleans's Italian community. Five concentric colonnades focus the visitor's attention on an elaborate fountain, part of which is shaped like the Italian peninsula, projecting into the circular piazza. Each colonnade displays a different classical order but the result has much less of the decorum usually associated with classical design. Moore recast the orders in whimsical ways using a variety of water effects and visual puns such as "wetopes" (instead of metopes) for the Doric order. Neon lights outline the arches and columns to create a gaudy effect at night. Throughout this exuberant design, the familiar is handled in surprising ways and there is something to delight novice admirers of architecture and cognoscenti alike.

Piazza d'Italia neatly captures the postmodern attitude to the past: interested in historical models yet unwilling to reproduce them literally. The playfulness of

Moore's design offended some critics who dismissed it as kitsch, and the piazza became one of the most controversial projects of the late 1970s. The rise of post-modernism laid bare not only the dullness of too many modernist buildings but also the unease that highbrow critics still felt when confronted with designs that took their cues from lowbrow culture.

Ricardo Bofill

Beginning in the mid-1970s, Ricardo Bofill (b. 1939) of the Spanish–French archi-tectural firm Taller de Arquitectura designed a series of large housing projects in France that relied on Baroque planning principles for their site plans and incorpo-rated classical elements in their facade designs. At Les Echelles du Baroque in Paris, for example, seven-story apartment blocks define three linked plazas, each with a different geometric form (fig. 7.11). Postmodernism promoted the use of ele-ments drawn from traditional architecture: Bofill incorporated enormous columns, pedimented windows, and projecting cornices in his design. Postmodern architects, however, avoided the literal imitation of historical models, and Bofill exaggerated the scale and subverted the traditional reading of classical elements. Rather than solid elements, the giant columns of the courtyard elevation are faced with glass and serve as bay windows for the apartments. These "palaces for the people" avoid the mind-numbing monotony of so many modernist housing schemes; rather, Bofill's eccentric handling of classical imagery creates a surreal monumentality that overwhelms any sense of human scale.

The emergence of a postmodern sensibility in Europe was confirmed in an important architectural exhibition entitled "The Presence of the Past," staged as

7.12 (opposite) Strada Novissima, from the exhibition "The Presence of the Past," Venice Biennale, Italy, 1980.

7.11 Ricardo Bofill, Les Echelles du Baroque housing project, 14th district, Paris, France, 1979–83.

part of the 1980 Venice Biennale. In his catalog essay, the exhibit's chief organizer, Paolo Portoghesi, described post-modernism as "the end of prohibitionism," that is, the end of an era in which architects were prohibited from engaging in a creative dialogue with the past because of the anti-historicism of modernist design theory. The central feature of the exhibit was the so-called Strada Novissima, a seventy-meter-long "street" lined by facades designed by an international array of architects (fig. 7.12). A broad spectrum of design orientations were represented in the selection of architects. Unlike the Museum of Modern Art's "International Style" exhibition of 1932 which sought to codify a particular style, the Strada Novissima celebrated diversity. Portoghesi was correct; the era when a single way of thinking about design could dominate the theory and practice of architecture was over. The end of prohibitionism ushered in a new era of pluralism and lively debate about the appropriate architecture for the late twentieth century.

Michael Graves and the Walt Disney Company

Early examples of postmodernism were unsettling for many design critics because work departed radically from the prevailing paradigms of modernist design theory. Outside of the design profession, however, the visual humor, distinctive color schemes, and the inclusion of images drawn from history or popular culture typical of postmodern designs were far less provocative. Indeed, these qualities proved to be attractive to clients eager to brand their buildings with bold, recognizable identities. Many of the same design strategies that the authors of *Learning from Las Vegas* had noted in their analysis of American commercial vernacular—exaggerated size, iconic shapes, and thematic use of decoration—now returned as emblematic features of high design. The career of Michael Graves (b. 1934) serves as an example of the impact of postmodernism.

When, in 1978, Michael Graves won a competition for the Portland Public Services Building, advocates of postmodernism hailed his victory as validation of the postmodern position. In place of the abstract language of modernist architecture, Graves provided a colorful design festooned with swags, giant keystones, and an enormous sculpture meant to symbolize the progressive spirit of this Oregon city. Completed in 1982, the Portland building, like Moore's Piazza d'Italia, proved to be one of the most controversial designs of the period. Critics dismissed the decoration as little more than arbitrary and superficial trappings draped unconvincingly over a banal box, and they disapproved of the building's small windows and cramped interior spaces.

In a media-saturated society, controversy creates celebrities more often than it resolves fundamental issues concerning what is appropriate in the civic realm and more large-scale commissions soon came to Graves. In 1986 he began design work on two new hotels for Walt Disney World Resort in Florida. In his master plan he sited the hotels on opposite sides of a crescent-shaped lake and linked them with a pedestrian causeway over the water. He created distinct yet related identities for each through a heraldic use of two exotic animals: a swan and a dolphin. For this postmodern *gesamtkunstwerk*, Graves also designed or selected furniture and furnishing for the hotels.

Michael Graves was not the only high-profile architect commissioned by The Walt Disney Company; indeed Disney's architectural patronage serves as an excellent example of the emergence of a new, more figurative corporate architecture. From a single amusement park, Disneyland, opened in 1955, The Walt Disney Company evolved into a sprawling, full-service resort, merchandising, and entertainment giant. In 1984 Michael Eisner became chairman and chief executive of The Walt Disney Company. Eisner rejected the cool, abstract forms of postwar corporate architecture and commissioned new buildings from prominent architects including Frank Gehry (b. 1929), Michael Graves, Arata Isozaki (b. 1931), Antoine Predock (b. 1936), and Robert A. M. Stern (b. 1939). Disney's architectural programs provide a revealing index of changing attitudes in architectural criticism as well as design. In 1965 Charles Moore published an essay in the Yale architectural journal *Perspecta*, praising the original Disneyland Park in southern California as "the most important single piece of construction in the West in the past several decades." Moore discussed Disneyland as a model of a stimulating yet comprehensible public space. By the mid-1980s, however, such naïve enthusiasm had given way to darker assessments by many cultural commentators of the "Disneyification" of public space in America. Today critical opinion is sharply divided about Disney's impact on contemporary architecture. Sensitive about its public image, the Disney Corporation attempts to maintain tight control over the use of Disney-related images. (Disney refused, for example, to grant permission to reproduce illustrations of the Swan and Dolphin Hotels here without prior approval of this text, a condition rejected by the author as unacceptable.)

Deconstructivism

Postmodern architecture was only one manifestation of the phenomenon that Portoghesi so aptly described as the end of prohibitionism. Challenges within design culture to the hegemony of modernism paralleled similar challenges to prevailing social and political norms elsewhere within contemporary society. In field after field, questions were raised concerning the fundamental assumptions on which different disciplines and practices were predicated. In 1988 Philip Johnson and Mark Wigley organized the exhibition "Deconstructivist Architecture" for the Museum of Modern Art that attempted to probe some of the central assumptions regarding architecture's deepest cultural significance. In his catalog essay Mark Wigley wrote:

> Architecture has always been a central cultural institution valued above all for its provision of stability and order. These qualities are seen to arise from the geometric purity of its formal composition. . . . The projects in this exhibition mark a different sensibility, one in which the dream of pure form has been disturbed.
>
> (Johnson & Wigley, p. 10)

Wigley employed the term Deconstructivism to label this sensibility. Deconstructivism is the conflation of two words: deconstruction and Constructivism. Deconstruction is an approach to reading and language that seeks to uncover the multiple and often conflicting levels of meaning inherent in texts of all kinds. In the 1970s the work of the French philosopher Jacques Derrida served as the primary source for many architectural theorists interested in the application of deconstruction to architecture. Constructivism is one of the terms used originally to describe Soviet avant-garde architecture of the immediate post-Revolutionary years in Russia (see chapter 4). In Deconstructivist designs, Wigley argued, architects employ the radical forms of the early-twentieth-century Soviet avant-garde to represent some of the theoretical ideas of deconstruction. Nevertheless, some of the architects categorized as Deconstructivist were reluctant to explain their work solely as the conjunction of late twentieth-century literary theories with early-twentieth-century avant-garde designs.

In contrast to the epigrammatic clarity of early-twentieth-century architectural programs and manifestos, the literature on Deconstructivism displayed a convoluted and abstruse writing style characteristic of the worst in academic prose. Ironically, language became a barrier rather than a bridge between architectural form and public comprehension. Reviews of the exhibition were mixed and even the exhibit's organizers acknowledged the tenuous quality of the concept of Deconstructivism. In his catalog essay, Wigley refused to claim the status of an organized movement for the work selected. Instead he described the exhibition in the following terms:

> It is a curious point of intersection among strikingly different architects moving in different directions. The projects are but brief moments in the independent programs of the artists.

(Johnson & Wigley, p. 19)

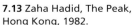

7.13 Zaha Hadid, The Peak, Hong Kong, 1982.

In the mid-1970s Hadid studied architecture at the Architectural Association in London, a school with a tradition of encouraging bold experimental design. She subsequently worked in the Office of Metropolitan Architecture (OMA) with Rem Koolhaas before establishing her own practice in 1979, three years before The Peak.

In 1932 the Museum of Modern Art's "International Style" exhibition established a popular definition of modern architecture that would endure for decades. By the late 1980s, however, there was less enthusiasm for defining normative conditions in the arts or anointing a limited selection of work as canonical. It was challenging enough for cultural institutions to illuminate "brief moments."

Projects by seven different architects were included in the Deconstructivist exhibition: Frank Gehry, Daniel Libeskind (b. 1946), Rem Koolhaas (b. 1944), Peter Eisenman (b. 1932), Zaha Hadid (b. 1950), Coop Himmelbau (the name for the joint practice of Wolf Prix [b. 1968] and Helmut Swiczinsky [b. 1944]), and Bernard Tschumi (b. 1944). Zaha Hadid's design for The Peak, an exclusive Hong Kong club, conveys the formal qualities that characterized work selected for the exhibition (fig. 7.13). Conceptually, the building consists of a horizontal stack of tubes. No clear hierarchy among the parts is apparent and the complexity of the scheme defies quick comprehension. Each level is skewed in its relationship to adjacent levels in an effort to negate any hint of orthogonal order. Hadid presented the building as a sequence of knifelike forms that appear to shred rather than compose the site as they slice into the hillside setting. While the lack of conventional order is at first unsettling, the intricate layering of the scheme and the manic intensity with which it was rendered is a compelling demonstration of architecture's ability to function as a form of philosophical speculation. Indeed, many of the buildings designed by Hadid and the other architects included in the exhibition possess an eloquence that their writings unfortunately lack.

The Deconstructivist architecture exhibition represented a preliminary attempt to label a new design orientation. Despite the awkwardness of the word, "Decon" entered the vocabulary of contemporary criticism because it answered the need for a term to describe a body of work that could neither be considered modern in the conventional sense nor postmodern in terms of its visual imagery and cultural references. Two architects whose work proved to be central to the crystalization of a new architectural approach were Peter Eisenman and Rem Koolhaas. Both architects effectively combined writing and designing to establish international reputations. Their work called into question the continued viability of classical and modernist design strategies and suggested the outlines of a new architectural aesthetic.

Peter Eisenman

For a quarter of a century following the end of World War II, developments in material and building technologies served as crucial points of reference for many architects. However, the political and social turmoil of the late 1960s called into question values and beliefs once considered sacrosanct. The nature of truth and authority along with the power of social conventions to define normative conditions became the subject of heated debates in a wide variety of domains. Peter Eisenman's architecture evolved in tandem with his reading in various intellectual fields. By the time of the Deconstructivist exhibition at the Museum of Modern Art, he had developed an approach to design influenced by linguistic theories and the philosophical arguments of poststructuralism. He began to appreciate architecture's role in providing persuasive images of authority for social institutions in an era when truth, authority, and beauty were increasingly described as socially constructed rather than universally valid conditions. In an essay published in the July

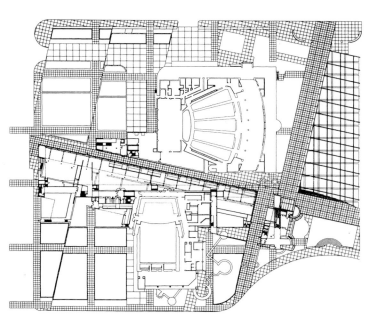

7.14 Peter Eisenman,
Wexner Center,
Ohio State University,
plan, Columbus, Ohio,
1983–89.

1987 issue of the Japanese magazine *Architecture and Urbanism* Eisenman wrote:

Architecture, because it is bricks and mortar, holds out the promise of reality, authenticity, and genuine truth in a surreal world where truth is a managed item developed by committees, produced by writers, and sold by media spokesmen. Our only source of value today is a memory of value, a nostalgia; we live in a relativist world, yet desire absolute substance, something that is incontrovertibly real. Through its being, architecture has become, in the unconscious of society, the promise of this something real.

(Nesbitt, p. 176)

In his writing and his architecture, Eisenman argues that architects must reinvent architecture so that instead of validating social institutions and cultural beliefs, buildings can call them into question.

In 1983 Eisenman won a competition for the design of the Wexner Center for the Visual Arts at Ohio State University in Columbus, Ohio, and with this commission had his first opportunity to build on an institutional rather than a domestic scale. Completed in 1989, the Wexner Center includes exhibition and performance spaces, a lecture hall, and a library—all intended to support experimental programs in the visual and performing arts (fig. 7.14 and see p. 200). Eisenman made the building an essay on the arbitrary nature of order and the dubious role of context in architectural design. He marshaled the conventional tools all architects use to impose order and ensure legibility in a building, but he applied them in unconventional ways. The dominant axis of the building is aligned with the municipal grid of Columbus rather than the campus grid (the alignment of the two grids is off by 12.25 degrees). As a result, the visitor has the distinct impression of different geometries colliding within the building. Instead of responding to the existing surroundings, Eisenman erected castellated brick towers at one corner to evoke the memory of a nineteenth-century armory, destroyed by fire in 1958, that once occupied part of the site. Since these design cues are obscure rather than apparent, the logic of the architect's decisions is lost on the visitor who arrives unprepared to decipher the dissonant features of the building. The Wexner Center continually prods the visitor, prepared or not, to confront his or her expectations concerning the relationship between visual order and spatial experience.

Rem Koolhaas

Dissonance, an anathema in most design aesthetics, is one of the intriguing qualities of "Decon" architecture. An appreciation for dissonance emerged as a response to the congestion of contemporary cities and the evident failure of decades' worth of schemes advanced by modernist architects and planners to manage the modern metropolis. Beginning with the publication of *Delirious New York* in 1978, Rem Koolhaas has been writing about the implications of the density, congestion, and sheer gigantism of the twentieth-century metropolis. With a keen eye for the state of

modern urbanism and sensitive to the temperament of his generation, he summed up the situation in a 1993 lecture in Toronto. To identify the different design orientations within his generation Koolhaas contrasted the classical urbanism of Leon Krier (whose work will be discussed later in this chapter) with the Deconstructivist schemes of Coop Himmelblau:

> I also want to talk about my generation, as a kind of caricature of the generation of May 1968 which shouldn't be taken too seriously but shouldn't be ignored. Our generation has had two reactions to this contemporary urban condition. One basically ignored it, or to give it a more positive interpretation, courageously resisted it, as Leon Krier's big theoretical reconstruction of Washington. . . . Where Leon Krier and his half of the generation are rebuilding the city, Coop Himmelbau and the other half is abandoning any claims that the city can be rebuilt, throwing up their arms about our ability to even reconstruct any recognizable form of the city. Out of this debate, they make spectacle—a rhetorical play where instead of a series of formal axes there is just composition, inspired on the unconscious and essentially chaotic aesthetic.

(Nesbitt, p. 333)

7.15 Rem Koolhaas, The Netherlands Dance Theater, The Hague, Netherlands, 1984–87.

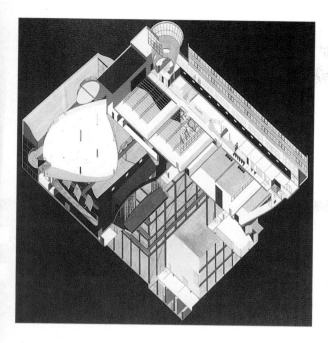

Rem Koolhaas came to architecture with a background in journalism and film, and he first achieved public prominence as a theoretician. Beginning in the 1980s, while practicing with Elias and Zoe Zenghelis and Madelon Vriesendorp under the name of the Office for Metropolitan Architecture (OMA), Koolhaas began to secure commissions that allowed him to advance his own conception of an architecture appropriate for the late twentieth century.

Completed in 1987, OMA's Netherlands Dance Theater occupies a very unpromising site wedged between an elevated highway and several bland office buildings (figs. 7.15, 7.16). The theater is filled with dramatic gestures such as an undulating roof and an ovoid platform that appears to balance precariously on a single beam. In order to maximize the size of the lobby, Koolhaas incorporated the area under the auditorium's raked seating into it. The sloping roof of this part of the lobby combined with curve walls creates an eccentrically shaped space that further complicates attempts to comprehend the theater's spatial order. There is no classical model of axial order or modernist system of gridded discipline to mold the collection of colorful shapes and quirky spaces into a simple, legible order. The dance theater endows the neighborhood with a theatrical flair and evokes the restless energy of contemporary urban life.

7.16 Rem Koolhaas, The Netherlands Dance Theater, cross-section, The Hague, Netherlands, 1984–87.

Information rather than theatrics provided the theme for Koolhaas's 1989 design for the National Library of France competition (fig. 7.17). The Industrial Revolution ushered in the age of the machine, and early modern architects were concerned with the design implications of the machine. The cybernetic revolution of the late twentieth century ushered in the age of information, and Koolhaas's generation was the first to grapple with the spatial implications of information and methods of organization based on computer logic. In cyberspace the familiar shapes of Euclidean geometry no longer serve as the only model. Forms that begin as shapeless blobs can be stretched out, rotated and twisted so as to defy the conventional wisdom about building and introduce a new dialectic between orthogonal and non-orthogonal configurations of space. This tension between alternative conceptions of space is at the heart of Koolhaas's design.

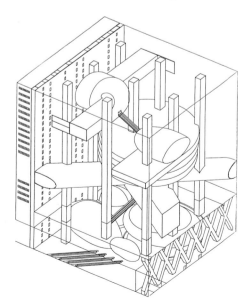

7.17 Rem Koolhaas, National Library of France, section, Paris, France, 1989.

The program for the National Library of France called for five separate collections, with holdings in a variety of formats, to be housed in a single structure. Koolhaas envisioned the library as a solid block of information with the major public spaces treated as voids carved out of the solid. A stack of identical floors contains storage areas for library material and occupies the majority of the block's volume. In section, the public spaces appear as a series of eccentrically shaped voids distributed throughout the block. Koolhaas's description of the reading rooms as embryos "floating in memory . . . each with its own technological placenta" suggests a new spatial vocabulary emerging from the womb of the old.

The Return of Classicism

Architecture provides shelter and facilitates many different human activities. It also expresses cultural values and it is as champions of traditional values that classical architects returned to the international arena in the late 1970s and 1980s. Although classicism had never entirely disappeared from the architectural scene, it had clearly receded in importance after World War II until it was little more than a residual element in contemporary design culture. Slowly, classicism began to attract new adherents.

Young architects took out the old texts on classical composition and began to relearn the principles of proportion, the orders, and traditional tectonics. When, in the passage quoted above (p. 216), Rem Koolhaas referred to Leon Krier (b. 1946) and "his half" of a generation, he was acknowledging the existence of a design orientation dramatically different from the one highlighted by the Museum of Modern Art's review of contemporary developments in its Deconstructivist architecture exhibition. Koolhaas, however, was too generous in his description of the new classicists as representing half of his generation. The actual number of committed classicists constituted only a small minority of the generation coming to professional maturity in the last quarter of the century. Numbers, however, are not the critical issue since emerging movements initially represent, by definition, a minority within the dominant professional culture.

Classicists were, of course, not the only ones to point out the manifest failures of modernism; modern architecture was being assailed from many different quarters during the 1970s and 1980s. The Neo-Rationalist critique of modernist urbanism outlined by Aldo Rossi in his *The Architecture of the City*, for example, stimulated interest in traditional typologies which, in turn, led at least some young architects to investigate the enduring heritage of classical design. But neither Rossi nor postmodernists such as Charles Moore ever embraced classical models as literally as the new generation of classicists, represented here by the European polemicist Leon Krier and the American architect and educator Thomas Gordon Smith.

Leon Krier

In the late 1970s Leon Krier began to gain recognition as a passionate critic of modern and postmodern approaches to architecture. Along with Demetri Porphyrios (b. 1949), Allan Greenberg (b. 1938), and Leon's brother Rob Krier (b. 1938), he advocated a return to the principles of classicism. Krier's rhetorical skills as a polemicist soon gave him a prominent voice in international design debates. Like Rem Koolhaas, Krier's appreciation of modern architecture was shaped by the postwar transformation of European cities. Defined in demographic terms, Krier and Koolhaas belong to the same generation; Koolhaas was born in 1944 in the Netherlands and Krier two years later in Luxembourg. Both recognized the discrepancy between the utopian promise of early-twentieth-century modernism and the gritty actuality of late-twentieth-century building. In a 1985 essay entitled "The Terrifying Beauty of the Twentieth Century," Rem Koolhaas described postwar European cities as textbooks of flawed design efforts: "the European metropolis is like a reef on which each intention, each ambition, each solution, each question, each answer implacably runs aground."

This is an assessment with which Krier certainly concurred, but here the parallels begin to diverge. Rather than recoil from congestion and the formal disorder of the contemporary city, Koolhaas remains fascinated by it: "Europe is now, almost everywhere, ridiculously beautiful," he concluded. What Koolhaas perceives as ridiculously beautiful, Leon Krier finds hideously ugly. Using the harshest possible language, Krier describes the postwar transformation of Luxembourg as a devastation:

> The rape of that beautiful birthplace became for me what genocide must mean for a persecuted people. I took it very personally. Here was a menace on a global scale.
>
> (Economakis, p. 7)

Krier has become one of the leading spokespersons for the position that nothing can be salvaged from the great experiment in design and life known as modernism. Only by turning away from the illusory promises of modernism can order, harmony, and beauty be restored to the built environment.

Krier illustrated his lectures and publications with his own trenchant drawings, but until the late 1980s he had built practically nothing. In the 1980s he was invited to be a design consultant for a new town in Florida called Seaside. The story of Seaside belongs to Chapter 8; here it is sufficient to note that Krier's involvement led to his first major executed work: the Krier/Wolff House, completed in 1989 (fig. 7.18). In plan and massing, the house is built up from a series of units. One of the distinctive features found in many of the houses in Seaside is a rooftop terrace from which the residents can enjoy the stunning sunsets common in this coastal location. Krier developed his rooftop terrace as a classical tempietto poised serenely atop the building.

He drew upon both classical and vernacular models for his design and the effect does much to explain the appeal of classicism in the late twentieth century. In place of dissonance, classical architects speak of beauty; in place of the cult of the new, they stress continuity with the past through the adoption of the classical language of architecture. In classical design theory, the anthropomorphic basis of proportions is an affirmation, in architectural terms, of human dignity and value. Within design culture, the backward-looking nature of these arguments became the object of derision and scorn. Outside of professional circles, however, these themes struck a responsive chord in many people baffled and alienated by the latest examples of modern, postmodern, and Deconstructivist architecture.

7.18 Leon Krier, Krier/Wolff House, Seaside, Florida, 1989.

Thomas Gordon Smith

The same year Krier finished his house in Seaside, Thomas Gordon Smith was appointed head of the School of Architecture at the University of Notre Dame. Smith received international attention after his participation in the 1980 "Presence of the Past" exhibition, and his appointment marked the first time in decades that the direction of a professional degree program in an American university was entrusted to an architect committed to the revival of the classical tradition. Smith introduced the model of paradigmatic education. In place of the Bauhaus approach to education through experimentation (see Chapter 3), the paradigmatic approach is based on education through the emulation of noteworthy examples of traditional architecture. In this approach, students learn the principles of classical composition through the study of masterworks from the canon of great buildings.

Smith's scholarly investigation of the classical tradition is evident in his own house, designed in 1989 on a small lot in an existing residential neighborhood in South Bend, Indiana (fig. 7.19). He synthesized elements drawn from a variety of sources. The main image of the house as a pedimented block flanked by one-story wings is related to nineteenth-century American Greek Revival houses. The proportions of the pedimented portico and main interior space draw upon Vitruvian and Palladian sources. Smith's goal of achieving the harmonic integration of material from many sources has a polemical edge that can be fully appreciated only when his designs are considered next to Deconstructivist designs from the same period.

7.19 Thomas Gordon Smith, Smith House, South Bend, Indiana, 1989–90.
For the pedimented portico Smith uses the classical formula of Ionic columns *in antis* (aligned with the side walls rather then projecting forward). The flanking wings are articulated with a Doric entablature. Metopes illustrate incidents from the Labors of Herakles.

Challenge and Adaptation

Thus far, this chapter has traced the unraveling of the postwar modernist hegemony in architecture by examining developments in Europe and North America. Even Zaha Hadid's design for The Peak in Hong Kong (see fig. 7.13) reveals more about Western architectural debates than it does about developments in either China or Hadid's native Iraq. In the twentieth century, however, modernism as a cultural phenomenon and agent of economic modernization exercised global impact. It is important to acknowledge that in the Third World, too, modernism encountered challenges and demonstrated a pattern of adaptation.

Hassan Fathy

In 1945 the Egyptian architect Hassan Fathy (b. 1899) received the commission for the design of a new village to house 7,000 residents of an existing village scheduled for relocation. The village of Gourna was located near the archaeological site at Luxor and villagers were suspected of profiting from the illegal trafficking in antiquities. Egyptian officials saw the creation of New Gourna at a location distant from the archaeological zone as an effective way to suppress the plundering of ancient sites. Fathy saw the design and construction of New Gourna (figs. 7.20, 7.21) as an

opportunity to assert the enduring wisdom of vernacular building traditions in the face of the pressure to adapt Western models of economic and physical development. He lamented the failure of modern architects to heed the lessons of vernacular building concerning materials and forms responsive to local climate and existing levels of technology.

Fathy proposed to build New Gourna out of mud bricks and to incorporate time-tested features of Egyptian architecture such as the *malkaf* (a "wind-catcher" that ventilates a house naturally) and *mashrabiyas* (timber lattice screens over windows). Fathy described his agenda for New Gourna in great detail in his book *Gourna: A Tale of Two Villages*, published in Cairo in 1969. The story of New Gourna acquired an international significance when an English translation of this under the title *Architecture for the Poor: An Experiment in Rural Egypt* appeared in the United States in 1973. Fathy's critique of modern architecture's inadequacies as a model for developing countries added to the drum beat of criticism being leveled at modernism.

Fathy recognized the erosion of the vernacular traditions he admired as local craftsmen abandoned their methods in favor of newer, Western techniques. In his design for the village center, he made provisions for a mosque, a village hall to house municipal offices, a theater, and a *khan* or commercial hall patterned after the caravanserai which had for centuries served as important trading centers in Islamic communities. Fathy hoped the provision of a *khan*

7.20 Hassan Fathy, New Gourna, plan and elevation, Egypt, 1948.

In his gouache renderings for New Gourna, Fathy combined a conventional plan and elevation with decorative motifs and symbols borrowed from Pharaonic wall painting to convey an indigenous and timeless quality. The cow visible here is a representation of Hathor, the ancient goddess of fertility.

7.21 Hassan Fathy, New Gourna, Egypt, 1948.

would stimulate the reestablishment of traditional, craft-based production by providing a center for village artisans to sell their goods. New Gourna reflected Fathy's conception of the role of the architect in the Third World:

> An architect is in a unique position to revive the peasant's faith in his own culture. If, as an authoritative critic, he shows what is admirable in local forms, and even goes so far as to use them himself, then the peasants at once begin to look on their own products with pride. What was formerly ignored or even despised becomes suddenly something to boast about.
>
> (Fathy, p. 43)

There is, however, another aspect to the story of New Gourna. The village residents refused to play the role assigned to them by Fathy and the Egyptian authorities, and actively resisted the reforming efforts of the "authoritative critic." Despite Fathy's efforts, New Gourna did not become a model for an architecture in the service of the poor. Residents began to modify and eventually abandoned the mud-brick construction central to Fathy's vision of the village. Recent accounts of New Gourna have noted cases in which residents have rebuilt their mud-brick houses in concrete. "The world has changed," residents are quoted as saying. "We wanted something modern, with a modern look."

Charles Correa

The theme of resistance to an alien but dominant world view is recast in different terms by the Indian architect Charles Correa (b. 1930) in his design for the Jawahar Kala Kendra in Jaipur, India (fig. 7.22). Commissioned in 1986 as a cultural center and craft museum, the Jawahar Kala Kendra is a contemporary interpretation of an ancient cosmic model. Correa based his plan on the nine-square *navagraha* mandala in which each square is associated with a different planet (fig. 7.23). Each of the nine squares in the Jawahar Kala Kendra measures thirty meters square and houses different programmatic elements. Correa carefully paired each discrete

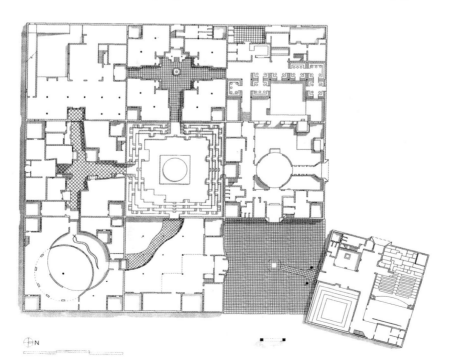

7.22 (left) Charles Correa, Jawahar Kala Kendra, Jaipur, Rajasthan, India, 1986–92.

7.23 (right) Charles Correa, Jawahar Kala Kendra, plan, Jaipur, Rajasthan, India, 1986–92.

component of the program with the appropriate planetary symbol. Thus the library is housed in the square dedicated to Jupiter, the planet associated with knowledge gained through meditation; the administrative offices are located in the square dedicated to Mars as the symbol of power; and so forth through the entire mandala. The decorative motifs and color scheme of each square follow the attributes of the corresponding planets as recorded in the ancient Vedic literature.

A second level of significance is added to this cosmic symbolism. Jaipur, the capital of the state of Rajasthan, was founded in 1727 by Maharaja Sawai Jai Singh; the original city plan also was based on the *navagraha* mandala. However, Jai Singh was forced to shift the location of one of the nine planetary squares in order to avoid impinging on an existing hill. In his plan for the Jawahar Kala Kendra, Correa shifted one square out of the grid to acknowledge the particular history of Jaipur as a complement to the universal symbolism of the mandala.

Born in India and educated in the United States at the University of Michigan and MIT, Correa blends local and global references in his work. For example, the plan of Jawahar Kala Kendra is based on the repetitive use of a basic geometric form, a plan type emblematic of modern architecture. At the same time, the design acquires a compelling sense of presence and significance because of its relationship to Indian traditions. Correa has written about the importance of open-to-sky spaces in Indian architecture. Rather than conform to the Western model of the self-contained, climate-controlled box, the circulation system of the Jawahar Kala Kendra moves the visitor through a sequence of outdoor spaces. In ways both large and small, the experience of being in the museum is unmistakably Indian in character. Modernism has been accused by critics of leveling cultural differences and relentlessly eroding regional identities. In preserving and celebrating the distinctive cultural heritage of Rajasthan, Correa demonstrated the power of architecture to resist this process of homogenization.

Organic Form and Craft-Building

It would be a mistake to assume that the emergence of postmodernism and Deconstructivism and the revival of classicism signaled the demise of all other conceptions of the modern tradition in architecture. The final two examples to be considered in this chapter testify to the continued vitality of two important design orientations in twentieth-century architecture: organic form and craft-based building.

The Pietiläs

In 1978 the husband-and-wife partnership of Raili (b. 1926) and Reima (1923–1993) Pietilä won a competition for a new city library in Tampere, Finland. The result (fig. 7.24), opened in 1986, belongs to a tradition of idiosyncratic and highly expressive architecture that includes the work of Hugo Häring and Hans Scharoun (1893–1972) in Europe and Frank Lloyd Wright and Bruce Goff in America. The rounded profiles of the copper-clad dome and roof have been compared to the shell of marine animals in the same way that Wright's Guggenheim Museum frequently is. Using an equally vivid but very different image, some critics have described the low, compact library as a flying saucer that has settled to earth. Both metaphors

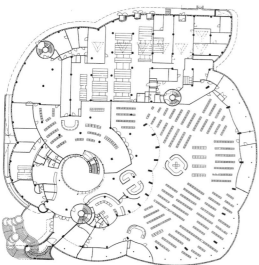

7.24 (above) Raili and Reima Pietilä, Tampere Main Library, Tampere, Finland, 1978–86.

7.25 (left) Raili and Reima Pietilä, Tampere Main Library, plan, Tampere, Finland, 1978–86.

identify the library as a provocative presence in the cityscape. The fluid swirling character of the design is evident in the plan as well (fig. 7.25). The Pietiläs cited the shape of a male wood-grouse ruffling its plumage as their formal inspiration for the plan.

Seen from the entry foyer, the interior unfolds in a series of expanding spaces; no single axis establishes the visitor's route through the library or fixes a spatial hierarchy within the building. By tilting the shallow dome to admit more light, the architects created an interior that seems to open to the sky rather than rigidly fixing the boundary between inside and out. Such unconventional forms are difficult to ignore and elicit strong responses from the visitor but, in the Tampere Library, the result is engaging rather than dissonant. The Pietiläs' combination of immediate sensory stimulation with allusive forms that reveal their metaphorical richness only after thoughtful observation is typical of the organic tradition in twentieth-century architecture. The Tampere Library can be deciphered as a romantic interpretation of regional myths and images or experienced viscerally as a marvelous orchestration of space, light, and material.

Peter Zumthor

At first sight, the work of the Swiss architect Peter Zumthor lacks the attention-grabbing character of the Tampere Library. His work draws its power to attract from the subtle appeal of craft-based building with its emphasis on the integrity of the well-made artifact. Zumthor is the son of a cabinetmaker and his studio in Haldenstein, finished in 1986, reflects his own early training as a furniture maker (fig. 7.26). The simple, barnlike structure is constructed of wood according to the local building tradition. A thin shell of larch-wood slats encases the structure and endows the studio with the aura associated with a fine piece of furniture.

7.26 Peter Zumthor, Studio, Haldenstein, Graubünden, Switzerland, 1985–86.
  Zumthor's studio contains a single large room on the ground floor, a drafting room above, and archival space in the cellar. While the north elevation contains a single door and a narrow band of windows, an enormous opening on the building's south side provides views onto a garden with a grove of cherry trees.

Zumthor's appreciation of the role of building in contemporary life is shaped by his reading of the philosopher Martin Heidegger. In a 1991 essay, "The Hard Core of Beauty," Zumthor explained the links between Heidegger's ideas and his own work:

> In an essay entitled "Building, Dwelling, Thinking," Martin Heidegger wrote "Living among things is the basic principle of human existence," which I understand to mean that we are never in an abstract world but always in a world of things, even when we think. . . . The concept of dwelling, understood in Heidegger's wide sense of living and thinking in places and spaces, contains an exact reference to what reality means to me as an architect.
>
> (Zumthor, p. 24)

In an age saturated with superficial images generated by electronic media, Zumthor strives to provide an authentic experience of being in the world. This commitment to nurturing a profound awareness of place and materiality is, for Zumthor, a way of resisting the loss of meaning he sees as characteristic of contemporary culture. In his 1988 essay "A Way of Looking at Things," Zumthor articulated a conception of the role of the architect by describing how he confronted reality in his own work: "I carefully observe the concrete appearance of the world, and in my buildings I try to enhance what seems to be valuable, to correct what is disturbing, and to create anew what we feel is missing."

As the dominant ideology of modernism in architecture gave way to emergent design orientations such as postmodernism and Deconstructivism and a revived classical tradition, architects operated in an increasingly pluralistic design culture. Zumthor's call for architects to enhance the valuable, correct the flawed, and create again what has been lost sets a compelling and timely agenda for contemporary architecture.

Chapter 8

Reconfiguring the City

In the twentieth century the story of architecture unfolded in tandem with the story of urbanism as architects claimed professional expertise essential to the development of the modern city. Architectural design could, architects argued, facilitate the process of modernization, integrate the disparate parts of the modern metropolis, and even advance a social agenda based on improving living and working conditions for city residents. The explicit link between architecture and urbanism so forcefully insisted upon by modern architects means that changes in architectural design thinking have inevitably had repercussions on urban design. Chapter 7 described the loosening of a narrowly defined modernist architectural orthodoxy in the 1960s and the emergence in the 1970s and 1980s of a pluralist design culture in which postmodern, poststructuralist, and classical conceptions of architecture coexisted. This chapter examines the impact of this new architectural diversity on concepts and approaches to urban design.

Just as developments in architecture affected urban design, changes in the character of traditional cities influenced the way architecture was incorporated into major campaigns of urban regeneration. As the global economy was reconfigured in the last quarter of the twentieth century, information processing and financial services supplanted industrial manufacturing and commodities exchange as the driving force in many urban economies. European centers such as Paris, London, and Berlin were no longer the capitals of colonial empires extracting from their colonies abroad the resources necessary to sustain their industrial establishments at home. In the developed countries of Europe and North America many cities had to scramble to fill the void left by the dispersal of manufacturing activities around the globe.

Design campaigns conceived on an urban scale now addressed an expanded set of goals as service industries, information management, and tourism emerged as major determinants of planning priorities. Design served as a crucial form of municipal therapy for cities adjusting to new global conditions and, in a number of cases, still coping with the lingering effects of damage sustained during World War II. Design programs constituted an integral part of the promotional efforts of cities eager to attract new economic activity. Finally, confronted with profound changes on a global scale, many cities focused their attention once more on their urban images in an effort to reaffirm traditional notions of cultural superiority. As it has been throughout history, architecture would be a major component of ambitious new urban visions.

Canary Wharf, Isle of Dogs, Docklands, London, England, 1990s.

London

Daniel Burnham, one of the leading figures of the City Beautiful movement (see Chapter 1), advised his peers "Make no small plans for they have no magic to stir men's blood." The sweeping character of planning schemes in the early twentieth century that celebrated the modern metropolis as a center of culture and political power reflects this design ethos. The prominent urban schemes of the last decades of the century are shaped by a different agenda as the example of London's Docklands illustrates.

The Docklands

Encompassing an enormous area (2,226 hectares) stretching eastward along the Thames river from the city center, the Docklands historically had served as London's center for maritime trade. By the 1970s financial and service industries had supplanted manufacturing and trade as the driving force in the economy. The election of the Conservative Margaret Thatcher as prime minister in 1979 ushered in a new era in British planning. In 1981 the government created the London Docklands Development Corporation (LDDC) to supervise the redevelopment of former docks.

The ability of local councils to regulate new developments was greatly reduced and the LDDC was invested with broad powers to attract private developers through the creation of special enterprise zones. The LDDC represented a new type of planning agency endowed with powers unavailable to Daniel Burnham when he

8.1 (opposite) Nicholas Grimshaw & Partners, *Financial Times* Printing Works, 240 East India Dock Road, London, England, 1988.
 Grimshaw designed the building around the linear printing process. Huge rolls of newsprint are positioned at one end of the building, and printed newspapers are loaded onto trucks in a special dispatch bay at the other end. The simplicity of the layout and the regularity of the structural system meant that design and construction could be completed in one year.

8.2 (above) John Outram Associates, Storm Water Pumping Station, Stewart Street, Isle of Dogs, London, England, 1988.

presented the 1909 Plan for Chicago. Canary Wharf on the Isle of Dogs illustrates the LDDC approach (see page 228). Olympia and York, a Canadian development company, obtained the rights to develop the property. Olympia and York hired the American firm of Skidmore, Owings and Merrill to prepare a master plan for the twenty-nine-hectare site and commissions for individual buildings were awarded to an international roster of architects.

In the emerging global economy of the late twentieth century, developers no longer turned to local context for their models. Canary Wharf owes more to such North American mega-developments as Manhattan's Battery Park City or Toronto's First Canadian Place than it does to the urban traditions of London. Not surprisingly, therefore, much of the criticism surrounding Canary Wharf involves a lament for the loss of a distinctive sense of place and scale in favor of a generic business district of tall office buildings, restaurants, and retail outlets catering to an equally generic class of urban professionals. The degree to which urban form is shaped by financial concerns rather than civic idealism is an equally strong thread in the criticism of Canary Wharf.

Critical opinion concerning the architectural merits of new buildings in the Docklands can be summed up by quoting the opening paragraphs of one popular architectural guidebook to the area.

> London's Docklands contains one of the worst collections of late twentieth-century building to be seen anywhere in the world. It is a marvel, if it were not so embarrassing, that so many bad buildings from the same period can be found in such a comparatively small area of the city . . . And yet it is to the Docklands that you must go to find some of the best British architecture of the 1980s. The gems are few, but compared to anywhere else in the UK today, the concentration is high and the quality rare.
>
> (Williams, p. 8)

The "gems" indicate how no single design approach dominated the architectural image of the city in the late twentieth century. Nicholas Grimshaw's (b. 1939) Printing Works for the *Financial Times* (fig. 8.1) recasts the modernist paradigm of the glazed box in contemporary terms. The building is a huge steel-framed industrial shed housing the printing presses for the *Financial Times*. From a distance, the transparent skin of the building reveals the giant presses in the modernist tradition of celebrating technology by revealing mechanical processes. Up close, the observer is drawn to the articulation of the glass curtain wall. In place of postwar metal and glass-curtain-wall systems that tended to conceal the means of assembly, Grimshaw chose to expose the system of attachment. One need not possess an engineering degree to appreciate intuitively how the glass is held in place by steel plates attached to steel pieces cantilevered from the structural frame.

Completed the same year as the *Financial Times* Printing Works, 1988, John Outram's (b. 1943) Storm Water Pumping Station (fig. 8.2) reveals a very different approach. Like the *Financial Times* building, the pumping station is basically an industrial shed erected to protect machinery. Outram houses the giant pumps in a colorful brick box. The oversized column capitals supporting a pediment pierced by an enormous industrial fan reflect a postmodern sense of form and composition.

Paris

The opening, in 1977, of the Pompidou Center focused the spotlight of international attention on Paris. The glamor and notoriety surrounding the new cultural center whetted the appetite of French authorities for more, and proposals for new buildings quickly followed. In the 1980s Paris was the subject of international press coverage and design commentary as a result of a sustained campaign to build major new civic and cultural monuments known collectively as *les grands projets*. Preliminary work on some of the individual buildings later identified as part of the *grands projets* began during the administration of President Valéry Giscard d'Estaing.

It was, however, during the presidency of François Mitterand, who succeeded Giscard d'Estaing in 1981, that the *grands projets* assumed their definitive form as building programs and as emblems of a renewed French prestige. Kings, emperors, and presidents have long recognized the power of architecture to immortalize the memory of ambitious leaders and the socialist Mitterand was no exception. He embarked on an ambitious program of new construction that grew to encompass nine major projects. Four projects were initiated during the previous administration and confirmed, with revisions, by Mitterand: the Musée d'Orsay, the Museum of Science and Technology, the Arab World Institute, and the Great Arch at La Défense. Five new projects were added to this list: the remodeling of the Louvre Museum, a new home for the Ministry of Finance, a new opera house, a park at La Villette, and a new home for the National Music Conservatory.

The *grands projets* were intended, in part, to commemorate the 1989 bicentenary of the French Revolution. The ensemble of new buildings was also intended to identify Paris as a center of innovative design thinking and signal the city's importance as an international center of culture. Finally, Mitterand envisioned the *grands projets* as a model for a new kind of city that was already busy preparing in the last decades of one century for the dawning of the next. Mitterand used the phrase "a new equilibrium" to describe his conception:

> It is a city of imagination, ideas, youth. . . . The major projects mark an important step in the urban development of the end of the 20th century. Disturbed and often devastated by industrial evolution, economic crises, demographic changes and immigration, our cities must find a new equilibrium. . . . I also intended that these major projects provide meeting places for different kinds of people, for different forms of knowledge and for art. A new form of public facility must address a larger public . . . Only in this way can we grasp the continuous movement of invention and thought and be prepared for technological, cultural and social change.
>
> (Fachard, p. 8)

In Mitterand's "city of imagination, ideas, youth," architecture's role was to provide dramatic, tangible proof that innovation and creativity were alive and flourishing in Paris.

Louvre Pyramid

For centuries the Louvre has served as the architectural representation of French authority in both the political and cultural realms, first as the royal residence and later as one of the world's foremost museums. Thus the decision to undertake a major reconfiguration of the building signaled the importance of the *grands projets*. In 1981 President Mitterand awarded the commission for the remodeling of the Louvre to the American architect I. M. Pei (b. 1917), one of the leading modernists of his generation who had recently completed a major addition to the National Gallery in Washington DC. Plans called for the Ministry of Finance, which shared space in the Louvre with the museum, to be relocated to a new building and the museum's facilities to be modernized and substantially enlarged. Historic parts of the structure were refurbished and new space created by excavating the Louvre's enormous forecourt and inserting various public services including a new lobby below ground.

The signature piece of Pei's design is a glass pyramid that rises out of the Cour Napoleon (fig. 8.3). Twenty-one meters high and thirty-three meters to a side at the base, the pyramid serves as the museum's main entrance and allows natural light to reach the lower level of the public spaces. In a reversal of a tradition stretching back to ancient Egypt, the Louvre pyramid is a transparent volume instead of a massive solid. Surrounded by the ornate architecture of the Louvre, the pyramid is an ethereal presence in its historic setting; its design combines formal abstraction with technologically advanced construction. The Louvre pyramid affirmed the continued vitality of the formal language of modernism in an era of postmodern

8.3 I. M. Pei, Louvre, glass pyramid, Paris, France, 1989.

8.4 (left) Victor Laloux, Gare d'Orsay Railway Station, Paris, France, interior before remodeling, 1900.

8.5 (below) Victor Laloux and Gae Aulenti, Gare d'Orsay Railway Station, Paris, France, interior after remodeling, 1986.

Gae Aulenti described her design as a building within a building. The contrast between the new museum walls and the old train station emphasizes the difference between nineteenth- and twentieth-century architecture. The low walls installed by Aulenti can be seen as geometric abstractions of the railroad cars that once filled the train shed.

pluralism; it also served notice that French authorities would not shrink from controversy. The bold character of the *grands projets* ensured that they remained the center of international debates about the condition of contemporary design.

Musée d'Orsay

Across the Seine from the Tuilleries, another of the *grands projets*, the Musée d'Orsay, opened in 1986. Conceived as a museum of French art from the years 1848 to 1914, the collection is housed in the former Gare d'Orsay erected in 1900. Designed originally by Victor Laloux (1850–1937), the station is an example of Beaux-Arts architecture adapted to accommodate the modern program of rail travel (fig. 8.4). By 1939, however, railroad technology had rendered the station obsolete and its future unclear. The destruction in the early 1970s of Les Halles, the famous central food markets, sparked new interest in the preservation of Parisian monuments. As a result, in 1973 President Giscard d'Estaing declared the Gare d'Orsay a national monument, but it remained a monument without a purpose. Five years later, plans to install the great collection of French nineteenth-century art in the building were announced and the museum commission was awarded to the French firm ACT Architecture.

ACT's proposal called for the refurbishment of the building's exterior. The Beaux-Arts style of Laloux's railroad station was now enlisted to project the aura of a cultural monument. However, initial plans for the interior of the new museum soon encountered strong criticism and in 1980 the Italian designer Gae Aulenti (b. 1927) was brought in to develop a gallery plan. One of the challenges in any renovation of a historic structure involves establishing a dialogue between the past and the present. This issue acquired particular significance in the 1970s as a result of postmodern commentaries on the relationship between modern and historical design languages. Aulenti refused to defer to the Beaux-Arts character of Laloux's station; instead she installed a series of low granite walls within the lofty space of the old train shed (fig. 8.5). The result is a provocative tension between the restrained detailing and lithic solidity of the new walls and the ornate character of Laloux's design. This tension, Aulenti writes, is intentional:

> The principle of composition adopted is one of deliberate and systematic contrast and not one of either natural or stylistic symbiosis. In this way the buildings within the building appear to profit from the decomposition–fragmentation process and develop their own language.

(Fachard, p. 65)

As the Musée d'Orsay demonstrates, the design of exhibition space is critical to the intellectual program of any museum and serves as a revealing index of contemporary museological concerns.

Arab World Institute

While the Musée d'Orsay pointedly raises the issue of how the present looks at the past, the Arab World Institute, designed by Jean Nouvel (b. 1945) and opened in 1987, explored the possibility of a design dialogue between European and Arab cultures. Located in the Latin Quarter, the Arab World Institute was conceived as a center for Arab studies; the facility includes library, auditorium, museum, and

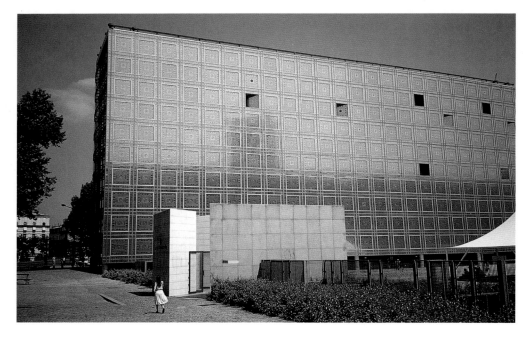

exhibition spaces. The selection of materials and prismatic volumes of Nouvel's design reflect the European tradition of modernist architecture. The southern facade of the building is fabricated of aluminum and glass panels (fig. 8.6). Set within these panels are twenty-seven thousand adjustable diaphragms regulated by light-sensitive photo-electric cells. Like the shutter of a camera, these diaphragms open and close to control the amount of light filtering through the wall. The intricate patterns of light and dark created by the diaphragms provide a modern equivalent to the *mashrabiya* (latticework screen for windows) which is a common building element found throughout the Arab world. Using modern technology, Nouvel recast the traditional Arab screening device in a way that suggests the potential for a design dialogue between industrialized and vernacular approaches to building.

Previously, European architects had appropriated elements of non-Western building cultures in ways that reinforced the dominant status of colonial powers. Chapter 4, for example, included a discussion of the Netherlands Pavilion at the 1931 "Paris Exposition Coloniale Internationale" in which bits and pieces of indigenous architecture from the Dutch-controlled East Indies were assembled in an elaborate pastiche that catered to a European taste for the exotic. Nouvel's desire to explore a more complex relationship between different traditions provides a European parallel to the design efforts of Charles Correa discussed in Chapter 7.

La Villette

The quest for a "new equilibrium" was not confined to Paris's historic core. Several of the *grands projets* are located in the city's nineteenth arrondissement because the relocation of the nineteenth-century slaughterhouses opened up an area encompassing

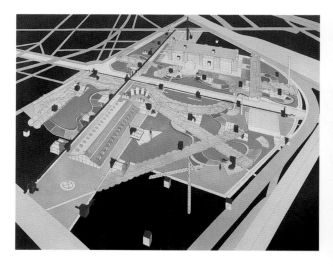

8.9 (right) Bernard Tschumi, Parc de La Villette, Paris, France, 1984–89.

Tschumi tries to strike a balance between individuality and uniformity. Each park pavilion is unique although all have the same bright-red metallic skin. They combine features drawn from eighteenth-century follies, nineteenth-century industrial installations, and Russian constructivist designs of the early twentieth century.

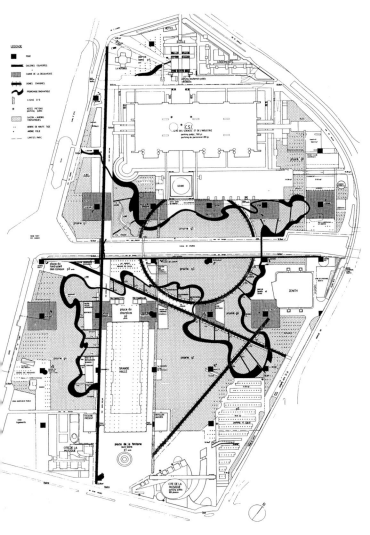

fifty-five hectares in the working-class neighborhood of La Villette. In 1983 Bernard Tschumi (b. 1944) won an international competition for the design of a new park covering thirty-five hectares (figs. 8.7, 8.8, 8.9). Tschumi seized the opportunity to propose what he described in the following words as model urban park for the twenty-first century:

> The fact that Paris is a concentration of tertiary or professional employment argues against passive "esthetic" parks of repose in favor of new urban parks based on cultural invention, education and entertainment. The inadequacy of the civilization vs. nature polarity under modern city conditions has invalidated the time-honored prototype of the park as an image of nature. It can no longer be conceived as an undefiled Utopian world-in-miniature, protected from vile reality.

(Fachard, p. 131)

Geometry in the form of points, lines, and planes rather than nature serves as Tschumi's point of departure. The Parc de La Villette is based on the superimposition of three different ordering systems. The "points" consist of a set of pavilions (labeled "follies" by Tschumi) arranged in a grid pattern within the park. A series of paths and canals create a network of "lines" and a broad expanse of flat green lawn constitutes the "plane" of the composition. The most distinctive elements of the Parc de La Villette are the bright

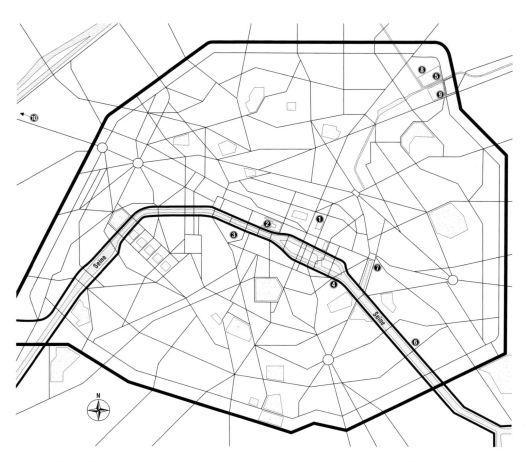

red follies distributed throughout the park and meant to be read conceptually as points in the multilayered geometry of the design. Tschumi distributed various services such as refreshments, sports center, media laboratory, and nursery throughout the park using the follies. Like the multiple alignments of Eisenman's Wexner Center, the coexistence of separate organizing devices (points, lines, and planes) on a single site calls into question the architect's ability to impose an all-embracing order and regulate human activity through design.

This discussion of the *grands projets* could be continued project by project. The design of each building involves a unique set of programmatic issues, constraints, and opportunities. In a chapter devoted to urban considerations, however, the significance of what Mitterrand labeled the "new equilibrium" resides in the contrast between the *grands projets* and earlier urban visions. Whether one is discussing the civic idealism of the City Beautiful movement, the rationalistic urbanism of the CIAM, or the awesome display of power at the heart of imperial and totalitarian designs, the whole (the city) is greater than the sum of its parts (the buildings). The totality of the urban vision is expressed with a diagrammatic clarity in plan. Mapping the location of the *grands projets* onto the city of Paris reveals no such comprehensive and unified urban configuration (fig. 8.10). The urban character of the *grands projets* is closer to the prescient urbanism of Antonio Sant'Elia and the Futurist city of isolated monuments.

How then do the *grands projets* convey the image of Paris as a center of creativity and culture? Through the camera's eye. The popular as well as professional design press saturated the media with images of the new Paris; fashion and travel magazines reproduced photographs coupled with captions describing the latest developments. People who never visited Paris read or watched programs about the latest French architectural *cause célèbre*. In the "global village" media images rather than urban spaces told the story of the city in the late twentieth century.

Berlin

Internationale Bauausstellung (IBA)

In the late 1970s Berlin entered a significant new phase in its tumultuous history. Devastated in the final battles of World War II, partitioned in the peace that followed, and exploited by both sides during the Cold War, Berlin struggled to regain control of its own destiny. In West Berlin the main impetus for the rejuvenation of the urban scene came from the Internationale Bauausstellung (IBA) founded in 1979. Like the Hansaviertel scheme of the mid-1950s (see Chapter 5), the IBA attracted an international roster of prominent architects and made West Berlin once again a showcase for contemporary design. The IBA had a significantly new approach to developing the city. With the motto "The Inner City as a Place to Live," the IBA combined much needed new housing initiatives with an urban design agenda that broke decisively with the CIAM-inspired practice of segregating different functions of the city in separate zones. In contrast to postwar programs of urban renewal that wiped out existing neighborhoods, the IBA advocated mixed-use developments and the restoration of existing housing stock where possible. It pursued a two-pronged approach, with new construction under the general supervision of Josef Kleihues (b. 1933) and "careful urban renewal," which mandated the renovation of existing structures, under the direction of Hardt-Waltherr Hämer.

If careful was one key word in the vocabulary of Berlin planners, critical was another. The collapse of the Berlin Wall in 1989 added a new sense of urgency and purpose to debates concerning Berlin's future. The relationship between the city's past and its future figured prominently in this debate and the term "critical reconstruction" emerged as the key concept guiding design efforts. In the context of urban design in the 1980s and 1990s, the word critical meant architects were challenged to question the assumptions of modernist planners concerning urban space. Hans Stinmann, City Building Director in the late 1980s, explained the concept in the following words:

> Following years of failed urban experiments, the prevailing wish was not for an entirely new city but for a return to traditional urbanism. . . . The purpose of critical reconstruction is not to recreate historical conditions or a nostalgic landscape, but rather to achieve a differentiated, contemporary urban structure. Berlin should once again be made perceptible in its historical scales and layerings . . . but also as a site of contemporary architecture and of economic conditions.
>
> (Balfour, p. 51)

Rather than treat the city as a tabula rasa to be configured according to modernist design principles, critical reconstruction required architects to work within a set of guidelines designed to promote a dialogue between the past and present concerning the urban form and architectural character of the city. New projects were required to observe height limitations and restore the outlines of old streets and squares obliterated by wartime destruction or eroded by postwar modernist schemes. This desire to reconnect with the city's distinctive urban history constitutes a genuine postmodern alternative to the urban theories of modernism.

Zaha Hadid

Some critics warned that the emphasis on reconstructing the urban fabric of prewar Berlin would impose a straightjacket on creativity and encourage a nostalgic fixation on premodern conditions. As buildings rose throughout the 1980s and 1990s, however, the results indicated that the critics missed their mark. In 1986 Zaha Hadid designed an apartment building in the South Friedrichstadt area of the city. Her scheme consists of an eight-story tower rising over a low base that defines the edge of the street (figs. 8.11, 8.12, 8.13). Rather than replicate the block forms typical of many IBA projects, Hadid exploited the triangular shape of the corner site. The viewer's initial impression is of a slablike form twisted and torqued until it matches the geometry of the site. Surface patterns created by the seams of the anodized sheet-metal cladding and the window mullions are skewed as well. The building has the same unsettled quality as her design for The Peak in Hong Kong

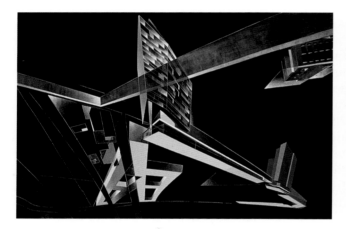

8.11 (above) Zaha Hadid, IBA housing complex, drawing, Berlin, Germany, 1994.

8.12 (right) Zaha Hadid, IBA housing complex, Dessauerstrasse 40, Berlin, Germany, 1994.

8.13 (far right) Zaha Hadid, IBA housing complex, Stessemannstrasse 109, Berlin, Germany, 1994.

which was included in the Museum of Modern Art's 1988 "Deconstructivist Architecture" exhibition. The flexed massing and apparent distortions of the orthogonal order inscribed on the surface of Hadid's design for Berlin suggests a barely contained energy that threatens to force the building apart. During the Cold War, the modern designs of the Hansaviertel apartment blocks were held up as architectural exemplars of freedom and rationality. It is difficult, if not impossible, however, to invest Hadid's IBA project with the same type of political significance.

"Green" Design

Like Paris with the completion of the *grands projets*, Berlin can now boast of a collection of signature buildings by some of the most prominent architects in international design circles. The IBA, however, included another kind of accomplishment which is indicative of Germany's investment in innovative approaches to energy management and environmental issues. Several of the IBA projects demonstrated a concern for what, in the 1980s, began to be called "green" design. One residential complex completed in 1987 in the South Friedrichstadt neighborhood, for example, included a miniature wetlands as part of an integrated system for water management. The development at the corner of the Bernburgerstrasse and Dessauerstrasse includes 106 residential units in a series of five- and six-story apartment blocks designed by four different German architectural offices. An urban wetlands created within the large city block allows the residents to purify and reclaim "gray water," thus reducing resource consumption (fig. 8.14). The planning and implementation of this integrated approach to energy and waste management involved extensive resident participation. Complementary efforts to develop ecologically sophisticated solutions to managing the energy consumption of new housing were undertaken elsewhere in Berlin.

8.14 Christoph Langhof et al, IBA housing complex, Bernburgerstrasse 22–26, Berlin, Germany, 1985–87.

The program of critical reconstruction in Berlin combined a respect for traditional urban design with an interest in innovative solutions to social and environmental problems. Here architects took advantage of Berlin's large urban blocks. They arranged housing along the perimeter in a traditional manner but developed the block's interior as an urban wetland for conservation purposes.

The IBA projects and the program of critical reconstruction demonstrate a significant effort to recalculate the balance between the construction of new housing, the renovation of existing building stock, and the implementation of energy-conscious design features characteristic of postwar urban renewal.

Frankfurt am Main

Berlin was not the only German city to attract international attention in the 1980s as a laboratory for new urban design initiatives. Frankfurt am Main also experienced a major urban renaissance in the 1980s and early 1990s (fig. 8.15). The huge convention facilities and the proliferation of tall office buildings on Frankfurt's skyline identified the city as a center of business and finance and earned for it the nickname of Manhattan am Main. In an effort to project an image of a city of culture as well as commerce, internationally prominent architects were commissioned to design a series of new museums on the Schaumainkai, a riverfront boulevard across the Main river from the city's historic center.

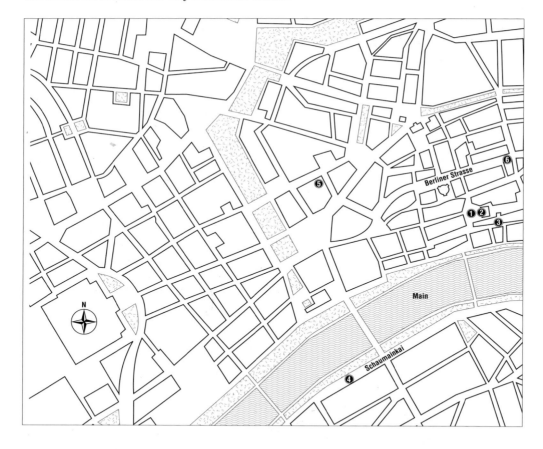

8.15 Map of Frankfurt am Main, Römerberg, Saalgasse, and Berlinerstrasse, Frankfurt am Main, Germany, 1980s.

1 Römerberg
2 Ostzeile
3 Saalgasse-rowhouses
4 Schaumainkai Museums
5 Commerzbank-skyscaper
6 Berlinerstrasse

Saalgasse and Ostzeile Townhouses

A row of twelve townhouses on the Saalgasse designed by various German, Italian, and American architects added to the city's collection of distinguished contemporary architecture (fig. 8.16). The Saalgasse is located in the city's historic core

known as the Römerberg. This part of town was completely destroyed in Allied air raids in March 1944. Although the medieval town hall was quickly rebuilt following the war, most of the Römerberg remained a vacant lot for decades. In a bold departure from the International Style modernism characteristic of the immediate postwar era, the city council approved a plan prepared by Ernst Schirmacher for the rebuilding of the Römerberg in a manner that took into account its prewar character. The Ostzeile, a row of six patrician houses spanning the city's Gothic and Renaissance eras, was reconstructed thus restoring the prewar spatial configuration to the area in front of the town hall (fig. 8.17).

An intriguing aspect of postmodern urbanism with its commitment to establishing a design dialogue between past and present conceptions of architecture are the various ways the Ostzeile and Saalgasse townhouses reflect a fidelity to their historic models. The Ostzeile houses represent an attempt literally to reconstruct the past. The literalness of the effort is compromised, however, by the decision to reconstruct the Ostzeile with half-timbered facades. Prewar photographs indicate the building fronts were finished with shingles rather than half-timbering. Thus the past is "improved upon" and a more picturesque, postcard-like effect achieved. Despite the evident postmodernity of their style, the Saalgasse townhouses reflect an appreciation for the distinctive character of Frankfurt am Main's

8.16 (above) Townhouses (no. 18 by Charles Moore; 16 by N. Berghof, M. Landes, and W. Ranger; 14 by D. Unglaub and W. Horvath), Saalgasse, Frankfurt am Main, Germany, 1980s.

This row of postmodern townhouses is a permanent equivalent to the temporary Strada Novissima erected for the 1980 Venice Biennale (see fig. 7.12). Postmodernists reject the modernist emphasis on uniformity and regularity in favor of variety and eccentricity. Unlike the restoration of the nearby Ostzeile (fig. 8.17), the Saalgasse townhouses do not attempt to emulate literally any premodern examples.

8.17 (right) E. Schirmacher, Ostzeile restoration, Römerberg, Frankfurt am Main, Germany, 1983.

historic urban fabric. Frankfurt am Main's premodern architecture can be described as homogenous in terms of the materials, building construction, and continuity of mural surfaces. At the same time, the old streets were filled with eccentric details, odd angles, and irregular building alignments. In keeping with a postmodern interest in the eccentric rather than the normative, the varied facades along the Saalgasse respect and reinterpret the architectural traditions of Frankfurt am Main in contemporary terms.

The Ostzeile and the Saalgasse townhouses, indicative of what the Italian critic Paolo Portoghesi called the "end of prohibitionism," represent different facets of postmodernism in German architecture. While they did much to open up the debate about postmodernism in Germany, they also represent the conclusion of a different chapter in Frankfurt am Main's history, one that deals with the rebuilding of the city's historic core following the devastation of the war.

Barcelona

Barcelona provides an excellent example of the conflation of factors driving design and urban planning planning in the 1980s. Evolving patterns of industrialization, significant political changes, and the impetus provided by special events propelled planning efforts in Barcelona. The death of Spanish dictator Francisco Franco in 1975 ushered in a new era in Spanish politics and cultural life. In the early 1980s Barcelona embarked on an urban renewal campaign that distributed small projects throughout the city rather than concentrating efforts on a single area. New parks, plazas, and streets were created, existing ones were refurbished, and derelict lots were reclaimed for new neighborhood facilities. The goal of this initial campaign, according to Pasqual Maragall, mayor of Barcelona from 1982 to 1997, was "to restore a sense of dignity to the urban landscape." The architect Oriol Bohigas (b. 1925) was appointed councillor to the mayor for Urban Design and provided the design vision and professional expertise required.

The Historic Port, Montjuïc Hill, and Nova Icària

Parallel with this program of design therapy for neighborhoods was the growing realization that Barcelona's historic port was increasingly unable to cope with changes in maritime traffic. New, larger, and more efficient port facilities were developed elsewhere, but the fate of the old Mediterranean port remained unclear. Barcelona's bid to host the 1992 Olympic Games galvanized the city's planning efforts. In an effort to prepare for the summer games, the city modernized its transportation network including new highways and an enlarged airport, upgraded the infrastructure for telecommunications networks, installed a new sewer system, remodeled existing athletic facilities, and erected new ones. As justifications for major new building campaigns, special events such as the Olympic Games are a mixed blessing. While such special events provide a focus for new construction and help generate public support, the necessity to meet unchangeable deadlines accelerates the pace of construction. As Barcelona discovered, the pressure to complete multiple projects on time can strain resources and produce cost overruns.

Venues for competitions were dispersed throughout the city and neighboring towns. The largest Olympic sports facilities are located on Montjuïc Hill overlook-

8.18 (above) 1992 Olympics sports facilities, Montjuïc, Barcelona, Spain.

8.19 (below) Oriol Bohigas and MBMP, Nova Icària Olympic Village, plan, Barcelona, Spain, 1990s.

ing Barcelona and the Mediterranean (fig. 8.18). The Montjuïc sporting complex reflects a diversity of architectural approaches ranging from the sophisticated space-frame technology of Arata Isozaki's (b. 1931) Sant Jordi Sports Pavilion to the classical aspirations of Ricardo Bofill's Institute of Physical Education. A broad esplanade serves as the spine for the complex and attempts to unify the disparate buildings on the site. However, the stylistic unity of groups of buildings that figures so prominently in urban visions dating from the first quarters of the century is no longer in evidence.

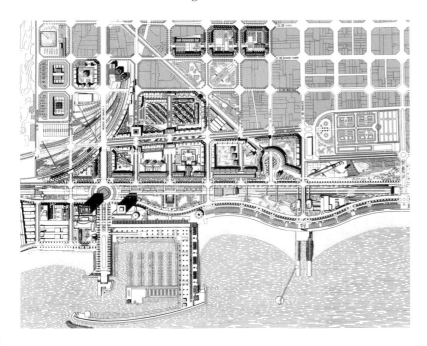

Athletes were housed in an Olympic Village conceived as part of the transformation of the old industrial zone near the port. Oriol Bohigas with his firm Martorell, Bohigas, Mackay, Puigdomènech (MBMP) prepared the masterplan for this area, renamed Nova Icària (fig. 8.19). For the new neighborhood, the plan extended a modified version of Barcelona's famous street grid based on the Eixample Plan developed in the mid-nineteenth century by Ildefonso Cerdà (1815–1876). The Bohigas plan created a series of superblocks by combining three of Cerdà's blocks into a single planning unit. The new super-blocks are defined by perimeter buildings that establish a uniform street frontage; in the interior various housing configurations were developed.

Thirty-eight different architects were involved in the design of new housing and neighborhood facilities, and the former industrial waterfront was converted into a seaside esplanade.

Nova Icària demonstrates how traditional urban morphologies could be modified to transform a former industrial zone into an area catering to a mix of residential, recreational, tourist, and service industries characteristic of the late twentieth century. Tradition and innovation are combined here in a way that distinguishes this (and similar urban design campaigns elsewhere) from more strictly modernist urban design approaches characteristic of the initial postwar period.

Traditional Architecture and the Reconstruction of the European City

In the wake of the Neo-Rationalist critique of CIAM-inspired urbanism (see Chapter 7), some historians, theorists, and architects began to develop a new appreciation for the value of traditional architecture and urbanism. For a generation educated in curricula dominated by the design theories and cultural values of modernism, the very act of looking to the past for lessons applicable in the present was subversive. During the postwar decades, the modernist design program had acquired an aura of inevitability that was finally, in the second half of the 1970s, beginning to dissipate. No longer the sole way to think about the built environment, modernism was now recognized as one among several possible ways to design.

In 1976 the architectural historian Anthony Vidler (b. 1941) published an influential essay entitled "The Third Typology" in which he examined different paradigms that shaped the production of architecture since the eighteenth century. The first typology, rooted in the rationalist philosophy of the Enlightenment, posited nature as the model for architecture; the second, a product of nineteenth-century industrialization, sought its model for the production of buildings in modern technologies. The third typology took as its model the form of the traditional (i.e. pre-industrial) city. Vidler arranged his three typologies in an oppositional rather than evolutionary relationship to each other and identified the third typology as an explicit critique of the modernist approach:

> While the Modern Movement found its hell in the closed, cramped and insalubrious quarters of the old industrial cities, and its Eden in the uninterrupted sea of sunlit space filled with greenery—a city become a garden—the new typology as a critique of modern urbanism raises the continuous fabric, the clear distinction between public and private marked by the walls of street and square, to the level of principle. Its nightmare is the isolated building set in an undifferentiated park.
>
> (Vidler, pp. 3–4)

Vidler's essay, which appeared originally in the American journal *Oppositions*, soon began to circulate internationally. Two years later it was reprinted in *Architecture rationnelle: la reconstruction de la ville européene*; this dual-language publication (French and English) brought together the work of a handful of European architects who were united in their belief that the principles of traditional architecture and urbanism remained valid for contemporary designers. The rhetorical stance of this nascent movement was one of adamant opposition to the legacy of modernist planning.

Leon and Rob Krier

In the late 1970s and 1980s Leon Krier emerged as one of the most vocal of the new traditionalists. In "Charter for the Reconstruction of the European City" (fig. 8.20), which he first drafted in 1978 and subsequently revised and expanded, Krier laid out his argument in concise and pointed language. The city, he argued, is "a moral project," not just a product of economic activity, and the design of the city should be directed to nobler ends than profit maximization or technological modernization. Krier equated modernism with the industrialization of building and dismissed it as "a technical, political and cultural failure." What is needed, he suggests, is a return to a craft-based culture of building. In his lectures and writings, the eloquently simple diagrams he used to illustrate his points reduce the complexity of the contemporary metropolis to a fundamental conflict between good and evil. This conflict is manifest in the contrast between (good) traditional and (bad) modernist designs.

Like the manifestos of the early twentieth-century avant-garde, the reductive simplicity of Krier's argument is both its greatest strength and its greatest weakness. His diagnosis of the problems plaguing contemporary cities strikes a responsive chord in people disillusioned with the achievements of modernist design and unconvinced by postmodernist and deconstructivist alternatives to the status quo. Yet Leon Krier's idealization of the pre-industrial city remains problematic because he drains the past of its own complex social reality and assumes that issues surrounding ethnic, class, and gender identities or the problems of economic restructuring can be subsumed neatly within the framework of the traditional town.

In the early 1980s the new traditionalists began to gain opportunities to apply their ideas. In 1984 Rob Krier won an

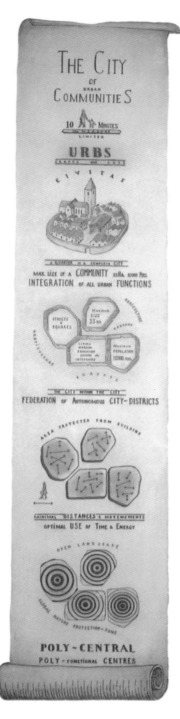

8.20 Leon Krier, "Charter for the Reconstruction of the European City," from *Building Classical*, edited by R. Economakis, Academy Editions, 1993, pp. 28–29.

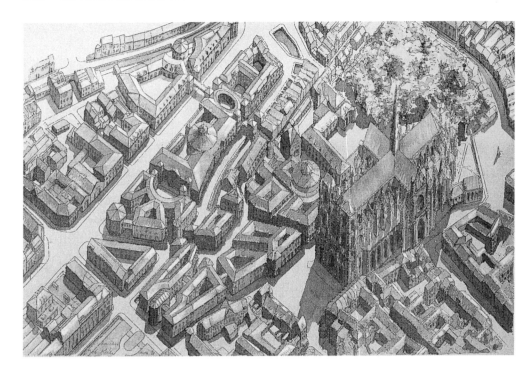

8.21 (left) Rob Krier, Amiens reconstruction, masterplan, France, 1984–92.

8.22 (below) Rob Krier, Amiens reconstruction, France, 1984–92.

urban design competition for a new "masterplan" for part of Amiens, France (fig. 8.21). During World War II an area adjacent to the city's cathedral, one of the masterpieces of French Gothic architecture, was severely damaged. The devastation encompassed an area of 140 hectares stretching north and west from the cathedral square and, in the early 1980s, this zone still had not recovered its former vitality and completeness.

In contrast to the superblocks of Nova Icària, which represent the modernization of Barcelona's nineteenth-century scheme of urban blocks, Krier's plan for Amiens is an attempt to reinstate the traditional morphology of the town. The Krier plan does not call for the literal reproduction of the prewar buildings in the same manner that Ernst Schirmacher proposed for Frankfurt's Ostzeile. Instead, Krier calls for respecting the premodern scale, density, and building typologies of the former neighborhood and adapting these features for new construction. As a result of Krier's plan, streets and public spaces are defined by buildings, blocks are penetrated by a series of pedestrian paths, and a variety of functions are accommodated in the same neighborhood.

Krier's plan does not ignore the requirements of modern life; provisions, for example, are made for parking needs. For Rob Krier, good urbanism demonstrates a respect for the past and attempts to weave old and new parts of the urban fabric together. Rather than isolate the cathedral, Krier draws the church and neighborhood together by enclosing the square in front of the cathedral with new buildings (fig. 8.22). In Krier's plan for Amiens we see many of the features that become hallmarks of the movement to revive traditional urbanism in the 1980s: a rejection of the modernist legacy of urban design, a concern for pedestrian scale, and a clear preference for traditional typologies and building materials.

John Simpson: The Paternoster Square Debate

Rob Krier's scheme for Amiens took shape in the context of a concrete opportunity to reconstruct the urban fabric of the city. Some of the most significant urban designs of the twentieth century were created as abstract planning exercises independent of specific commissions. Antonio Sant'Elia's Futurist drawings of the Città Nuova and Le Corbusier's Plan Voisin for Paris are two examples of such "paper visions."

In 1987 the British architect John Simpson (b. 1955) presented a plan for Paternoster Square in London, the area to the north of Saint Paul's Cathedral, which became the focal point of a heated debate (fig. 8.23). Simpson offered his scheme as a polemical counterproposal to published plans for the redevelopment of the area. Simpson's classicism differed sharply from the modernist character of the official proposals and gained additional prominence when the Prince of Wales, who began to speak out publicly about the direction of contemporary British architecture in the mid-1980s, added his voice to the Paternoster Square debate. In a speech in London's Mansion House on December 1, 1987, Prince Charles delivered a stinging rebuke to the architects and planners responsible for postwar commercial architecture in the nation's capital. They had, in the prince's words, "wrecked the London skyline and desecrated the dome of Saint Paul's."

Prince Charles's harsh criticism attracted a great deal of attention. While classicists rallied to his side, the prince's critics maintained that he lacked the requisite professional expertise to intervene and that his social position gave his words unwarranted weight. Prince Charles addressed this criticism in the Mansion House speech and presented himself as the *vox populi*:

> I believe I have been accused of setting myself up as a new, undemocratic hurdle in the planning process—a process we are supposed to leave to the professionals. . . . Everywhere I go, it is one of the things people complain about most and, if there is one message I would like to deliver this evening, in no uncertain terms, it is that large numbers of us in this country are fed up with being talked down to and dictated to by the existing planning, architectural and development establishment.

(Jencks, *The Prince*, p. 48)

The role of the Prince of Wales in the design debates of the 1980s is intriguing and raises important questions concerning who has a voice in planning policy. In Chapter 1 the shift in emphasis from artistic ability to technical skills as an element of professional identity was noted in the discussion of the CIAM. In the last quarter of the twentieth century, however, the design professions began to encounter the same growing skepticism about claims to authority based on technical expertise as other

scientific and managerial professions. Once the faith in modernism's power to rationally calculate and improve the built environment began to wane, alternative approaches, such as the emulation of traditional models, grew more attractive.

The New Urbanism in the United States

In the last quarter of the twentieth century the suburb, once hailed as a bucolic alternative to dirty and overcrowded urban neighborhoods, came under harsh scrutiny from sociologists, ecologists, and designers. The list of complaints about suburban design addressed a variety of issues. Critics noted a depressing sameness to suburban architecture across the country and bemoaned the loss of a distinctive sense of place. The absence of significant civic spaces was interpreted as emblematic of a decline in shared civic values and lost opportunities for communal experiences.

Studies of suburban life-styles increasingly pointed to the burden of isolation imposed on both the very old and the very young as a result of the necessity to drive everywhere in order to get anywhere. The energy needed to sustain this automotive life-style was only one part of a larger environmental critique of the

8.23 John Simpson and Partners, Paternoster Square reconstruction, masterplan, London, 1992.

What is missing is as revealing of the architect's intention as what is depicted here. Simpson envisions public spaces filled with people rather than cars, and surrounded by masonry buildings rather than steel, glass, and concrete structures. No skyscrapers spoil the skyline and only the pedestrians' clothing indicates that this scene is set in the late twentieth century.

suburban settlement pattern. Close-cropped grassy lawns, the hallmark of so many suburban landscapes, came under increasing attack for the chemical load they placed on the environment as a result of the use of fertilizers and the water required to maintain them in many arid regions of the country. Rather than perpetuate the existing pattern of mono-functional development in which residential areas and commercial districts were separated, a new model of community planning that integrated the activities of daily life was needed.

Seaside, Florida

In the 1980s a new town on Florida's gulf coast attracted international attention because it was conceived and promoted as an alternative to the conventional post-war developments in America. Seaside, Florida was founded by the developer Robert Davis; in the early 1980s he commissioned the husband-and-wife firm of Andres Duany (b. 1949) and Elizabeth Plater-Zyberk (b. 1950) (DPZ) to prepare a masterplan for the eighty-acre site. The DPZ concept for Seaside is a seminal example of what came to be called the New Urbanism (fig. 8.24). Small lots, compact planning, and provisions for small retail outlets in the town center encourage walking within the community. Central to the success of the Seaside plan are the urban and architectural codes developed by DPZ in 1982. Rather than the conventional land-use zoning diagrams, DPZ created an urban code based on distinct building typologies. Eight different building types are specified for different parts of Seaside. Complementing this urban code, tectonic details such as window and roof specifications and appropriate constructional materials are delineated in an architectural code. Critical ingredients of both codes are derived from a careful study of the region's vernacular architecture. This reflects the recognition by Davis, Duany, and Plater-Zyberk that the accumulated wisdom of experience is embodied in vernacular design and available to anyone willing to learn from the experience of previous generations.

8.24 DPZ, Odessa Street, Seaside, Florida, 1980s.

Despite its dependence on small southern towns as models, Seaside is not an exercise in historic recreation as some critics have suggested; it is a hybrid community, more urban, more complex, with greater architectural diversity and a higher density than small towns typically display. The architectural historian Neil Levine (b. 1941) acknowledged this complexity and Seaside's seminal position in American design debates of the 1980s in his essay "Questioning the View: Seaside's Critique of the Gaze of Modern Architecture." Levine wrote:

> Seaside can be read in many ways—as a proposition about urban design, as a discourse on developer/architect relations, as an argument for the vernacular, as a descriptive account of place, as a demonstration of the increasing role of women in the architectural profession, as an essay on resort culture, or as a critique of modernism.
>
> (Mohney, p. 240)

Levine's reference to the increasing role of women is based on the significant number of houses in Seaside designed by women architects. In a 1989 interview, Elizabeth Plater-Zyberk expressed a less sanguine view of the status of women in the profession and reflected on some of the frustrations and impediments that still confront female practitioners:

> Women are not yet on an equal footing with men in architecture anywhere, not just at Seaside. . . . some of us [women] measure ourselves and our work against an ideal objective standard, shrinking from its impossibility . . . However, I think Neil is correct in saying that there probably have been few building projects of any scale in recorded history where women have been as prominent as here.
>
> (Mohney, p. 84)

Jaime Lerner: Curitiba, Brazil

From the first chapter this book has presented design discourse in the twentieth century as an ongoing, passionate debate between competing visions of the modern world. However one may describe the twentieth century, it was not a century of consensus; its myriad voices have alternated between optimistic and pessimistic assessments of present situations and future prospects. In the last decades of the twentieth century, the relentless pressure of population growth, resource depletion, environmental degradation, and social conflict combined to make the problems of the contemporary city appear intractable. Architects, however, are optimists by profession; to build is a vote of confidence in the future. In a 1994 interview in the American journal *Progressive Architecture*, the Brazilian architect Jaime Lerner (b. 1937) rejected the suggestion that large cities were now beyond the control of planners:

> Throughout the world there exists a tragic view of the city, and often those responsible for planning speak as if there were no solution to urban problems. There's a misconception that the larger cities, whether third world or first, have become unworkable. This is not true. Scale cannot be used as an excuse.
>
> (Lerner, p. 84)

Lerner's comments are noteworthy because of his role in transforming Curitiba, Brazil, into a model of environmentally sensitive planning during his three terms as mayor. Trained as an architect, Lerner was appointed mayor of Curitiba for the first

8.25 Jaime Lerner, bus stop, Curitiba, Brazil, 1970s.

Good design integrates large-scale environmental concerns with practical solutions to small-scale problems. Effective mass transit is a major component of Curitiba's approach to environmental planning. Buses run in dedicated lanes. Passengers pay at turnstiles in special boarding stations with elevated floor levels that match the height of the bus floor.

time in 1971 and held that office intermittently throughout the 1970s and 1980s. Lerner's career coincided with decades of explosive growth during which Curitiba, capital of the Brazilian state of Paraná, grew from a city with a population of 500,000 in the early 1960s to more than 1.6 million people by the mid-1990s (with a projected population of 2.7 million by 2020).

In devising a strategy to cope with the environmental and social stresses of rapid growth, Lerner's administration focused on developing an effective mass-transit system, increasing the amount of green space within the city, instituting recycling programs, and working with the residents of poor neighborhoods to improve the habitability of their *favelas*. Lerner himself designed the city's distinctive bus shelters which accommodate specially designed buses and facilitate rapid loading and unloading of passengers (fig. 8.25). Design, as both the process of problem-solving and as the final image of the solution, is critical to Lerner's approach whether it is a park facility built with recycled timber or the special bus shelters. As a process, design discussions allow for resident involvement in the decision-making process. As an image, the design of shelters becomes emblematic of the city's commitment to maintaining the public realm. The Curitiba experience has been hailed as a model of "green" design and as a powerful reminder of design's potential for sustaining both the natural and the built environments.

Chapter 9

The Present as History

Throughout this book, the history of twentieth-century architecture has been presented as an ongoing discussion concerning an appropriate architecture, and the closing decades of the century conform to the model of history as the record of passionate debate. However, writing the history of the recent past is a problematic venture. Historians often rely on a perspective that comes with the passage of time when they assert particular buildings to be seminal examples of architecture. The reassurance that comes from hindsight is not available for those writing about the last decades of the twentieth century and questions inevitably surround any account. Is, for example, a particular design selected for discussion the greatest or only the latest work by the architect in question? Should the amount of press coverage a new building attracts be interpreted as an indication that it is a work of enduring significance or merely the sign of a successful media blitz? Will an emerging technology fundamentally alter the conceptualization of form and the construction of buildings or be incorporated smoothly into existing patterns of design activity?

Local circumstances, programmatic requirements, and the architect's personal sensibility inevitably shape individual projects. Yet, within the broad panorama of contemporary architecture, it is possible to discern pervasive themes that serve to organize design discourse. Thus, this chapter explores the various ways in which late-twentieth-century architecture addresses issues of physical context, environmental concerns, and cultural memory.

Building Technologies

The rapid pace of technological development in the twentieth century ensured that the relationship between architectural design and building technology remained a central topic of design debate. The term building technologies identifies a set of factors influencing architectural design: building materials, design tools, methods of structural analysis, and environmental control systems. After decades of assuming energy was a limitless resource, the overdue recognition of environmental issues has prompted a new concern for energy management among architects.

Advances in building technology affect more than the architect's design of environmental control systems. Digital technologies have created new design tools for architects and opened up new formal possibilities for designers. When, for

Cesar Pelli, Petronas Towers, Kuala Lumpur, Malaysia, 1998.

example, Jørn Utzon began working on the original design for the Sydney Opera House in 1957, the architect's imagination exceeded the engineer's ability to calculate and erect the desired forms. Modifications of Utzon's original concept were necessary in order to build the opera house. Today, new design tools such as Computer-Aided Design (CAD) and Computer-Aided Manufacturing (CAM) programs ensure that technology can stimulate rather than inhibit the architect's imagination. Starting in the 1980s, the availability of CAD–CAM software packages forced architects to reconsider some of the central tenets of architectural modernism. In a 1998 lecture, Renzo Piano, one of the architects of the Pompidou Center in Paris, described the impact of computers on the design profession's understanding of standardization:

> Thirty years ago when I was at school, we learned that, with standardization and modulor construction, you could not modify a single element, because if you did, everything would become too expensive. Today we live in a different world in which the computer permits all sorts of modifications. . . . To have an intelligent sense of structural unity today you no longer have to make each piece identical. Everything has changed today, including the concept of standardization.

(Frampton, *Technology, Place, and Architecture*, p. 135)

Formerly, architects were taught that the industrial production of architecture operated most efficiently when buildings were constructed using a limited set of regular, uniform structural elements. With the advent of CAD–CAM software packages which can calculate and manufacture irregular shapes, however, eccentrically shaped designs are no longer prohibitively expensive to manufacture and construct.

Coop Himmelblau and the Enduring Appeal of Novelty

In an era when, as Piano suggests, everything has changed, there are nonetheless threads of continuity that connect the developments at the end of the twentieth century with the ideals and goals outlined at the beginning. Projects that initially appear to be shaped by design debates of the 1980s and 1990s can also be understood in terms of themes articulated decades earlier. In 1898, for example, Josef Olbrich crowned the solid-looking Secession building with a perforated metal sphere and inscribed over the main entrance the motto "To the Age its Art — to Art its Freedom." Almost nine decades later, the rooftop of another Viennese building demonstrates the continuing relevance of the Secession's motto. In 1987 the Viennese firm Coop Himmelblau, headed by Wolf Prix (b. 1942) and Helmut Swiczinsky (b. 1944), created a rooftop addition for a law office housed in a traditional building (fig. 9.1). The design, which Prix described as an inverted bolt of lightning tearing open the roof, consists of a steel and glass volume, vaguely zoomorphic in character, perched precariously on top of a sedate apartment block. Rather than harmonize with the existing building, the taut skeletal form of the addition, like an abstract rendition of a giant insect or bird of prey, appears completely at odds with its immediate surroundings. The inclusion of this project in the Museum of Modern Art's 1988 "Deconstructivist Architecture" exhibition is not hard to understand; it possesses the edgy, unsettled quality that characterized so much of the work in that exhibition. Wolf Prix defended the design in the following terms:

> Many people say that we are inordinately aggressive and that we destroy our architecture. This is an error, it is like confusing Deconstructivism and destruction. I believe it

9.1 Wolf Prix and Helmut Swiczinsky (Coop Himmelblau), Schuppich, Sporn, and Winischhofer law offices, rooftop conference room addition, Vienna, Austria, 1987.

The name "Coop Himmelblau" (Blue-Sky Cooperative) captures the anarchic spirit evident in the firm's free-form designs. Nothing could be further from the sober, decorous image traditionally associated with lawyers' offices than this jagged pile of steel and glass.

is wrong to speak of destruction. If we destroy something, like this old roof, for instance, it is only in order to create new spaces, spaces more differentiated and exciting than what was there before.

(Noever, p. 24)

Coop Himmelblau's conception of architecture as a tool for creating vivid spatial experiences that interrupt the mind-numbing tedium of routine has deep roots in the modernist design tradition. Beyond its connection with Deconstructivism, the pedigree of the faceted form of Coop Himmelblau's design can be traced back to the Expressionist design language of Bruno Taut's Alpine Architecture (see Chapter 1). It remains another demonstration of the ongoing commitment of the avant-garde to energize the space of the modern metropolis through the creation of novel and shocking forms.

Domestic Design

Glenn Murcutt

The detached, single-family house continues to serve architects as a vehicle to explore a wide range of issues and as an opportunity for personal expression. The Australian architect Glenn Murcutt's (b. 1936) work has been described as the

manifestation of a regionalist sensibility in design. On one level, regionalism can be recognized as the creation of picturesque alternatives to the insistent international-ism of modern architecture and reduced to the quotation of local vernacular models and materials. Murcutt's work, however, reveals a more profound, environmentally aware, and culturally diverse conception of regionalism that draws upon a wide range of source materials. His Ball-Eastaway House of 1983 is based on his rigorous analysis of the constituent features and prevailing patterns of its site on the edge of the Marramarra National Park outside of Sydney (fig. 9.2). The design is shaped by Murcutt's appreciation of earth, water, air, and fire not only as environmental aspects of the immediate context to be accommodated but as primal forces of nature that need to be revealed. The house sits lightly on the earth; rooflines and openings are calculated to ensure maximum cross-ventilation and optimal light conditions in various seasons. A special sprinkler system provides fire protection in case of brush fires. His use of corrugated metal sheets reflects a vernacular tradition in Australian architecture.

A description of the house as a response to site conditions and local traditions reveals only part of the story. Murcutt is an astute student of architectural history as well as natural history. The Ball-Eastaway House, like a number of Murcutt's early works, represents his response to Mies van der Rohe's modernist paradigm of mini-malist design: the Farnsworth House (see fig. 6.2). In the Farnsworth House, Mies van der Rohe idealized the concept of a steel and glass pavilion at the expense of the reality of living in a glass box; the result is beautiful but uncomfortable. Murcutt recasts the Miesian model in a form that takes into account the role of nature as well as culture in shaping human experience and the consciousness of place.

9.2 Glenn Murcutt, Ball-Eastaway House, Glenorie, north Sydney, New South Wales, Australia, 1983.

Stanley Tigerman

In its sensitive contextualism, Murcutt's work holds out the promise of achieving a harmonic resolution of the orders of nature and culture. But architects could also employ the design of a single-family house to suggest a contrary view. In a 1989 project for a private residence in Illinois, Chicago, architect Stanley Tigerman (b. 1930) orchestrated the design as the disintegration of an original and ideal unity (fig. 9.3). Rather than arrange the various elements of the domestic program as smaller volumes (rooms) within a single large volume (the house), each room is expressed as a discrete geometric form. The visitor approaches the house across a paved circular court which represents an image of perfect order embodied in geometry (in Tigerman's own words, "a metaphysical Garden of Eden"). As one exits this circular "Eden" and enters the house, the rest of the design appears to disintegrate as the rooms rotate in different directions destroying the geometric order and purity of the whole.

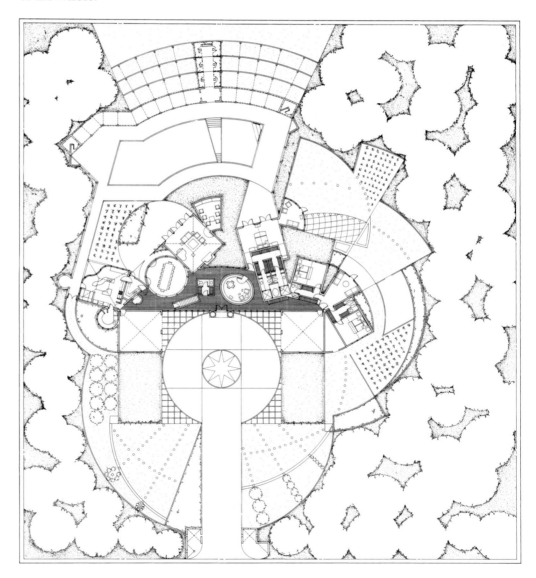

9.3 Stanley Tigerman, private residence, plan, near Chicago, Illinois, 1989.

Tigerman's interest in evoking the unraveling of order acquires its significance in the context of late twentieth-century design discourse. Earlier in the century, modernists and traditionalists shared the conviction that design could establish order and harmony in the built environment although each side proposed different strategies for achieving its particular vision of what that order should be. In contrast, many design critics and theorists in the closing decades of the century called into question the notion that an enduring order, harmony, and logic could be discovered in the diversity of contemporary society. This argument is rooted in post-structuralist philosophy and criticism which tends to evaluate systems of social and aesthetic order as thinly veiled attempts to manage the network of power relationships at the heart of social and political life. Tigerman seizes the opportunity presented by the design of a house to suggest how such theoretical concepts can be applied to architecture.

Frank Gehry

In the late 1970s, Frank Gehry (b. 1929) began to remodel a 1920s house in Santa Monica, California, for his own use (fig. 9.4). Rather than meekly blend the new with the old, he established an explosive relationship between the disparate elements of the composition. The domestic decorum of the original house is literally overwhelmed by the addition of new eccentric volumes defined by chain-link fencing, galvanized metal siding, and exposed plywood. Viewed through the filter of

9.4 Frank Gehry, Gehry House, Santa Monica, California, 1977. Frank Gehry's house combines international themes drawn from twentieth-century avant-garde art together with local references. The jarring assemblage of different materials and eccentric shapes can be seen as an expression of the underlying instability of earthquake-prone California and of the state's precarious cultural balance as seen in the polyglot population of Los Angeles.

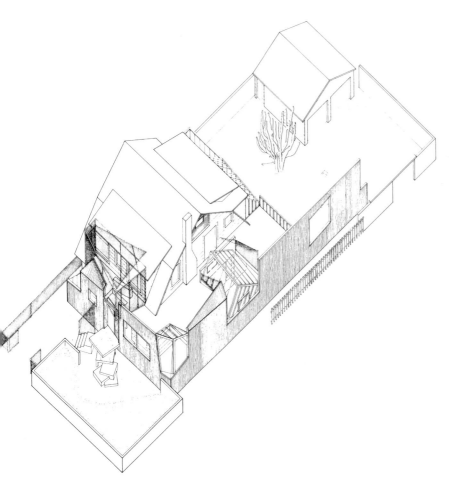

9.5 Frank Gehry, Gehry House, axonometric drawing, Santa Monica, California, 1977.

poststructuralist criticism, Gehry's house appears to support the thesis that the only message left for architecture to convey in a pluralist era is one of cultural fragmentation.

The inclusion of this house in the Museum of Modern Art's 1988 exhibition "Deconstructivist Architecture" seemed to confirm an affinity between Gehry's work and the intellectual argument of Deconstructivism. However, an alternate reading is possible, one closer to Gehry's own intentions. In interviews and lectures Gehry often speaks of his involvement in the contemporary art world of painters and sculptors. Substitute the "combine paintings" of Robert Rauschenberg or the Merz pieces by Kurt Schwitters for the philosophical speculations of Deconstruction as the critical point of reference, and one can appreciate Gehry's house as a contribution to the vital twentieth-century tradition of collage. Gehry framed the volume of the new kitchen so that it appears as if a huge cube is tumbling into the house (fig. 9.5). The tumbling cube, inspired by early twentieth-century Russian art (Gehry designed the installation for an important 1980 exhibition of Russian avant-garde art in Los Angeles), injects the subversive spirit of the early avant-garde into the quiet, residential neighborhood.

That same neighborhood, however, provides its own set of references for Gehry's house. While his arrangement of elements is unorthodox, his selection of materials is oddly in harmony with the material environment of backyard fences, recreational vehicles, and boat trailers evident elsewhere in the neighborhood. A house that draws together references as diverse as Russian avant-garde art, mixed-media work by Rauschenberg, and bits and pieces of contemporary life-styles culled from the driveways and garages of local streets reflects a design sensibility shaped by an idiosyncratic spirit of adventure as much as it is determined by any particular philosophical system.

R. Scott Johnson

Unique projects by Murcutt, Tigerman, and Gehry cannot be represented as typical of the dominant trends in the production of single-family homes. As they have throughout the century, however, architect-designed houses serve as a useful index of the themes, concerns, and experiments with which designers are engaged. The last house to be considered in this chapter reminds us that the emergence of post and neo "isms" such as postmodernism or Deconstructivism does not signal the end of modernism as a creative force in architecture.

In the early 1990s R. Scott Johnson (b. 1951) began designing a house for his family on a hilltop site near Saint Helena in California's Napa Valley (figs. 9.6, 9.7). Johnson's previous commercial work demonstrated his command of a variety of formal idioms; in describing his approach to this design he admitted:

> Modern architecture is the most intriguing to me. . . . But I'm interested in its ambiguities and in achieving a rooted, tactile brand of modernism—not the icy-cold variety.
>
> (Viladas, p. 153)

The front of the house appears as a series of opaque wooden boxes painted different colors. From the entry, the interior of the house slowly opens up culminating in a extensively glazed living area at the far end of the scheme offering the visitor a panoramic view of the landscape. There is an insistent materiality to the design. Just as the spatial character of the houses shifts from sheltering to expansive, finishes range from the rough textures of concrete block, exposed wooden ceiling, and plywood paneling through smooth flagstone floors and slate tiles to walls covered with a delicate white-gold leaf. Throughout the house, surfaces are animated by light.

This is not an example of the house as a machine to regulate life, nor does it advance the argument that design is a tool with which humankind can dominate the natural environment, although such themes can be found within the modernist tradition. It is a demonstration of how architecture can focus and intensify experience. Modernism offered twentieth-century architects the freedom to explore new strategies for manipulating space, material, and light—the elemental ingredients of architecture—and as the Johnson House makes clear, it remains an important element in the mix of contemporary design culture.

Office Buildings

Richard Rogers: Lloyd's of London

While diversity has been a hallmark of twentieth-century domestic architecture, the design of office space has evolved in strict conformity to the dictates of the commercial real-estate market. In London, three very different projects demonstrate a growing diversity in approaches to the configuration of office buildings. The first of this trio, a new headquarters for Lloyd's of London (completed in 1986), brought the high-tech image of the recently completed Pompidou Center to the City of London (fig. 9.8). Richard Rogers and Renzo Piano terminated their joint practice after the completion of the Pompidou Center and Lloyd's commissioned Rogers, now working alone, to design its new facility.

The project brief specified large open-floor areas capable of accommodating new office technologies. Typically, office floor plans are arranged around central service cores containing elevator shafts and duct work for the mechanical systems. Rogers turned this model inside out; he clustered building services and arranged structural elements around the periphery of the plan thus opening up the structure's interior. The result has the diagrammatic clarity of Louis Kahn's servant and served spaces and the exhibitionist bravado previously seen in the work of Archigram. Rather than encase the whole in a single, prismatic volume, Rogers produced a highly

9.6 (above) R. Scott Johnson, family home, Saint Helena, California, 1994.

9.7 (right) R. Scott Johnson, family home, interior, Saint Helena, California, 1994.

9.8 (left) Richard Rogers, Lloyd's Building, City of London, England, 1979–86.
The high-tech image of Lloyd's of London demonstrates how building technology can provide not only the practical means but also the expressive language of design. By turning the building inside out and exposing elevators, plumbing lines, and ventilation ducts on the exterior, Rogers reveals what most buildings conceal.

articulated design in which the building's various components are clearly differentiated like the parts of a giant mechanical device.

Quinlan Terry: Richmond Riverside

Quinlan Terry (b. 1937) is one of the new generation of British classicists. His design for the Richmond Riverside Development (completed in 1988) (fig. 9.9) establishes a different relationship between building tectonics, office technology, and urban context than Rogers applied to Lloyd's of London. Rather than one large building, Terry developed his design to read as a series of varied and smaller buildings along a traditional street. The details are drawn from a variety of historical sources including Georgian, Palladian, and Baroque architecture. He took advantage of the riverfront site with a series of terraces that step down to the river and create a great public outdoor room for the surrounding neighborhood.

9.9 Quinlan Terry, Richmond Riverside Development, Richmond, Surrey, England, 1984–88.

As one moves inside, the traditional design of the facades is replaced by thoroughly modern office spaces equipped with the building systems necessary to support the latest in telecommunications and work-station technologies. The Lloyd's of London design vocabulary is consistent throughout the building. The Richmond project thus speaks different languages inside and out. This design dichotomy has prompted some critics to suggest that the design's beauty is only skin deep; it is, however, a very thick skin. In keeping with the classical commitment to traditional modes of construction, the outer walls of the development are built using load-bearing masonry with no internal cavities or expansion joints; in places they are eighteen inches thick.

Ralph Erskine: The Ark

The third project to be considered, Ralph Erskine's 1992 speculative office building dubbed The Ark, occupies a site in Hammersmith as ugly as Richmond Riverside's is attractive (fig. 9.10). Wedged between an elevated motorway and railroad tracks, there is little reason to face outward and try to engage the surroundings. Instead, Erskine turned the building in on itself and organized the interior around a central atrium (fig. 9.11). The outer walls wrap around the interior like a protective carapace and the building's volume expands as it rises. The result is an ungainly shape that lacks the precise machinelike image of Lloyd's of London or Richmond Riverside's picturesque charm.

What The Ark does offer is a distinctive approach to the design of office space. Erskine is keenly aware that space shapes experience and that corporate

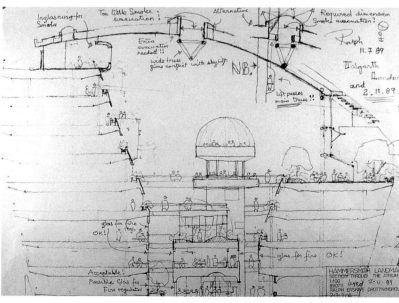

9.10 (left) Ralph Erskine, The Ark, London, England, 1996.

9.11 (below) Ralph Erskine, The Ark, cross-section, London, England, 1996. Drawing by Ralph Erskine.
   Erskine's sketch reveals how the atrium space expands as it nears the top of the building. This ensures that natural light will penetrate the building from above as well as from the sides.

hierarchies and organizational structures are encoded in the arrangement of offices and work-stations. In recent decades, however, new attitudes to office planning have emerged and corporations have adopted planning models designed to promote more free-form types of interaction within organizations. Rigid chains of command and strict compartmentalization are giving way to more flexible spatial arrangements that allow working groups to be reconfigured quickly. The Ark's central atrium provides a variety of areas to accommodate informal interaction among workers and within the building's barrel-like envelope a variety of different floor plans and office types are possible.

Skyscrapers

In the 1990s a new generation of skyscrapers appeared on urban skylines around the world. Emblems of national pride as well as centers of commerce, the appearance of tall buildings in such cities as Kuala Lumpur, Malaysia, and Shanghai, China, signaled profound changes in the global economic order. "We need something to express our towering ambition" declared Mahathir Mohamad, prime minister of Malaysia at the formal opening of the Petronas Towers in Kuala Lumpur in 1998. Rising 452 meters over the Malaysian capital, the Petronas Towers claimed the title of world's tallest skyscraper and boldly staked Malaysia's claim to be a major Asian player in the emerging global economic system (see p. 254).

The drive for height has been an important part of the story of skyscrapers since their invention in the late nineteenth century. But height was not the only thing that distinguished the skyscrapers erected in the waning years of the twentieth century from their predecessors. As the set of buildings reviewed here illustrates, the tall buildings of the 1990s differed significantly from earlier skyscrapers in terms of their layouts, construction, and operations. Indeed, the innovations in skyscraper design were so far-reaching that such architects as Norman Foster and Kenneth Yeang described their efforts as nothing less than the reinvention of the skyscraper.

Norman Foster: Commerzbank

Frankfurt's Commerzbank, designed by the English architect Norman Foster (b. 1935) , is an excellent example of the new paradigm in skyscraper design (fig. 9.12). Towering sixty stories (261 meters) over Frankfurt's central business district, the Commerzbank, completed in 1997, is considered the tallest skyscraper in Europe. With its sleek metal and glass exterior skin, the building resembles at first sight a typical modern skyscraper.

Germany, however, is a leader in environmentally responsible architectural design and the reduction of energy consumption was a major goal of the design effort. Foster, therefore, reconsidered the standard formulas for skyscraper design. The typical skyscraper floor plan with office space arranged around a central service core emerged early in the century. After World War II, improvements in mechanical systems such as air conditioning prompted the development of sealed metal and glass curtain walls, so that the building's occupants were now totally dependent upon artificial climate control of interior spaces. Foster turned this design formula inside out. Instead of a single service core in the center of the building, he arranged service elements into three towers and repositioned them at the corners of his triangular plan thus creating a central atrium rising the full height of the tower (fig. 9.13).

In place of a hermetically sealed curtain wall, Foster's design for the exterior skin consists of double-glazed windows which can be opened to allow fresh air into the building. The atrium facilitates ventilation by allowing fresh air to rise through the building. Landscaped "sky gardens" four stories tall are positioned at regular intervals within the building. These garden serve as "local" centers and social spaces within the enormous tower and freshen the interior atmosphere naturally. In order to maximize the advantages of natural ventilation techniques, new

9.12 (left) Norman Foster & Partners, Commerzbank, Frankfurt am Main, Germany, 1997.

In traditional skyscraper construction, a regular grid of columns and beams creates a three-dimensional structural skeleton. For the Commerzbank, Foster designed special structural masts positioned at the corners of the building. These support eight-story-high beams on which the individual floors rest. The result is office space uninterrupted by structural columns, and enormous open-sky courts throughout the tower.

9.13 (opposite above) Norman Foster & Partners, Commerzbank, floor plan, Frankfurt am Main, Germany, 1997.

9.14 (opposite) Kenneth Yeang, Menara Mesiniaga Building, Kuala Lumpur, Malaysia, 1991.

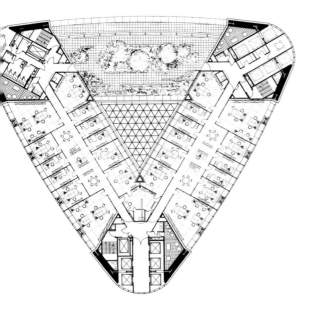

computerized Building Management Systems (BMS) monitor environmental conditions, adjusting the volume of outside air drawn into the building as temperature and air quality conditions change during the course of a day. BMS technology is also employed automatically to adjust lighting levels within the building thus reducing energy consumption and the heat gain attributable to lighting fixtures. The Commerzbank demonstrates how a combination of ancient techniques for natural ventilation and modern technology for measuring environmental conditions precisely can be combined to improve the energy performance of tall buildings.

Kenneth Yeang: Menara Mesiniaga

Technology, energy, and local character are three important themes in the work of the Malaysian architect Kenneth Yeang (b. 1948). His 1991 Menara Mesiniaga Building for IBM in Kuala Lumpur illustrates Yeang's conception of what he calls the bioclimatic skyscraper (fig. 9.14). The logic of the design begins not with an abstract idea about the symbolic role of architecture in the modern era but as a concrete response to local environmental conditions. The positions of exterior sun screens, landscaped terraces, service towers, and lobby areas open to the breeze are carefully calculated to enhance the quality of interior office space and reduce energy consumption through natural ventilation (fig. 9.15). In Yeang's conception of a regionally appropriate design approach, geography and climate are the critical variables. Improvements in energy performance are achieved by adjusting the building's design to local climatic conditions. This emphasis on local conditions, Yeang argues, has some important implications for the ways in which architects think about modern technology:

We might compare the high-rise building with the 747 aircraft in that like the airplane, it has become an international piece of technology which every nation's economy possesses. Even some of the poorest countries in the world have their own national fleet of 747s and a number of high-rises in their urban areas. The question then becomes how do we personalise and make use of this international machinery in a way that it can be related to its geographical context?

(Yeang, *Space Design*, p. 20)

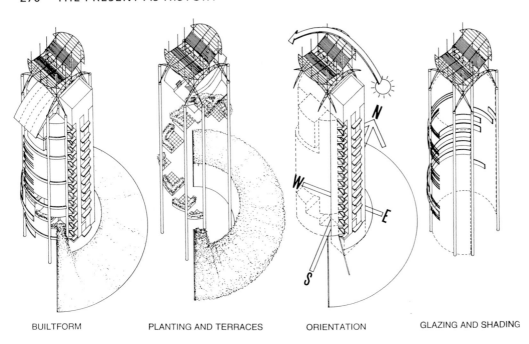

BUILTFORM   PLANTING AND TERRACES   ORIENTATION   GLAZING AND SHADING

9.15 Kenneth Yeang, Menara Mesiniaga building, plan, Kuala Lumpur, Malaysia, 1991.

In this analytical diagram, Yeang pulls the Menara Mesiniaga apart visually to reveal how different elements of the tower are positioned to take advantage of the building's orientation to the sun. The earth berm around the base and the landscaped terraces on different levels are integral parts of the tower's energy-management and climate-control systems.

Cesar Pelli: Petronas Towers

Yeang's bioclimatic approach to skyscraper design is only one way that architects have attempted to answer the question of how contemporary architecture can respond to distinctive features of the local context. Kuala Lumpur is also home to the Petronas Towers designed by Cesar Pelli (b. 1926) (see page 254). The twin towers serve as the centerpiece of the city's new commercial center. The development program called for a design that would express the culture and heritage of Malaysia. There are, however, no obvious precedents in the history of South Asian architecture for a modern skyscraper.

Malaysia is a predominately Muslim country and Pelli turned to the traditional Islamic design practice of creating intricate patterns using simple geometric forms. The Petronas Towers are configured from two intersecting squares that form an eight-pointed star in plan and create a faceted shape in elevation. Curved bays are inserted between the eight points to create an alternating rhythm of curved and angular surfaces. In contrast to the Islamic-inspired geometry of the building, the design of the steel metal and glass curtain wall owes more to state-of-the-art technology than it does to cultural traditions.

Less noticeable than the building's form and surfaces but equally important is its structural system. For most of the twentieth century, skyscrapers were built using a steel-framed skeleton to support the weight of the structure. As a result of improvements in the strength and performance of reinforced concrete, however, the Petronas Towers, like many of the skyscrapers erected in the last two decades of the century, are concrete rather than steel structures.

Kohn, Pederson, Fox: Shanghai World Financial Center

Early in the twentieth century, the story of skyscrapers centered on developments in American cities such as Chicago and New York. Until the completion of the

Petronas Towers, for example, the title of world's tallest building was held by Chicago's Sears Tower (443 meters) designed by Skidmore, Owings, and Merrill and completed in 1974. By the end of the century, however, Asian cities had emerged as major centers of new skyscraper construction. The tall building symbolized the new strength and global importance of Asian economies. To encourage economic growth, Chinese authorities designated Shanghai's Pudong district as a special economic zone and in less than a dozen years scores of new towers were built. The Pudong district is located across the Huangpu river from the Bund, Shanghai's famous waterfront boulevard, and the contrast between the two riverbanks is vivid evidence of the dramatic changes that occurred in China during the 1990s. Just as Tian'anmen Square represented in architectural terms the triumph of China's political revolution after World War II, the Pudong district now symbolizes China's economic revolution.

In 1997 work began on the Shanghai World Financial Center designed by the American firm of Kohn, Pederson, Fox Associates (KPF) (fig. 9.16). The architectural plans call for the building to be 460 meters tall thus surpassing the 452-meter-tall Petronas Towers as world's tallest skyscraper. After its height, the most distinctive feature of the KPF design is an enormous circular opening at the top of the tower. This opening reduces the lateral stress generated by high winds blowing against the side of the building and provides a unique identifying feature for the tower. Like Cesar Pelli, KPF struggled to find some way to stamp this skyscraper with an indigenous character, thus this circular opening has been compared to the Moon Gate motif of traditional Chinese garden architecture.

9.16 Kohn, Pederson, Fox Associates, Shanghai World Financial Center, Shangai, China, 1997–.

The Shanghai World Financial Center is an excellent example of the global nature of contemporary design practice. KPF, an American architectural firm, is designing the world's tallest building for a site in China with financing and supervision provided by a wholly owned subsidiary of the Mori Building Company, one of Japan's leading real-estate and construction firms. Coordinating the contributions of Chinese, Japanese, and American personnel and managing the construction effort in a project of this magnitude are major challenges. Architectural, engineering, and financial considerations are inextricably linked in skyscrapers, and in the world of commercial architecture financial considerations often overshadow design issues. Fourteen months after the beginning of construction, work halted when fluctuations in Asian financial markets prompted investors to reconsider the project's financing; completion is now scheduled for "sometime early" in the twenty-first century.

Antonio Ismael: Citra Niaga Center

It is easy to be mesmerized by the towering new skylines of such cities as Shanghai, Hong Kong, Singapore, or Kuala Lumpur and to conclude that they represent Asia today. In Samarinda, Indonesia, the provincial capital of East Kalimantan, however, a different kind of tower reveals another aspect of contemporary Asian architecture: small-scale, community friendly development that addresses local needs. A timber-framed tower decorated with elaborate carvings crowns a simple two-story pavilion that serves as the focal point for a small commercial development covering 2.7 hectares (fig. 9.17). The scheme includes small shops, kiosks, and sidewalk stalls and functions as the commercial center for Samarinda's Citra Niaga neighborhood.

9.17 Antonio Ismael, Citra Niaga project, Samarinda, Indonesia, 1980s.

In the 1970s Samarinda experienced a tremendous growth in population which subjected the economy and social fabric of the city's neighborhoods to enormous stress. The Citra Niaga project was conceived as an effort to ease problems of congestion, provide much needed neighborhood services, and promote community cohesion. The developer, Didik Soewandi, and the designer, Antonio Ismael, involved local residents in the planning and administration of the project. The scheme functions much like a small village market and enhances rather than disrupts the neighborhood.

Compared to Cesar Pelli or KPF's efforts to build the tallest buildings in the world or Kenneth Yeang's attempt to fundamentally rethink the design formulas for skyscrapers, Citra Niaga is a modest project. Materials and construction techniques, for example, were carefully selected to take advantage of local building practices. The quality of urban life, however, depends on modestly scaled projects like Citra Niaga as much as it does on the collection of gleaming skyscrapers in "special economic zones" or new business parks.

Government Buildings

Geoffrey Bawa: Sri Jayawardenepura

Recent political architecture demonstrates the same range and diversity we have noted elsewhere in the architectural production of the century's closing decades. Architects continue to provide a variety of answers to the design question: How do you represent the nature of political institutions architecturally? For the Sri Jayawardenepura, the National Parliament building of Sri Lanka, the architect Geoffrey Bawa (b. 1919) rejected the abstract language of modernism. Instead, he turned to the architectural heritage of Sri Lanka for inspiration (fig. 9.18).

However, looking to the past is not an uncomplicated design strategy. In a country composed of multiple ethnic and religious groups, the answer to the question "whose past?" has the potential to divide rather than unite as different groups within society can feel excluded by the selective use of history. Acutely aware of this dilemma, Bawa skipped over Sri Lanka's recent colonial past and chose instead models from the island nation's Anuradhapura era (third century BCE to the tenth century CE). Inevitably, ancient models require modification to fit contemporary needs. Although he is speaking of the specific case of Sri Lanka, Bawa's description of this process of creative adaptation neatly sums up the challenge facing architects committed to a creative dialogue between the past and the present:

9.18 Geoffrey Bawa, National Parliament, Kotte, Sri Lanka, 1982.

> When you look at the better examples of what remains of these earlier buildings you find they all have met the essentials of life in Sri Lanka, but although the past gives lessons it does not give the whole answer to what must be done now. . . . We must now design for a society living in a framework of a difficult economy, a much faster life—sometimes a freer one—new conventions and a greater liberality of belief to all the dictates of ever-changing needs. But there is, against this background of life, the great constant of the climate.
>
> (Taylor, p. 16)

Bawa imitated Anuradhapura models by siting the parliament complex on an island in the middle of an artificial lake, reached by a long causeway. The processional axis established by the causeway continues across a forecourt and then through a series of ceremonial doors executed in bronze and silver before culminating in the legislative chamber at the center of the complex. Traditional Sri Lankan design elements, such as small pavilions arranged around the large central hall and porticos shaded by deep overhangs, are reworked to accommodate modern needs. The result is a building that appeals to ancient traditions and satisfies contemporary programmatic requirements in a uniquely Sri Lankan way.

Kenzo Tange: Tokyo Metropolitan Government Headquarters

Modern technologies not ancient building types provide the models for the new Tokyo Metropolitan Government Headquarters, opened in 1991. Kenzo Tange designed an enormous civic center with two skyscrapers housing administrative offices, a smaller seven-story assembly building, and a semi-oval public plaza (fig. 9.19). The size of the complex is a response to the scale and complexity of the contemporary metropolis and the buildings are designed to function as efficiently as business machines. All three are equipped with state-of-the-art building management systems and other so-called "smart technologies" capable of monitoring internal air quality, temperature, lighting levels, and energy consumption as well as security conditions. All three structures are wired with the latest information-processing technologies.

Instead of the overt references to historical architecture that Geoffrey Bawa provided for the Sri Jayawardenepura, Tange pursued a subtle approach of double-coding elements in his design. The term double-coding describes situations in which a single feature refers simultaneously to different sources. For Tange, the latticelike pattern created by the vertical and horizontal lines of the towers' facades refers both to traditional Japanese timber-framed buildings and to the geometric patterns visible on the surface of computer circuit boards. Neither reference is immediately obvious and the balance between traditional and contemporary cultural references is tipped decidedly in favor of the latter. More than anything, the Tokyo Metropolitan Government Headquarters recalls Antonio Sant'Elia's 1914 Futurist drawings (see fig. 1.7). Like Sant'Elia's *Città Nuova*, Tange's design features skyscrapers connected by elevated bridges rising over multileveled roadways.

Norman Foster: Reichstag

In 1993 Norman Foster emerged as the winner of an international competition for the Reichstag, the German parliament building in Berlin (fig. 9.20), He faced a different kind of design challenge from that confronting the architects of the

9.19 Kenzo Tange, New Tokyo Metropolitan Government Head-quarters, Shinjuku, Tokyo, Japan, 1991.

Monumental architecture requires both inventive designers and ambitious patrons able to marshall the required resources. This new center for municipal government was part of a building campaign by Tokyo's Governor Suzuki Shun'ichi to enhance the city's image. Other new facilities include a museum, gymnasium, aquarium, and cultural center.

Sri Lankan parliament or the Tokyo Metropolitan Government Headquarters complex. Rather than design a new building, Foster was expected to insert the necessary parliamentary facilities into the shell of the existing Reichstag building.

Originally completed in 1894 according to the Neo-Renaissance design of Paul Wallot (1841–1912), the history of the Reichstag paralleled the tumultuous history of Germany in the twentieth century. The seat of the imperial and later the republican parliament, the building was burned down in 1933, an incident that the Nazis exploited to consolidate their grip on power. As Berlin became a battleground in the closing days of World War II, the building was reduced to shattered hulk. During the Cold War, it received only minimal restoration because of its position near the Berlin Wall and the politically sensitive issue of national symbols in a divided Germany. German reunification and the decision to return the seat of national government to Berlin added one more politically charged layer of history to the Reichstag. The remodelled Reichstag was inaugurated in 1999.

Foster's Reichstag design addresses three critical issues: political symbolism, the building's history, and architecture's environmental impact. Foster employed the architectural metaphor of transparency to suggest the openness and accessibility of democratic government. He replaced the heavy, solid dome of Wallot's original design with a shimmering glass cupola over the legislative chamber located at the center of the building. Helical ramps around the inside of the dome carry visitors to the top of the building. From above they can look down on the legislators at work below or gaze out over the city's skyline. Rather than bury the building's dramatic history beneath new surfaces, Foster left the scars of war, including shell marks and graffiti scrawled by victorious Russian soldiers, exposed on some of the interior walls. In this way, the building's own history becomes a reminder to all who use it of the ravages of war. Finally, the building serves as an exemplary demonstration of how technology can be employed to soften architecture's environmental impact. A huge inverted cone is suspended beneath the glass dome (fig. 9.21). The cone's mirrored surface reflects natural light down into the legislative chamber. The cone also acts like a convection chimney drawing hot air up and out through the top of the dome as part of a natural ventilation system. In place of fossil fuels, the buildings's

9.20 Norman Foster and Partners, The Reichstag, Berlin, Germany, 1992–99.

9.21 Norman Foster and Partners, The Reichstag, cross-section, Berlin, Germany, 1992–99.

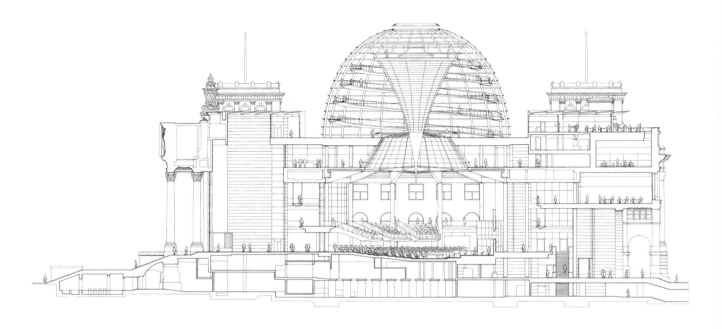

heating and cooling plant burns refined vegetable oils for power and excess heat is stored for future use in an aquifer located three hundred meters beneath the Reichstag. All of these systems combined result in a significant reduction of the energy consumed and the pollution generated by the Reichstag.

Foster is keenly aware of the role influential public buildings can play in promoting a more efficient use of energy. In a 1997 interview he said:

> Prophets like Buckminster Fuller many years ago predicted the kind of global crises which are now the subject of international summits and media headlines. We know that buildings currently consume half the world's energy and significantly add to the spiral of pollution through the consumption of non-renewable fossil fuels—a major factor in global warming. Given the symbolic importance of the Reichstag we suggested that it could be an inspiration to the nation and the world at large—as an ecological flagship. I also suggested that this approach should be justified on moral grounds—but if that was not acceptable then, given the very high energy costs of running the Reichstag at that time (that is, before 1993), then there was a strong economic argument for doing so anyway.
>
> (Quantrill, *The Norman Foster Studio*, p. 218)

Foster's transparent cupola, conceived as the crowning feature of "an ecological flagship," and the massive dome proposed by Albert Speer for the Great Hall of the Third Reich (see chapter 4) provide two very different models of political architecture and encapsulate two different chapters in modern German history.

Railroad Stations

Nicholas Grimshaw: Channel Tunnel Railway Terminal

The interplay between architectural design and structural engineering is an important theme in twentieth-century architecture. Often, however, engineering advances are invisible to the casual observer because structural features are covered by a building's walls and ceilings. This is not the case for building types such as railroad stations. The necessity to enclose large volumes without obstructing the traffic flow favors station designs with roofs that span long distances.

Two railroad stations completed in the early 1990s, one in London and one near Lyon, France, rely on the revelation of dramatic structural forms for their visual impact. For the Channel Tunnel Railway Terminal at London's Waterloo station, Nicholas Grimshaw designed a train shed over four hundred meters long. A narrow site and the necessity to cover a track on the extreme western edge of the station resulted in a multilevel station spanned by an asymmetrical truss system supporting the roof (figs. 9.22, 9.23). Until recently, the difficulty of calculating precisely

9.22 Nicholas Grimshaw, Waterloo International Terminal, cross-section, London, England, 1990–93.

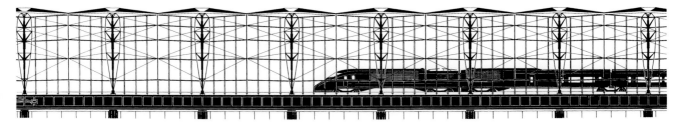

the stress patterns generated by eccentrically shaped structural members was a serious obstacle for designers. In the 1980s the advent of digitalized graphic software for modeling designs and computer programs capable of analyzing eccentric shapes greatly enhanced the ability of architects and engineers to solve complex structural equations. The structural skeleton of Grimshaw's design, visible thanks to its glass skin, is the product of sophisticated engineering calculations, but the design cannot be explained solely in terms of numbers or formulas. In a 1992 interview, Grimshaw described the effect he was after in his design for the Channel Tunnel Station:

> A building has to have atmosphere. It has to have appeal as you go into it. . . . You don't want to just hurry and scuffle into a train. You want to have some kind of feeling of wonder at being in the space.

(Moore, p. 245)

Site conditions and programmatic requirements determined the basic layout at Waterloo, but the building's special "atmosphere" comes from its artful marriage of brute strength and delicate balance (fig. 9.24).

9.23 (above) Nicholas Grimshaw, Waterloo International Terminal, cross-section, London, England, 1990–93.

9.24 (below) Nicholas Grimshaw, Waterloo International Terminal, London, England, 1990–93.

Santiago Calatrava: Lyon-Satolas TGV Railway Station

9.25 (above) Santiago Calatrava, TGV Railway Station, Lyon, France, 1989–92.

9.26 (below) Santiago Calatrava, TGV Railway Station, interior, Lyon, France, 1989–92.

Provoking a sense of wonder is important also to the Spanish architect and engineer Santiago Calatrava (b. 1951). He is responsible for the design of the TGV railway station of Lyon-Satolas. This station serves as a link between rail and air travel and connects Lyon with the airport at Satolas forty kilometers away. Like Grimshaw, Calatrava has taken advantage of sophisticated new analytical tools to create designs for bridges and stations that would have presented insurmountable difficulties for engineers a generation earlier. For Calatrava, calculation should support rather than constrain the designer's imagination: "I understand technology," Calatrava once said in an interview, "as a support for the lyricism of architecture."

Critics consistently use the word poetic to differentiate his evocative forms from more mundane examples of engineering. Calatrava's poetry is metaphorical in character; the viewer is tempted constantly to draw parallels between the structural forms of a Calatrava-designed building and the skeletal features of animals such as ribs and vertebrae or body parts such as wings and legs. The soaring roof of his Lyon-Satolas station, for example, suggests the metaphor of unfolding wings (figs. 9.25, 9.26). This birdlike form recalls Eero Saarinen's TWA Terminal in New York and the imaginative designs of Antonio Gaudí.

Cultural Institutions

Renzo Piano: Jean-Marie Tjibaou Cultural Center, Nouméa, New Caledonia

The appearance of novel forms made possible by new technologies is not restricted to transportation facilities. Patrons eager to project an image of innovation and creativity for their cultural institutions provide architects with high-profile opportunities to develop new shapes. In 1991 the French government commissioned Renzo Piano to design the Jean-Marie Tjibaou Cultural Center in Nouméa, on the Pacific island of New Caledonia (figs. 9.27, 9.28). The program called for an exhibition space, an auditorium, a library, and meeting facilities.

   Like his former partner Richard Rogers, Piano built an international reputation

9.27 Renzo Piano, Jean-Marie Tjibaou Cultural Center, Nouméa, New Caledonia, 1991–98.

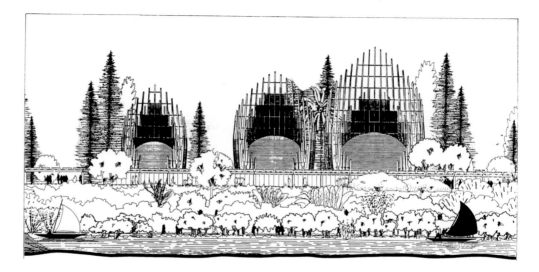

9.28 Renzo Piano, Jean-Marie Tjibaou Cultural Center, Nouméa, cross-section, New Caledonia, 1991–98.

based on a series of high-tech designs. For the cultural center, he employed late twentieth-century technologies to recast traditional features of the island's architecture. The cultural center's various departments are housed in separate pavilions. Piano wrapped each of these functional units in tall wooden screens made of laminated timber ribs set in cast aluminum footings and covered with light wooden slates. The screens (or "cases" as Piano calls them) are modeled abstractly on the traditional house type of the island's Kanak people. Clustered together, the tall cases evoke the image of a Kanak village. The cases act as wind screens, and louvers positioned in the base of the building can be adjusted to provide natural ventilation for interior spaces under different weather conditions. Computer modeling of preliminary designs allowed Piano to refine his original concept for combining traditional and contemporary forms in a solution uniquely tailored for its location.

The Nouméa cultural center raises, once again, the question of how architects combine formal design languages rooted in different cultural contexts. In his design for the Viceroy's House in New Delhi, discussed in chapter 4, Lutyens tried to blend elements of Western and Indian architectural traditions. Substitute high-tech for classical and much the same situation applies to Piano's attempt to fuse images, materials, and environmental control techniques from two different cultures: one indigenous to the Pacific island of New Caledonia, the other European in origin, global in scope, and advanced in terms of its level of technological development. As in the Viceroy's House in New Delhi, the balance between imported and indigenous elements is tipped decisively in favor of the former. However, if reports from Piano's office are to be believed, the islanders have responded enthusiastically to the design and critics should be wary of using interpretive models based on an alleged opposition between First and Third World sensibilities.

Movies, popular music, and television programs cross national borders with impunity and the isolation that once ensured cultural differentiation is disappearing under the impact of communication media that did not exist a century ago. At the beginning of the twenty-first century, the global circulation of ideas, images, and technologies is facilitating the development of novel, hybrid designs that fuse elements from different cultures. Unlike the classical orders of Greco-Roman antiquity that inevitably bear the stamp of a European–Mediterranean heritage, high-tech architecture increasingly escapes national or continental associations. Renzo Piano was born in Italy but his architecture belongs much more to this new global culture than it does to the venerable tradition of Italian architecture.

Frank Gehry: Guggenheim Museum, Bilbao, Spain

In 1997 the Solomon R. Guggenheim Foundation, based in New York City, opened a
new art museum in Bilbao, Spain (fig. 9.29). The Guggenheim's New York facility
designed by Frank Lloyd Wright remains one of the most famous examples of
modern architecture. However, it is not the only facility operated by the foundation; there are Guggenheim collections on display in Berlin, Bilbao, and Venice.
The story of the Bilbao Guggenheim is part of a larger story involving Bilbao's transformation from a gritty industrial seaport to a cosmopolitan center with a post-
industrial economy oriented to tourism, culture, and service industries. The
economic decline in the 1970s and 1980s of Bilbao's industrial and maritime sectors forced the city to reinvent itself in the 1990s. Port facilities, formerly located
along the Nervión river near the center of town, were relocated downstream closer
to the Bay of Biscay. This move allowed the city to reclaim the enormous site of the
former port for new development.

Like Frankfurt and Barcelona, Bilbao turned to famous architects as a way of
attracting international attention. Cesar Pelli was commissioned to prepare a masterplan for the Abandoibarra zone (the name of the former port area) and Norman
Foster designed stations for the city's new metro system. Santiago Calatrava
designed a dramatic pedestrian bridge spanning the Nervión in the area of the

9.29 (above) Frank Gehry,
Guggenheim Museum,
Bilbao, Spain,1997.

9.30 (opposite) Frank
Gehry, Guggenheim
Museum, CATIA model,
Bilbao, Spain,1997.

former port and a new terminal for the city's airport. Other projects by an international cast of designers are still to come.

Gehry's Guggenheim, the centerpiece of the entire urban renewal effort, has established Bilbao as a pilgrimage spot for anyone interested in contemporary architecture. Bilbao has experienced a fivefold increase in tourism since the Guggenheim opened and surveys indicate that 80 percent of visitors to Bilbao now come expressly to visit the museum. The financial impact on the local economy has been enormous and the city recouped its investment in the project in less than two years.

Located on the site of the former river port, the Bilbao Guggenheim appears as a shimmering pile of eccentrically shaped forms. Like Wright's New York Guggenheim, the plan unfolds around a central atrium; here, however, the similarities end. In place of Wright's image of organic unity, the Bilbao Guggenheim appears to be on the verge of flying apart. The design eludes prosaic description; it cannot easily be described as a composition of simple geometric forms or understood in terms of historical references. From every angle the building appears different. The viewer, therefore, is forced back into his or her own imagination in order to comprehend the building. It is as if the intellectual and emotional energy invested in the artwork inside has generated an enormous vortex that draws parts of the building toward the center before flinging them up and out into the surrounding city. Like leaping tongues of flame, titanium-clad curved shapes twist and turn around stone-clad rectangular volumes. Many critics hailed the building as a celebration of the power of the human imagination. Reviewing the building for the *New York Times*, Herbert Muschamp wrote:

> The most divine of all human qualities—empathy—is the source of meaning in Frank Gehry's designs. His aim is not to found a school, not to create a style. Rather, he is possessed by the gaga 19th century notion that by exercising their imagination artists can inspire others to use their own.

(Muschamp, p. 58)

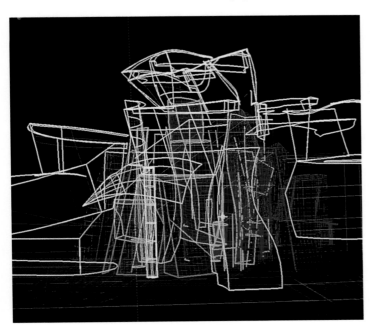

A vivid imagination, however, is not enough to create a great building. The success of the Bilbao Guggenheim must be attributed, in part, to a new design tool Gehry used to translate his vision into reality: digitalized imaging software (fig. 9.30). Until the 1980s, the difficulty of calculating the stress patterns of irregularly shaped structures combined with the high cost of constructing complex, curved shapes imposed severe limitations on what was feasible in terms of architectural design. In short, the ability to construct odd shapes lagged behind the architect's capacity to imagine them. Specialists in Gehry's office, however, use CATIA, a software program originally developed in France for use in the aerospace industry, to translate the eccentric forms of his designs into polynomial equations, that is, they turned shapes into numbers. A special digital wand is used to trace the surfaces of three-dimensional design models. The digital record of this form is then used to generate wire-frame images of the design on the computer which, in turn, are used to prepare the technical drawings needed to build the museum. Jim Glymph, one of Gehry's associates responsible for adapting Catia for architectural use, sums up the impact of this new design tool in the following words:

> Many of the forms he [Gehry] is developing now are only possible through the computer. Bilbao is a perfect example. Prior to the development of the computer applications in the office ... we would never be able to build it. Bilbao could have been drawn with a pencil and straight-edge, but it would take us decades.

(Van Bruggen, p. 138)

Materials as well as software contribute to the Guggenheim's novel appearance. The curved exterior walls of the Bilbao Guggenheim are sheathed with titanium panels so thin they flutter in strong wind. The shiny, rippling surfaces of the museum react to changing light conditions and transform the building into a giant light sculpture.

Thomas Beeby: Harold Washington Library, Chicago

In contrast to the emphasis on innovative forms and unconventional applications of materials, the design for the Chicago public library fits the postmodernist paradigm of a return to history. In 1987 Thomas Beeby (b. 1941) won a competition for the design of a new main library for Chicago. Named in honor of the city's first African-American mayor, the Harold Washington Library occupies an entire city block in Chicago's Loop district (fig. 9.31). Chicago is home to some of the most important buildings in the history of modern American architecture and within the radius of a fifteen-minute walk from the new library are some of the city's most famous landmark structures.

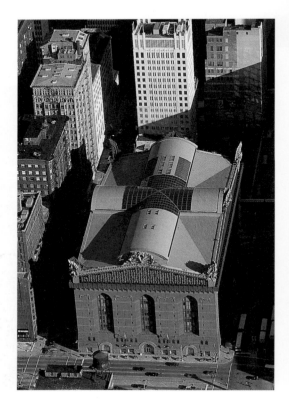

9.31 Hammond, Beeby, & Babka Associates, Harold Washington Library, Chicago, Illinois, 1992.

Cognizant of this important history, Beeby produced a complex design that draws on different aspects of the city's rich architectural heritage. The tall, round arches and deep, red-brick color of the new building recalls such nineteenth-century Chicago monuments as Adler and Sullivan's Auditorium Building and the Rookery Building by Burnham and Root. An elaborately decorated elevation wraps around three sides of the library. However, on the building's west side, which runs along a narrow street, a plain metal and glass curtain wall appears instead. This west elevation is a homage to the post-World War II generation of metal and glass buildings designed by Mies van der Rohe and his contemporaries. The abrupt shift from masonry to metal undermines the unity of the design, but by refusing to stick to a single design vocabulary the library acknowledges the city's rich diversity. The metaphor of a public building that "speaks" with multiple voices is related to a model of cultural pluralism understood as a sustained conversation among different traditions. The building's iconographic program includes references to libraries in general as repositories of knowledge as well as to the Harold Washington Library's specific identity as a Chicago building. The enormous statues of owls posed in front of giant palmettes perched on the library's rooftop symbolize the flowering of wisdom.

Architecture and Memory

Since the invention of pyramids, architecture has served as a vehicle for memory. The history of nations, communities, and individuals provides the answer to the question: What must be remembered? Architects, through their designs, answer the question: How to remember? The last set of buildings to be considered, a crematorium, a memorial, and a museum, illustrates different ways in which architecture gives form to memory. It covers the design spectrum from projects intended to serve small groups of people gathered together to say farewell to a deceased loved one to entire nations trying to come to terms with the past.

9.32 Fumihiko Maki, Kaze-No-Oka Crematorium, Nakatsu, Japan, 1997.

Maki was a student of Kenzo Tange (see fig. 5.5) and one of the founding members of the Metabolist group. Here he uses simple geometric shapes to explore the theme of differentiation within unity. Each major room of the crematorium has its own geometric form but the broad green lawn serves as a unifying element.

Fumihiko Maki: Kaze-No-Oka Crematorium

Cemeteries and memorials constitute the formal settings in which private and public rituals of remembrance occur. Often it is the rituals themselves that guide the architectural design. For the Kaze-No-Oka crematorium in the southern Japanese city of Nakatsu, Fumihiko Maki (b. 1928) arranged his design to conform to the various stages in the funeral ritual. There is a hall for the funeral service, the crematorium proper, and an area set aside for families waiting to collect the ashes. Each of these areas is expressed with a different geometric shape (fig. 9.32). The parklike setting of the crematorium includes several ancient burial mounds and the various

components of Maki's design appear as abstract sculptural forms embedded in the earth. Maki varied the quality of light in each area in order to establish different moods that correspond to different stages in the funeral ceremony. As one moves further into the crematorium, the sense of distance from the outside world grows and natural light, which one took for granted in the park above, becomes precious and creates a peaceful, meditative aura (fig. 9.33).

Maya Lin: Vietnam Veterans Memorial, Washington, DC

Only a short distance physically separates the Vietnam Veterans Memorial and the Lincoln Memorial in Washington DC. Conceptually, however, the two memorials stand at opposite ends of the spectrum in terms of design. In contrast to the rich classicism, prominent position, and heroic monumentality of Henry Bacon's Lincoln Memorial (see fig. 4.25), the Vietnam Veterans Memorial, designed by Maya Lin (b. 1959), has a quieter, more abstract, and intimate quality (fig. 9.34). While she was a still an architectural student, Lin won a national competition for the memorial in 1981. The competition brief called for an apolitical design that would make no partisan statement regarding the war and specified that the memorial must include the names of the 58,183 Americans lost in the conflict.

9.33 Fumihiko Maki, Kaze-No-Oka Crematorium, interior, Nakatsu, Japan, 1997.

However, few events in recent American history have been as divisive for the country as the Vietnam War and the controversy surrounding the war eventually would swirl around the memorial as well. Lin proposed a V-shaped wall of polished black granite set into the earth on which the names of the deceased would be inscribed in chronological (based on the date of death) rather than alphabetical order. In an essay entitled "Making the Memorial" she describes the genesis of the design:

> I imagined taking a knife and cutting into the earth, opening it up, an initial violence and pain that in time would heal. The grass would grow back, but the initial cut would remain a pure, flat surface in the earth with a polished, mirrored surface . . . It would be an interface, between our world and the quieter, darker, more peaceful world beyond.

(Lin, p. 33)

The question of how to remember those killed in the war was soon complicated by issues of race and gender. While some people expressed reservations about the abstract nature of the design, others objected to awarding the commission to an Asian–American female. Like many female designers before her, Lin was forced to confront a kind of hostility seldom faced by male architects:

> I remember [Lin wrote] reading the article in *The Washington Post* referring to "An Asian Memorial for an Asian War" and I knew we were in trouble. . . . Ironically, one side attacked the design for being "too Asian," while others saw its simplicity and understatement, not as an intention to create a more Eastern meditative space, but as a minimalist statement which they interpreted as being nonreferential and disconnected from human experience.

(Lin, p. 35)

9.34 Maya Lin, Vietnam Veterans Memorial, Washington, DC, 1982.

Materials as well as styles can acquire political significance. The memorial is faced with black granite. Although Canada and Sweden are both providers of this stone for world markets, the committee responsible for building the memorial objected to purchasing material from countries that provided haven for American men who left the USA rather than serve in the military.

The criticism of the memorial as "disconnected from human experience" because of its abstract design is a familiar theme in conservative critiques of modern architecture. According to this line of reasoning, the public neither understands the forms nor is willing to make the effort required to comprehend abstraction. Maya Lin's design, however, proved the critics wrong and today the Vietnam Veterans Memorial is recognized as one of the most powerful and emotionally compelling memorials in the nation's capital.

Daniel Libeskind: Jewish Museum, Berlin

In 1988 the Berlin Museum, devoted to the history of the city, announced a design competition for a new wing to the existing building to house an exhibit detailing the history of Berlin's Jewish community. One year later, Daniel Libeskind (b. 1946) was selected as the winner of the competition. By the time the museum opened a decade later Berlin was transformed from a city divided between rival foreign powers to the capital of a united Germany, and Libeskind's addition was the focus of international attention.

Over any account of Berlin's Jewish community hangs the shadow of the holocaust; the challenge for the architect was to find a form capable of doing justice to the story the museum was charged with telling. Rather than take his design cues from the existing museum building, or from the history of museum architecture, the architect pursued an esoteric approach that he admits defies rational explanation:

> In my view, the best works of the contemporary spirit come from the irrational, while what prevails in the world, what dominates and often kills, does so always in the name of Reason. The irrational as a nonbeginning of this project was my starting point.
>
> (Noever, p. 63)

Libeskind uses the phrase "between the lines" to describe the theme of his design. In a complicated process of fabricating connections between different aspects of Jewish life in Berlin he created a network of invisible lines which he used to establish the outline of the Jewish Museum. On a map of Berlin, he plotted the addresses of important figures in the history of the Jewish community thus establishing the spatial coordinates of Jewish life in Berlin before World War II. He connected these plotted points with lines and from this random diagram (labeled an "irrational nexus" by Libeskind) he generated the zigzag plan of the building (fig. 9.35). Running straight through the meandering arrangement of museum galleries is a series of stark, empty spaces. These voids are powerful, spatial symbols of what was lost in the holocaust. The curious pattern of openings on the zinc-clad exterior of the Jewish Museum adds another layer to the building's enigmatic iconography (fig. 9.36). On a traditional facade, windows typically conform to the arrangement of interior spaces and make it possible to count the number of stories. No such logic governs the positioning of openings in the Jewish Museum; instead narrow window strips slice diagonally through the building's skin. Like undecipherable hieroglyphs or ancient runes inscribed on the monuments of a lost civilization, the design of the Jewish Museum defies simple explanation, as does the holocaust itself.

But Libeskind does not surrender to despair. The adjacent gardens are an integral part of the entire scheme. Forty-nine concrete planters arranged in a seven

9.35 Daniel Libeskind, Jewish Museum, plan, Berlin, Germany, 1989–96.
Libeskind's zig-zag addition to the site plan is adjacent to the original U-shaped museum building. The two buildings are connected by an underground corridor. The analytical diagram reveals the internal volumes of the addition and the corridors that take the visitor to the Holocaust Tower and the gardens.

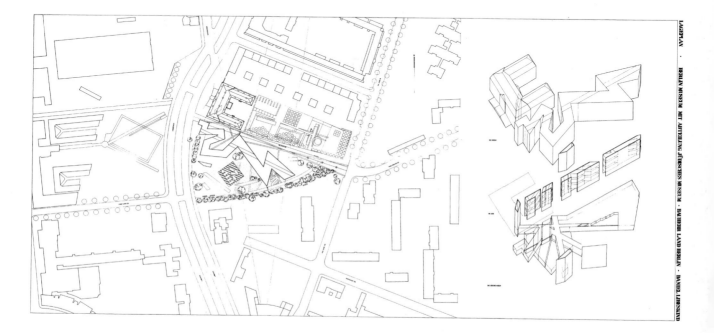

9.36 Daniel Libeskind, Jewish Museum, Berlin, Germany, 1989–96.

by seven grid establish a grove of trees. Forty-eight of the planters are filled with earth excavated in Berlin and stand for 1948, the year Israel was established. The forty-ninth planter, in the center of the grid, contains soil from Jerusalem. Roses, the only flower permitted to be cultivated in the ancient city of Jerusalem according to a tradition cited by Libeskind, are used to create an arbor around the edge of the garden. Thus nature provides the emblems of rebirth and renewal that balance the sense of destruction and loss evoked so viscerally by the convoluted plan and lacerated elevations of the architecture.

This book began by describing daring visions of the future. It ends by describing equally bold attempts to remember the past. Throughout the twentieth century architects have provided more than simple shelter; they have developed new or adapted existing design tools in order to create a built environment that responds to more than the physical needs of human beings. Architects have tried to provide architectural images and spatial metaphors that help people comprehend the world around them, inhabit it with some degree of dignity, and find pleasure and stimulation in the buildings they create. This is a noble and ambitious design agenda for the architectural profession and one that has provoked continued passionate debate concerning the elements of an appropriate architecture for the twentieth century. As the twenty-first century dawns, this debate continues.

Timeline

Architecture and Artworks

Pre-1900

Philip Webb, Red House, Bexley Heath, Kent, 1859 **(2.1)**
H. P. Berlage, Amsterdam Exchange, Amsterdam, 1897–1903 **(1.17)**
Ebenezer Howard, Garden City diagram, *Tomorrow: A Peaceful Path to Real Reform*, 1898 **(1.1)**

Joseph Olbrich, Secession Building, Vienna, 1898 **(1.32)**
Otto Wagner, Karlsplatz Stadtbahn, Vienna, 1899 **(3.8)**
Edwin Lutyens, Deanery Garden, Sonning, Berkshire, 1899–1902 **(2.2)**

1900

Alfred Messel, Wertheim Department Store, Berlin, 1900s **(1.22)**
Victor Laloux and Gae Aulenti, Gare d'Orsay, Paris, 1900 **(8.4, 8.5)**
Hector Guimard, Porte Dauphine, Paris, 1900 **(p. 76)**
Frank Lloyd Wright, "A Home in a Prairie Town," *Ladies' Home Journal*, 1901 **(2.5)**
Eliel Saarinen et al, Villa Hvitträsk, near Helsinki, 1901–03 **(2.14, 2.15)**
Auguste Perret, apartment building, Paris, 1902–03 **(1.27)**
Ragnar Östberg, Town Hall, Stockholm, 1902–23 **(4.1, 4.2)**
Charles Rennie Mackintosh, Hill House, Helensburgh, 1903 **(2.9, 2.10)**
Otto Wagner, Postal Savings Bank, Vienna, 1904–06 **(1.16)**
Eliel Saarinen, Railway Station, Helsinki, 1904–19 **(3.4, 3.5)**
Albert Kahn, Packard Motor Car Company, Detroit, 1905 **(4)**
Robert Maillart, Tavanasa Bridge, Grisons, c. 1905 **(3.27)**

Josef Hoffmann, Palais Stoclet, Brussels, 1905–11 **(2.11, 2.12, 2.13)**
Antonio Gaudí, Casa Milá, Barcelona, 1905–11 **(1.25)**
Wivi Lönn, Central Fire Station, Tampere, 1908 **(1.29)**
Charles and Henry Greene, Gamble House, Pasadena, CA, 1908–09 **(2.3, 2.4)**
Peter Behrens and Karl Bernhard, AEG turbine factory, Berlin, 1908–09 **(3.19)**
Frank Lloyd Wright, Robie House, Chicago, IL, 1908–10 **(2.6, 2.7, 2.8)**
Charles A. Platt, Villa Turicum, Lake Forest, IL, 1908–18 **(2.17, 2.18)**
Daniel Burnham and Edward Bennett, Chicago plan, 1909 **(1.3, 1.4)**
Herbert Baker, Union Building, Pretoria, 1909 **(4.7)**
Adolf Loos, Goldman & Salatsch Building, Vienna, 1909–11 **(1.26)**

1910

Aston Webb, Admiralty Arch, London, 1910 **(4.10)**
Paul Bonatz and Friedrich Scholer, Railway Station and Hotel, Stuttgart, 1911–28 **(3.6)**
Henry Bacon, Lincoln Memorial, Washington, DC, 1912–22 **(4.25)**
Edwin Lutyens, Viceroy's House, New Delhi, 1912–31 **(4.8, 4.9)**
Grand Central Terminal and Hotel Commodore, New York, 1913 **(3.2, 3.3)**
Michel De Klerk, Eigen Haard, Amsterdam, 1913–19 **(1.11)**
Antonio Sant'Elia, from *Una Città Nuova*, 1914 **(1.7)**
George Metzendorf, Margarethenhöhe, Essen, 1914 **(1.2)**
Walter Gropius and Adolf Meyer, factory and office building, "Deutscher Werkbund Exhibition," Cologne, 1914 **(3.21)**

Bruno Taut, Glass Pavilion, "Deutscher Werkbund Exhibition," Cologne, 1914 **(3.22)**
Le Corbusier, Dom-ino House, 1914–15 **(2.22)**
Equitable Building, New York, 1915 **(1.18)**
Howard Van Doren Shaw, Market Square, Lake Forest, IL, 1916 **(6.12)**
Tony Garnier, from *Une Cité industrielle*, 1917 **(1.6)**
Eliel Saarinen, King's Avenue from proposed Helsinki plan, 1917 **(1.5)**
Erik Gunnar Asplund, Villa Snellman, Djursholm, 1917–18 **(2.19, 2.20)**
Bruno Taut, from *Alpine Architektur*, 1919 **(1.8)**
Vladimir Tatlin, Project for Monument to the Third International, 1919–20 **(4.12)**

1920

Erik Gunnar Asplund, Public Library, Stockholm, 1920–28 **(1.33)**
Erich Mendelsohn, Rudolf Mosse Building, Berlin, 1922 **(1.15)**
Edwin Lutyens, Gledstone Hall, Yorkshire, 1922–26 **(2.16)**
Bertram Goodhue, Nebraska State Capitol, Lincoln, NE, 1922–32 **(4.27)**
Frank Lloyd Wright, Ennis House, Los Angeles, CA, 1923 **(2.32, 2.33)**
Louis Boileau, Bon Marché Pavilion, Paris, 1925 **(1.21)**
Le Corbusier, "The City of Tomorrow," from *Urbanisme*, 1925 **(1.10)**
Fritz Lang, from *Metropolis*, 1926 **(1.9)**
Paul Frankl, bookcase as skyscraper, c. 1926 **(1.20)**
Julia Morgan, YWCA, Honolulu, 1926 **(1.30, 1.31)**
John Eberson, Tampa Theatre, Tampa, FL, 1926 **(1.38)**
Grete Schütte-Lihotzky, "Frankfurt Kitchen," 1926 **(2.38)**
Walter Gropius, Bauhaus, Dessau, 1926 **(3.23)**
Laszlo Moholy-Nagy, *Bauhausbauten Dessau* book jacket (Gropius's Törten housing project), Dessau, 1926–28 **(3.25)**
Johannes A. Brinkman et al, Van Nelle Tobacco Factory, Rotterdam, 1926–30 **(3.17, 3.18)**
Ernst May, Römerstadt, Frankfurt am Main, 1927 **(1.13)**
R. Buckminster Fuller, 4-D Tower, 1927 **(2.40)**

Ludwig Mies van der Rohe, Weissenhof housing development, "Deutscher Werkbund Exhibition," Stuttgart, 1927 **(3.20)**
Konstantin Melnikov, Rusakov Workers' Club, Moscow, 1927–8 **(4.13)**
Richard Neutra, Lovell House, Los Angeles, CA, 1927–9 **(2.31 and p. 44)**
Karl Ehn, Karl-Marx-Hof, Vienna, 1927–30 **(1.14)**
Marcello Piacentini, Monument to Victory, Bolzano, 1928 **(4.17)**
John and Donald Parkinson, Bullock's–Wilshire Department Store, Los Angeles, CA, 1928 **(1.23)**
William van Alen, Chrysler Building, New York, 1928–30 **(1.19)**
Erich Mendelsohn, Schocken Store, Chemnitz, 1928–30 **(1.24)**
Le Corbusier, Villa Savoye, Poissy, 1928–31 **(2.23, 2.24, 2.25)**
Willem Dudok, Town Hall, Hilversum, 1928–31 **(4.5, 4.6)**
George Howe and William Lescaze, PSFS Building, Philadelphia, PA, 1928–32 **(1.37)**
R. Buckminster Fuller, project for Dymaxion House, 1929 **(2.41)**
William Mooser, Santa Barbara Courthouse, CA, 1929 **(4.26)**
Ludwig Mies van der Rohe, Barcelona Pavilion, "International Exhibition," Barcelona, 1929 **(2.22)**
Le Corbusier, from *The City of Tomorrow*, New York, 1929 **(3.1)**
Moisei Ginzburg, Narkomfin House, Moscow, 1929 **(4.14)**

Architectural Publications

Pre-1900

John Ruskin, *The Seven Lamps of Architecture* (London), 1849
Eugène Emmanuel Viollet-le-Duc, *Entretiens sur l'architecture* (Paris), 1863–72
Ebenezer Howard, *Tomorrow: A Peaceful Path to Real Reform* (London), 1898
Otto Wagner, *Moderne Architektur* (Vienna), 1898

1900

Camillo Sitte, *Der Städte-bau nach seinen kunstlerischen Grundsätzen* (Vienna), 1901
Barry Parker, *The Art of Building a Home: A Collection of Lectures and Illustrations by Barry Parker and Raymond Unwin* (London), 1901
Frank Lloyd Wright, "The Art and Craft of the Machine," 1901
Hendrik Petrus Berlage, *Gedanken über Stil in der Baukunst* (Leipzig), 1905
Adolf Loos, "Ornament and Crime," 1908
Raymond Unwin, *Town Planning in Practice: An Introduction to the Art of Designing Cities and Suburbs* (London), 1909
Commercial Club of Chicago, *Plan of Chicago*. Prepared under the Direction of the Commercial Club by Daniel Burnham and Edward H. Bennett (Chicago), 1909
Gustav Stickley, *Craftsman Homes* (New York), 1909

1910

Frank Lloyd Wright, *Ausgeführte Bauten und Entwürfe von Frank Lloyd Wright* (Berlin), 1910
Frederick Winslow Taylor, *The Principles of Scientific Management* (New York), 1911
Frank Lloyd Wright, *The Japanese Print: An Interpretation* (Chicago), 1912
Antonio Sant'Elia, "Manifesto of Architecture," 1914
Geoffrey Scott, *The Architecture of Humanism* (London), 1914
Tony Garnier, *Une cité industrielle: Etude pour la construction des villes* (Paris), 1917
Christine Frederick, *Household Engineering: Scientific Management in the Home* (Chicago), 1919
Walter Gropius, "Program of the Staatliches Bauhaus in Weimar," 1919
Bruno Taut, *Alpine Architektur* (Hagen), 1919

1920

Adolf Loos, *Ins Leere gespochen* (Paris), 1921
Le Corbusier, *Vers une architecture* (Paris), 1923
Louis Sullivan, *A System of Architectural Ornament According with a Philosophy of Man's Powers* (New York), 1924
Walter Gropius, *Internationale Architektur* (Munich), 1925
Le Corbusier, *L'Art décoratif d'aujourd'hui* (Paris), 1925
Erich Mendelsohn, *Amerika: Bilderbuch eines Architekten* (Berlin), 1926
Louis Sullivan, *The Autobiography of an Idea* (New York), 1926
Walter Behrendt, *Der Sieg des neuen Baustils* (Stuttgart), 1927
Le Corbusier, *Urbanisme* (Paris), 1927
Richard Neutra, *Wie baut Amerika?* (Stuttgart), 1927
Gustav Platz, *Die Baukunst der Neuesten Zeit* (Berlin), 1927
Hugh Ferriss, *The Metropolis of Tomorrow*, 1929
Henry Russell Hitchcock, *Modern Architecture: Romanticism and Reintegration* (New York), 1929
Erich Mendelsohn, *Russland, Europa, America: Ein architektonischer querschnitt* (Berlin), 1929
Laszlo Moholy-Nagy, *Von Material zu Architektur* (Munich), 1929
Bruno Taut, *Die neue Baukunst in Europa und Amerika* (Stuttgart), 1929

Contemporary Events and Technologies

Pre-1900

Marx and Engels publish *Communist Manifesto*, 1848
Elisha Otis develops safety elevator for passenger use, 1852
Henry Bessemer develops process for steel mass-production, 1856
Oil discovered in Pennsylvania, 1859
Alexander Graham Bell invents telephone, 1876
Thomas Edison invents electric incandescent light bulb, 1879

1900

Charles Seeberger develops escalator for safe public use, 1900
Harmon Palmer develops system for concrete blocks mass-production, 1900
Guglielmo Marconi achieves first wireless radio transmission, 1901
Oil discovered in Texas, 1901
Netherlands Housing Act, 1902
Wright Brothers achieve first powered airplane flight, 1903
Russo-Japanese War, 1904-05
Julius Kahn invents improved method of reinforced concrete construction, 1905
Pure Food and Drug Act passed by United States Congress, 1906
Ford Model T in production, 1908
Filippo Tommaso Marinetti founds Futurism, 1909
Louis Blériot flies airplane across English Channel, 1909

1910

Norwegian Roald Amundsen reaches South Pole, 1911
The *Titanic* sinks, 1912
Henry Ford builds first moving assembly line, Detroit, 1913
Standard Oil of California launches first chain of service stations, 1914
World War I, 1914–18
Zoning ordinance passed regulating height/bulk of tall office buildings, New York, 1916
Russian Revolution, 1917
US enters World War I, 1917
Women in the UK over age 30 gain right to vote (voting age for men is 21), 1918
Infuenza epidemic kills 20 million people worldwide, 1918–19
Weimar Republic founded in Germany, 1919
Benito Mussolini founds Fascist Party, Italy, 1919

1920

League of Nations established, 1920
19th Amendment to US Constitution grants women right to vote, 1920
Commercial Radio Broadcasting begins, 1920
National Socialist German Workers' Party (NAZI) founded, 1920
Immigration controls introduced in US, 1921
Irish Free State established, 1921
Oil discovered in Venezuela, 1922
Elizabeth Boyd Lawton founds National Committee for Restriction of Outdoor Advertising in US, to promote cause of roadside beauty, 1923
Ernst May begins 5-year term as city architect for Frankfurt am Main, responsible for housing estates (*siedlungen*), 1926
Robert Goddard launches first liquid-fuel rocket, 1926
Charles Lindbergh flies New York to Paris non-stop, 1927
First TV broadcast in US, 1928
Dr. Alexander Fleming discovers penicillin, 1928
Women in the UK gain equal voting rights with men, 1928
First 5-Year Plan in USSR to promote industrialization and agricultural collectivization, 1928
The Great Depression, 1929–34

Architecture and Artworks

1930

Charles Holden, Arnos Grove Station, London, 1930s (3.9)
John C. Wenrich, Rockefeller Center, New York, 1930s (1.41)
Ernest Lewis, New Victoria Cinema, London, 1930 (1.39)
Coffee Pot, Tacoma, Washington, 1931 (3.11)
Netherlands Pavilion, "Colonial Exhibition," Paris, 1931 (4.11)
J. S. Sirén, National Parliament Building, Helsinki, 1931 (4.3, 4.4)
Richard Shreve et al, Empire State Building, New York, 1931 (p. 2)
J. J. P. Oud, Blijdorp housing project, Rotterdam, 1931 (1.12)
"Modern Architecture: International Exhibition," MOMA, New
     York, 1932 (1.36)
Hans Scharoun, Villa Schminke, Löbau, 1932–33 (2.26, 2.27)
Giuseppe Terragni, Casa del Fascio, Como, 1932–36 (4.18, 4.19)
Wallis Gilbert, Hoover Factory, Perivale, London, 1932–38 (3.16)
Roland Wank, Norris Dam, 1933–36 (4.28, 4.29)
Boris Iofan, Palace of the Soviets, 1934 (p. 102)
Alexander Klein, "Functional Housing for Frictionless Living,"
     Modern Housing (Catherine Bauer), 1934 (2.37)
Konstantin Melnikov, People's Commissariat of Heavy Industry,
     Moscow, 1934 (4.15)
Frank Lloyd Wright, Falling Water, Bear Run, PA,
     1934–37 (2.34, 2.35, 2.36)
John and Donald Parkinson, Union Passenger RR Terminal,
     Los Angeles, CA, 1934–39 (3.7)

John and Donald Parkinson, Union Passenger RR Terminal,
     Los Angeles, CA, 1934–39 (3.7)
Berthold Lubetkin, Highpoint One, London, 1935 (1.28)
Robert Derrah, Coca Cola Bottling Plant and Office,
     Los Angeles, CA, 1936 (3.15)
Frank Lloyd Wright, Herbert Jacobs House, Madison, WI,
     1936–37 (6.8, 6.9)
Ernst Sagebiel, Tempelhof Airport, Berlin, 1936–39 (4.23, 4.24)
Lester Beall, "Wash Day," 1937 (2.39)
Jupp Weirtz, *2 Days to Europe*, 1937 (1)
Golden Gate Bridge, San Francisco, CA, 1937 (3.26)
Albert Kahn, Half-ton truck plant, Dodge Division, Warren, MI,
     1937 (3.13, 3.14)
John Russell Pope and Otto R. Eggers, *The National Gallery of Art*,
     Washington, DC, 1937 (1.34)
Giovanni Guerrini et al, EUR, Rome, 1937–42 (4.20)
Albert Speer, Grand Avenue, Dome, Arc de Triomphe, and Great
     Hall, Berlin plans, 1937–43 (4.21, 4.22)
Aalvar Aalto, Villa Mairea, Noormarkku, 1938–39 (2.28, 2.29, 2.30)
S. Charles Lee, Academy Theater, Inglewood, CA, 1939 (1.40)
Philip Goodwin and Edward Stone, MOMA, New York,
     1939 (1.35)
Norman Bel Geddes, General Motors Pavilion, 1939–40 (1.42)

1940

Sigfried Giedion, *Space, Time, and Architecture*, Harvard
     University Press, 1941 (3.24)
Frank Lloyd Wright, Taliesin West, Scottsdale, AR, 1942 (6.6, 6.7)
Frank Lloyd Wright, Guggenheim Museum, New York,
     1943–52 (6.23, 6.24)
R. R. Burns, Jr., Ranch house, Chicagoland Prize Homes
     Competition, *Chicago Tribune*, 1945 (6.10)
Charles and Ray Eames, Eames House, Santa Monica, CA, 1945–49
     (6.4 and p. 166)
Le Corbusier, Unité d'habitation, Marseilles, 1945–52 (5.24, 5.25)
Mario Ridolfi et al, from *Manuale dell'Architetto*, 1946 (5.9)
Ludwig Mies van der Rohe, Edith Farnsworth House, Plano, IL,
     1946–51 (6.2)
Daniel Brenner, Concert Hall Project, 1946 (6.1)
Wallace Harrison and Max Abramovitz, United Nations HQ,
     New York, 1947–50 (5.4)

Eduardo Paolozzi, *It's a Psychological Fact Pleasure Helps Your
     Disposition*, 1948 (6.13)
Hassan Fathy, New Gourna, 1948 (7.20, 7.21)
Walter Gropius, Harkness Commons, Harvard University,
     Cambridge, MA, 1948 (6.17)
Walter Dorwin Teague, Texaco Gas Station, Milwaukee, WI,
     1948 (3.10)
State University, Lenin Hills, Moscow, 1948 (6.22)
Grigorii Zakharov and Zinaida Chernysheva, Kurskaya metro
     station, Moscow Central Hall, 1949 (4.16)
Philip Johnson, Glass House, New Canaan, CT,
     1949–50 (6.3)
Alvar Aalto, Town Hall, Säynätsalo, 1949–52 (5.18, 5.19)
Eero Saarinen, General Motors Technical Center, Warren, MI,
     1949–55 (6.33)
Stalinallee, former East Berlin, 1949–57 (5.13)

1950

Por San Maria, Ponte Vecchio, Florence (5.10)
Tian'anmen Square, Beijing, 1950s (5.12)
Bruce Alonzo Goff, Eugene Bavinger House, Bartlesville, OK,
     1950 (6.5)
Le Corbusier, Notre Dame du Haut, Ronchamp,
     1950–54 (6.30, 6.31, 6.32)
Kenzo Tange, Peace Center, Hiroshima, 1950–56 (5.5)
Basil Spence, Cathedral, Coventry, 1950–62 (6.29)
Le Corbusier, Chandigarh, 1950–65 (5.15, 5.16)
Ludwig Mies van der Rohe, North Lake Shore Drive Apartments,
     Chicago, IL, 1951 (5.28)
"Festival of Britain," London, 1951 (5.30)
Skidmore, Owings, and Merrill, Lever House, New York,
     1951–52 (5.29)
Juan O'Gorman and Gustavo Saavedra, Library, Ciudad
     Universitaria, Mexico City, 1951–53 (6.21)
Wallace Harrison and Max Abramovitz, Alcoa Technical Center,
     Pittsburgh, PA, 1952 (5.1, 5.2)
Alison and Peter Smithson, Golden Lane Housing Project,
     London, 1952 (5.26)
Oscar Niemeyer, Niemeyer House, Canoa, Rio de Janeiro,
     1953 (6.14, 6.15)
Felix Candela, Church of Miraculous Virgin, Mexico City,
     1953 (6.28)

Juan O'Gorman, O'Gorman House, El Pedregal, Mexico City,
     1953–56 (6.16)
Victor Gruen, Northland Center, Detroit, MI, 1954 (6.11)
Per Ekholm and Sidney White, Baronbackarna housing project,
     Örebro, 1953–57 (5.23)
Skidmore, Ownings, and Merrill, Air Force Academy, Colorado
     Springs, CO, 1954 (6.18)
Louis Kahn, Bathhouse, Trenton, NJ, 1955 (7.4)
Hansaviertel, "Interbau Housing Exhibition," former West Berlin,
     1955–61 (5.14)
Otto Apel, Berlinerstrasse 25, Frankfurt am Main, 1956 (5.11)
Carlo Scarpa, Museo Castelvecchio, Verona, 1956 (6.27)
Lucio Costa, Brasilia, 1957 (5.17)
Jørn Utzon, Opera House, Sydney, 1957–73 (5.3)
Oscar Niemeyer, Plaza of the Three Powers, Brasilia,
     1958 (p. 130)
Raymond Erith, Provost's Lodgings, Queen's College, Oxford
     University, 1958–59 (5.8)
Richard Nixon and Nikita Khrushchev, "American National
     Exhibition," Sokolniki Park, Moscow, 1959 (2)
Charles and Ray Eames, *Glimpses of the USA*, from "American
     National Exhibition," Moscow, 1959 (5.31)
Louis Kahn, Jonas Salk Institute for Biological Sciences,
     La Jolla, CA, 1959–65 (7.5, 7.6)

Architectural Publications

1930

Sheldon Cheney, *The New World Architecture*
(New York), 1930
Lazar Markovich Lissitzky, *Russland, die Rekonstruktion der
Architektur in der Sowjetunion* (Vienna), 1930
Pietro Maria Bardi, *Rapporto sull'architettura* (Rome), 1931
Norman Bel Geddes, *Horizons* (Boston), 1932
Henry Russell Hitchcock and Philip Johnson, *The International
Style: Architecture Since 1922* (New York), 1932
Charles George Ramsey, *Architectural Graphic Standards for
Architects, Engineers, Decorators, Builders and Draftsmen*
(New York), 1932
Albert Sartoris, *Gli elementi dell'architettura funzionale, sintesi
panoramica dell'architettura moderna* (Milan), 1932
Le Corbusier, *La Ville radieuse* (Paris), 1933
Catherine Bauer, *Modern Housing* (Boston), 1934
Lewis Mumford, *Technics and Civilization* (New York), 1934
Agnoldomenico Pica, *Nuova architettura nel mondo*
(Milan), 1936
Curt Behrendt, *Modern Building* (London), 1937

1940

J. M. Richards, *An Introduction to Modern Architecture*
(Harmondsworth, UK), 1940
Sigfried Giedion, *Space, Time and Architecture: The Growth of a
New Tradition* (Cambridge, MA), 1941
Eliel Saarinen, *The City: Its Growth, Its Decay, Its Future*
(New York), 1943
Frank Lloyd Wright, *An Autobiography* (New York), 1943
Gyorgy Kepes, *Language of Vision* (Chicago), 1944
Ernesto Rogers, "Programma: Domus, la casa dell'uomo" (*Domus*,
January), 1946
Paul and Percival Goodman, *Communitas: Means of Livelihood
and Ways of Life* (Chicago), 1947
Philip Johnson, *Mies van der Rohe* (New York), 1947
Laszlo Moholy-Nagy, *Vision in Motion* (Chicago), 1947
Sigfried Giedion, *Mechanization Takes Command: A Contribution
to Anonymous History* (New York), 1948

1950

Bruno Zevi, *Storia dell'architettura moderna* (Turin), 1950
Bruno Zevi, *Towards an Organic Architecture* (London), 1950
Sigfried Giedion, *A Decade of the New Architecture*
(Zurich), 1951
Talbot Faulkner Hamlin, *Forms and Functions of Twentieth-
Century Architecture* (New York), 1952
Thomas Howarth, *Charles Rennie Mackintosh and the Modern
Movement* (London), 1952
Lewis Mumford, *Art and Technics* (New York), 1952
Martin Heidegger, "Bauen Wohnen Denken," 1954
Philip Johnson, "The Seven Crutches of Modern
Architecture," 1954
Richard Neutra, *Survival Through Design* (New York), 1954
Walter Gropius, *The Scope of Total Architecture* (New York), 1955
Vincent Scully, *The Shingle Style: Architectural Theory and
Design from Richardson to the Origins of Wright*
(New Haven, CT), 1955
Giulio Carlo Argan, "Architettura e ideologia," 1957
Edmund De Zurko, *Origins of Functionalist Theory*
(New York), 1957
John Summerson, "The Case for a Theory of Modern
Architecture," 1957
Henry Russell Hitchcock, *Architecture: Nineteenth and Twentieth
Centuries* (Harmondsworth, UK), 1958

Contemporary Events and Technologies

1930

Oil discovered in Kuwait, 1930
Technicolor launches full-color film, 1930
Japan occupies Manchuria, 1931
Oil discovered in Bahrain, 1932
Maiden flight of first modern airliner, Boeing 247, 1933
Fall of Weimar Republic; Hitler's National Socialists gain
power, 1933
Franklin Delano Roosevelt's New Deal administration, featuring
ambitious regional planning programmes, 1933
Works Progress Administration (WPA) and Federal Arts Project
established, 1935
Ocean liner *Normandie* crosses Atlantic in 107 hours and
33 minutes, 1935
War begins between Japan and China, 1936
Spanish Civil War, 1936–39
Zeppelin *Hindenburg* crashes in New Jersey, 1937
General Motors auto workers unionize, 1937
William Carothers invents nylon, 1938
Orson Welles produces radio broadcast of H. G. Wells's *War of
the Worlds*, 1938
World War II begins in Europe, 1939

1940

First network television broadcasts in the US, 1941
Japanese attack on Pearl Harbor brings US into World War II, 1941
Orson Welles' *Citizen Kane*, 1941
First nuclear chain reaction achieved, 1942
Atomic bombs dropped on Hiroshima and Nagasaki, Japan, 1945
World War II ends, 1945
United Nations established, 1945
First transistor invented, 1947
Pan-Am begins global commercial flights, 1947
Marshall Plan for European recovery, 1947
Oil discovered in Saudi Arabia, 1948
State of Israel founded, 1948
Mahatma Gandhi assassinated, 1948
Berlin divided into East and West Berlin, 1948
Soviet blockade of West Berlin, 1948–49
The North Atlantic Treaty Organization (NATO) founded, 1949

1950

German Democratic Republic (East Germany) issues planning
directive, "Sixteen Principles for the Restructuring of
Cities," 1950
Chinese Communist Party announces 5-year plan for
transformation of Beijing, 1950
Korean War, 1950–53
US Census Bureau acquires first UNIVAC computer, 1951
"Festival of Britain," London, 1951
Color television available in US, 1952
Edmund Hillary of New Zealand and Tenzing Norgay of Nepal
reach top of Mount Everest, 1953
Francis Crick and James Watson identify DNA double-helix
structure, 1953
McCarthyism at its height, 1953–54
Dr. Jonas Salk discovers vaccine for polio, 1954
Racial segregation banned in US schools, 1954
McDonald's fast-food restaurant chain launched, 1955
First transatlantic telephone cable laid, 1956
Soviet Union launches Sputnik, 1957
European Common Market established, 1957
Chinese Communist Party announces Great Leap Forward,
including rebuilding of Tian'anmen Square, 1958
US nuclear submarine *Nautilus* cruises under North Pole, 1958
Microchip introduced, 1959

Architecture and Artworks

1960

Kenzo Tange, Tokyo, 1960 **(5.20)**
The Monas, Medan Merdeka Square, Jakarta, 1961–72 **(5.6)**
Eero Saarinen, TWA Terminal, JFK Airport, New York, 1962 **(6.34, 6.35)**
Robert Venturi, Vanna Venturi House, Chestnut Hill, PA, 1962–63 **(7.8)**
Giancarlo De Carlo, Nuovi Collegi, Urbino, 1962–83 **(6.19, 6.20)**

Peter Cook, Plug-In City, 1964 **(5.21)**
Kenzo Tange, National Gymnasium, Olympics, Tokyo, 1964 **(5.7)**
Louis Kahn, Kimbell Art Museum, Fort Worth, TX, 1966–72 **(7.7)**
Ralph Erskine, Byker Wall, Newcastle-upon-Tyne, 1968–74 **(7.2)**

1970

Jaime Lerner, bus stop, Curitiba, 1970s **(8.25)**
Aldo Rossi, San Cataldo Cemetery, Modena, 1971–73 **(7.1)**
Richard Rogers and Renzo Piano, Centre Georges Pompidou, Paris, 1971–77 **(6.25, 6.26)**
Superstudio, Micro-event/Micro-environment, 1972 **(5.22)**
Robert Venturi et al, from *Learning from Las Vegas*, MIT Press, 1972 **(7.9)**
Minoru Yamasaki, Pruitt-Igoe Housing Project being demolished, St. Louis, MO, 1972 **(5.27)**

Aldo van Eyck, Hubertshuis, Amsterdam, 1973–81 **(7.3)**
Charles Moore, Piazza d'Italia, New Orleans, LO, 1975–80 **(7.10)**
Frank Gehry, Gehry House, Santa Monica, CA, 1977 **(9.4, 9.5)**
Raili and Reima Pietilä, Main Library, Tampere, 1978–86 **(7.24, 7.25)**
Ricardo Bofill, Les Echelles du Baroque Housing Project, Paris, 1979–83 **(7.11)**
Richard Rogers, Lloyd's Building, London, 1979–86 **(9.8)**
"Les Grands Projets de l'Etat à Paris," Paris, 1979–89 **(8.10)**

1980

Townhouses, Saalgasse, Frankfurt am Main, 1980s **(8.16)**
Antonio Ismael, Citra Niaga project, Samarinda, 1980s **(9.17)**
DPZ, Odessa Street, Seaside, FL, 1980s **(8.24)**
Map of Römerstadt, Frankfurt am Main, 1980s **(8.15)**
Strada Novissima, Venice Biennale, 1980 **(7.12)**
Jean Nouvel, Arab World Institute, Paris, 1981–87 **(8.6)**
Zaha Hadid, The Peak, Hong Kong, 1982 **(7.13)**
Maya Lin, Vietnam Memorial, Washington, DC, 1982 **(9.34)**
Geoffrey Bawa, National Parliament, Kotte, Sri Lanka, 1982 **(9.18)**
Bernard Tschumi, Parc de La Villette, Paris, 1982–89 **(8.7, 8.8, 8.9)**
E. Schirmacher, Ostzeile restoration, Römerberg, Frankfurt am Main, 1983 **(8.17)**
Glenn Murcutt, Ball-Eastaway House, Glenorie, Sydney, 1983 **(9.2)**
Peter Eisenman, Wexner Center, Ohio State University, Columbus, OH, 1983–89 **(7.14 and p. 200)**
Rem Koolhaas, The Netherlands Dance Theater, The Hague, 1984–87 **(7.15, 7.16)**
Quinlan Terry, Riverside Development, Richmond, Surrey, 1984–88 **(9.9)**

Rob Krier, Amiens reconstruction, Amiens, 1984–92 **(8.21, 8.22)**
Peter Zumthor, Studio, Haldenstein, Graubünden, 1985–86 **(7.26)**
Christoph Langhof, IBA housing complex, Berlin, 1985–87 **(8.14)**
Charles Correa, Jawahar Kala Kendra, Jaipur, Rajasthan, 1986–92 **(7.22, 7.23)**
Wolf Prix et al (Coop Himmelblau), Schuppich, Sporn, and Winischhofer law offices, Vienna, 1987 **(9.1)**
Nicholas Grimshaw & Partners, *Financial Times* Building, London, 1988 **(8.1)**
John Outram Associates, Storm Water Pumping Station, Isle of Dogs, London, 1988 **(8.2)**
Rem Koolhass, National Library of France, Paris, 1989 **(7.17)**
I. M. Pei, glass pyramid, Louvre, Paris, 1989 **(8.3)**
Leon Krier, Krier/Wolff House, Seaside, FL, 1989 **(7.18)**
Stanley Tigerman, private residence, near Chicago, IL, 1989 **(9.3)**
Thomas Smith, Smith House, South Bend, IN, 1989–90 **(7.19)**
Santiago Calatrava, TGV Railway Station, Lyon, 1989–92 **(9.25, 9.26)**
Daniel Libeskind, Jewish Museum, Berlin, 1989–96 **(9.35, 9.36)**

1990

Shenzen, China, 1990s **(3)**
Canary Wharf, Docklands, London, 1990s **(p. 228)**
Oriol Bohigas and MBMP, Nova Icària Olympic Village, Barcelona, 1990s **(8.19)**
Nicholas Grimshaw, Waterloo International Terminal, London, 1990–93 **(9.22, 9.23, 9.24)**
Kenneth Yeang, Menara Mesiniaga building, Kuala Lumpur, 1991 **(9.14, 9.15)**
Kenzo Tange, New Tokyo Metropolitan Government HQ, Tokyo, 1991 **(9.19)**
Renzo Piano, Jean-Marie Tjibaou Cultural Center, Nouméa, 1991–98 **(9.27, 9.28)**
Olympic sports facilities, Montjuïc, Barcelona, 1992 **(8.18)**
John Simpson et al, Paternoster Square reconstruction, London, 1992 **(8.23)**

Hammond, Beeby & Babka, Harold Washington Library, Chicago, IL, 1992 **(9.31)**
Norman Foster et al, The Reichstag, Berlin, 1992–99 **(9.20, 9.21)**
Leon Krier, "Charter for the Reconstruction of the European City," *Building Classical*, Academy Editions, 1993 **(8.20)**
Zaha Hadid, IBA housing complex, Berlin, 1994 **(8.11, 8.12, 8.13)**
R. Scott Johnson, family home, Saint Helena, CA, 1994 **(9.6, 9.7)**
Ralph Erskine, The Ark, London, 1996 **(9.10, 9.11)**
Norman Foster et al, Commerzbank, Frankfurt am Main, 1997 **(9.12, 9.13)**
Frank Gehry, Guggenheim Museum, Bilbao, 1997 **(9.29, 9.30)**
Fumihiko Maki, Kaze-No-Oka Crematorium, Nakatsu, 1997 **(9.32, 9.33)**
Kohn, Pederson, Fox Associates, World Financial Center, Shanghai, 1997– **(9.16)**
Cesar Pelli, Petronas Towers, Kuala Lumpur, 1998 **(p. 254)**

Architectural Publications

1960

Lewis Mumford, *The City in History* (New York), 1961
Victor Gruen, *The Heart of Our Cities* (New York), 1964
Reyner Banham, *The New Brutalism* (New York), 1966
Michel Foucault, *Les mots et les choses: une archéologie des sciences humaines* (Paris), 1966
Aldo Rossi, *L'architettura della città* (Padua), 1966
Robert Venturi, *Complexity and Contradiction in Architecture* (New York), 1966

1970

Victor Papanek, *Design for the Real World* (New York), 1971
Dennis Sharp, *A Visual History of Twentieth-Century Architecture* (London), 1972
Robert Venturi, Denise Scott Brown, and Steven Izenour, *Learning From Las Vegas* (Cambridge, MA), 1972
Charles Jencks, *Modern Movements in Architecture* (London), 1973
Rob Krier, *Stadtraum* (Stuttgart), 1975
David Watkin, *Morality and Architecture* (Oxford), 1977

1980

Kenneth Frampton, *Modern Architecture. A Critical History* (New York), 1980
Tom Wolfe, *From Bauhaus to Our House* (New York), 1981
Gwendolyn Wright, *Building the Dream: A Social History of Housing in America* (New York), 1981
William Curtis, *Modern Architecture Since 1900* (London), 1982
Leon Krier, *Albert Speer's Architecture, 1932–1942* (Brussels), 1985
Vittorio Magnago Lampugnani, *Architecture and City Planning in the Twentieth Century* (New York), 1985
Reyner Banham, *A Concrete Atlantis: U.S. Industrial Buildings and European Modern Architecture, 1900–1925* (Cambridge, MA), 1986
George R. Collins and Christiane Crasserman Collins, *Camillo Sitte: The Birth of Modern Town Planning* (New York), 1986
Marshall Berman, *All That Is Solid Melts Into Air: The Experience of Modernity* (New York), 1988
Philip Johnson and Mark Wigley, *Deconstructivist Architecture* (New York), 1988
Thomas Gordon Smith, *Classical Architecture: Rule and Invention* (Layton, UT), 1988

1990

Peter Calthorpe, *The Next American Metropolis* (New York), 1993
Kenneth Yeang, *Bioclimatic Skyscrapers* (London), 1994
William J. Mitchell, *City of Bits: Space, Place and the Infobahn* (Cambridge, MA), 1995
Mark Wigley, *White Walls, Designers Dresses: The Fashioning of Modern Architecture* (Cambridge, MA), 1995
Kate Nesbitt, *Theorizing a New Agenda for Architecture: An Anthology of Architectural Theory 1965–1995* (New York), 1996
Karsten Harries, *The Ethical Function of Architecture* (Cambridge, MA), 1997
Peter Noever, *Architecture in Transition: Between Deconstruction and New Modernism* (New York), 1997
Adrian Forty, *Words and Buildings: A Vocabulary of Modern Architecture* (New York), 2000
Anthony Vidler, *Warped Space: Art, Architecture and Anxiety in Modern Culture* (Cambridge, MA), 2000

Contemporary Events and Technologies

1960

World population exceeds 3 billion, 1960
Berlin Wall erected, 1961
Cuban Missile Crisis, 1962
President John F. Kennedy assassinated, 1963
Civil Rights Act, US, 1964
American troops begin offensive operations in Vietnam, 1965
Oil discovered in Alaska, 1968
Concorde supersonic aircraft makes first flight, 1969

1970

Gilbert Hyatt invents microprocessor, 1970
Boeing introduces first jumbo jet, 1970
Watergate scandal, 1972–74
American combat troops leave Vietnam, 1973
OPEC oil crisis, 1973
President Richard Nixon resigns, 1974
Fall of Saigon, 1975
Apollo-Soyuz project, 1975
Bill Gates and Paul Allen form Microsoft, 1975

1980

CNN begins broadcasting, 1980
World Health Organization announces effective eradication of smallpox, 1980
Egyptian president Anwar Sadat assassinated, 1981
World's fastest train, TGV, begins service between Paris and Lyons, 1981
IBM introduces personal computer for home use, 1981
Space Shuttle Columbia launched, 1981
Falklands War, 1982
Compact discs introduced, 1982
Acquired Immune Deficiency Syndrome (AIDS) identified, 1983
Apple Macintosh computer introduced, 1984
Soviet Union launches MIR space station, 1986
Laptop computers introduced, 1986
World population exceeds 5 billion, 1987
Political dissidents in Tian'anmen Square, Beijing, crushed, 1989
Vietnam Veterans Memorial erected to the 58,183 killed American servicemen, 1982
Berlin Wall torn down, 1989

1990

Hubble space telescope launched, 1990
Nelson Mandela released from prison in South Africa, 1990
Gulf War, 1990–91
Collapse of Soviet Union, 1991
Barcelona Olympics, 1992
IBM supercomputer "Deep Blue" defeats chess champion Gary Kasparov, 1992
Channel Tunnel connecting England and France opened, 1994
Nelson Mandela elected President of South Africa, 1994
Prime Minister Yitzhak Rabin of Israel assassinated, 1995
Political control of Hong Kong returned to China, 1997
"Pathfinder" spacecraft transmits images from surface of Mars, 1997
Entire human code of human chromosome mapped, 1999
Euro currency introduced, 1999

Bibliography

Introduction

Berman, Marshall, *All That Is Solid Melts Into Air. The Experience of Modernity.* Harmondsworth, Middlesex, England: Penguin Books, 1988.

Betsky, Aaron, *Building Sex: Men, Women, Architecture, and the Construction of Sexuality.* New York: William Morrow, 1995.

Coleman, Debra, Elizabeth Danze, and Carol Henderson, eds, *Architecture and Feminism.* New York: Princeton Architectural Press, 1996.

Colomina, Beatriz, ed, *Sexuality and Space.* New York: Princeton Architectural Press, 1992.

Curtis, William, *Modern Architecture Since 1900,* 3rd ed. Upper Saddle River, NJ: Prentice Hall, 1996.

Duncan, Alistair, *Art Deco.* New York: Thames and Hudson, 1998.

Ferguson, Russell, ed, *At the End of the Century: One Hundred Years of Architecture.* New York: Harry N. Abrams, Inc, 1998.

Frampton, Kenneth, *Modern Architecture: A Critical History,* 3rd ed. London, England: Thames and Hudson, 1992.

Frampton, Kenneth, *Studies in Tectonic Culture,* ed John Cava. Cambridge, MA: MIT Press, 1995.

Hobsbawm, Eric, *The Age of Empire, 1875–1914.* London, England: George Weidenfeld and Nicolson Ltd, 1987.

Hobsbawm, Eric, *The Age of Extremes: A History of the World, 1914–1991.* London, England: Michael Joseph, 1994.

Jester, Thomas, ed, *Twentieth-Century Building Materials: History and Conservation.* New York: McGraw-Hill, 1995.

Kern, Stephen, *The Culture of Time and Space, 1880–1918.* Cambridge, MA: Harvard University Press, 1983.

Margolin, Victor, and Richard Buchanan, eds, *The Idea of Design.* Cambridge, MA: MIT Press, 1995.

Peter, John, *The Oral History of Modern Architecture: Interviews with the Greatest Architects of the Twentieth Century.* New York: Harry N. Abrams, Inc, 1994.

Pevsner, Nikolaus, *Pioneers of Modern Design from William Morris to Walter Gropius,* rev ed. Harmondsworth, Middlesex, England: Penguin, 1966.

Tafuri, Manfredo, and Francesco Dal Co, *Modern Architecture.* New York: Harry N. Abrams, 1979.

Torre, Susanna, ed, *Women in American Architecture: A Historic and Contemporary Perspective.* New York: Whitney Library of Design, 1977.

Twombly, Robert, *Power and Style: A Critique of Twentieth-Century Architecture in the United States.* New York: Hill and Wang, 1995.

Chapter 1

Allan, John, *Berthold Lubetkin: Architecture and the Tradition of Progress.* London, England: RIBA Publications, 1992.

Banham, Reyner, *Theory and Design in the First Machine Age.* London, England: Architectural Press, 1960.

Blau, Eve, *The Architecture of Red Vienna, 1919–1934.* Cambridge, MA: MIT Press, 1998.

Boutelle, Sarah Holmes, *Julia Morgan: Architect.* New York: Abbeville Press, 1988.

Burnham, Daniel H., and Edward Bennett, *Plan of Chicago.* New York: Princeton Architectural Press, 1993.

Dal Co, Francesco, *Figures of Architecture and Thought: German Architectural Culture, 1880–1920.* New York: Rizzoli, 1990.

Fishman, Robert, *Urban Utopias in the Twentieth Century: Ebenezer Howard, Frank Lloyd Wright, and Le Corbusier.* New York: Basic Books, 1977.

Greenhalgh, Paul, ed, *Modernism in Design.* London, England: Reaktion Books, Ltd, 1990.

Hall, Peter, *Cities of Tomorrow. An Intellectual History of Urban Planning and Design in the Twentieth Century,* rev ed. Cambridge, MA: Blackwell Publishers Ltd, 1996.

Hillier, Bevis, and Stephen Escritt, *Art Deco Style.* London, England: Phaidon, 1997.

Hitchcock, Henry-Russell, and Philip Johnson, *The International Style: Architecture Since 1932.* New York: W.W. Norton & Company, 1932.

Howard, Ebenezer, *Garden Cities of Tomorrow.* Cambridge, MA: MIT Press, 1965.

Le Corbusier, *The City of Tomorrow and Its Planning,* trans Frederick Etchells. New York: Payson & Clarke Ltd, 1929; Mineola, New York: Dover Publications, 1987.

Le Corbusier, *Towards a New Architecture,* trans Frederick Etchells. New York: Praeger, 1960.

Mumford, Eric, *The CIAM Discourse on Urbanism, 1928–1960.* Cambridge, MA: MIT Press, 2000.

Nikula, Riitta, *Architecture and Landscape. The Building of Finland.* Helsinki, Finland: Otava Publishing Company Ltd, 1993.

Poggioli, Renato, *The Theory of the Avant-Garde.* Cambridge, MA: The Belknap Press, 1968.

Rollins, William, *A Greener Vision of Home. Cultural Politics and Environmental Reform in the German Heimatschutz Movement, 1904–1918.* Ann Arbor, MI: University of Michigan Press, 1997.

Sutcliffe, Anthony, *Metropolis 1890–1940.* London, England: Mansell Publishing Ltd, 1984.

Tafuri, Manfredo, *The Sphere and the Labyrinth: Avant-Gardes and Architecture from Piranesi to the 1970s.* Cambridge, MA: MIT Press, 1987.

Valentine, Maggie, *The Show Starts on the Sidewalk: An Architectural History of the Movie Theater.* New Haven, CT: Yale University Press, 1994.

Wagner, Otto, *Modern Architecture.* Santa Monica, CA: The Getty Center Publication Program, 1988.

Ward, Stephen, ed, *The Garden City: Past, Present and Future.* London, England: E. & F. N. Spon, 1992.

Willis, Carol, *Form Follows Finance: Skyscrapers and Skylines in New York and Chicago.* New York: Princeton Architectural Press, 1995.

Wright, Gwendolyn, *Building the Dream: A Social History of Housing in America.* New York: Pantheon Books, 1981.

Zukowsky, John, *The Many Faces of Modern Architecture: Building in Germany Between the World Wars.* New York: Prestel-Verlag, 1994.

Chapter 2

Brooks, H. Allen, *The Prairie School: Frank Lloyd Wright and His Midwest Contemporaries.* Toronto: University of Toronto Press, 1972.

Brooks, H. Allen, *Writings on Wright: Selected Comment on Frank Lloyd Wright.* Cambridge, MA: MIT Press, 1981.

Friedman, Alice, *Women and the Making of the Modern House: A Social and Architectural History.* New York: Harry N. Abrams, Inc, 1998.

Hayden, Dolores, *The Grand Domestic Revolution: A History of Feminist Designs for American Homes, Neighborhoods, and Cities.* Cambridge, MA: MIT Press, 1981.

Hussey, Christopher, *The Life of Sir Edwin Lutyens.* London, England: Country Life, 1950

Jones, Peter Blundell, *Hans Scharoun.* London, England: Phaidon, 1995.

Kaplan, Wendy, ed, *Charles Rennie Mackintosh.* New York: Abbeville Press, 1996.

Kaufmann, Edgar, and Ben Raeburn, eds. *Frank Lloyd Wright: Writings and Buildings.* Cleveland, OH: Meridian Books, 1960.

Marks, Robert, *The Dymaxion World of Buckminster Fuller.* New York: Reinhold Publishing Corp, 1960.

Quantrill, Malcolm, *Finnish Architecture and the Modernist Tradition.* London, England: E. & F. N. Spon, 1995.

Rowe, Colin, *The Mathematics of the Ideal Villa and Other Essays.* Cambridge, MA: MIT Press, 1976.

Sekler, Eduard, *Josef Hoffmann: The Architectural Work.* Princeton, NJ: Princeton University Press, 1985.

Wright, Gwendolyn, *Moralism and the Model Home: Domestic Architecture and Cultural Conflict in Chicago, 1873–1913.* Chicago, IL: University of Chicago Press, 1980.

Chapter 3

Billington, David, *The Tower and the Bridge. The New Art of Structural Engineering.* Princeton, NJ: Princeton University Press, 1983.

Bucci, Federico, *Albert Kahn: Architect of Ford.* New York: Princeton Architectural Press, 1993.

Campbell, Joan, *The German Werkbund: The Politics of Reform in the Applied Arts.*

Princeton, NJ: Princeton University Press, 1978.

Conrads, Ulrich, ed, *Programs and Manifestos on 20th-Century Architecture*. Cambridge, MA: MIT Press, 1970.

Giedion, Sigfried, *Space, Time, and Architecture: The Growth of a New Tradition*, 5th ed. Cambridge, MA: Harvard University Press, 1967.

Greenhalgh, Paul, ed, *Art Nouveau 1890–1914*. London, England: V & A Publications, 2000.

Hochman, Elaine, *Bauhaus: Crucible of Modernism*. New York: Fromm International, 1997.

Jennings, Jan, *Roadside America. The Automobile in Design and Culture*. Ames, IA: Iowa State University Press, 1990.

Kahn, Albert, "Industrial Architecture—An opportunity and a Challenge," *The Architectural Forum*, vol 73, no 6, December 1940, pp. 501–03.

Naylor, Gillian, *The Bauhaus Reassessed: Sources and Design Theory*. New York: E. P. Dutton, 1985.

Pommer, Richard, and Christian Otto, *Weissenhof 1927 and the Modern Movement in Architecture*. Chicago, IL: University of Chicago Press, 1991.

Schwartz, Frederic, *The Werkbund: Design Theory and Mass Culture Before the First World War*. New Haven, CT: Yale University Press, 1996.

Skinner, Joan, *Form and Fancy: Factories and Factory Buildings by Wallis, Gilbert, & Partners, 1916–1939*. Liverpool, England: Liverpool University Press, 1997.

Zukowsky, John, ed, *Building for Air Travel: Architecture and Design for Commercial Aviation*. New York: Prestel, 1996.

Chapter 4

Al Sayyad, Nezar, ed, *Forms of Dominance: On the Architecture and Urbanism of the Colonial Enterprise*. Avebury, Aldershot, England: Avebury, imprint of Ashgate Publishing Group, 1992.

Doordan, Dennis, *Building Modern Italy: Italian Architecture 1914–1936*. New York: Princeton Architectural Press, 1988.

Etlin, Richard, *Modernism in Italian Architecture, 1890–1940*. Cambridge, MA: MIT Press, 1991.

Ginzburg, Moisei, *Style and Epoch*. Cambridge, MA: MIT Press, 1982.

Golomstock, Igor, *Totalitarian Art in the Soviet Union, The Third Reich, Fascist Italy, and the People's Republic of China*. London, England: Collins Harvill, 1990.

Gouda, Frances, *Dutch Culture Overseas: Colonial Practice in the Netherlands Indies, 1900–1942*. Amsterdam, Netherlands: Amsterdam University Press, 1995.

Hinz, Berthold, *Art in the Third Reich*. New York: Pantheon Books, 1979.

Hudson, Hugh D. Jr, *Blueprints and Blood: The Stalinization of Soviet Architecture, 1917–1937*. Princeton, NJ: Princeton University Press, 1994.

Irving, Robert Grant, *Indian Summer: Lutyens, Baker, and Imperial Delhi*. New Haven, CT: Yale University Press, 1981.

Jaskot, Paul, *The Architecture of Oppression: The SS, Forced Labour, and the Nazi Monumental Building Economy*. London, England: Routledge, 2000.

Khan-Magomedov, Selim, *Pioneers of Soviet Architecture: The Search for New Solutions in the 1920s and 1930s*. New York: Rizzoli, 1987.

Krier, Leon, *Albert Speer: Architecture 1932–1942*. Brussels, Belgium: Archives d'Architecture Moderne, 1985.

Metcalf, Thomas, *An Imperial Vision: Indian Architecture and Britain's Raj*. Berkeley, CA: University of California Press, 1989.

Miller-Lane, Barbara, *Architecture and Politics in Germany, 1918–1945*. Cambridge, MA: Harvard University Press, 1968.

Morton, Patricia A., *Hybrid Modernities: Architecture and Representation at the 1931 Colonial Exposition, Paris*. Cambridge, MA: MIT Press, 2000.

Taylor, Brandon, and Wifried van der Will, eds, *The Nazification of Art: Art, Design, Music, Architecture, and Film in the Third Reich*. Winchester, Hampshire, England: The Winchester Press, 1990.

Upton, Dell, *Architecture in the United States*. New York: Oxford University Press, 1998.

Wright, Gwendolyn, *The Politics of Design in French Colonial Urbanism*. Chicago, IL: University of Chicago Press, 1991.

Chapter 5

_____ "In Search of a New Monumentality: A Symposium," *Architectural Review*, vol 104, no 621, September 1948.

Albrecht, Donald, ed, *World War II and the American Dream: How Wartime Building Changed a Nation*. Cambridge, MA: MIT Press, 1995.

Banham, Reyner, *A Critic Writes. Essays by Reyner Banham*. Berkeley, CA: University of California Press, 1996.

Banham, Reyner. *Megastructure: Urban Futures of the Recent Past*. London, England: Thames and Hudson, 1976.

Caldenby, Claes, Jöran Lindvall, and Wifried Wang, eds, *Sweden: Twentieth-Century Architecture*. New York: Prestel, 1988.

Cook, Peter, "Cook's Grand Tour," *Architectural Review*, vol xxxx, no 1040, October 1983, pp. 32–43.

Diefendorf, Jeffry, *In the Wake of the War. The Reconstruction of German Cities after World War II*. New York: Oxford University Press, 1993.

Fairbanks, Wilma, *Liang and Lin: Partners in Exploring China's Architectural Past*. Philadelphia, PA: University of Pennsylvania Press, 1994.

Fry, Maxwell, and Jane Drew, *Tropical Architecture in the Humid Zone*. New York: Reinhold Publishing Corporation, 1956.

Gropius, Walter, *Scope of Total Architecture*. New York: Harper, 1955.

Hooker, Virginia Matheson, ed, *Culture and Society in New Order Indonesia*. New York: Oxford University Press, 1993.

Jacobs, Jane, *The Death and Life of Great American Cities*. New York: Random House, 1961.

Jencks, Charles, *Modern Movements in Architecture*, 2nd ed. Harmondsworth, Middlesex, England: Penguin Books, 1985.

Khilnani, Sunil, *The Idea of India*. New York: Farrar, Strauss, & Giroux, 1997.

King, Anthony, *Global Cities: Post-Imperialism and the Internationalization of London*. London, England: Routledge, 1990.

Kurokawa, Kisho, *Metabolism in Architecture*. Boulder, CO: Westview Press, 1977.

Mumford, Lewis, *From the Ground Up*. New York: Harcourt Brace Jovanovich, 1956.

Nas, Peter J. M., ed, *Urban Symbolism*. Leiden, Germany: E. J. Brill, 1993.

Nichols, Sarah, ed, *Aluminum by Design*. New York: Harry N. Abrams, Inc, 2000.

Ockman, Joan, ed, *Architecture Culture 1943–1968: A Documentary Anthology*. New York: Rizzoli, 1993.

Schildt, Görn, ed, *Alvar Aalto in His Own Words*. New York: Rizzoli, 1998.

Sommer, Degenhard, Ove Arup, & Partners, *Engineering the Built Environment: Philosophy, Projects, Experience*. Basel, Switzerland: Birkhäuser Verlag, 1994.

Stewart, David, *The Making of a Modern Japanese Architecture: 1868 to the Present*. New York: Kodansha International Press, 1987.

Chapter 6

_____ "The Architect's Place in the Suburban Retail District," *Architectural Forum*, vol 93, no 2, August 1950, pp. 110–21.

Bruegmann, Robert, ed, *Modernism at Mid-Century: The Architecture of the United States Air Force Academy*. Chicago, IL: University of Chicago Press, 1994.

Burian, Edward R. *Modernity and the Architecture of Mexico*. Austin, TX: University of Texas Press, 1997.

Gordon, Elizabeth, "The Threat to the Next America," *House Beautiful*, vol 95, April 1953, pp. 126–130, 250–251.

Jackson, Kenneth, *Crabgrass Frontier: The Suburbanization of the United States*. New York: Oxford University Press, 1985.

Lasdun, Denys, *Architecture in the Age of Scepticism*. London, England: Heinemann, 1984.

Leighey, Marjorie, "A Testimony to Beauty": The Pope-Leighey House. ed Terry B. Morton. Washington, DC: National Trust for Historic Preservation, 1983.

Nelson, George, *Tomorrow's House: How to Plan Your Post-War Home Now*. New York: Simon & Schuster, 1945.

Richards, J. M., "Coventry," *Architectural Review*, vol 111, no 661, January 1952, pp. 3–7.

Riley, Terence, ed, *Frank Lloyd Wright, Architect*. New York: Museum of Modern Art, 1994.

Rogers, Ernesto, *La Chapelle de Notre Dame du Haut à Ronchamp de Le Corbusier*. Milan, Italy: Editoriale Domus, 1955.

Saarinen, Aline, ed, *Eero Saarinen on His Work*, rev ed. New Haven, CT: Yale University Press, 1968.

Saliga, Pauline, and Mary Woolever, eds, *The Architecture of Bruce Goff, 1904–1982: Design for the Continuous Present*. New York: Prestel-Verlag, 1995.

Schulze, Franz, *Mies van der Rohe: A Critical Biography*. Chicago, IL: University of Chicago Press, 1985.

Schulze, Franz, *Philip Johnson: Life and Work*. New York: Alfred Knopf, 1994.

Sergeant, John, *Frank Lloyd Wright's Usonian Houses: The Case for Organic Architecture*. New York: Whitney Library of Design, 1976.

Smith, Clive Bamford, *Builders in the Sun*. New York: Architectural Book Publishing Company, 1967.

Smithson, Alison and Peter, *Without Rhetoric: An Architectural Aesthetic, 1955–1972*. Cambridge, MA: MIT Press, 1974.

Smithson, Peter, "Just a Few Chairs and a House: An Essay on the Eames-aesthetic," *Architectural Design*, vol 36, no 9, September 1966.

Spence, Basil, *Phoenix at Coventry*. London, England: Geoffrey Bles Ltd, 1962.

Underwood, David, *Oscar Niemeyer and Brazilian Free-Form Modernism*. New York: Braziller, 1994.

Wright, Lance, "Coventry Cathedral Six Years Later," *American Institute of Architects*, vol 50, no 2, August 1968, pp. 50–55.

Chapter 7

Betsky, Aaron, *Violated Perfection: Architecture and the Fragmentation of the Modern*. New York: Rizzoli, 1990.

Correa, Charles, *Charles Correa*. London, England: Thames and Hudson, 1996.

Dunlop, Beth, *Building a Dream: The Art of Disney Architecture*. New York: Harry N. Abrams, 1996.

Economakis, Richard, ed, *Leon Krier: Architecture and Urban Design 1967–1992*. London, England: Academy Editions, 1992.

Fathy, Hassan, *Architecture for the Poor: An Experiment in Rural Egypt*. Chicago, IL: University of Chicago Press,1973.

Ghirardo, Diane, *Architecture After Modernism*. London, England: Thames and Hudson, 1996.

Hadid, Zaha, *Zaha Hadid: The Complete Buildings and Projects*. New York: Rizzoli, 1998.

Hays, K. Michael, ed, *Architectural Theory Since 1968*. Cambridge, MA: MIT Press, 1998.

Jencks, Charles, *Architecture Today*. New York: Harry N. Abrams, 1988.

Jencks, Charles, *The Language of Post-Modern Architecture*, 6th ed. New York: Rizzoli, 1991.

Jencks, Charles, *What Is Post-Modernism?* 4th ed. London, England: Academy Editions, 1996.

Johnson, Philip, and Mark Wigley, *Deconstructivist Architecture*. New York: Museum of Modern Art, 1988.

Koolhaas, Rem, *Delirious New York*. New York: Oxford University Press, 1978.

Koolhaas, Rem, and Bruce Mau, ed Jennifer Sigler. *S, M, L, XL*: O. M. A. Rotterdam, Netherlands: Uitgeverij 010 Publishers, 1995; New York: The Monacelli Press, 1995.

Latour, Alessandra, ed, *Louis I. Kahn: Writings, Lectures, Interviews*. New York: Rizzoli, 1991.

Marder, Tod, ed, *The Critical Edge: Controversy in Recent American Architecture*. Cambridge, MA: MIT Press, 1985.

Nesbitt, Kate, ed, *Theorizing a New Agenda for Architecture: An Anthology of Architectural Theory 1965–1995*. New York: Princeton Architectural Press, 1996.

Norris, Christopher, and Andrew Benjamin, *What is Deconstruction?* London, England: Academy Editions, 1988.

Rossi, Aldo, *The Architecture of the City*. Cambridge, MA: MIT Press, 1982.

Smith, Thomas Gordon, *Classical Architecture: Rule & Invention*. Layton, UT: Gibbs M. Smith, Inc, 1988.

Stern, Robert A. M., *Modern Classicism*. New York: Rizzoli, 1988.

Tzonis, Alexander, and Liane Lefaivre, *Architecture in Europe: Memory and Invention Since 1968*. London, England: Thames and Hudson, 1992.

Venturi, Robert, *Complexity and Contradiction in Architecture*. New York: Museum of Modern Art, 1966.

Venturi, Robert, Denise Scott Brown, and Steve Izenour, *Learning from Las Vegas: The Forgotten Symbolism of Architectural Form*. Cambridge, MA: MIT Press, 1972.

Vidler, Anthony, "The Third Typology," *Oppositions* 7, Winter 1976, pp. 1–4.

Zumthor, Peter, *Thinking Architecture*. Baden, Germany: Lars Müller Publishers, 1998.

Chapter 8

Balfour, David, ed, *Berlin*. London, England: Academy Editions, 1995.

Ellin, Nan, *Postmodern Urbanism*, rev ed. New York: Princeton Architectural Press, 1996.

Fachard, Sabine, ed, *Paris 1979–1989*. New York: Rizzoli, 1988.

Jencks, Charles, *The Prince, the Architects, and New Wave Monarchy*. New York: Rizzoli, 1988.

Katz, Peter, *The New Urbanism: Toward An Architecture of Community*. New York: H. Holt, 1988.

Kleihues, Josef, and Heinrich Klotz, eds, *International Building Exhibition, Berlin 1987: Examples of a New Architecture*. New York: Rizzoli, 1987.

Lerner, Jaime, "Architect, Mayor, Environmentalist: An Interview with Jaime Lerne," *Progressive Architecture*, vol 75, no 7, July 1994, pp. 84–85, 110.

Mohney, David, and Keller Easterling, *Seaside: Making a Town in America*. New York: Princeton Architectural Press, 1991.

Saliga, Pauline, and Martha Thorne, eds, *Building in a New Spain: Contemporary Spanish Architecture*. Chicago, IL: Art Institute of Chicago, 1992.

Sexton, Richard, *Parallel Utopias: Sea Ranch and Sea Side*. San Francisco, CA: Chronicle Books, 1995.

Williams, Stephanie, *Docklands*, rev ed. London, England: Phaidon, 1993.

Chapter 9

Coaldrake, William, *Architecture and Authority in Japan*. London: Routledge, 1996.

Davis, Colin, and Ian Lambot, *Commerzbank, Frankfurt: Prototype for an Ecological High-Rise*. Basel, Switzerland: Birkhäuser, 1997.

Foster, Norman, *Rebuilding the Reichstag*. Woodstock, NY: The Overlook Press, 2000.

Frampton, Kenneth, ed, *Technology, Place, and Architecture: The Jerusalem Seminar in Architecture*. NewYork: Rizzoli, 1998.

Friedman, Mildred, ed, *Gehry Talks: Architecture + Process*. New York: Rizzoli, 1999.

Jencks, Charles, and Karl Kropf, eds, *Theories and Manifestos of Contemporary Architecture*. Chichester, England: Academy Editions, 1997.

Ladd, Brian, *The Ghosts of Berlin: Confronting German History in the Urban Landscape*. Chicago, IL: University of Chicago Press, 1997.

Lin, Maya, "Making the Memorial," *The New York Review of Books*, November 2, 2000, pp. 33–35.

Moore, Rowan, ed, *Structure, Space, and Skin: The Work of Nicholas Grimshaw & Partners*. London: Phaidon, 1993.

Muschamp, Herbert, "Miracle in Bilbao," *The New York Times Magazine*, September 7, 1997, pp. 54–59, 72, 82.

Noever, Peter, *Architecture and Transition: Between Deconstruction and New Modernism*. Munich: Prestel-Verlag, 1991.

Piano, Renzo, *Renzo Piano Logbook*. New York: Monacelli Press, 1997.

Quantrill, Malcolm, *The Norman Foster Studio: Consistency Through Diversity*. London, England: E. & F. N. Spon, 1999.

Powell, Robert, *Rethinking the Skyscraper: The Complete Architecture of Ken Yeang*. New York: Whitney Library of Design, 1999.

Steele, James, ed, *Architecture for Islamic Societies Today*. London, England: Academy Editions, 1994.

Taylor, Brian Brace, *Geoffrey Bawa*. Singapore, Indonesia: Concept Media, 1986.

Thorne, Martha, ed, *The Pritzker Architecture Prize: The First Twenty Years*. New York: Harry N. Abrams, 1999.

Vale, Lawrence, *Architecture, Power, and National Identity*. New Haven, CT: Yale University Press, 1992.

Van Bruggen, Coosje, *Frank O. Gehry Guggenheim Museum, Bilbao*. New York: The Guggenheim Museum, 1998.

Viladas, Pilar, "Lyrical Cubism in the Napa Valley," *Architectural Digest*, vol 53, no 3, March 1996, pp. 150–59.

Yeang, Kenneth, "Bioclimatic Skyscrapers," *Space Design*, no 354, March 1994, pp. 18–23.

Zukowsky, John, and Ian Wardropper, *Austrian Architecture and Design: Beyond Tradition in the 1990s*. Chicago, IL: Art Institute of Chicago, 1991.

Zukowsky, John, and Martha Thorne, eds, *Skyscrapers: The New Millennium*. New York: Prestel-Verlag, 2000.

Picture Credits

Index

Note: **bold** page numbers refer to illustrations.